Solaris System Administrator's Guide, Third Edition

Janice Winsor

Sun Microsystems Press
A Prentice Hall Title

PH PTR

10 9 8 7 6 5 4 3

ISBN 0-13-027702-9
Printed in the United States of America
Editorial/production supervisor: Wil Mara
Cover design director: Jerry Votta
Cover designer: Kavish & Kavish Digital Publishing and Design
Manufacturing manager: Alexis R. Heydt
Marketing manager: Bryan Gambrel
Acquisitions editor: Gregory G. Doench
Sun Microsystems Press
Marketing manager: Michael Llwyd Alread
Publisher: Rachel Borden

Sun Microsystems Press
A Prentice Hall Title

CONTENTS

4 Administering User Accounts and Groups 119

ACKNOWLEDGMENTS

Many people contributed to the design, writing, and production of the third edition of this book. Sun Microsystems Press would particularly like to acknowledge the following people for their contributions.

Peter Gregory, HartGregory Group, for reviewing the technical information in this book and for useful suggestions about adding new information.

Linda Gallops, Sun Microsystems, Inc., for technical help.

Mary Lautner, Sun Microsystems, Inc., for providing useful information about the Solaris 8 release.

John Stearns, Technical Publications Manager, SSE Group, Sun Federal, Sun Microsystems, Inc., for providing answers to questions about Role-Based Access Control (RBAC) features.

Mary Lautman, Sun Microsystems, Inc., for providing answers to questions about Role-Based Access Control (RBAC) features and providing valuable input to Chapter 5.

Larissa Brown, Sun Microsystems, Inc., for helping put me in contact with the right people to help with new Solaris 8 functionality.

Those writers from Sun Technical Publications who contributed to the *Solaris System Adminsitration Guides Volumes I, II, and III*, which were used as a technical reference resource.

The author would especially like to thank Rachel Borden of Sun Microsystems Press and Greg Doench, Senior Editor, Prentice Hall, for their unfailing enthusiasm, support, and friendship, Mary Lou Nohr for editing this manuscript with her usual skill and tact, and Wil Mara of Prentice Hall for production.

The author would also like to thank her husband, Maris, for his continued love and support.

Thanks to the following people, who contributed to the second edition of this book.

Brett Bartow, Acquisitions Editor, Macmillan Technical Publishing, for his enthusiasm and support on this project.

Mary Lautner, Program Manager, Sun Microsystems, Inc., for her invaluable help and assistance in providing the author with documentation and answers to numerous questions. Without Mary's help and the information she provided, the author would have been unable to complete this project.

Those writers from SunSoft Technical Publications who contributed to the *Solaris System Adminsitration Guide*, which was used as a technical reference resource.

Lisa Gebken of Macmillan Technical Publishing for editing this manuscript.

Tobin Crockett, for networking the author's SPARCstation 10 and Macintosh PowerPC and setting up a network printer.

Rob Johnston, System Support Specialist, Sun Microsystems Computer Company, for installing Solaris 2.6 and troubleshooting hardware and software problems.

Tien Nguyen, System Support Specialist, SunSoft, Inc., for help in troubleshooting hardware and software problems.

Linda Gallops, SunSoft SQA, for help in tracking down information about modems.

Ken Erickson of SunSoft, for allowing the author to pester him with occasional technical questions.

The author would especially like to thank Rachel Borden and John Bortner of Sun Microsystems Press for their unfailing enthusiasm, support, and friendship.

Thanks to the following people, who contributed to the first edition of this book.

Connie Howard and Bridget Burke, SunSoft Publications managers, for their support and encouragement.

Randy Enger, SunSoft Engineering Manager, for help in gaining early access to the Solaris 2.1 administration tools. Special thanks are also due to Gordon Kass, Solaris 2.1 Product Manager, and Steve Hanlon, SunSoft Marketing.

Patrick Moffitt, SunOS Ambassador, for providing background information about the Service Access Facility. Patrick Moffitt and Cindy Swearingen, Technical Education Services, for providing a modem procedure that worked.

Rick Ramsey, SunSoft Technical Writer, for source information about NIS+, and for many discussions about good technical writing.

Keith Palmby, SunSoft Technical Writer, for source information about user environments.

Charla Mustard-Foote, SunSoft Technical Writer, for providing source information and the conversion table for Appendix A, and for calmly helping make software available for screen shots.

Bruce Sesnovich, SunSoft Technical Writer, for providing background information about the Service Access Facility and modem procedures.

Tom Amiro, SunSoft Technical Writer, for providing background information about administering user accounts and printers, and for early access to information about the Solaris 2.1 administration tools. Tom also deserves thanks for help in making software available for screen shots.

John Pew, Writing Consultant, for providing information and filters for converting raster files to GIF format.

Bill Edwards, Dave Miner, Jeff Parker, Chuck Kollars, Ken Kane, and Paul Sawyer—SunSoft Engineers in Billerica, MA—deserve thanks for reviewing information about NIS+ security, Administration Tool security, Database Manager, and User Manager.

Sam Cramer, SunSoft Engineer, for help with file system information. Bill Shannon, SunSoft Distinguished Engineer, for help with backup and restore information.

Pat Shriver, SunSoft Engineer, Robin Greynolds, SunSoft System Administrator, and Craig Mohrman, SunSoft Engineer, for technical review.

Karin Ellison, SunSoft Press, for parenting this book and for extraordinary assistance, including providing a Solaris 2.0 system for use on this project.

Thanks are also due to Melinda Levine, our editor at Ziff-Davis Press, and to Cheryl Holzaepfel, Managing Editor, for being so easy to work with.

And lastly, thanks to the engineers, writers, and marketing folks at SunSoft who helped with the SunSoft version of this book.

PREFACE

This book is for beginning system administrators, system administrators new to the Solaris™ Operating Environment, or any user who wants a task-oriented quick-reference guide to basic administrative commands.

A Quick Tour of the Contents

Chapter 1, "Introducing Solaris System Administration," describes basic administration tasks and superuser status. It tells how to communicate with users, start up and shut down systems, and monitor processes. It also introduces some frequently used commands and the new Administration Tools in the Solaris 8 Operating Environment.

Chapter 2, "Using Basic OS Commands," describes basic commands for finding user and environment information, creating and editing files, combining commands and redirecting output, displaying manual pages, and determining disk data.

Chapter 3, "Understanding Shells,"describes some commands common to all shells and provides basic information about the Bourne, C, Korn, Bourne-Again, TC, and Z shells. *New!*

Chapter 4, "Administering User Accounts and Groups," describes how to add and remove user accounts and how to set up new group accounts.

Chapter 5, "Administering Roles," introduces the Role-Based Access Control (RBAC) security feature, new in the Solaris 8 Operating Environment, that enables you to assign a subset of superuser privileges to one or more users. *New!*

Chapter 6, "Administering File Systems," describes the types of file systems provided in the Solaris 8 Operating Environment, the default file system, the virtual file system table, and the file system administrative commands. It shows you how to make file systems available and how to back up and restore file systems.

Chapter 7, "Administering Devices," describes how to use tapes and diskettes to store and retrieve files and how to administer disks. It also introduces the Service Access Facility and provides instructions for setting up port monitors for printers and modems.

Chapter 8, "Administering Systems," describes commands to display system-specific information, configure additional swap space without reformatting a disk, and create a local mail alias.

New! Chapter 9, "Administering Network Services," describes commands to check on remote system status, log in to remote systems, and transfer files between systems. It describes how to use the Solaris AdminSuite™ 3.0 tools to make changes to NIS+ databases once NIS+ is up and running. This chapter also introduces the IPv6 internet protocol and describes how to display network statistics and configuration information.

Chapter 10, "Administering Printing," introduces the LP print service, describes how to set up printing services, and explains how to use the printing commands.

Chapter 11, "Recognizing File Access Problems," provides information on how to recognize problems with search paths and with permissions and ownership.

The Glossary contains basic system administration terms and definitions.

Important: Read This Before You Begin

Because we assume that the root path includes the `/sbin`, `/usr/sbin`, `/usr/bin`, and `/etc` directories, the steps show the commands in these directories without absolute path names. Steps that use commands in other, less common directories show the absolute path in the example.

The examples in this book are for a basic Solaris software installation without the Binary Compatibility Package installed and without `/usr/ucb` in the path.

CAUTION. If `/usr/ucb` *is included in a search path, it should always be at the end. Commands like* `ps` *or* `df` *are duplicated in* `/usr/ucb` *with different formats and options from those of Solaris ommands.*

This book does not contain all the information you need to administer systems. Refer to the complete system administration documentation for comprehensive information.

Because the Solaris Operating Environment provides the Bourne (default), Korn, and C shells, examples in this book show prompts for each of the shells.

The default C shell prompt is `system-name%`. The default Bourne and Korn shell prompt is `$`. The default root prompt for all shells is a pound sign (#). In examples that affect more than one system, the C shell prompt (which shows the system name) is used to make it clear when you change from one system to another.

Conventions Used in This Book

Commands

In the steps and the examples, the commands to be entered are in bold type. For example: "Type **su** and press Return." When following steps, press Return only when instructed to do so, even if the text in the step breaks at the end of a line.

Variables

Variables are in an italic typeface. When following steps, replace the variable with the appropriate information. For example, to print a file, the step instructs you to "type **lp *filename*** and press Return." To substitute the file named `quest` for the ***filename*** variable, type **lp quest** and press Return.

Mouse-Button Terminology

This book describes mouse buttons by function. The default mouse button mapping is shown below.

- SELECT is Left.
- ADJUST is Middle.
- MENU is Right.

Use the SELECT mouse button to select unselected objects and activate controls. Use the ADJUST mouse button to adjust a selected group of objects, either adding to the group or deselecting part of the group. Use the MENU mouse button to display and choose from menus.

Platform Terminology

New!

In this document, the term IA (Intel Architecture) is used instead of x86 to refer to the Intel 32-bit processor architecture, which includes the Pentium, Pentium Pro, Pentium II, Pentium II Xeon, Celeron, Pentium III Xeon processors, and comparable microprocessor chips made by AMD and Cyrix.

Storage-Medium Terminology

In this book, we distinguish between three different types of media storage terminology in the following way.

- *Disc* is used for an optical disc, CD-ROM, or DVD disc.
- *Disk* is used for a hard-disk storage device.
- *Diskette* is used for a floppy diskette storage device. (Note: Sometimes, screen messages and mount points use the term *floppy*.)

Icons

New!

Marginal icons mark information that is new in this edition. The new information may be new with the Solaris 7 Operating Environment or new with the Solaris 8 Operating Environment.

Other new information may have been available in previous releases but was not included in the second edition. Where possible, the text indicates the release number where the command or functionality was added.

SPARC and IA Information

This book provides system administration information for both SPARC and IA systems. Unless otherwise noted, information throughout this book applies to both types of systems. Table A summarizes the differences between the SPARC and IA system administration tasks.

Table A SPARC and IA System Administration Differences

Category	SPARC Platform	IA Platform
System operation before kernel is loaded	A programmable read-only memory (PROM) chip with a monitor program runs diagnostics and displays device information. The PROM is also used to program default boot parameters and to test the devices connected to the system.	The basic input/output system (BIOS) runs diagnostics and displays device information. A Solaris Device Configuration Assistant boot diskette with the Multiple Device Boot (MDB) program is used to boot from nondefault boot partitions, the network, or the CD-ROM.

Table A SPARC and IA System Administration Differences (Continued)

Category	SPARC Platform	IA Platform
Booting the system	Commands and options at the PROM level are used to boot the system.	Commands and options at the MBD, primary, and secondary boot subsystems level are used to boot the system.
Boot programs	`bootblk`, the primary boot program, loads `ufsboot`. `ufsboot`, the secondary boot program, loads the kernel.	`mboot`, the master boot record, loads `pboot`. `pboot`, the Solaris partition boot program, loads `bootblk`. `bootblk`, the primary boot program, loads `ufsboot`. `ufsboot`, the secondary boot program, loads the kernel.
System shutdown	The `shutdown` and `init` commands can be used without additional operator intervention.	The `shutdown` and `init` commands are used but require operator intervention to type any key to continue the prompt.
Disk controllers	SCSI	SCSI and IDE
Disk slices and partitions	A disk may have a maximum of eight slices, numbered 0-7.	A disk may have a maximum of four `fdisk` partitions. The Solaris `fdisk` partition may contain up to 10 slices, numbered 0–9, but only 0–7 can store user data.
Diskette drives	Desktop systems usually contain one 3.5-inch diskette drive.	Systems may contain two diskette drives: a 3.5-inch and a 5.25-inch drive.

Solaris System Software Evolution

To help you understand how Solaris is evolving, Table B provides a list of the major system administration feature differences for each release.

Table B Solaris System Software Evolution

Release	New Features
Solaris 1.0	Berkeley (BSD) UNIX contains Solaris 4.x functionality.
Solaris 2.0 (SunOS 5.0)	A merger of AT&T System V Release 4 (SVR4) and BSD UNIX. To facilitate customer transition, Solaris uses SVR4 as the default environment, with BSD commands and modes as an option. Administration Tool provides a graphical user interface Database Manager and Host Manager.
Solaris 2.1 (SunOS 5.1)	Administration Tool adds a graphical user interface Printer Manager and User Account Manager.
Solaris 2.2 (SunOS 5.2)	Volume management integrates access to CD-ROM and diskette files with the File Manager and provides a command-line interface. Users no longer need superuser privileges to mount CD-ROMs and diskettes. Solaris 2.0 and 2.1 procedures do not work with volume management because volume management controls and owns the devices.
Solaris 2.3 (SunOS 5.3)	Volume management changes Solaris 2.2 mount point naming conventions.
	Administration Tool adds a graphical user interface Serial Port Manager with templates that provide default settings, which makes adding character terminals and modems much easier.
	The automounter is split into two programs: an automounted daemon and a separate automount program. Both are run when the system is booted. The `/tmp_mnt` mount point is not displayed as part of the path name, and the local path is displayed as `/home/`*`username`*. Additional predefined automount map variables are provided. (Refer to the *Solaris Advanced System Administrator's Guide*.)
	Online: Backup 2.1 is included with the release. (Not documented in this book.)

Table B Solaris System Software Evolution (Continued)

Release	New Features
	Pluggable Authentication Model (PAM) is included with the release. PAM provides a consistent framework to enable access control applications, such as `login`, to be able to choose any authentication scheme available on a system, without concern for implementation details. (Not documented in this book.)
	C2 Security is included in this release. (Not documented in this book.)
	The `format`(1) command changes for SCSI disks. (Not documented in this book.)
	PPP network protocol product that provides IP network connectivity over a variety of point-to-point connections is included in this release. (Not documented in this book.)
	Cache File System (CacheFS) for NFS is included in this release. CacheFS is a generic, nonvolatile caching mechanism to improve performance of certain file systems by using a small, fast, local disk.
	New NIS+ setup scripts are included in this release. The `nisserver`(1M), `nispopulate`(1M), and `nisclient`(1M) scripts enable you to set up an NIS+ domain much more quickly and easily than if you used the individual NIS+ commands to do so. With these scripts, you can avoid a lengthy manual setup process.
Solaris 2.4 (SunOS 5.4)	New Motif GUI for Solaris software installation is added. (Not documented in this book.)
Solaris 2.5 (SunOS 5.5)	New `pax`(1M) portable archive interchange command for copying files and file systems to portable media is added.
	Admintool is used to administer only local systems. Solstice AdminSuite product is available for managing systems in a network for SPARC and IA systems.
	New process tools are available in `/usr/proc/bin` that display highly detailed information about the active processes stored in the process file system in the `/proc` directory.

Table B Solaris System Software Evolution (Continued)

Release	New Features
	Telnet client is upgraded to the 4.4 BSD version. `rlogin` and `telnetd` remote login capacity are improved. (Not documented in this book.)
Solaris 2.5.1 (SunOS 5.5.1)	The limit on user ID and group ID values is raised to 2147483647, or the maximum value of a signed integer. The `nobody` user and group (60001) and the no access user and group (60002) retain the same UID and GID as in previous Solaris releases.
Solaris 2.6 (SunOS 5.6)	Changes to the Solaris 2.6 printing software provide a better solution than the LP print software in previous Solaris releases. You can easily set up and manage print clients by using the NIS or NIS+ nameservices to enable centralization of print administration for a network of systems and printers. New features include redesign of print packages, print protocol adapter, bundled SunSoft Print Client software, and network printer support.
	New `nisbackup` and `nisrestore` commands provide a quick and efficient method of backing up and restoring NIS+ namespaces.
	New patch tools, including `patchadd` and `patchrm` commands, add and remove patches. These commands replace the `installpatch` and `backoutpatch` commands that were previously shipped with each individual patch. (Refer to the *Solaris Advanced System Administrator's Guide*.)
	New `filesync` command ensures that data is moved automatically between a portable computer and a server. (Not documented in this book.)
	The previous flat `/proc` file system is restructured into a directory hierarchy that contains additional subdirectories for state information and control functions. This release also provides a watchpoint facility to monitor access to and modifications of data in the process address space. The `adb`(1) command uses this facility to provide watchpoints.

Table B Solaris System Software Evolution (Continued)

Release	New Features
	Large files are supported on UFS, NFS, and CacheFS file systems. Applications can create and access files up to one Tbyte on UFS-mounted file systems and up to the limit of the NFS server for NFS- and CacheFS-mounted file systems. A new `-mount` option disables the large-file support on UFS file systems. Using the `-mount` option enables system administrators to ensure that older applications that are not able to safely handle large files do not accidentally operate on large files.
	NFS Kerberos authentication now uses DES encryption to improve security over the network. The kernel implementations of NFS and RPC network services now support a new RPC authentication flavor that is based on the Generalized Security Services API (GSS-API). This support contains the hooks for future stronger security of the NFS environment. (Refer to the *Solaris Advanced System Administrator's Guide*.)
	The PAM authentication modules framework enables you to "plug in" new authentication technologies. (Refer to the *Solaris Advanced System Administrator's Guide*.)
	Font Admin enables easy installation and use of fonts for the X Window System. It supports TrueType, Type0, Type1, and CID fonts for multibyte languages and provides comparative font preview capability. It is fully integrated into the CDE desktop. (Not documented in this book.)
	TrueType fonts are supported through X and Display PostScript. Font Admin enables easy installation and integration of third-party fonts into the Solaris environment. (Not documented in this book.)
	The Solaris 2.6 operating environment is year 2000 ready. It uses unambiguous dates and follows the X/Open guidelines where appropriate. (Not documented in this book.)
	WebNFS software enables file systems to be accessed through the Web with the NFS protocol. This protocol is very reliable and provides greater throughput under a heavy load. (Not documented in this book.)

Table B Solaris System Software Evolution (Continued)

New!

Release	New Features
	The Java Virtual Machine 1.1 integrates the Java platform for the Solaris Operating Environment. It includes the Java runtime environment and the basic tools needed to develop Java applets and applications. (Not documented in this book.)
	For IA systems, the Configuration Assistant interface is part of the new booting system for the Solaris (Intel Platform Edition) software. It determines which hardware devices are in the system, accounts for the resources each device uses, and enables users to choose which device to boot from.
	For IA systems, the `kdmconfig` program configures the mouse, graphics adapter, and monitor. If an `owconfig` file already exists, `kdmconfig` extracts any usable information from it. In addition, `kdmconfig` retrieves information left in the `devinfo` tree by the `defconf` program and uses that information to automatically identify devices. (Not documented in this book.)
	Release is fully compliant with X/Open UNIX 95, POSIX standards. (Not documented in this book.)
Solaris 7 (SunOS 5.7)	Solaris 64-bit operating environment is added (SPARC Platform Edition only). (Not documented in this book.)
	UFS logging improves file system support.
	Lightweight Directory Access Protocol (LDAP) protocol improves managing name databases. (Not documented in this book.)
	Java Development Kit for Solaris significantly improves scalability and performance for Java applications. (Not documented in this book.)
	Dynamic reconfiguration significantly decreases system downtime.
	AnswerBook2 server runs on a Web server. (Not documented in this book.)
	Unicode locales enhanced with multiscript capabilities and six new Unicode locales are added.

Table B Solaris System Software Evolution (Continued)

Release	New Features
	RPC security is enhanced with integrity and confidentiality. (Not documented in this book.)
	The Solaris Common Desktop Environment (CDE) contains new tools to make it easy to find, manipulate, and manage address cards, applications, e-mail addresses, files, folders, hosts, processes, and Web addresses. (Not documented in this book.)
Solaris 8 (SunOS 5.8)	IPv6 adds increased address space and improves Internet functionality by using a simplified header format, support for authentication and privacy, autoconfiguration of address assignments, and new quality-of-service capabilities.
	The Solaris Operating Environment provides the Naming Service switch back-end support for Lightweight Directory Access Protocol (LDAP) based directory service. (Not documented in this book.)
	The Java2 Software Development Kit for Solaris significantly improves scalability and performance of Java applications. (Not documented in this book.)
	The Solaris 8 Installation CD provides a graphical, wizard-based, Java-powered application to install the Solaris Operating Environment and other software. (Not documented in this book.)
	The Solaris 8 Operating Environment supports the Universal Disk Format (UDF) file system, enabling users to exchange data stored on CD-ROMs, disks, diskettes, DVDs, and other optical media.
	The Solaris Smart Card feature enables security administrators to protect a computer desktop or individual application by requiring users to authenticate themselves by means of a smart card. (Not documented in this book.)
	The PDA Synchronization (PDA Sync) application synchronizes the data from applications such as Desktop Calendar, Desktop Mail, Memo, and Address, with data in similar applications on a user's Personal Digital Assistant (PDA). (Not documented in this book.)

New!

Table B Solaris System Software Evolution (Continued)

Release	New Features
	The Solaris 8 Software CDs and Languages CD include support for more than 90 locales, covering 37 languages. (Not documented in this book.)
	The Solaris Common Desktop Environment (CDE) contains new and enhanced features that incorporate easy-to-use desktop productivity tools, PC interoperability, and desktop management tools. (Not documented in this book.)
	The X Server is upgraded to the X11R6.4 industry standard that includes features to increase user productivity and mobility, including remote execution of X applications through a Web browser on any Web-based desktop, Sinerama, Color Utilization Policy, EnergyStar support, and new APIs and documentation for the developer tool kits. (Not documented in this book.)
	Role-Based Access Control (RBAC) enables system administrators to create specific roles by which they can assign superuser privileges for specific tasks to one or more individual users.

New! Freeware

The following freeware tools and libraries are included in the Solaris 8 release.

- `bash`—`sh`-compatible command language interpreter.
- `bzip2`—Block-sorting file compressor.
- `gpatch`—Applies patch files to originals.
- `gzip`—GNU zip compression command.
- `less`—A pager similar to `more`.
- `libz`—Also known as `zlib`. A library that performs compression, specifically, RFCs 1950-1952.
- `misofs`—Builds a CD image, using an iso9660 file system.
- `rmp2cpio`—Transforms a package in RMP format (Red Hat Package Manager) to a `cpio` archive.
- `tcsh`—C shell with file-name completion and command-line editing.
- `zip`—Compression and file packaging command.

- `zsh`—Command interpreter (shell) usable as an interactive login shell and as a shell script command processor.

1

INTRODUCING SOLARIS SYSTEM ADMINISTRATION

Winchester Mystery House [in San Jose, California] . . . was designed to baffle the evil spirits that haunted Sarah Winchester, eccentric heiress to the Winchester Arms fortune and mistress of the house. With 160 rooms and 2,000 doors, 13 bathrooms, 10,000 windows, 47 fireplaces, blind closets, secret passageways, and 40 staircases, the house is so complex that even the owner and servants needed maps to find their way.

—AAA, California/Nevada TourBook, 1991

Sarah Winchester, listening to the advice of psychics, believed that if she kept adding rooms to the house, she would not die and be subject to the influences of spirits who had been killed with the Winchester rifles manufactured by her husband.

The UNIX operating system is much like the Winchester Mystery House without, we hope, the evil spirits. The original operating system has been continually enhanced and expanded. There are many ways to get about, and, like the owner and the servants in the Winchester house, system administrators frequently need a map to help them get from place to place.

To add to the complexity, there are many versions of the UNIX operating system based on either Berkeley (or BSD) UNIX or AT&T's System V. This book serves as a map to some of the most frequently used "rooms" of the Solaris Operating Environment, which is an enhanced implementation of UNIX System V, Release 4 (usually referred to as SVR4).

Defining the System Administrator's Job

The system administrator's job is to keep the software (and perhaps hardware) functioning for a stand-alone system or for a set of systems on a network so that others can use the systems.

Typical duties of system administrators vary, depending on the number of systems supported and how the duties are divided up. It is not uncommon for system administrators to be experts in administering one or more areas and be inexperienced in others. Some administrators specialize in network administration; others in user accounts; and still others in areas such as printing.

The following list of typical system administration duties are described in part or in full in this book.

- Understanding shells.
    - Using generic shell commands.
    - Using Bourne shell commands.
    - Using C shell commands.
    - Using Korn shell commands.
- Administering user and group accounts.
    - Adding users.
    - Removing users.
    - Changing user information.
    - Creating new group accounts.

- Administering roles.
    - Granting users superuser permissions for specific tasks.
    - Creating, modifying, and deleting roles.
- Administering file systems.
    - Understanding the types of file systems.
    - Mounting and unmounting file systems.
    - Checking file-system consistency.
    - Backing up and restoring files and file systems.
    - Creating cache file systems.
- Administering devices.
    - New! Understanding device autoconfiguration.
    - New! Using DVD-ROM devices.
    - Using tape cartridges.

    - Formatting diskettes.
    - Monitoring disk use.
    - Administering disks.
    - Understanding the Service Access Facility.
    - Setting up a bidirectional modem.
- Administering systems.
    - Finding system information.
    - Creating local mail aliases.
    - Configuring additional swap space.
    - Administering the system date and time.
- Administering network services.
    - Finding network information.
    - Transferring files between systems.
    - Administering NIS+ databases.
    - Displaying network statistics.
    - Displaying network configuration information.

- Administering printing.
    - Setting up a print client and print server.
    - Using printing commands.
- Recognizing file access problems.
    - Identifying roblems with search paths.
    - Solving problems with permission and ownership.
    - Locating problems with network access.

The organization of this book matches the tasks listed above. To accomplish these tasks, you need to know when and how to perform the following tasks.

- Gain full access to all file systems and resources.
- Communicate with users.
- Shut down and start up systems.
- Monitor processes.

However, information about the following system administration tasks is beyond the scope of this book.

- Installing system software.
- Installing third-party software.
- Setting up and administering network services.
- Setting up and administering mail services.

- Adding and removing hardware.
- Administering security and accounting.
- Monitoring system and network performance.

The rest of the sections in this chapter, which describe how to accomplish the system administrator's tasks, introduce some basic commands and administrative tools.

Understanding Superuser Status

The *superuser* is a privileged user with unrestricted access to all files and commands. The superuser has the special UID (user ID) 0. The user name for this account is *root*. Note that the terms *root* and *superuser* have the same meaning and are used interchangeably in this book. You must be root to perform many system administration tasks, such as mounting and unmounting file systems, changing ownership or permissions for a file or directory you do not own, backing up and restoring file systems, creating device files, and shutting down the system.

You can become superuser in one of two ways.

- When logged in as another user, by typing the **su** (switch user) command with no arguments, and then typing the root password.
- From a login prompt, by typing **root** and then typing the root password.

When you have superuser privileges, the shell provides a special # (pound sign) prompt to remind you that you have extra access to the system. The system keeps a log that records each time the `su` command is used and who uses it. You can keep track of who is using the superuser account by consulting the `/var/adm/sulog` log file.

Become superuser only when it is required, and avoid doing your routine work as superuser. Occasionally, you may need to log out of your user account and log in again as root. When a task in this book requires you to log in as root, you are instructed to do so. You should switch user (**su**) to root, perform the required tasks, and exit superuser status when the tasks are complete.

Because unauthorized access to root can be a serious security breach, always add a password to the root account. For enhanced security, change the root password frequently.

NOTE. The default shell for root is the Bourne shell. See Chapter 3, "Understanding Shells," for more information on shells.

Becoming Superuser (su)

Become superuser only when you need to perform a task that requires root permissions. Use the following steps to become superuser.

1. At the shell prompt ($ or %), type **su** and press Return. You are prompted for the superuser (root) password, if one has been set up.
2. Type the superuser password and press Return. If you enter the password correctly, you have superuser (root) access to the system and the root prompt (#) is displayed.

```
oak% su
Password:
#
```

NOTE. If you want to use root's environment variables, type **su -** *and press Return.*

Exiting Superuser Status

To exit superuser status, simply type **exit** and press Return. The shell prompt is redisplayed.

```
# exit
oak%
```

Logging In as Root

To log in as root, the system must be at a login prompt.

1. At a login prompt, type **root** and press Return. You are prompted for the root password.
2. Type the root password and press Return. If you enter the password correctly, you have superuser (root) access to the system, and the root prompt (#) is displayed in all open terminal windows.

```
login: root
Password:
```

With the Role-Based Access Control (RBAC) security feature, new in the Solaris 8 Operating Environment, you can assign a subset of superuser privileges to a role and assign one or more users to that role. See Chapter 5, "Administering Roles," for more information. If you are a member of a role New!

that assigns a subset of superuser privileges, you log in by using the role name and the password assigned to that role.

Communicating with Users

An important part of your job as a system administrator is communicating with users to let them know that a task you are performing can affect their ability to use a system. Always let users know when you are about to perform a task that affects them, such as rebooting a system, installing new software, or changing the environment in some way.

You can communicate with users by personal visit or phone, but the most common way is by using the system to notify users in one of the following ways.

- Display a system-specific message at login by using the message of the day.
- Send a message directly to an individual user's terminal by using the `write` command.
- Send a message to all users on a system by using the `wall` command.
- Send a message to all users on a network by using the `rwall` command.
- Send a message to an individual or a group of users by electronic mail.

Displaying System-Specific Messages at Login (motd)

Each time a user logs in to a system, the message of the day in the file `/etc/motd` is displayed. The message is not displayed to users who are already logged in and are using the system. Use `motd` to give users system-specific information that someone logging in would want to know. This information might include the release number of the installed operating system, changes to system software, the name of the newly installed (or deleted) third-party software, or a list of scheduled downtimes.

Be sure to keep the `motd` file current. If `motd` displays outdated messages, users may begin to ignore all the messages, thereby missing critical information when it is presented. Keep the message short: If the message is longer than a screenful of information, users won't be able to read the beginning.

Root should own the `/etc/motd` file and be the only user who has write permission to it.

```
oak% ls -l /etc/motd
-rw-r--r--   1 root     sys      49 Jan  1  1970 /etc/motd
oak%
```

NOTE. When the system software is installed, several files, including `/etc/motd`*, have a time stamp of "Jan 1 1970." This date is the beginning of UNIX time. When you edit these files, the time stamp is updated.*

The default `/etc/motd` file contains information about the Solaris release level. The following example shows the default `/etc/motd` file for Solaris 8.

```
paperbark% more /etc/motd
Sun Microsystems Inc.   SunOS 5.8          Generic  February 2000
paperbark%
```

Creating a Message of the Day

Use the following steps to create a message of the day.

1. Become superuser.
2. Use an editor such as `vi` to edit the `/etc/motd` file.
3. Delete any existing messages and type the new one.
4. Save the changes.

   The message is changed and is displayed the next time a user logs in to the system.

Sending a Message to an Individual User

You can send a message to the terminal of an individual user by using the `write` command. When a windowing system such as CDE or OpenWindows, is used, each window is considered a separate login. If the user is logged in more than once, the message is directed to the console window.

NOTE. In the CDE environment, users typically do not use a console window. If the console window is not open, the user never sees the message because it is not displayed if the user opens a console window after the `write` *message has been received.* New!

Typing a Short Message to an Individual User (write)

Use the following steps to send a short, one-time message to an individual user.

1. Type **`write`** ***`username`*** and press Return. *`username`* is the login name of the user.
2. Type the message you want to send.
3. When the message is complete, press Control-D.

   The message is displayed in the user's console window.

The following example shows a message a system administrator might type.

```
# write winsor
winsor is logged on more than one place.
You are connected to "console".
Other locations are:
pts/3
pts/4
pts/5
pts/6
pts/7
I'll come by at 12:00 to look at your problem.
#
```

As you can see, `winsor` is logged in to more than one place and `write` tells you that it is sending the message to the console window. The message is displayed in the user's console window, as shown in the following example.

```
paperbark%
        Message from winsor on paperbark (pts/6) [ Tue Mar  7 16:40:09 ] ...
I'll come by at 12:00 to look at your problem.
<EOT>
```

Sending a Message from a File to an Individual User (write)

If you have a longer message that you want to send to a number of users, use the following steps to create the message in a file and then use the file name as an argument to the `write` command.

1. Create a file containing the text of the message you want to send.
2. Type **`write`** ***`username < filename`*** and press Return.

In the following example, the system administrator uses the `cat` command to create a file named `message` that contains a short message and then uses the `write` command to send the message.

```
oak% cat > message
I'll come by at 12:00 to look at your problem.
oak% write ignatz@elm < message
write: ignatz logged in more than once ... writing to console
oak%
```

If the user is logged in to more than one window, the message is displayed in the user's console window, as shown below.

```
Message from fred@oak on ttyp1 at 11:20 ...
I'll come by at 12:00 to look at your problem.
EOF
```

As you can see, the user doesn't see any difference in the output created from a typed message and the message included from a file. The user can initiate a dialogue by using the `write` command to respond, but the dialogue is not truly interactive. Two `write` paths are open, one in each direction. See the `write`(1) manual page for more information. For more information about manual pages, see "Using Manual Pages" on page 94.

Sending a Message to All Users on a System or Network (wall, rwall)

You can use the `wall` (write all) command to simultaneously send a message to every user on a system. You can use the `rwall` (remote write all) command to simultaneously send a message to the console window of every user on a network.

NOTE. In the CDE environment, users typically do not use a console window. If the console window is not open, the user never sees the message because it is not displayed if the user opens a console window after the `wall` *message has been received.* New!

Use the following steps to send a message to all users on a system.

1. Type **`wall`** and press Return.
2. Type the message you want to send.
3. When the message is complete, press Control-D. The message is displayed in the console window of each user on the system.

The following example shows a message a system administrator might type.

```
oak% wall
System will be rebooted at 12:00.
oak%
```

The message is displayed in the users' console window, as shown below.

```
Broadcast message from root on console ...
System will be rebooted at 12:00.
EOF
```

NOTE. Use the `rwall` *command carefully because it consumes extensive system and network resources.*

Use the following steps to send a message to all users on a network.

1. Type **`rwall -n`** ***`netgroup`*** and press Return.
2. Type the message you want to send.
3. When the message is complete, press Control-D. The message is displayed in the console window of each user on the system.

The following example shows a message the system administrator might type to send to all members of the netgroup `Eng`.

```
oak% rwall -n Eng
System oak will be rebooted at 12:00.
oak%
```

The message is displayed in the users' console windows, as shown below.

```
Broadcast message from root on console ...
System will be rebooted at 12:00.
```

You can also use the `rwall` command to send a message to all users on a system by typing **`rwall`** ***`hostname`***.

Sending a Message by E-Mail

E-mail is an effective way to communicate some system administration informational messages. However, this book does not describe how to use electronic mail. See the `mail`(1), `mailtool`(1), `mailx`(1), and `dtmail`(1X) manual pages for information about the mail programs.

Starting Up and Shutting Down Systems

Starting up and shutting down systems is an integral part of performing system administration tasks. This section describes procedures for routinely starting up and shutting down systems. If a system does not start up gracefully, see your system documentation for information on how to diagnose booting problems.

The Solaris Operating Environment is designed to be left running continuously so that the e-mail and network software can work correctly. You must, however, halt or shut down a system when performing the following tasks.

- Turning off system power.
- Installing a new release.
- Preparing for a power outage.
- Adding hardware to a system.
- Performing maintenance on a file system.

Choosing an Init State

The init state (also called run level) determines what programs are started or initialized when a system is booted. A system can be in only one init state at a time. The Solaris Operating Environment has eight init states; the default init state for each system is specified in the `/etc/inittab` file. The default `init` state for the Solaris Operating Environment is run level 3. Table 1 shows the available run levels and the state of the system at each level.

Table 1 System Init States

Init State	Function
`0`	Power-down state.
`S, or s`	Single-user state. All file systems mounted.
`1`	Administrative state. All file systems mounted and user logins allowed.
`2`	Multiuser state (resources not exported). All daemons are running except the NFS server daemons.
`3`	Multiuser state. NFS resource-sharing available.
`4`	Alternative multiuser state (currently unused).

Table 1 System Init States (Continued)

New!

Init State	Function
5	Power-down state. Shut down the operating system so that it is safe to turn off power to the system. If possible, turn off power on systems that support this feature.
6	Reboot. Shut down the system to init state 0 and then reboot to the multiuser state defined in the `inittab` file.

The `/sbin/init` command is responsible for keeping the system running correctly and is the command you use to change init states. You can also use the init states (with the `-i` option) as arguments to the `shutdown` command. The four types of system states are described below.

New!

- Power-down (run levels 0 and 5).
- Single-user (run levels 1 and s or S).
- Multiuser (run levels 2 and 3).
- Reboot (run level 6).

When preparing to do a system administration task, you need to determine which init state is appropriate for the system and the task at hand.

New!

The /etc/inittab File

When you boot a system or use the `init` or `shutdown` command to change run levels, the `init` daemon starts processes by reading information from the `/etc/inittab` file. This file defines the following important items for the `init` process.

- The default run level for the system.
- The processes to start, monitor, and restart if they terminate.
- Actions to take when the system enters a new run level.

Each entry in the `/etc/inittab` file has the following fields.

```
id:rstate:action:process
```

Table 2 describes the fields in the /etc/inittab file.

Table 2 Fields in the inittab File

Field	Description
id	A unique identifier for the entry.
rstate	A list of run levels to which this entry applies.
action	How the process specified in the process field is to be run. Possible values include initdefault, sysinit, boot, bootwait, wait, and respawn.
process	The command to execute.

The following example shows a default /etc/inittab file.

```
ap::sysinit:/sbin/autopush -f /etc/iu.ap
ap::sysinit:/sbin/soconfig -f /etc/sock2path
fs::sysinit:/sbin/rcS sysinit          >/dev/msglog 2<>/dev/msglog </dev/console
is:3:initdefault:
p3:s1234:powerfail:/usr/sbin/shutdown -y -i5 -g0 >/dev/msglog 2<>/dev/msglog
sS:s:wait:/sbin/rcS                    >/dev/msglog 2<>/dev/msglog </dev/console
s0:0:wait:/sbin/rc0                    >/dev/msglog 2<>/dev/msglog </dev/console
s1:1:respawn:/sbin/rc1                 >/dev/msglog 2<>/dev/msglog </dev/console
s2:23:wait:/sbin/rc2                   >/dev/msglog 2<>/dev/msglog </dev/console
s3:3:wait:/sbin/rc3                    >/dev/msglog 2<>/dev/msglog </dev/console
s5:5:wait:/sbin/rc5                    >/dev/msglog 2<>/dev/msglog </dev/console
s6:6:wait:/sbin/rc6                    >/dev/msglog 2<>/dev/msglog </dev/console
fw:0:wait:/sbin/uadmin 2 0             >/dev/msglog 2<>/dev/msglog </dev/console
of:5:wait:/sbin/uadmin 2 6             >/dev/msglog 2<>/dev/msglog </dev/console
rb:6:wait:/sbin/uadmin 2 1             >/dev/msglog 2<>/dev/msglog </dev/console
sc:234:respawn:/usr/lib/saf/sac -t 300
co:234:respawn:/usr/lib/saf/ttymon -g -h -p "`uname -n` console login: " -T sun
 -d /dev/console -l console -m ldterm,ttcompat
```

Run Control Scripts

New!

The init command uses a different script for each run level instead of grouping all of the run levels together. The files named by a run level are located in the /sbin directory.

The following listing shows the default run control scripts in the /sbin directory.

```
paperbark% ls -l /sbin/rc*
-rwxr--r--   3 root     sys         2792 Jan  6 07:55 /sbin/rc0
-rwxr--r--   1 root     sys         3177 Jan  6 07:55 /sbin/rc1
-rwxr--r--   1 root     sys         2885 Jan  6 07:55 /sbin/rc2
-rwxr--r--   1 root     sys         2341 Jan  6 07:55 /sbin/rc3
-rwxr--r--   3 root     sys         2792 Jan  6 07:55 /sbin/rc5
-rwxr--r--   3 root     sys         2792 Jan  6 07:55 /sbin/rc6
-rwxr--r--   1 root     sys         9973 Jan  6 07:55 /sbin/rcS
paperbark%
```

Run control files are located in the /etc/init.d directory. These files are linked to corresponding run control files in the /etc/rc.etc and

/etc/rc*.d directories. The files in the /etc directory define the sequence in which the scripts are performed within each run level. For example, the /etc/rc2.d directory contains files, listed below, that start and stop processes for run level 2.

```
paperbark% ls /etc/rc2.d
K07dmi           S47asppp            S73nfs.client   S88sendmail
K07snmpdx        S48ppp              S74autofs       S88utmpd
K16apache        S69inet             S74syslog       S89bdconfig
K28nfs.server    S70uucp             S74xntpd        S90wbem
README           S71ldap.client      S75cron         S92volmgt
S01MOUNTFSYS     S71rpc              S75savecore     S93cacheos.finish
S05RMTMPFILES    S71sysid.sys        S76nscd         S94ncalogd
S20sysetup       S72autoinstall      S80PRESERVE     S96ab2mgr
S21perf          S72inetsvc          S80lp           S99audit
S30sysid.net     S72slpd             S80spc          S99dtlogin
S40llc2          S73cachefs.daemon   S85power
paperbark%
```

The scripts are always run in ASCII sort order. The names of the scripts have the form [K,S][0-9][A-Z][0-99]. Files beginning with K are run to terminate (kill) some system process. Files beginning with S are run to start a system process. The actions of each run-level control script are summarized in the following sections.

The /sbin/rc0 Script The /sbin/rc0 script performs the following tasks.

- Stop system services and daemons.
- Terminate all running processes.
- Unmount all file systems.

The /sbin/rc1 Script The /sbin/rc1 script runs the /etc/rc1.d scripts to perform the following tasks.

- Stop system services and daemons.
- Terminate all running processes.
- Unmount all file systems.
- Bring the system up in single-user mode.

New!

The /sbin/rc2 script The /sbin/rc2 script runs the /etc/rc2.d scripts to perform the following tasks.

- Mount all local file systems.
- Enable disk quotas if at least one file system was mounted with the quota option.
- Save editor temporary files in /usr/preserve.
- Remove any files in the /tmp directory.
- When boot -r is used, create device entries in /dev for new disks.
- Configure system accounting.

- Configure default router.
- Set NIS domain and `ifconfig` netmask.
- Reboot the system from the installation media or a boot server if either `/.PREINSTALL` or `/AUTOINSTALL` exists.
- Start `inetd` and `rpcbind` and `named`, if appropriate.
- Start Kerberos client-side daemon, `kerbd`.
- Start NIS daemons (`ypbind`) and NIS+ daemons (`rpc.nisd`), depending on whether the system is configured for NIS or NIS+ and whether the system is a client or a server.
- Start `keyserv`, `statd`, `lockd`, `xntpd`, and `utmpd`.
- Mount all NFS entries.
- Start `cscd` (nameservice cache daemon).
- Start `automount`, `cron`, LP print service, `sendmail`, `utmpd`, and `vold` daemons.

NOTE. Many of the system services and applications started at run level 2 depend on what software is installed on the system.

The /sbin/rc3 Script The `/sbin/rc3` script runs the `/etc/rc3.d` scripts to perform the following tasks.

- Clean up `sharetab`.
- Start `nfsd`.
- Start `mountd`.
- If the system is a boot server, start `rarpd`, `rpc.bootparamd`, and `rpld`.
- Start `snmpdx` (Solstice Enterprise Agent process).

The /sbin/rc5 and /sbin/rc6 Scripts The `/sbin/rc5` and `/sbin/rc6` scripts run the `/etc/rc0d/K*` scripts to perform the following tasks.

- Kill all active processes.
- Unmount the file systems.

The /sbin/rcS script The `/sbin/rcS` script runs the `/etc/rcS.d` scripts to bring the system to run level S and perform the following tasks.

- Establish a minimal network.
- Mount `/usr` if necessary.
- Set the system name.
- Check the root and `/usr` file systems.
- Mount pseudofile systems (`/proc` and `/dev/fd`).
- Rebuild the device entries for reconfiguration boots.
- Check and mount other file systems to be mounted in single-user mode.

Finding the Run Level for a System

To find the run level for a system, type **who -r** and press Return. The run level, date and time, process termination status, process ID, and process exit status are displayed.

New!

In the following example, the system named `paperbark` is at the default multiuser run level (3), the date and time of the last run level change is `May 2 08:34`, the process termination status is `3`, the number of times at this run level since the last reboot is `0`, and the previous run level is `S`.

```
paperbark% who -r
   .       run-level 3  May  2 08:34     3      0  S
paperbark%
```

The next sections describe how you might use each init state.

Using Power-Down State, Run Level 0

Use run level 0 to shut down the operating system so that it is safe to turn off the power to the system.

Using Single-User State, Run Level s and S

Use run level s or S when performing administrative tasks that require you to be the only user on the system with all file systems mounted and accessible. The terminal from which you issue the `init 1` command becomes the console. No other users are logged in.

New!

NOTE. In the Solaris 7 release, Bug ID 1154696 was fixed so that you can cleanly bring a system to run level S (or single-user mode) by using the `shutdown -s` *or the* `init -s` *command. The* `inittab` *file and the* `rc` *scripts in the* `/etc/init.d` *directory and the* `/etc/rcn.d` *directories have been modified to ensure system run-level transitions are made cleanly and efficiently.*

Using Administrative State, Run Level 1

Use run level 1 as a single user to access all available file systems with user logins allowed.

Using Multiuser State, Run Level 2

Use run level 2 for normal operations. Multiple users can access the system and the entire file system. All daemons are running except for NFS server, `syslog`, and remote file sharing.

NOTE. A daemon *is a special type of program that, once activated, starts itself and carries out a specific task without any need for user input. Daemons typically are used to handle jobs, such as printing, mail, and communication, that have been queued.*

Using Remote Resource-Sharing State, Run Level 3

Use run level 3 for normal operations with NFS resource-sharing available.

Using Alternative Multiuser State, Run Level 4

Run level 4 is an alternative multiuser state, currently not used.

Using Power-Down State, Run Level 5

Use run level 5 to shut down the operating system so that it is safe to turn off power to the system. If possible, automatically turn off power on systems that support this feature. New!

Using Reboot State, Run Level 6

Use run level 6 to shut down the system to run level 0, and then reboot to multiuser level (or to whatever level is the default in the `inittab` file).

Changing Run Levels

Use either the `telinit` or `init` command to change run levels. The `telinit` command takes a one-character argument that tells `init` what run level to use. Although you can use the `init` command directly, `telinit` is the preferred command to use to change system run states.

Use the following steps to change run levels.

1. Become superuser.
2. Type **`telinit n`** and press Return. Replace the variable *n* with the number of the init state you want to use.

The following example shuts down the system.

```
oak% su
Password:
# telinit 0
```

The following example changes the system to single-user state.

```
oak% su
Password:
# telinit 1
```

The following example changes to multiuser state, with no NFS server daemons running.

```
oak% su
Password:
# telinit 2
```

The following example changes to multiuser state, with NFS server daemons running.

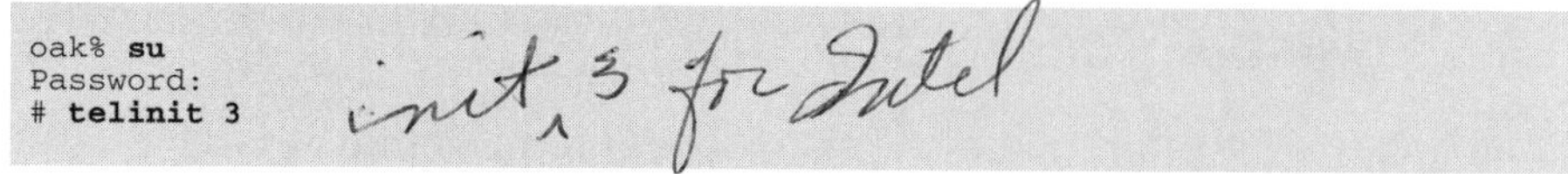

```
oak% su
Password:
# telinit 3
```

The following example shuts down and reboots a system.

```
oak% su
Password:
# telinit 6
```

Choosing Which Shutdown Command to Use

When preparing to do a system administration task, you need to determine which shutdown command is appropriate for the system and the task at hand. The next sections describe how you might use each of the available shutdown commands.

- `/usr/sbin/shutdown`
- `/etc/telinit` and `/sbin/init`
- `/usr/sbin/halt`
- `/usr/sbin/reboot`
- `/usr/sbin/uadmin`

These commands initiate shutdown procedures, kill all running processes, write out any new data to the disk, and shut down the Solaris Operating Environment to the appropriate run level.

shutdown

Use the `shutdown` command when shutting down a system with multiple users. The `shutdown` command sends a warning message to all users who are logged in, waits 60 seconds (the default), and then shuts down the system to single-user state. You can choose a different default wait time.

telinit and init

Use the `telinit` or `init` command to shut down a single-user system or to change its run level. The `init` command changes the run level of the system. The `telinit` command tells `init` what run level you want. You can use the commands interchangeably, but `telinit` is the preferred command. You can use `telinit` to place the system in power-down state (`init 0`) or in single-user state (`init 1`).

NOTE. Use `telinit/init` *and* `shutdown` *as the preferred method of changing system state. These programs are the most reliable way to shut down a system because they use a number of* `rc` *scripts to kill running processes.*

halt

Use the `halt` command when the system must be stopped immediately and it is acceptable not to warn any current users. The `halt` command shuts down the system without any delay and does not warn any other users on the system. The `halt` command does not run the `rc` shutdown scripts and is not the preferred method for shutting down a system.

reboot

Use the `reboot` command to shut down a system that does not have multiple users and to bring it back into multiuser state. The `reboot` command does not warn users on the system, does not run the `rc` scripts, and is not the preferred method for shutting down a system.

The Boot PROM (SPARC Platforms)

New!

Each SPARC system has a programmable read-only memory (PROM) chip with a program called the *monitor*. The monitor controls operation of the system before the kernel is available. When you turn a system on, the monitor runs a quick self-test procedure to check things such as the hardware and memory on the system. If the monitor finds no errors, the system begins the automatic boot process.

NOTE. Some older systems may require PROM upgrades before they will work with the Solaris Operating Environment. Contact your local service provider for more information.

The boot process consists of the boot PROM, boot programs, kernel initialization, and system initialization phases. These phases are summarized in Table 3.

Table 3 Description of the SPARC Boot Process

Boot Phase	Description
Boot PROM	The PROM displays system identification information and then runs self-test diagnostics to verify the hardware and memory of the system.
	Then, the PROM loads the `bootblk` primary boot program, which loads the secondary boot program from the default boot device located in the UFS fie system.
Boot programs	The `bootblk` program finds and executes the `ufsboot` secondary boot program and loads it into memory.
	After the `ufsboot` program is loaded, `ufsboot` loads the kernel.
Kernel initialization	The kernel initializes itself and begins loading modules, using `ufsboot` to read the files. When the kernel has loaded enough modules to mount the root file system, it terminates the `ufsboot` program and continues by using its own resources.
	The kernel creates a user process and starts the `/sbin/init` process, which starts other processes by reading the `/etc/inittab` file.
`init`	The `/sbin/init` process starts the run control (`/sbin/rc*`) scripts, which execute a series of other scripts (`/etc/rc*.d/S*`). These scripts check and mount file systems, start various processes, and perform system maintenance tasks.

The OpenBoot Interface

The OpenBoot firmware on the SPARC PROM not only initiates the boot process but also provides a command-line interface. OpenBoot provides two modes. The restricted monitor mode, which displays the > prompt, provides only three commands. These commands enable you to boot the operating system (`b` *`specifiers`*), resume the execution of a halted program (`c`), or enter the Forth Monitor (`n`).

The Forth Monitor, also referred to as *new command mode*, is the default mode of the OpenBoot firmware. The Forth Monitor displays the `ok` prompt. This monitor enables you to access an extensive set of diagnostic commands for hardware and software. Anyone who has access to the system console can access these functions. To access the restricted monitor, at the ok PROM prompt, type **old-mode** and press Return.

Displaying the PROM Release for a System To display the PROM release for a system, at the ok PROM prompt type **banner** and press Return. Hardware configuration information, including the release number of the PROM is displayed, as shown in the following example.

```
ok banner
     Sun Ultra 2 UPA/Sbus (UltraSPARC 168MHz, Keyboard Present
     OpenBoot 3.11, 128 MB memory, installed, Serial #8223188.
     Ethernet address 8:0:20:7d:79:d4, Host ID 807d79d4
```

OpenBoot Configuration Information OpenBoot configuration parameters are listed in Table 4.

NOTE. Not all OpenBoot systems support all parameters. Defaults can vary depending on the system and the PROM revision.

Table 4 Boot Configuration Parameters

ansi-terminal?	
	Configuration variable to control the behavior of the terminal emulator. The value false makes the terminal emulator stop interpreting ANSI escape sequences, instead of just echoing them to the output device. Default is true.
auto-boot?	If true, boot automatically after power-on or reset. Default is true.
boot-command	
	Command executed if auto-boot? is true. Default is boot.
boot-device	
	Device from which to boot. boot-device can contain zero. or more device specifiers separated by spaces. Each device specifier can be either a PROM device alias or a PROM device path. The boot PROM tries to open each successive device specifier in the list, beginning with the first device specifier. The first device specifier that opens successfully is used as the device to boot from. Default is disk net.
boot-file	File to boot (an empty string lets the secondary booter choose default). Default is an empty string.
boot-from	Boot device and file (OpenBoot PROM version 1.x only). Default is vmunix.

Table 4 Boot Configuration Parameters (Continued)

boot-from-diag	
	Diagnostic boot device and file (OpenBoot PROM version 1.x only). Default is `le()unix`.
com*X*-noprobe	
	Where *X* is the number of the serial port, prevent device probe on serial port *X*.
diag-device	
	Diagnostic boot source device. Default is `net`.
diag-file	File from which to boot in diagnostic mode. Default is an empty string.
diag-level	Diagnostics level. Values include `off`, `min`, `max`, and `menus`. There may be additional platform-specific values. When set to `off`, POST is not called. If POST is called, the value is made available as an argument to, and is interpreted by, POST. The default value is platform dependent.
diag-switch?	
	If `true`, run in diagnostic mode. Default is `true`.
fcode-debug?	
	If `true`, include name parameter for plug-in device FCodes. Default is `false`.
hardware-revision	
	System version information. If `true`, include name parameter for plug-in device FCodes. Default is `false`.
input-device	
	Input device used at power-on (usually `keyboard`, `ttya`, or `ttyb`). Default is `keyboard`.
keyboard-click?	
	If `true`, enable keyboard click. Default is `false`.
keymap	Keymap for custom keyboard.
last-hardware-update	
	System update information.
load-base	Default load address for client programs. Default value is `16384`.

Table 4 Boot Configuration Parameters (Continued)

local-mac-address?	
	If true, network drivers use their own MAC address, not system's. Default is false.
mfg-mode	Manufacturing mode argument for POST. Possible values include off or chamber. The value is passed as an argument to POST. Default is off.
mfg-switch?	
	If true, repeat system self-tests until interrupted with STOP-A. Default is false.
nvramrc	Contents of NVRAMRC. Default is empty.
oem-banner	Custom OEM banner (enabled by setting oem-banner? to true). Default is an empty string.
oem-banner?	
	If true, use custom OEM banner. Default is false.
oem-logo	Byte-array custom OEM logo (enabled by setting oem-logo? to true). Displayed in hexadecimal.
oem-logo?	If true, use custom OEM logo (else, use Sun logo). Default is false.
output-device	
	Output device used at power-on (usually screen, ttya, or ttyb). Default is screen.
sbus-probe-list	
	Which SBus slots are probed and in what order. Default is 0123.
screen-#columns	
	Number of on-screen columns (characters/line). Default is 80.
screen-#rows	
	Number of on-screen rows (lines). Default is 34.
scsi-initiator-id	
	SCSI bus address of host adapter, range 0-7. Default is 7.
sd-targets	Map SCSI disk units (OpenBoot PROM version 1.x only). Default is 31204567, which means that unit 0 maps to target 3, unit 1 maps to target 1, and so on.

Table 4 Boot Configuration Parameters (Continued)

security-#badlogins		
	Number of incorrect security password attempts. This property has no special meaning or behavior on IA-based systems.	
security-mode		
	Firmware security level (options: none, command, or full). If set to command or full, system prompts for PROM security password. Default is none. This property has no special meaning or behavior on IA-based systems.	
security-password		
	Firmware security password (never displayed). Can be set only when security mode is set to command or full. This property has no special meaning or behavior on IA-based systems.	
selftest-#megs		
	Megabytes of RAM to test. Ignored if diag-switch? is true. Default is 1.	
skip-vme-loopback?		
	If true, POST does not do VMEbus loopback tests. Default is false.	
st-targets	Map SCSI tape units (OpenBoot PROM version 1.x only). Default is 45670123, which means that unit 0 maps to target 4, unit 1 maps to target 5, and so on.	
sunmon-compat?		
	If true, display Restricted Monitor prompt (>). Default is false.	
testarea	One-byte scratch field, available for read/write test. Default is 0.	
tpe-link-test?		
	Enable 10baseT link test for built-in twisted pair Ethernet. Default is true.	
ttya-mode	TTYA (baud rate, #bits, parity, #stop, handshake). Default is 9600,8,n,1,-.	
	Fields, in left-to-right order, are described below.	
	baud rate	110, 300, 1200, 4800, 9600...

Table 4 Boot Configuration Parameters (Continued)

	data bits	5, 6, 7, 8
	parity	n (none), e (even), o (odd), m (mark), s (space)
	stop bits	1, 1.5, 2
	handshake	- (none), h (hardware: rts/cts), s (software: xon/xoff)
ttyb-mode	TTYB (baud rate, #bits, parity, #stop, handshake). Default is 9600,8,n,1,-.	
	Fields, in left-to-right order, are described below.	
	baud rate	110, 300, 1200, 4800, 9600...
	data bits	5, 6, 7, 8
	stop bits	1, 1.5, 2
	parity	n (none), e (even), o (odd), m (mark), s (space)
	handshake	- (none), h (hardware: rts/cts), s (software: xon/xoff)
ttya-ignore-cd		
	If true, operating system ignores carrier-detect on TTYA. Default is true.	
ttyb-ignore-cd		
	If true, operating system ignores carrier-detect on TTYB. Default is true.	
ttya-rts-dtr-off		
	If true, operating system does not assert DTR and RTS on TTYA. Default is false.	
ttyb-rts-dtr-off		
	If true, operating system does not assert DTR and RTS on TTYB. Default is false.	
use-nvramrc?		
	If true, execute commands in NVRAMRC during system start-up. Default is false.	
version2?	If true, hybrid (1.x/2.x) PROM comes up in version 2.x. Default is true.	
watchdog-reboot?		
	If true, reboot after watchdog reset. Default is false.	

You can display and set the list of OpenBoot commands from Solaris by using the `eeprom` command or display the list at the `ok` PROM prompt by typing **`printenv`** and pressing Return.

The following example uses the `eeprom` command without arguments to display the current settings.

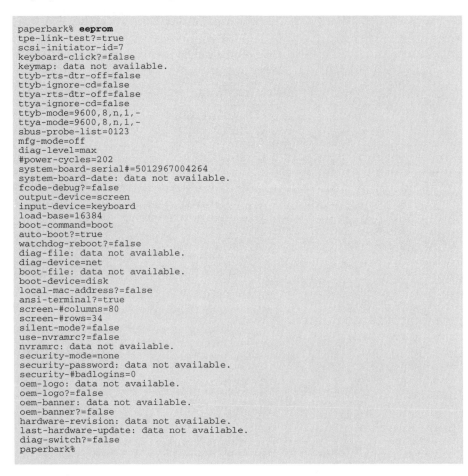

```
paperbark% eeprom
tpe-link-test?=true
scsi-initiator-id=7
keyboard-click?=false
keymap: data not available.
ttyb-rts-dtr-off=false
ttyb-ignore-cd=false
ttya-rts-dtr-off=false
ttya-ignore-cd=false
ttyb-mode=9600,8,n,1,-
ttya-mode=9600,8,n,1,-
sbus-probe-list=0123
mfg-mode=off
diag-level=max
#power-cycles=202
system-board-serial#=5012967004264
system-board-date: data not available.
fcode-debug?=false
output-device=screen
input-device=keyboard
load-base=16384
boot-command=boot
auto-boot?=true
watchdog-reboot?=false
diag-file: data not available.
diag-device=net
boot-file: data not available.
boot-device=disk
local-mac-address?=false
ansi-terminal?=true
screen-#columns=80
screen-#rows=34
silent-mode?=false
use-nvramrc?=false
nvramrc: data not available.
security-mode=none
security-password: data not available.
security-#badlogins=0
oem-logo: data not available.
oem-logo?=false
oem-banner: data not available.
oem-banner?=false
hardware-revision: data not available.
last-hardware-update: data not available.
diag-switch?=false
paperbark%
```

The following example changes the number of megabytes of RAM that the system tests from `1` to `2`.

```
# eeprom selftest-#megs
selftest-#megs=1
# eeprom selftest-#megs=2
selftest-#megs=2
#
```

The following example sets the method for setting the `auto-boot?` parameter to `true`. You may need to enclose the command in double quotation marks to prevent the shell from interpreting the question mark.

```
# eeprom "auto-boot?"=true
#
```

Alternatively, you can precede the question mark with an escape character (`\`) to prevent the shell from interpreting the question mark.

Commands Used to View or Modify Configuration Variables Table 5 describes the commands you can use from the `ok` PROM prompt to view or modify the OpenBoot configuration variables.

Table 5 Commands to View or Modify Configuration Variables

Command	Description
`help [`*`category`*`]`	Display a list of help categories. Help for an individual category is displayed if you specify a *`category`* argument.
`printenv [`*`variable`*`]`	Display the variable, the current value, and the default value. If you specify a variable, the values for that variable are displayed.
`setenv` *`variable value`*	Set *`variable`* to the specified numeric or text value. Changes are permanent, but often do not take effect until after you reset or reboot the system.
`set-default` *`variable`*	Reset the value of the variable to the factory default.
`set-defaults`	Reset all variable values to the factory defaults.
`password`	Set security-password.

Openboot Firmware Security Levels The OpenBoot firmware provides three levels of system security: `none`, `command`, and `full`.

For the `none` security level, no password is required. Users can change all OpenBoot settings, including the boot disk partition and execute any command. By default, Sun systems are shipped with the OpenBoot security level set to `none`.

For the `command` security level, a password is required for all commands except `boot` and `go` (continue system operation after a Stop-A, L1-A, or Break sequence).

For the `full` security level, a password is required for all OpenBoot commands except `go`.

You can set the OpenBoot security level either while running Solaris or from the `ok` PROM prompt.

Use the following steps to set the OpenBoot security level from Solaris.

1. Become superuser.
2. Type **`eeprom security-mode=`*`level`*** and press Return.

   The security level is set as specified by the *`level`* argument.

In the following example, the security level is set to `command`.

```
paperbark% su
Password:
# eeprom security-mode=command
```

To set the OpenBoot security level at the `ok` PROM prompt, type **`security-mode`** ***`level`*** and press Return.

In the following example, the security level is set to `full`.

```
ok security-mode full
```

For more information, refer to the `eeprom`(1M) manual page or to the OpenBoot documentation available from Sun Microsystems.

New!

The PC BIOS (IA Platforms)

For IA platforms, before the kernel is started, the system is controlled by the read-only-memory (ROM) Basic Input/Output System (BIOS), which is the firmware interface on a PC.

Hardware adapters can have an onboard BIOS that displays the physical characteristics of the device and that can be used to access the device. During the startup sequence, the PC BIOS checks for the presence of an adapter BIOS and, if found, loads and executes each one. The BIOS for each individual adapter runs self-test diagnostics and displays device information.

Boot Subsystems

You can make the choices about booting a system at three times during the Solaris IA boot process, as described below.

- Primary Boot Subsystem (Partition Boot Menu)—This first menu is displayed if multiple bootable `fdisk` partitions exist on the disk. The menu enables you to boot from one of the `fdisk` partitions. By default, the active partition is booted if you take no action. Note that if you boot a non-Solaris partition, the next two menus are never displayed.
- Interrupt the Autoboot Process—If you interrupt the autoboot process, you can access the Configuration Assistant, which enables you to boot the Solaris Operating Environment from a different boot device, configure new or misconfigured hardware, or perform other device- or boot-related tasks.
- Current Boot Parameters Menu—This menu has two forms, one for a normal Solaris boot and one for a Solaris installation boot.
    - The normal Current Boot Parameters menu enables you to boot the Solaris system with options or to enter the boot interpreter.
    - The install Current Boot Parameters menu enables you to choose the type of installation to be performed or to customize the boot.

Table 6 describes the IA Platform boot subsystems.

Table 6 IA Platform Boot Subsystems

Boot Subsystem	Description
Primary Boot Subsystem	This menu is displayed if the disk you are booting from contains more than one `fdisk` partition in addition to the Solaris `fdisk` partition.
Secondary Boot Subsystem	This menu is displayed each time you boot the Solaris Operating Environment. The Solaris Operating Environment is booted automatically unless you interrupt it to run the Solaris Device Configuration Assistant.
Solaris Device Configuration Assistant/Boot Diskette	You can access the Solaris Device Configuration Assistant menu by using the Solaris Device Configuration Assistant Boot Diskette to boot the system or by interrupting the autoboot process when booting the Solaris Operating Environment from an installed disk.
Current Boot Parameters Menu	This menu is displayed when you boot from a disk with the Solaris Operating Environment installed or if you want to install the Solaris release from the Solaris installation CD or the network. In either case, this menu presents a list of boot options.

When booting an IA platform, the Configuration Assistant performs the following tasks during the device identification phase.

- Scans for devices installed on the system.
- Displays the identified devices.
- Enables you to perform optional tasks such as choosing a keyboard type and editing devices and their resources.

During the boot phase, the system displays a list of devices from which to boot. The asterisk (*) marks the default boot device. You can perform optional tasks, such as editing autoboot and property settings.

The boot process consists of the BIOS, boot programs, kernel initialization, and system initialization phases. These phases are summarized in Table 7.

Table 7 Description of the IA Boot Process

Boot Phase	Description
BIOS	When the system is turned on, the PC BIOS runs self-test diagnostics to verify the hardware and memory on the system. If the BIOS finds no errors, the system begins to boot automatically. If errors are found, error messages are displayed describing recovery options.
	BIOS for additional hardware devices are run.
	The BIOS boot program tries to read the first physical sector from the boot diskette or hard drive. This first disk sector contains the `mboot` master boot record, which is loaded and executed. If BIOS finds no `mboot` program, an error message is displayed.
Boot programs	The `mboot` program contains disk information needed to find the active partition and the location of the `pboot` Solaris boot program. `mboot` loads and executes `pboot`.
	`pboot` loads `bootblk`, which is the primary boot program. `bootblk` loads the secondary boot program located in the UFS file system.
	If the disk has more than one bootable partition, `bootblk` reads the `fdisk` table to locate the default boot partition and builds and displays a menu of available partitions. You have a 30-second timeout interval during which you can choose an alternate partition from which to boot. This step occurs only if more than one bootable partition is present on the system.

Table 7 Description of the IA Boot Process (Continued)

Boot Phase	Description
	`bootblk` finds and executes either the `boot.bin` or `ufsboot` secondary boot program in the root file system. At this point, you have a 5-second timeout interval during which you can interrupt the autoboot to start the Configuration Assistant.
	`boot.bin` or `ufsboot` starts a command interpreter that executes the `/etc/bootrc` script, which provides a menu of choices for booting the system. The default action is to load and execute the kernel. You have a 5-second timeout interval during which you can specify a boot option or start the boot interpreter.
Kernel initialization	The kernel initializes itself and begins loading modules, using `boot.bin or ufsboot` to read the files. When the kernel has loaded enough modules to mount the root file system, it terminates the secondary boot program and continues by using its own resources.
	The kernel creates a user process and starts the `/sbin/init` process, which starts other processes by reading the `/etc/inittab` file.
`init`	The `/sbin/init` process starts the run control (`/sbin/rc*`) scripts, which execute a series of other scripts (`/etc/rc*.d/S*`). These scripts check and mount file systems, start various processes, and perform system maintenance tasks.

Booting a System

If a system is powered off, turning it on starts the multiuser boot sequence. The following procedures tell you how to boot in different states from the `ok` PROM prompt. If the PROM prompt is >, type **n** to display the `ok` prompt, and then follow the appropriate steps.

NOTE. The PROM prompt description is for SPARC systems.

Table 8 describes commands for booting a system for different reboot reasons.

Table 8 Commands for Booting a System

Reboot Reason	Boot Instructions
Turning off system power because of anticipated power outage.	Turn on system power.
Changing kernel parameters in the `/etc/system` file.	Reboot to run level 3 (multiuser mode with NFS resources shared) (`boot`). See "Booting in Multiuser State" on page 33 for more information.
Performing file system maintenance, such as performing a backup or restoring system data.	Use Control-D from run level S to bring the system back to run level 3.
Repairing a system configuration file such as `/etc/system`.	Interactive boot (`boot -a`). See "Booting Interactively" on page 33 for more information.
Changing pseudodevice parameters in the `/etc/system` file.	Reconfiguration boot (`boot -r`). See "Booting After Adding New Hardware" on page 35 for more information.
Adding or removing hardware from the system.	Reconfiguration boot (`boot -r`) plus turning on system power after adding or removing hardware. See "Booting After Adding New Hardware" on page 35 for more information.
Booting the kernel debugger to track down a system problem.	Boot `kadb`. See "Booting the System with the Kernel Debugger" on page 36.
Repairing an important system file that is causing system boot failure.	Recovery boot (SPARC Platform, `sync`; IA platform, `kadb`). See "Booting a System for Recovery Purposes (SPARC Platform) and "Booting a System for Recovery Purposes (IA Platform)" on page 37.

Table 8 Commands for Booting a System (Continued)

Reboot Reason	Boot Instructions
Recovering from a hung system and forcing a crash dump.	Recovery boot (SPARC Platform, `sync`; IA platform, `kadb`). See "Booting a System for Recovery Purposes (SPARC Platform) and "Booting a System for Recovery Purposes (IA Platform)" on page 37.

Booting in Multiuser State

To boot in multiuser state, at the `ok` PROM prompt, type **boot** and press Return. The automatic boot procedure starts on the default drive, displaying a series of start-up messages. The system is brought up in multiuser state.

Booting in Single-User State

To boot in single-user state, at the `ok` PROM prompt, type **boot -s** and press Return. The system boots to single-user state and prompts you for the root password.

```
ok boot -s

INIT: SINGLE USER MODE
Type Ctrl-d to proceed with normal start-up,
(or give root password for system maintenance)
Type the root password and press Return.
```

NOTE. To continue the process and bring the system up in multiuser state, press Control-D.

Booting Interactively

You may boot interactively if you want to make a temporary change to the system file or the kernel. In this way, you can test your changes and recover easily if you have any problems.

1. At the `ok` PROM prompt, type **boot -a** and press Return. The boot program prompts you interactively.
2. Press Return to use the default kernel `/kernel/unix`, or type the name of the kernel to use for booting.
3. Press Return to use the default modules directory path, or type the default path for the modules and press Return.
4. Press Return to use the default `/etc/system` file, or type the name of the system file and press Return.

5. Press Return to use the default root file system. Type **ufs** for local disk booting or **nfs** for diskless clients.
6. Press Return to use the default physical name of the root device, or type the device name.

In the following example, the user accepted the default choices (shown in square brackets [ ]) by pressing Return.

```
ok boot -a
(Hardware configuration messages)
rebooting from -a
Boot device: /sbus/esp@0,800000/sd@0,0 File and args: -a
Enter filename [/kernel/unix]:
Enter default directory for modules [/platform/SUNW,Ultra-2/kernel
  /platform/sun4u/kernel /kernel /usr/kernel]:
Name of system file [/etc/system]:
(Copyright notice)
root filesystem type [ufs]
Enter physical name of root device
[/sbus@if,0/SUNW,fas@e,8800000/sd@0.0:a]:
Swap filesystem type [swapfs]
Configuring IPv4 interfaces:  le0
Hostname: paperbark
The system is coming up. Please wait.
(fsck messages)
(Startup messages)
paperbark login:
```

New!

Looking at the Boot Messages

The most recent boot messages are stored in the /var/adm/messages file. To see these messages after you have booted the system, type **more /var/adm/messages** and press Return. The /usr/sbin/dmesg command is obsolete; however, you can still use it to display boot messages.

NOTE. You can now view /usr/sbin/dmesg *text from a CDE terminal window, which was not possible in previous releases.*

Because the /var/adm/messages file is maintained in chronological order, the most current boot messages are at the end of the file. The following example shows the last 30 lines of the /var/adm/messages file.

```
paperbark% tail -30 /var/adm/messages
Mar  7 18:11:15 paperbark swapgeneric: [ID 308332 kern.info] root on
  /sbus@1f,0/SUNW,fas@e,8800000/sd@0,0:a fstype ufs
Mar  7 18:11:16 paperbark sbus: [ID 349649 kern.info] zs0 at sbus0: SBus0 slot
  0xf offset 0x1100000 Onboard device sparc9 ipl 12
Mar  7 18:11:16 paperbark genunix: [ID 936769 kern.info] zs0 is
  /sbus@1f,0/zs@f,1100000
Mar  7 18:11:16 paperbark sbus: [ID 349649 kern.info] zs1 at sbus0: SBus0 slot
  0xf offset 0x1000000 Onboard device sparc9 ipl 12
Mar  7 18:11:16 paperbark genunix: [ID 936769 kern.info] zs1 is
  /sbus@1f,0/zs@f,1000000
Mar  7 18:11:19 paperbark rootnex: [ID 349649 kern.info] ffb0 at root: UPA
  0x1e 0x0
Mar  7 18:11:19 paperbark genunix: [ID 936769 kern.info] ffb0 is
  /SUNW,ffb@1e,0
Mar  7 18:11:19 paperbark unix: [ID 987524 kern.info] cpu0: SUNW,UltraSPARC
  (upaid 0 impl 0x10 ver 0x22 clock 168 MHz)
```

```
Mar  7 18:11:22 paperbark hme: [ID 517527 kern.info] SUNW,hme0 : Sbus (Rev Id
  = 22) Found
Mar  7 18:11:22 paperbark sbus: [ID 349649 kern.info] hme0 at sbus0: SBus0
  slot 0xe offset 0x8c00000 and slot 0xe offset 0x8c02000 and slot 0xe offset
  0x8c04000 and slot 0xe offset 0x8c06000 and slot 0xe offset 0x8c07000
  Onboard device sparc9 ipl 6
Mar  7 18:11:22 paperbark genunix: [ID 936769 kern.info] hme0 is
  /sbus@1f,0/SUNW,hme@e,8c00000
Mar  7 18:11:24 paperbark genunix: [ID 454863 kern.info] dump on
  /dev/dsk/c0t0d0s1 size 512 MB
Mar  7 18:11:26 paperbark hme: [ID 517527 kern.info] SUNW,hme0 : Internal
  Transceiver Selected.
Mar  7 18:11:26 paperbark hme: [ID 517527 kern.info] SUNW,hme0 :
  Auto-Negotiated   10 Mbps Half-Duplex Link Up
Mar  7 18:12:01 paperbark pseudo: [ID 129642 kern.info] pseudo-device: pm0
Mar  7 18:12:01 paperbark genunix: [ID 936769 kern.info] pm0 is /pseudo/pm@0
Mar  7 18:12:01 paperbark pseudo: [ID 129642 kern.info] pseudo-device: tod0
Mar  7 18:12:01 paperbark genunix: [ID 936769 kern.info] tod0 is /pseudo/tod@0
Mar  7 18:12:02 paperbark sendmail[250]: [ID 702911 mail.crit] My unqualified
  host name (paperbark) unknown; sleeping for retry
Mar  7 18:12:03 paperbark pseudo: [ID 129642 kern.info] pseudo-device:
  devinfo0
Mar  7 18:12:03 paperbark genunix: [ID 936769 kern.info] devinfo0 is
  /pseudo/devinfo@0
Mar  7 18:12:06 paperbark sws.smc[290]: [ID 987397 daemon.notice] [1 admin.195
  0 (SW) NOTICE]: Running with SWS Configuration file
  "/etc/ehttp/server.conf".
Mar  7 18:12:10 paperbark sws.smc[290]: [ID 409041 daemon.error] [1
  servlet.353 0 (SW) ERR]: Servlet smc load error.
Mar  7 18:12:10 paperbark sws.smc[290]: [ID 420037 daemon.notice] [1
  servlet.919 0 (SW) NOTICE]: Servlet Engine (with JSDK2.0) started.
Mar  7 18:12:10 paperbark sws.smc[290]: [ID 111395 daemon.notice] [1 httpd.105
  0 (SW) NOTICE]: Sun_WebServer/2.1 server started.
Mar  7 18:12:15 paperbark sws.smc[290]: [ID 329940 daemon.notice] [1 httpd.135
  0 (SW) NOTICE]: Shutting down server.
Mar  7 18:12:18 paperbark sws.smc[368]: [ID 987397 daemon.notice] [1 admin.195
  0 (SW) NOTICE]: Running with SWS Configuration file
  "/etc/ehttp/server.conf".
Mar  7 18:12:19 paperbark sws.smc[368]: [ID 420037 daemon.notice] [1
  servlet.919 0 (SW) NOTICE]: Servlet Engine (with JSDK2.0) started.
Mar  7 18:12:19 paperbark sws.smc[368]: [ID 111395 daemon.notice] [1 httpd.105
  0 (SW) NOTICE]: Sun_WebServer/2.1 server started.
Mar  7 18:13:02 paperbark sendmail[250]: [ID 702911 mail.alert] unable to
  qualify my own domain name (paperbark) -- using short name
paperbark%
```

Booting After Adding New Hardware

New!

A reconfiguration boot tells the system to probe for all connected devices and build the names for them in the /devices and /dev directories. A reconfiguration boot formerly required you to issue the `boot -r` command.

With the Solaris 8 release, the `devfsadm` command manages the special device files in the /dev and /devices directories. The new `devfsadmd` daemon handles both processing of reconfiguration boot and updating of the /dev and /devices directories and responds to dynamic reconfiguration events. Because `devfsadmd` automatically detects device configuration changes generated by any reconfiguration event, you no longer need to perform a reconfiguration boot (`boot -r`) when you add new hardware to a system. See Chapter 7, "Administering Devices," for more information.

You can use the `-r` option to the `boot` command so that the operating system knows to look for new device drivers and incorporate them as part of the boot process.

1. Load the new device driver, following the instructions included with the hardware.
2. Shut down your system and install the new hardware.
3. Type **`boot -r`** and press Return. A reconfiguration script is run to load all the device drivers listed in the modules directories and to create the corresponding hardware nodes.

Alternatively, if you add another device with the driver already installed, you can use the following commands to tell the system to recognize the new device.

```
# touch /reconfigure
# _INIT_RECONFIG=YES /etc/init.d/drvconfig
# _INIT_RECONFIG=YES /etc/init.d/devlinks
```

New!

Forcing a Crash Dump and Rebooting the System

Sometimes you need to save crash dumps of the operating system. You use the `savecore` feature to enable crash dumps. See `savecore`(1M) for more information. This section describes only how to reboot the system when the `savecore` feature is enabled.

1. Type the stop key sequence for your system.

   The specific sequence depends on your keyboard type. For example, you can press Stop-A or L1-A. On terminals, press the Break key.
2. At the `ok` prompt, type **`sync`** and press Return.

   The disk is synchronized and a crash dump is written. After the crash dump is written to disk, the system continues to reboot.

New!

Booting the System with the Kernel Debugger

Use the following steps to boot the system by using the kernel debugger.

1. Type the stop key sequence for your system.

   The specific sequence depends on your keyboard type. For example, you can press Stop-A or L1-A. On terminals, press the Break key.
2. At the `ok` prompt, type **`sync`** and press Return.

   The disk is synchronized and a crash dump is written.
3. When you see the `syncing file systems...` message, press the abort key sequence again.
4. At the `ok` prompt, type **`boot kadb`** and press Return.

5. Review kadb booting messages (starting with `Rebooting with command: kadb`) to verify that the system is booting with the kernel debugger.

Refer to the kadb(1M) manual page for information about how to use the kernel debugger.

Booting a System for Recovery Purposes (SPARC Platform) New!

Use the following procedure on SPARC platforms when the boot process fails. The boot process can fail, for example, when an important file such as /etc/passwd has an invalid entry.

1. Boot from the installation CD-ROM (**boot cdrom -s**) or from an installation server on the network (**boot -net -s**) and press Return.
2. Type **mount /dev/dsk/*device-name* /a** and press Return.
3. Type **cd /a/*directory*** and press Return.
4. Type **term=sun;export TERM** and press Return.
5. Remove the invalid entry from the file with an editor such as vi.
6. Type **cd /** and press Return.
7. Type **umount /a** and press Return.
8. Type **init 6** and press Return.

   The system is rebooted.
9. Verify that the system boots to run level 3.

   The login prompt is displayed when the boot process has finished successfully.

The following example shows how to repair the **/etc/passwd** file after booting from a local CD-ROM.

```
ok boot cdrom -s
(Boot messages are displayed here)
# mount /dev/dsk/c0t3d0s0 /a
# cd /a/etc
# TERM=sun;export TERM
# vi passwd
(Remove or edit invalid entry)
# cd /
# umount /a
# init 6
```

Booting a System for Recovery Purposes (IA Platform) New!

Use the following procedure on IA platforms when the boot process fails. The boot process can fail, for example, when an important file such as /etc/passwd has an invalid entry.

1. Boot from the Solaris 2 installation CD or from the network. Use steps a-g. If you are booting from the network, skip step a.

   a. Insert the Solaris 2 installation CD into the CD-ROM drive.

   b. (Optional) If the disk you are booting from doesn't contain the Solaris 8 Intel Platform Edition or compatible version, insert the Configuration Assistant/Boot Diskette into the primary diskette drive (DOS drive A).

   c. If the system displays the `Type any key to reboot` prompt, press any key to reboot the system. At this prompt, you can also press the reset button. If the system is shut down, turn the system on with the power on/off switch.

   d. At the Solaris Device Configuration Assistant screen, press the F2 key (F2_Continue).

      Device identification is performed, and a screen identifying the devices is displayed.

   e. At the Identified Devices screen, press the F2 key (F2_Continue).

      Bootable drivers are loaded.

   f. From the Boot Solaris screen, select the CD-ROM drive or network as the boot device. Then, press the F2 key (F2_Continue)

      The Solaris boot option screen is displayed.

   g. At the `Select the type of installation:` prompt, type **`b -s`** and press Return.

      After a few minutes, the single-user mode # prompt is displayed.
2. Type **`mount /dev/dsk/`*`device-name`*` /a`** and press Return.

   The root file system is mounted.
3. Type **`cd /a/`*`directory`*** and press Return.
4. Type **`term=sun;export TERM`** and press Return.

   The terminal type is set and exported.
5. Remove the invalid entry from the file with an editor such as `vi`.
6. Type **`cd /`** and press Return.
7. Type **`umount /a`** and press Return.
8. Type **`init 6`** and press Return.

   The system is rebooted.
9. Verify that the system boots to run level 3.

   The login prompt is displayed when the boot process has finished successfully.

The following example shows how to repair the **/etc/passwd** file after you boot from a local CD-ROM.

```
Type any key to reboot
SunOS Secondary Boot version 3.00
Solaris Intel Platform Edition Booting System
Running Configuration Assistant...
Autobooting from Boot path: /pci@0,0/pci-ide@7,1/ide@0/cmdk@0,0:a
If the system hardware has changed, or to boot from a different
device, interrupt the autoboot process by pressing ESC.
Press ESCape to interrupt autoboot in 5 seconds.
      .
      .
      .
Boot Solaris
Select one of the identified devices to boot the Solaris kernel and
choose Continue.
To perform optional features, such as modifying the autoboot and property
settings, choose Boot Tasks.
An asterisk (*) indicates the current default boot device.
> To make a selection use the arrow keys, and press Enter to mark it [X].
[ ]  NET : DEC 21142/21143 Fast Ethernet
on Board PCI at Dev 3
[ ]  DISK: (*) Target 0, QUANTUM  FIREBALL1280A
on Bus Mastering IDE controller on Board PCI at Dev 7, Func 1
[ ]  DISK: Target 1:ST5660A
on Bus Mastering IDE controller on Board PCI at Dev 7, Func 1
[ ]  DISK: Target 0:Maxtor 9 0680D4
on Bus Mastering IDE controller on Board PCI at Dev 7, Func 1
[ ]  CD  : Target 1:TOSHIBA  CD-ROM XM-5602B  1546
on Bus Mastering IDE controller on Board PCI at Dev 7, Func 1
F2_Continue   F3_Back   F4_Boot Tasks   F6_Help
      .
      .
      .
               <<< Current Boot Parameters >>>
Boot path: /pci@0,0/pci-ide@7,1/ide@0/cmdk@0,0:a
Boot args: kernel/unix -r
Select the type of installation you want to perform:
1 Solaris Interactive
2 Custom JumpStart
3 Solaris Web Start
  Enter the number of your choice followed by <ENTER> the key.
  If you enter anything else, or if you wait for 30 seconds,
    an interactive installation will be started.
 Select type of installation:  b -s
      .
      .
      .
# mount /dev/dsk/c0t0d0s0 /a
      .
      .
      .
# cd /a/etc
# vi passwd
(Remove invalid entry)
# cd /
# umount /a
# init 6
```

Aborting a Booting Process

Occasionally, you may need to abort the booting process. The specific abort key sequence depends on your keyboard type. For example, you might press Stop-A or L1-A. On TTY terminals, press the Break key.

To abort the booting process, type the abort key sequence for your system. When you abort the boot process, the monitor displays the ok PROM prompt.

```
ok
```

Type **boot** and press Return to restart the boot process, or type **help** and press Return to display a list of help options. If your terminal shows the > monitor prompt, type **n** to get the ok prompt.

Shutting Down a System

The following sections describe how to use the shutdown and init commands to shut down a system.

Shutting Down a Multiuser System

Before shutting down a multiuser system, inform the other users on the system and give them time to complete critical procedures such as saving changes.

1. Type **who** and press Return.

   A list of all logged in users is displayed.
2. Type **ps -ef** and press Return.

   A list of system activities is displayed. If the activity is acceptable for running shutdown, go to the next step.
3. Become superuser.
4. Type **cd /** and press Return.

   You must be in the root directory to run the shutdown command.
5. Type **shutdown** and press Return.

   You are asked to confirm that you want to shut down the system.
6. Type **y**.

   A message is broadcast to all users. After a 60-second wait, the system is shut down to single-user state and you are prompted for the root password.
7. Type the root password.

   The system is in single-user state and you can perform any maintenance task.
8. Press Control-D to return to the default run system level.

```
paperbark% su
Password:
# cd /
# shutdown
```

```
Shutdown started.    Tue May  2 13:16:57 WST 2000

Broadcast Message from root (pts/7) on paperbark Tue May  2 13:16:59...
The system paperbark will be shut down in 1 minute

Broadcast Message from root (pts/7) on paperbark Tue May  2 13:17:29...
The system paperbark will be shut down in 30 seconds

Do you want to continue? (y or n):  y
Broadcast Message from root (pts/7) on paperbark Tue May  2 13:17:53...
THE SYSTEM paperbark IS BEING SHUT DOWN NOW! ! !
LOG OFF NOW OR RISK YOUR FILES BEING DAMAGED
(Shutdown messages)

INIT: SINGLE USER MODE
Type control-d to proceed with normal startup,
(or give root password for system maintenance):
```

Shutting Down a System: Alternative Ways

If you want to change the default actions of the `shutdown` command, choose one of the tasks in the following six sections.

Shutting Down a System Without Confirmation Use the following steps to shut down a system without confirmation.

1. Become superuser.
2. Type **`cd /`** and press Return.

   You must be in the root directory to run the `shutdown` command.
3. Type **`shutdown -y`** and press Return.

   The shutdown proceeds without asking you to type **`y`** to confirm.

Changing the Shutdown Grace Period The default is for the `shutdown` command to provide a 60-second grace period to enable users to save their changes. Use the following steps to change the shutdown 60-second grace period.

1. Become superuser.
2. Type **`cd /`** and press Return.

   You must be in the root directory to run the `shutdown` command.
3. Type **`shutdown -g`** ***`nnn`*** and press Return.

   The grace period is changed to the number of seconds you specify.

The following example changes the grace period to 120 seconds.

```
# cd /
# shutdown -g120
```

Shutting Down and Rebooting a Multiuser System Use the following steps to shut down and reboot a multiuser system.

1. Become superuser.
2. Type **`cd /`** and press Return. You must be in the root directory to run the `shutdown` command.
3. Type **`shutdown -i6`** and press Return. A message is broadcast to all users and the `rc` scripts are executed; the system is shut down to power-down state and then brought back up to multiuser state.

Shutting Down a Single-User System To shut down a single-user system, type **`telinit 0`** (or **`init 0`**) and press Return. The `init` command runs scripts that bring the system down cleanly. No warning messages are broadcast.

Shutting Down and Rebooting a Single-User System To shut down and reboot a single-user system, type **`telinit 6`** (or **`init 6`**) and press Return. Information is written to the disk, all active processes are killed, and the system is brought to a power-down state. The system is then rebooted to the default level (usually multiuser).

Shutting Down a System in a Hurry To shut down a system in a hurry, type **`uadmin 2 0`** and press Return. The system is brought to power-down state, displaying the PROM prompt.

Monitoring Processes

The programs that are running on a system at any one time are called *processes*. You can monitor the status of processes, control how much CPU time a process gets, find or signal processes, and suspend or halt the execution of a process.

Commands for Monitoring Processes

The `ps` (process status) command is your main tool for obtaining information about processes. You can use the `ps` command in combination with the `grep` command to focus your search for specific information.

You can also use the `dispadmin`, `priocntl`, `nice`, `renice`, `pgrep`, and `pkill` commands to manage processes. Table 9 lists the commands for managing processes.

Table 9 Commands for Managing Processes

Command	Description
ps	Check the status of active processes on a system and display detailed information about the processes.
dispadmin	List default scheduling policies.
priocntl	Assign processes to a priority class and manage process priorities.
nice	Raise or lower the priority of a timesharing process.
renice	Alter the scheduling priority of one or more running processes.
pgrep, pkill	Find or signal processes.

New!

New!

Refer to the ps(1), dispadmin(1M), priocntl(1), nice(1), renice(1), pgrep(1), and pkill(1) manual pages for complete information about these commands.

In addition, the /usr/proc/bin directory contains process tools that you can use to display highly detailed information about the processes listed in /proc. The /proc directory is also known as the process file system (procfs). It stores images of active processes by their process ID number. For more information about the /proc file system see "Types of File Systems" on page 199.

The process tools are similar to some options of the ps command, except that the output provided by the tools is more detailed. In general, the process tools

- Display more details about processes, such as fstat and fcntl information, working directories, and trees of parent and child processes.
- Provide control over processes, enabling users to stop or resume them.

Table 10 summarizes the /usr/proc/bin commands.

Table 10 Process Tools in the /usr/proc/bin Directory

Command	Description
pcred *pid*	Display credentials.
pfiles *pid*	Display fstat and fcntl information for open files.

Table 10 Process Tools in the /usr/proc/bin Directory (Continued)

Command	Description
`pflags` *pid*	Show `/proc` tracing flags, pending and held signals, and other status information for each LWP.
`pldd` *pid*	Show dynamic libraries linked into each process.
`pmap` *pid*	Show address map space.
`prun` *pid*	Restart the process.
`psig` *pid*	Display signal actions.
`pstack` *pid*	Display hex+symbolic stack trace for each LWP.
`pstop` *pid*	Stop the process.
`ptime` *pid*	Time the process, using microstate accounting.
`ptree` *pid*	Show process trees containing specified PIDs.
`pwait` *pid*	Wait for the specified processes to terminate.
`pwdx` *pid*	Display current working directory.

For a complete description of the process tools, refer to the `proc`(1) manual page. For information about how to use the process tools commands to display details about processes and how to start and stop them, see "Using the /usr/proc/bin Commands" on page 50.

The ps Command

You can use the `ps` command to determine which processes are running (or not running) and to get the following detailed information about an individual process.

- PID (process ID).
- UID (user ID).
- Priority.
- Control terminal.
- Memory use.
- CPU time.
- Current status.

The `ps` command takes a snapshot of system activity at the time you type the command. If you are monitoring system activity by time, be aware that the results are already slightly out-of-date by the time you read them.

Table 11 shows the most frequently used options for the ps command. See the ps(1) manual page for a complete list of options.

Table 11 Most Frequently Used Options for the ps Command

Option	Description
-e	Report on all processes.
-f	Show the owner of the process, by name instead of by UID, in the first column. This option turns off -l, -t, -s, and -r and turns on -a.
-l	Generate a long report, which includes all fields except STIME.

What the ps Command Reports

When you type **ps -e** and press Return, you get a report that looks like the following example.

```
oak% /usr/bin/ps -e
PID          TTY          TIME         COMD
0            ?            0:02         sched
1            ?            0:01         init
2            ?            0:00         pageout
192          ?            0:00         sac
79           ?            0:10         inetd
75           ?            0:01         in.route
136          ?            0:04         automoun
143          ?            0:01         cron
123          ?            0:01         statd
104          ?            0:01         rpcbind
106          ?            0:01         rpc.rwal
108          ?            0:01         rpc.ruse
110          ?            0:01         rpc.spra
113          ?            0:01         ypbind
115          ?            0:00         keyserv
117          ?            0:01         kerbd
127          ?            0:02         lockd
251          pts/0        0:00         ps
165          ?            0:00         sendmail
193          ?            0:01         ttymon
174          ?            0:03         syslogd
156          ?            0:01         lpsched
209          ?            0:02         in.rlogi
211          pts/0        0:03         csh
164          ?            0:00         lpNet
oak%
```

The columns are described in Table 12.

Table 12 Columns in the ps -e Report

Column	Description
PID	Process identification number.
TTY	The terminal from which the process (or its parent) started. If the process has no controlling terminal, this column contains a question mark (?). Processes with question marks usually are system processes.
TIME	The cumulative amount of CPU time used by the process.
COMD	The name of the command that generated the process. Note that for the `ps -e` command only the first eight characters of the file name are displayed.

When you type **`ps -el`** and press Return, you get a listing that looks like the following example.

```
oak% /usr/bin/ps -el
 F S   UID   PID  PPID  C PRI NI     ADDR     SZ    WCHAN TTY        TIME COMD
19 T     0     0     0 80   0 SY f010f1c8      0          ?          0:02 sched
 8 S     0     1     0251   1 20 ff1ad800     48 ff1ad9c4 ?          0:01 init
19 S     0     2     0  0   0 SY ff1ad000      0 ff1ad07d ?          0:00 pageout
 8 S     0   192     1 49   1 20 ff1f7000    238 ff2de348 ?          0:00 sac
 8 S     0    79     1 80   1 20 ff232800    291 f010f1a4 ?          0:10 inetd
 8 S     0    75     1 80   1 20 ff249000    258 f010f1a4 ?          0:01 in.route
 8 S     0   136     1 80   1 20 ff2c3000    327 f010f1a4 ?          0:04 automoun
 8 S     0   143     1149   1 20 ff293000    287 ff2de448 ?          0:01 cron
 8 S     0   123     1 80   1 20 ff28e000    270 f010f1a4 ?          0:01 statd
 8 S     0   104     1 80   1 20 ff25a000    301 f010f1a4 ?          0:01 rpcbind
 8 S     0   106     1 77   1 20 ff258800    272 f010f1a4 ?          0:01 rpc.rwal
 8 S     0   108     1 80   1 20 ff260800    272 f010f1a4 ?          0:01 rpc.ruse
 8 S     0   110     1 78   1 20 ff266800    272 f010f1a4 ?          0:01 rpc.spra
(Additional lines deleted from this example)
```

Table 13 describes the fields in the long listing report.

Table 13 Summary of Fields in a ps -el Report

Field	Description	
F	Hexadecimal flags, which, added together, indicate the process's current state.	
	00	The process has terminated. Its place in the process table is free.
	01	The process is a system process and is always in memory.
	02	The process is being traced by its parent.

Table 13 Summary of Fields in a ps -el Report (Continued)

Field	Description	
	`04`	The process is being traced by its parent and has been stopped.
	`08`	The process cannot be awakened by a signal.
	`10`	The process is currently in memory and is locked until an event completes.
	`20`	The process cannot be swapped.
`S`	The current state of the process, as shown by one of the following letters.	
	`O`	Currently running on the processor.
	`S`	Sleeping; waiting for an I/O event to complete.
	`R`	Ready to run.
	`I`	Idle; process is being created.
	`Z`	Zombie. The process has terminated and the parent is not waiting, but the dead process is still in the process table.
	`T`	Stopped because parent is tracing the process.
	`X`	Waiting for more memory.
`UID`	The user ID of the owner of the process.	
`PID`	The process identification number.	
`PPID`	The parent process's identification number.	
`C`	The process's CPU use (that is, an estimate of the percentage of CPU time used by the process).	
`PRI`	The process's scheduling priority. Higher numbers mean lower priority.	
`NI`	The process's `nice` number, which contributes to its scheduling priority. Making a process "nicer" means lowering its priority so it does not use up as much CPU time.	
`SZ`	The amount of virtual memory required by the process. This is a good indication of the demand the process puts on system memory.	
`TTY`	The terminal from which the process (or its parent) started, or a question mark to indicate there is no controlling terminal (which usually indicates a system process).	
`TIME`	The total amount of CPU time used by the process since it began.	
`COMD`	The command being run by the process.	

Using the ps Report

When you need to check on which processes or daemons are running, use the `ps -e` option. If you need more detailed information about a process, use the `ps -el` options. See the `ps`(1) manual page for a complete list of options. With experience, you will know how the report should look and be able to judge what is out of the ordinary.

The following guidelines can help you spot potential problems.

- Look for many identical jobs owned by the same user. This condition may result from someone running a script that starts a lot of background jobs without waiting for any of the jobs to terminate. Talk to the user to find out if that's the case. If necessary, use the `kill` command to terminate some of the processes. See the following section for more information on killing a process.
- Look at the `TIME` field for processes that have accumulated a large amount of CPU time. Such processes might be in an endless loop.
- Look at the `C` field to find unimportant processes that consume a large percentage of CPU time. If you do not think a process warrants so much attention, use the `priocntl` command to lower its priority. See the `priocntl`(1M) manual page for more information.
- Look at the `SZ` field for processes that consume too large a percentage of memory. If a process is a memory hog, you may need to kill the process. If many processes are using lots of memory, the system may need more memory.
- Watch for a runaway process that uses progressively more CPU time. You can check this by using the `-f` option to see the start time (`STIME`) of the process and by watching the `TIME` field for the accumulation of CPU time.

Killing Processes

Sometimes you need to eliminate a process entirely. Use the `kill` command to do this. The syntax of the `kill` command is `kill -`*`signal PID`*, where *`signal`* is a number or a name.

CAUTION. Kill a process only if you cannot get it to quit in the usual way.

Sometimes processes do not die when you use the `kill` command. The three most common cases are listed below.

- The process is waiting for a device, such as a tape drive, to complete an operation before exiting.

- The process is waiting for resources that are unavailable because of NFS problems. To kill such a process, type **kill -QUIT *PID***.
- The process is a zombie, as shown by the message `defunct` in the `ps` report. A zombie process is one that has had all its resources freed but has not received an acknowledgment from a parent process, receipt of which would ordinarily remove its entry from the process table. The next time a system is booted, zombie processes are cleared. Zombies do not affect system performance, and you do not need to remove them.

Use the following steps to kill a process.

1. Become superuser.

   You must be superuser to kill a process that you do not own.
2. Type **ps -e** and press Return.

   A list of the processes is displayed. Use the PID (process ID) number in the first column as input to the next step. If you know which process is causing the problem, you can type **ps -e | grep *process-name*** and press Return to focus your search.
3. Type **kill *PID*** and press Return.

   When you type **kill** with no signal argument, signal 15 is sent.
4. Type **ps -e** and press Return.

   Check to see if the process has terminated. If it's still there, go to step 5.
5. Type **kill -9 *PID*** and press Return.

   The process should be terminated. To see a description of the signals used by `kill`, type **man -s5 signal** and press Return.

In the following example, OpenWindows is frozen on the system `oak`. You must log in remotely from another system and kill the process.

```
elm% rlogin oak
Password:
oak% ps -e | grep openwin
PID TTY      TIME COMD
2212 pts/0   0:00 openwin
2213 pts/1    0:00 grep openwin
oak% su
Password:
oak# kill 2212
oak# exit
oak% logout
elm%
```

Using the /usr/proc/bin Commands

Starting with the Solaris 2.6 release, you can use a set of commands to display detailed, technical information about active processes. These commands are summarized in Table 14.

Table 14 Process Tools in the /usr/proc/bin Directory

Command	Description
`pcred` *pid**	Display credentials.
`pfiles` *pid**	Display `fstat` and `fcntl` information for open files.
`pflags` *pid**	Show `/proc` tracing flags, pending and held signals, and other status information for each LWP.
`pldd` *pid**	Show dynamic libraries linked into each process.
`pmap` *pid**	Show address map space.
`prun` *pid*	Restart the process.
`psig` *pid**	Display signal actions.
`pstack` *pid**	Display hex+symbolic stack trace for each LWP.
`pstop` *pid*	Stop the process.
`ptime` *pid*	Time the process using microstate accounting.
`ptree` *pid*	Show process trees containing specified PIDs.
`pwait` *pid*	Wait for specified processes to terminate.
`pwdx` *pid**	Display current working directory.

*Must be superuser to execute.

NOTE. If you use the `/usr/proc/bin` *commands frequently, add the process tool directory to your* `PATH` *variable to make the commands more easily accessible.*

All of the `/usr/bin/proc` commands use the process ID (PID) as the argument to the command. You can obtain the PID by using the `ps -e` and the `grep` commands to search for the name of the process you want more information about. The following example displays the PID for the `openwin` process in the first column.

```
oak% ps -e | grep openwin
PID TTY      TIME COMD
2212 pts/0   0:00 openwin
2213 pts/1    0:00 grep openwin
oak%
```

Displaying and Controlling Information About Processes

Use the following steps to display and control information about a process.

1. Type **ps -e | grep *process-name*** and press Return.

   The first column of the output displays the PID for the appropriate process name.
2. Become superuser to use pcred, pfiles, pflags, pldd, pmap, psig, pstack, and pwdx commands.
3. Type ***pcommand PID*** and press Return.

   The information for the specified command is displayed.

The following examples show the output for each of the /usr/proc/bin commands for the dtlogin PID of 283.

```
castle% ps -e | grep dtlogin
   283 ?        0:00 dtlogin
   270 ?        0:01 dtlogin
castle%
# /usr/proc/bin/pcred 283
283:    e/r/suid=0  e/r/sgid=0
        groups: 1 0 2 3 4 5 6 7 8 9 12
# exit
castle% /usr/proc/bin/ptime 283

real        0.016
user        0.000
sys         0.016
castle%
# /usr/proc/bin/pfiles 283
283:    /usr/dt/bin/dtlogin -daemon
  Current rlimit: 64 file descriptors
   0: S_IFDIR mode:0755 dev:32,24 ino:2 uid:0 gid:0 size:1024
      O_RDONLY|O_LARGEFILE
   1: S_IFDIR mode:0755 dev:32,24 ino:2 uid:0 gid:0 size:1024
      O_RDONLY|O_LARGEFILE
   2: S_IFREG mode:0644 dev:32,24 ino:326220 uid:0 gid:0 size:49
      O_WRONLY|O_APPEND|O_LARGEFILE
   3: S_IFCHR mode:0666 dev:32,24 ino:406038 uid:0 gid:3 rdev:13,12
      O_RDWR
   4: S_IFIFO mode:0666 dev:171,0 ino:4124779288 uid:0 gid:0 size:0
      O_RDWR|O_NONBLOCK
   5: S_IFREG mode:0644 dev:32,24 ino:326221 uid:0 gid:0 size:4
      O_WRONLY|O_LARGEFILE
      advisory write lock set by process 270
   7: S_IFSOCK mode:0666 dev:166,0 ino:32032 uid:0 gid:0 size:0
      O_RDWR
   8: S_IFDOOR mode:0444 dev:171,0 ino:4124780632 uid:0 gid:0 size:0
      O_RDONLY|O_LARGEFILE FD_CLOEXEC  door to nscd[174]
#
# /usr/proc/bin/pflags 283
283:    /usr/dt/bin/dtlogin -daemon
  /1:   flags = PR_PCINVAL|PR_ORPHAN|PR_ASLEEP [ wait() ]
#
# /usr/proc/bin/pldd 283
283:    /usr/dt/bin/dtlogin -daemon
/usr/openwin/lib/libXmu.so.4
/usr/openwin/lib/libX11.so.4
/usr/dt/lib/libDtSvc.so.1
/usr/lib/libresolv.so.2
/usr/lib/libdl.so.1
/usr/lib/libbsm.so.1
/usr/lib/libauth.so.1
/usr/lib/libsocket.so.1
/usr/lib/libnsl.so.1
/usr/dt/lib/libSDtFwa.so.1
```

```
/usr/lib/libc.so.1
/usr/openwin/lib/libXt.so.4
/usr/openwin/lib/libSM.so.6
/usr/openwin/lib/libICE.so.6
/usr/openwin/lib/libXext.so.0
/usr/lib/libm.so.1
/usr/openwin/lib/libtt.so.2
/usr/dt/lib/libXm.so.3
/usr/lib/libmp.so.2
/usr/lib/nss_files.so.1
/usr/lib/libpam.so.1
#
# /usr/proc/bin/pmap 283
283:    /usr/dt/bin/dtlogin -daemon
00010000    108K read/exec          /usr/dt/bin/dtlogin
0003A000     32K read/write/exec    /usr/dt/bin/dtlogin
00042000     80K read/write/exec      [ heap ]
EEE90000     12K read/shared        dev:32,24 ino:196384
EEEA0000     12K read/shared        dev:32,24 ino:196384
EEEB0000     12K read/shared        dev:32,24 ino:196384
EEEC0000      8K read/write           [ anon ]
EEF11000      4K read/write           [ anon ]
EEF89000      4K read/write           [ anon ]
EF001000      4K read/write           [ anon ]
EF060000     24K read/exec          /usr/lib/libpam.so.1
EF075000      4K read/write/exec    /usr/lib/libpam.so.1
(More information, not shown here)
EF7C0000      4K read/exec/shared   /usr/lib/libdl.so.1
EF7D0000    112K read/exec          /usr/lib/ld.so.1
EF7FB000      8K read/write/exec    /usr/lib/ld.so.1
EF7FD000      4K read/write/exec      [ anon ]
EFFF9000     28K read/write/exec      [ stack ]
 total     5480K
#
# /usr/proc/bin/psig 283
283:    /usr/dt/bin/dtlogin -daemon
HUP     ignored
INT     caught  RESETHAND,NODEFER
QUIT    ignored
ILL     default
TRAP    default
ABRT    default
EMT     default
FPE     default
KILL    default
BUS     default
SEGV    default
SYS     default
PIPE    ignored
ALRM    default
TERM    caught  RESETHAND,NODEFER
USR1    caught  RESETHAND,NODEFER
USR2    default
CLD     default NOCLDSTOP

PWR     default
WINCH   default
URG     default
POLL    default
STOP    default
TSTP    default
CONT    default
TTIN    ignored
TTOU    default
VTALRM  default
PROF    default
XCPU    ignored
XFSZ    ignored
WAITING default
LWP     default
FREEZE  default
THAW    default
CANCEL  default
LOST    default
RTMIN   default
RTMIN+1 default
```

```
RTMIN+2 default
RTMIN+3 default
RTMAX-3 default
RTMAX-2 default
RTMAX-1 default
RTMAX   default
#
# /usr/proc/bin/pstack 283
283:    /usr/dt/bin/dtlogin -daemon
 ef479154 wait     ()
 ef479154 _libc_wait (0, 3ec4c, 3b000, 12d, ef4e227c, 1e340) + 8
 0001e340 ManageSession (43000, 43000, 482f8, ef001230, 81010100, c) + 454
 00019348 StartDisplay (482f8, 3c954, 43000, 3b224, ef001240, ff00) + 7bc
 0001a324 ForEachDisplay (189a8, 0, 2400, 41800, 42e48, 17ca8) + 1c
 00017d54 main     (0, effffefc, efffff08, 3b000, 0, 0) + 228
 0001541c _start   (0, 0, 0, 0, 0, 0) + dc
#
# /usr/proc/bin/pwdx 283
283:    /
#
castle% /usr/proc/ptime 283

real        0.066
user        0.000
sys         0.032
castle%
castle% ptree 283
270   /usr/dt/bin/dtlogin -daemon
  283   /usr/dt/bin/dtlogin -daemon
    301   /bin/ksh /usr/dt/bin/Xsession
      311   /usr/openwin/bin/fbconsole
      346   /usr/dt/bin/sdt_shell -c unsetenv _ PWD;                unsetenv DT;
        349   -csh -c unsetenv _ PWD;               unsetenv DT;      setenv
 DISP
          366   /usr/dt/bin/dtsession
            373   dtwm
            374   dtterm -session dtOvPI0t -sdtserver
              387   /bin/csh
                407   ./textedit
                528   sh
              390   /bin/csh
              393   /bin/csh
                417   /usr/openwin/bin/cmdtool
                  420   /bin/csh
              531   /bin/csh
                553   ptree 283
            375   dtfile -session dtbfiQD_
              405   dtfile -session dtbfiQD_
            376   snapshot -Wp 781 588 -Ws 326 201 -WP 6 6 +Wi -f snapshot.rs
castle%
```

The Priority Control Command (priocntl)

You can use the `priocntl` command to display or set scheduling parameters of specified processes. You can also use it to display the current configuration information for the process scheduler of a system or to execute a command with specified scheduling parameters.

Each process has a distinct class with a separate scheduling policy assigned to each class. The following possible classes are configured on a system.

- System (`SYS`)
- Interactive (`IA`)

- Real-time (RT)
- Timesharing (TS)

For the timesharing class, the user-supplied priority ranges from –20 to +20. The priority of a timeshare process, referred to as the user-mode priority, is inherited from the parent process. The system looks up the user-mode priority in its timesharing dispatch parameter table, adds in any nice or priocntl (user-supplied) priority, and ensures a 0–59 range to create a global priority.

In the default configuration, a runnable real-time process runs before any other process. Inappropriate use of real-time processes can have a dramatic, negative impact on system performance.

Displaying Basic Information About Process Classes

Use the following procedure to display basic information about process classes.

- Type **priocntl -l** and press Return. The process class and scheduling parameters for the system are displayed.

In the following example, all classes except RT are defined.

```
paperbark% priocntl -l
CONFIGURED CLASSES
==================

SYS (System Class)

TS (Time Sharing)
        Configured TS User Priority Range: -60 through 60

IA (Interactive)
        Configured IA User Priority Range: -60 through 60
paperbark%
```

Displaying the Global Priority of a Process

You can use the ps -ecl command to display the global priority of a process. The global priority is listed under the PRI column.

The following example shows the output from the ps -ecl command. Data in the PRI column shows that pageout has the highest priority at 98, and cron and syslogd have the lowest at 10.

```
paperbark% ps -ecl
 F S   UID   PID  PPID  CLS PRI     ADDR     SZ    WCHAN TTY      TIME CMD
19 T     0     0     0  SYS  96 10416678    0            ?        0:00 sched
 8 S     0     1     0   TS  58 7032d580  199 7032d7b0 ?        0:00 init
19 S     0     2     0  SYS  98 7032ce58    0 10431e14 ?        0:00 pageout
19 S     0     3     0  SYS  60 7032c730    0 10437fb0 ?        0:09 fsflush
 8 S     0  2792     1   TS  58 704aa020  217 70385c5c ?        0:00 sac
 8 S  1001  2884     1   IA  59 708d8790  289 7014f1ba ?        0:00 dsdm
 8 S  1001  2939  2916   IA  32 70970078  112 70385adc ?        0:00 cat
```

```
8 S     0    44     1  TS  52 70360738    156 70360968 ?         0:00
devfseve
8 S     0    46     1  TS  41 70360010    280        ? ?         0:00
devfsadm
8 S     0  2787     1  TS  58 707f8050   1527 fec71e34 ?         0:03 java
8 S     0  2560     1  TS  58 7094ced0    201 7014fcfa ?         0:00
in.route
8 S  1001  2913  2898  IA  59 708d95e0    127 708d964c pts/3     0:00 sh
8 S     0  2765     1  TS  58 70912ec0    264 7014f0fa ?         0:00 snmpdx
8 S  1001  2881  2835  IA  59 707f8778    484 7014fcba pts/3     0:00
sdt_shel
8 S  1001  2924  2909  IA  43 709f8ee0    171 706573a6 pts/4     0:00 csh
8 S     0  2654     1  TS  50 707515b8    302 707517e8 ?         0:00 nscd
8 S  1001  2916     1  IA  22 70832058    226 708320c4 ?         0:00
sdtvolch
8 R     0  2682     1  TS  58 706b4760    125          ?         0:00 utmpd
8 S  1001  2848     1  IA  59 706e35a8    624 7014f27a ?         0:00
speckeys
8 S     0   212     1  TS  58 7057c750    167 7057c980 ?         0:00 powerd
8 S     0  2637     1  TS  10 7088b5d8    408 7014eefa ?         0:00 syslogd
8 S     0  2830     1  TS  58 708d8068    363 7014f43a ?         0:00
sendmail
8 S     0   226     1  TS  48 706e2e80    312 7014fafa ?         0:00 vold
8 S     0  1708     1  TS  53 709707a0    425 7014f4fa ?         0:00
rpc.ttdb
8 S  1001  2845  2835  IA  59 706e2758    286 7014f2fa ?         0:00
fbconsol
8 S     1   240     1  TS  35 706b55b0   1209 706b561c ?         0:00 dwhttpd
8 S     1   241   240  TS  58 706b4e88   2465 7014fa7a ?         0:28 dwhttpd
8 S  1001  2835  2809  IA  59 7057ce78    230 7057cee4 ?         0:00
Xsession
8 S  1001  2883  2881  IA  59 704aae70    174 704ab0a0 pts/3     0:00 csh
8 S     0  2769     1  TS  20 70912070    379 7014f5fa ?         0:00 dmispd
8 Z     0  2438   226       0                                         0:00
<defunct>
8 S     0  2663     1  TS  40 709135e8    380 7014f6ba ?         0:00 lpsched
8 S     0  2811     1  IA  59 704aa748    286 7014fdba ?         0:00
fbconsol
8 S     0  2712     1  TS  38 70912798    610 7014f33a ?         0:00 dtlogin
8 S     0  2643     1  TS  10 704c7590    234 70385e9c ?         0:00 cron
8 S     0  2793     1  TS  38 7088aeb0    217 7014f6fa console   0:00 ttymon
8 S     0  2770     1  TS  20 709715f0   5295 ff376b34 ?         0:03 java
8 S     0  2686     1  TS   0 704c6740    197 705c4294 ?         0:00
cimomboo
8 S  1001  2918  2910  IA  53 707955c0   2420 7014f13a ?         0:00
.netscap
8 Z     0  1854   226       0                                         0:00
<defunct>
8 S     0  2823  2765  TS  41 706b4038    290 708474f6 ?         0:03 mibiisa
8 Z     0   636   226       0                                         0:00
<defunct>
8 S  1001  2808  2712  IA  59 704c6e68  16107 7014f73a ?         0:25 Xsun
8 R     0  2929  2596  TS  58 709f87b8    222          ?         0:00
rpc.rsta
8 S     0  2596     1  TS  45 70361588    296 7014f3fa ?         0:00 inetd
8 S  1001  2912  2899  IA  59 709fc7b0    892 7014f17a ?         0:00
sdtperfm
8 S  1001  2931  2909  IA  53 70750040    171 7081c726 pts/6     0:00 csh
8 S     0   440     1  TS  55 7088a788    425 7014f47a ?         0:00
rpc.ttdb
8 S     1  2619     1  TS  50 709fd600    310 7014f8ba ?         0:00 statd
8 S  1001  2907  2899  IA  22 7057d5a0    548 7057d60c ?         0:00
netscape
8 S     0  2900  2596  TS  30 7094d5f8    425 7014f53a ?         0:00
rpc.ttdb
8 S  1001  2898     1  IA  59 70360e60    591 7014f3ba pts/3     0:00
ttsessio
8 S     0  2316     1  TS  58 70832780    424 7014fd7a ?         0:00
rpc.ttdb
8 S     0  2631     1  TS  58 709fc088    367 fee0be34 ?         0:00
automoun
8 S     0  2809  2712  IA  43 70794048    639 707940b4 ?         0:00 dtlogin
```

```
8 S  1001  2927  2909   IA  23 7057c028    171 7095875e pts/5    0:00 csh
8 S  1001  2910  2907   IA  48 7088a060   2922 7014f1fa ?        0:07
 .netscap
8 S  1001  2914  2913   IA  48 704c6018    852 7014fbba pts/3    0:00 dtpad
8 Z     0  1244   226        0                                       0:00
 <defunct>
8 S     0  2620     1   TS  40 708d8eb8    245 7014f07a ?        0:00 lockd
8 S  1001  2909  2899   IA  59 70794e98    944 7014f9fa ??       0:01 dtterm
8 O     0  3050  2934   IA  58 704ab598    117          pts/7    0:00 ps
8 S     0  1099     1   TS  54 707f95c8    425 7014f67a ?        0:00
 rpc.ttdb
8 S  1001  2906  2899   IA  59 707f8ea0   1091 7014ef7a ?        0:03 dtwm
8 S     0  2577     1   TS  59 7032c008    276 7014f03a ?        0:00 rpcbind
8 S     0  2795  2792   TS  58 70832ea8    217 708330d8 ?        0:00 ttymon
8 S  1001  2911  2907   IA  59 709f9608    562 7014f9ba ?        0:00
 netscape
8 S  1001  2899  2883   IA  48 70794770    952 7014efba pts/3    0:00
 dtsessio
8 S  1001  2934  2909   IA  59 706e2030    171 706e2260 pts/7    0:00 csh
8 S     0  2776     1   TS  58 70970ec8    449 70937ec6 ?        0:00
 snmpXdmi
paperbark%
```

You can also use the `/usr/sbin/dispadmin -l` command to display process scheduler information.

The following example shows the output from the `displadmin -l` command.

```
castle% /usr/sbin/dispadmin -l
CONFIGURED CLASSES
==================

SYS     (System Class)
TS      (Time Sharing)
IA      (Interactive)
castle%
```

For complete information, refer to the `dispadmin`(1M) manual page.

Designating a Process Priority

Use the following steps to designate a process priority.

1. Become superuser.
2. Type **`priocntl -e -c`** ***`class`*** **`-m`** ***`user-limit`*** **`-p`** ***`priority command-name`*** and press Return.

   The `-e` option executes the command, the `-c` class option specifies the class. Default classes are `TS` (timesharing) or `RT` (real-time). The `-m` *`user-limit`* option specifies the maximum amount you can raise or lower your priority with the `-p` option. The `-p` *`priority command-name`* option enables you to specify the relative priority, in the RT class for a real-time thread. For a timesharing process, the `-p` option enables you to specify the user-supplied priority, which ranges from –20 to +20.

3. While the process is running, in another terminal window, type **ps -ecl | grep *command-name*** and press Return.
4. Review the output of the PRI column to verify that you have changed the process status successfully.

The following example starts the find command with the highest possible user-supplied priority, and in a different terminal window, uses the ps -ecl command to display that priority.

```
# priocntl -e -c TS -m 20 -p 20 find / -name core -print
castle% ps -ecl | grep find
 8 S      0   632   528    TS  60 f5fa4b40     200 f5ff7ba0 pts/3     0:03 find
castle%
```

Changing the Scheduling Parameters of a Timeshare Process

Use the following steps to schedule the parameters of a timeshare process.

1. Become superuser.
2. Type **priocntl -s -m *user-limit [-p priority]* *-i id-type id-list*** and press Return.

   The -s option enables you to set the upper limit on the user priority range and change the current priority. The -m *user-limit* option specifies the maximum amount you can raise or lower your priority with the -p option. The -p *priority command-name option* enables you to designate a priority. The -i *id-type* and *id-list* option uses a combination of *id-type* and *id-list* to identify the process. The *id-type* specifies the type of ID, such as PID or UID.
3. While the process is running, in another terminal window, type **ps -ecl | grep *command-name*** and press Return.
4. Review the output of the PRI column to verify that you have changed the process status successfully.

The following example executes a command with a 500-millisecond time slice, a priority of 20 in the RT class, and a global priority of 120.

```
oak% priocntl -s -c RT -t 500 -p 20 myprog
oak%
```

Changing the Class of a Process

Use the following steps to change the class of a process.

NOTE. You must be superuser or working in a real-time shell to change the class of a process from or to real-time.

1. Become superuser.
2. Type **`priocntl -s -c`** ***`class`*** **`-i`** ***`id-type id-list`*** and press Return.

   The `-s` option enables you to set the upper limit on the user priority range and change the current priority. The `-c` class option specifies the class, `TS` or `RT`, to which you are changing the process. The `-i` *`id-type`* and *`id-list`* options use a combination of *`id-type`* and *`id-list`* to identify the process. The *`id-type`* specifies the type of ID, such as PID or UID.
3. While the process is running, in another terminal window, type **`ps -ecl | grep`** ***`command-name`*** and press Return.
4. Review the output of the PRI column to verify that you have changed the process status successfully.

The following example changes all the processes belonging to user `1001` to real-time processes.

```
# priocntl -s -c RT -i uid 1001
# ps -ecl | grep 1001
 8 S  1001   282   270   RT 100 f5e4c8a0   2392 f5d47806 ?        0:48 Xsun
 8 S  1001   311   301   RT 100 f5e6e1e8    471 f5d476ee ?        0:00
 fbconsol
 8 S  1001   301   283   RT 100 f5e6db28    392 f5e6db98 ?        0:01
 Xsession
 8 S  1001   349   346   RT 100 f5e6d468    256 f5e6d660 pts/2    0:00 csh
 8 S  1001   315     1   RT 100 f5e6cda8    982 f5d476c6 ?        0:00
 speckeys
 8 S  1001   366   349   RT 100 f5e6c6e8   1410 f5d47586 pts/2    0:01
 dtsessio
 8 S  1001   374   366   RT 100 f5e6c028   1814 f5d474be ??       0:24 dtterm
 8 S  1001   346   301   RT 100 f5ef38b0   1211 f5d47676 pts/2    0:00
 sdt_shel
 8 S  1001   347     1   RT 100 f5ef31f0    478 f5d47626 ?        0:00 dsdm
 8 S  1001   365     1   RT 100 f5ef2470    903 f5d475d6 pts/2    0:01
 ttsessio
 8 S  1001   375   366   RT 100 f5ef1db0   1702 f5d474e6 ?        0:03 dtfile
 8 S  1001   376   366   RT 100 f5ef16f0   1118 f5d4750e ?        0:01
 snapshot
 8 S  1001   373   366   RT 100 f5ef1030   1710 f5d4755e ?        0:06 dtwm
 8 S  1001   393   374   RT 100 f5f468b8    253 f5f93386 pts/5    0:00 csh
 8 S  1001   378     1   RT 100 f5f461f8    385 f5f46268 ?        0:00
 sdtvolch
 8 S  1001   405   375   RT 100 f5f45b38   1687 f5f76738 ?        0:00 dtfile
 8 S  1001   445   378   RT 100 f5f45478    193 f591aaf8 ?        0:00 cat
 8 S  1001   387   374   RT 100 f5f44db8    255 f5f44fb0 pts/3    0:00 csh
 8 S  1001   407   387   RT 100 f5f446f8   1140 f5d4732e pts/3    0:03
 textedit
 8 S  1001   390   374   RT 100 f5f44038    252 f5f93986 pts/4    0:00 csh
 8 S  1001   417   393   RT 100 f5fa58c0    916 f5d472de pts/5    0:01 cmdtool
 8 S  1001   420   417   RT 100 f5fa5200    252 f5fc2b96 pts/6    0:00 csh
 8 S  1001   531   374   RT 100 f5fa4480    256 f5ff62a6 pts/7    0:00 csh
 8 S  1001   634   374   RT 100 f5fa3dc0    252 f5ff68a6 pts/8    0:00 csh
#
```

Setting the Priority of a Process (nice)

You can use the `nice` command to raise or lower the priority of a command or a process. When you use the `nice` command without an argument, the default is to increase the `nice` number by four units, thus lowering the priority of the process.

NOTE. You must be superuser to change the priority of a process by using the `nice` *command.*

Use the following command to lower the priority of a command by four units (the default).

```
/usr/bin/nice command-name
```

Use the following command to lower the priority of a command by increasing the `nice` number by ten units.

```
/usr/bin/nice +10 command-name
```

NOTE. The plus sign (+) is optional for positive numbers. The minus sign (–) is required for negative numbers.

Use the following command to raise the priority of a command by lowering the `nice` number by ten units.

```
/usr/bin/nice -10 command-name
```

Use the following command to raise the priority of a command by lowering the `nice` number by ten units. The first minus sign is the option sign, and the second minus sign indicates a negative number.

```
/usr/bin/nice - -10 command-name
```

Changing the Priority of a Running Process (renice)

New!

If you want to alter the scheduling priority of one or more running processes, you can use the `renice` command. Specify the process IDs of the processes to be affected. If the first operand is a number within the range of priorities (–20 to 20), `renice` treats it as a priority. Otherwise, `renice` treats it as an ID.

Users other than superuser can alter the priority only of processes they own and can increase their `nice` value only within the range 0 to 19.

The following example adjusts the system scheduling priority so that process IDs 987 and 32 have a lower scheduling priority.

```
paperbark% renice -n 5 -p 987 32
paperbark%
```

New!

Finding or Signalling Processes (pgrep, pkill)

You can use the pgrep command to examine the active processes on the system and report the process IDs of the processes whose attributes match the command-line argument. The simplest way to use pgrep is to type the command with the name of the process as the argument.

```
pgrep process-name
```

Refer to the pgrep(1) manual page for a complete listing of options and arguments.

The following example uses pgrep to find the process ID of the sendmail command.

```
paperbark% pgrep sendmail
2830
paperbark%
```

The pkill command works in the same way as pgrep except that it signals each matching process as would kill(1) instead of displaying the process ID. You can specify a signal name or number as the first command-line option to pkill.

Refer to the pgrep(1) manual page for a complete listing of options and arguments for pkill.

The following example terminates the most recently created xterm.

```
paperbark% pkill -n xterm
paperbark%
```

Reviewing Essential Administration Tools

The Solaris Operating Environment provides three kinds of administration tools.

- The usual collection of operating system commands.
- An administration tool (Admintool) with a graphical user interface for administering database files on local systems.
- The Solaris Admin Pack, available as a free download from the Solaris System Administrator Portal at the following URL.

  `www.sun.com/bigadmin/content/adminPack`

  For an introduction to the Solaris Admin Pack, see "Introducing the Solaris 8 Admin Pack" on page 76.

Frequently Used Commands

The following sections briefly introduce basic Solaris commands that you are likely to use regularly as part of routine system administration; they are grouped by tasks. See Chapter 2, "Using Basic OS Commands," for additional frequently used commands.

Getting Around in the File System (pwd, cd)

The Solaris Operating Environment has a hierarchical file system. When administering systems, you need to know where you are in the file hierarchy and how to change to a different directory.

Finding Where You Are in the File System To find out where you are in the file system hierarchy, type **`pwd`** and press Return. The print working directory command displays the current directory.

```
oak& pwd
/etc
oak%
```

Changing Directories To change directories, type **`cd`** ***`pathname`*** and press Return. The change directory command moves the focus to the directory whose name you type.

```
oak% cd /usr
oak% pwd
/usr
oak%
```

If you type **`cd`** and press Return without typing a path name, focus is returned to the login home directory.

Finding Information About Files

Using the `ls` command, you can list the contents of a directory and display permissions, links, ownership, group, size (in bytes), modification date and time, and file name for files. Many user problems related to accessing files can be traced to problems with incorrect permissions or ownership. See Chapter 11, "Recognizing File Access Problems," for more information.

Displaying File Information (ls)

To display information about an individual file, type **`ls -l`** ***`filename`*** and press Return. Permissions, links, owner, group, file size in bytes, modification date and time, and the file name are displayed.

```
oak% ls -l /etc/passwd
-r--r--r--   1 root     sys          659 Feb 24 17:28 /etc/passwd
oak%
```

To see a complete list for all the files in the directory, type **`ls -l`** and press Return. See the `ls`(1) manual page for a complete list of options.

Finding a File (find)

To find a file by searching from the home directory, type **`find $HOME -name`** ***`filename`*** **`-print`** and press Return. The `$HOME` variable starts the search with the home directory. The `-name` option looks for the name specified in the *`filename`* variable. The `-print` option displays the results of the find. If the named file is not found, the prompt is redisplayed.

The following example shows the results of `find` looking for `core` files.

```
oak% find $HOME -name core -print
/home/ignatz/core
oak%
```

Table 15 shows some of the options to the `find` command that you can use to focus your searches.

Table 15 Options to the find Command

Option	Description
`-fstype` *`type`*	
	Find files of the file system type you specify (typically `ufs` or `nfs`).
`-prune`	Limit the search to the specified directory.
`-nouser`	Find files that belong to a user not in the `/etc/passwd` database.
`-nogroup`	Find files that belong to a group not in the `/etc/group` database.

Table 15 Options to the find Command (Continued)

Option	Description
`-atime` *n*	Find files that have been accessed within the last *n* days.
`-mtime` *n*	Find files that have been modified within the last *n* days.
`-ctime` *n*	Find files that have been changed within the last *n* days. Changes can include changes to its attribute such as the number of links, its owner, or its group.
`-Xdev`	Restrict search to one file system.

See the `find(1)` manual page for a complete list of options.

Finding the Type of a File (file)

Sometimes you need to determine the type of a file. To find the type of a file, type **`file`** ***`filename`*** and press Return. The output of the command makes an educated guess about the type of the file.

For example, if you are trying to execute an ASCII file that does not have execute permissions, or execute an empty file, displaying the file type tells you whether the system recognizes the file as a command.

In the following example, the file is empty.

```
anastasia% file junk1
junk1: empty file
anastasia%
```

In the following example, the file is an ASCII text file.

```
anastasia% file junk2
junk2: ascii text
anastasia%
```

In the following example, the file is a text file with executable permissions, so the `file` command reports that the file contains commands and is text.

```
anastasia% chmod 777 junk3
anastasia% file junk3
junk: commands text
anastasia%
```

NOTE. You can, of course, determine if the command has execute permissions with the `ls -l` *command.*

To show the file type for all files in a directory, type **`file *`** and press Return. The files are listed in alphabetical order followed by the file type.

```
$ file *

coterie:     directory
course:      ascii text
dead.letter  ascii text
ksyms        English text
people:      directory
personal:    directory
showrev:     ascii text
status:      directory
text:        directory
todo:        ascii text
$
```

Finding Information in Files (grep, egrep)

You can use the `grep` and `egrep` commands to search files and command output for specific information.

Searching Files for Text Strings To search files for a specific text string, type **`grep`** ***`search-string filenames`*** and press Return. Lines in the files containing the string are displayed.

In the following example, the `passwd` file is searched for lines containing `csh`.

```
oak% grep csh /etc/passwd
ignatz::6693:10:Iggy Ignatz 64607:/home/ignatz:/bin/csh
fred::14072:10:Fred Lux:/home/fred:/bin/csh
oak%
```

You can search more than one file by specifying a series of file names separated by spaces or by using *metacharacters* such as the asterisk (`*`) or question mark (`?`) together with (or in place of) the file name.

To print lines that do not contain the specified string, type **`grep -v`** ***`search-string filename`*** and press Return. Lines in the file that do not contain the string are displayed.

Searching Input for Lines with a Given Pattern You can use the `grep` command with pipes in combination with many administrative commands. For example, if you want to find all of a user's current processes, pipe the output of the `ps` command to `grep` and search for the user name, type **`ps -e | grep`** ***`name`*** and press Return. The listing for the name you specify is displayed. See "Combining Commands (|)" on page 93 for more information.

The following example finds the OpenWindows process.

```
oak% ps -e | grep openwin
PID TTY      TIME COMD
2212 pts/0    0:00 openwin
oak%
```

Looking at Files

You undoubtedly will spend lots of time looking at the content of files. When you need to look at the entire file, use the `more` command. When the information you need is at the end of the file (for example, in a log file), use the `tail` command to display the last lines (10 by default) of the file. When important information is at the beginning of the file, use the `head` command to display the first lines (10 by default) of the file.

Viewing a File (more)

To view a file, type **`more`** ***`filename`*** and press Return. The file is displayed one screen at a time. Press Return to display the next line. Press space to view the next screen.

To search for a specific string in a file you are viewing with `more`, type ***`/search-string`*** and press Return. The text scrolls to display the place in the file that contains the text of the *`search-string`* variable and displays the search string and the message `. . . skipping` at the top of the window. If no match is found, the message `Pattern not found` is displayed at the bottom of the window and the text does not scroll.

For example, to find the words **`Local aliases`** in the `/etc/mail/aliases` file, type **`/Local aliases`** and press Return.

```
/Local aliases
...skipping

########################
# Local aliases below #
########################
```

NOTE. You must use exact capitalization in the search string for the `more` *command. If you type* **`/local aliases`** *in the previous example, the pattern is not found.*

To search for the next occurrence of the search string, type **n**. To quit `more`, type **q**. The shell prompt is redisplayed.

Another way to quit `more`, if Control-C is set as your shell kill character, is to press Control-C. The shell prompt is redisplayed.

To display the shell intr (interrupt) character, type **stty -a** and press Return. A list of the stty settings is displayed. In the following example, ^C is the shell intr character.

```
castle% stty -a
ispeed 88840 baud; ospeed 88824 baud;
rows = 36; columns = 113; ypixels = 478; xpixels = 801;
eucw 1:0:0:0, scrw 1:0:0:0
intr = ^c; quit = <undef>; erase = ^h; kill = ^u;
eof = ^d; eol = <undef>; eol2 = <undef>; swtch = <undef>;
start = ^q; stop = ^s; susp = ^z; dsusp = ^y;
rprnt = ^r; flush = ^o; werase = ^w; lnext = ^v;
-parenb parodd cs8 cstopb hupcl cread -clocal loblk crtscts crtsxoff parext
-ignbrk -brkint -ignpar -parmrk -inpck -istrip -inlcr -igncr icrnl -iuclc
ixon -ixany ixoff -imaxbel
isig icanon -xcase echo echoe echok -echonl -noflsh
-tostop echoctl -echoprt echoke -defecho -flusho -pendin iexten
opost -olcuc onlcr -ocrnl -onocr -onlret -ofill -ofdel
castle%
```

Looking at the End of a File (tail)

To look at the end of a file, type **tail *filename*** and press Return. The last 10 lines of the file are displayed.

The following example shows the tail of the /etc/lp/Systems file:

```
castle% /usr/bin/tail /etc/lp/Systems
#
#ident  "@(#)Systems    1.8     97/06/09 SMI"   /* SVr4.0 1.2   */
# This file previously contained an LP private interface.  It's
# contents are no longer used by the printing system and therefore
# obsolete.  Expect the file to be removed in a subsequent release
# of Solaris, along with the lpsystem(1M) command.
+:x:-:bsd:-:n:10:-:-:Allow all connections
castle%
```

By default, the head and tail commands display 10 lines. You can change the number of lines displayed by using the -n option. Substitute the number of lines you want to display for the letter *n*. For example, to display the last 20 lines of a file, type **tail -20 *filename*** and press Return.

NOTE. tail *shows a maximum of 4096 bytes (about 400 lines).*

Looking at the Beginning of a File (head)

To look at the beginning of a file, type **head *filename*** and press Return. The first 10 lines of the file are displayed.

The following example shows the head of the /etc/passwd file.

```
paperbark% head /etc/passwd
root:x:0:1:Super-User:/:/sbin/sh
daemon:x:1:1::/:
bin:x:2:2::/usr/bin:
sys:x:3:3::/:
adm:x:4:4:Admin:/var/adm:
```

```
lp:x:71:8:Line Printer Admin:/usr/spool/lp:
uucp:x:5:5:uucp Admin:/usr/lib/uucp:
nuucp:x:9:9:uucp Admin:/var/spool/uucppublic:/usr/lib/uucp/uucico
listen:x:37:4:Network Admin:/usr/net/nls:
nobody:x:60001:60001:Nobody:/:
paperbark%
```

Changing File Ownership or Permissions (chown, chmod, chgrp)

Many user problems can be traced to file ownership or permissions problems. Use the `ls` command to check the permissions and ownership on a file. If you need to change one or both, use the `chown`, `chmod`, and `chgrp` commands.

Changing File Ownership You must own a file or directory (or have root permission) to be able to change its owner.

The operating system has a configuration option, `{_POSIX_CHOWN_RESTRICTED}`, to restrict ownership changes. When this option is in effect, even the owner of the file cannot change the owner ID of the file. Only superuser can arbitrarily change owner IDs regardless of whether this option is in effect. To set the `{_POSIX_CHOWN_RESTRICTED}` configuration option, include the following line in the `/etc/system` file. New!

```
set rstchown = 1
```

To disable the `{_POSIX_CHOWN_RESTRICTED}` option, include the following line in `/etc/system`.

```
set rstchown = 0
```

`{_POSIX_CHOWN_RESTRICTED}` is enabled by default. See `system`(4) and `fpathconf`(2).

Use the following steps to change the ownership of a file.

1. Type **`ls -l`** ***`filename`*** and press Return. The owner of the file is displayed in the third column.
2. Become superuser if necessary.
3. Type **`chown`** ***`new-owner filename`*** and press Return. Ownership is assigned to the new owner you specify:

```
oak% ls -l quest
-rw-r--r--  1 fred   staff    6023 Aug  5 12:06 quest
oak% su
Password:
# chown ignatz quest
# ls -l quest
-rw-r--r--  1 ignatz   staff    6023 Aug  5 12:06 quest
#
```

See Chapter 11, "Recognizing File Access Problems," for more information.

Changing File Permissions You can change file permissions by using the symbolic values `r`, `w`, `x`, and `-`. You can also change file permissions by using a set of octal numbers. Table 16 shows the octal values for setting file permissions. You use these numbers in sets of three to set permissions for owner, group, and other. For example, the value `644` sets read/write permissions for owner and read-only permissions for group and other.

Table 16 Octal Values for File Permissions

Value	Description
0	No permissions.
1	Execute-only.
2	Write-only.
3	Write, execute.
4	Read-only.
5	Read, execute.
6	Read, write.
7	Read, write, execute.

1. Type **`ls -l`** ***`filename`*** and press Return. The long listing shows the current permissions for the file.
2. Type **`chmod`** ***`nnn filename`*** and press Return. Permissions are changed according to the numbers you specify.

NOTE. You can change permissions on groups of files or on all files in a directory by using metacharacters such as `*` and `?` in place of file names or in combination with them.

The following example changes the permissions of a file from `666` (read/write, read/write, read/write) to `644` (read/write, read-only, read-only).

```
oak% ls -l quest
-rw-rw-rw-   1 ignatz   staff    6023 Aug  5 12:06 quest
oak% chmod 644 quest
oak% ls -l
-rw-r--r--   1 ignatz   staff    6023 Aug  5 12:06 quest
oak%
```

Changing File Group Ownership (chgrp)

To change the group ownership of a file, type **chgrp *gid filename*** and press Return. The group ID for the file you specify is changed.

```
$ ls -lg junk
-rw-r--r-- 1 other 0 Oct 31 14:49 junk
$ chgrp 10 junk
$ ls -lg junk
-rw-r--r-- 1 staff 0 Oct 31 14:49 junk
$
```

Group IDs are defined in the `Group` database or the local `/etc/group` file. See Chapter 4, "Administering User Accounts and Groups," for more information about groups.

Setting or Displaying the System Environment

The shell maintains an environment with a set of specifications that it gets from the shell initialization files. Users can also modify the shell environment for a session by issuing commands directly to the shell. The shell receives its information about the environment from environment variables. See Chapter 3, "Understanding Shells," for more information.

The Solaris Operating Environment provides several default environment variables.

- `PS1` defines the shell prompt. The default prompt for the Bourne and Korn shells is `$`. The default prompt for the C shell is `%`. The default prompt for root in either shell is `#`. Users can specify a different shell prompt in their `.profile`, `.login`, or `.cshrc` files.
- `HOME` defines the absolute path to the user's home directory. The default value for `HOME` is automatically defined and set to the login directory specified in the `/etc/passwd` file as part of the login process. The shell subsequently uses this information to determine the directory to change to when you type the `cd` command without an argument.
- `LOGNAME` defines the user's login name. The default value for `LOGNAME` is automatically defined and set to the login name specified in the `/etc/passwd` file as part of the login process.
- `PATH` lists, in order, the directories that the shell searches to find the program to run when the user types a command. If the directory is not in the search path, users must type the complete path name of a command. The default `PATH` is automatically defined and set as specified in `.profile` (Bourne or Korn shell), or `.cshrc` (C shell) as part of the login process. The order of the search path is very important. When identically named commands exist in different locations, the first command found with that name is used. For example, suppose that `PATH` is defined (in Bourne and Korn shell syntax) as

PATH=/bin:/usr/bin:/usr/sbin:$HOME/bin and a file named sample resides in both /usr/bin and /home/jean/bin. If the user types the command sample without specifying its full path name, the version found in /usr/bin is used.

- The LANG and LC environment variables specify the locale-specific conversions and conventions for the shell, such as time zones, collation order, and format of dates, time, currency, and numbers. In addition, you can use the stty command in a user-initialization file to set whether the system supports multibyte characters.

LANG sets all possible conversions and conventions for the given locale. If you have special needs, you can set various aspects of localization separately by using the following LC variables.

- LC_COLLATE
- LC_CTYPE
- LC_MESSAGES
- LC_NUMERIC
- LC_MONETARY
- LC_TIME

Table 17 lists the values for the LANG and LC environment variables.

Table 17 Values for LANG and LC Variables

Value	Locale
DE	German.
FR	French.
ISO_8859_1	English and European.
IT	Italian.
JAPANESE	Japanese.
KOREAN	Korean.
SV	Swedish.
TCHINESE	Taiwanese.

Other environment variables include the following.

New!

- ARCH sets the user's system architecture (for example sun4, i386). You can set this variable in the Bourne or Korn shells with ARCH = \`uname -p\` or in the C shell with setenv ARCH \`uname -p\`. No built-in behavior of the shell depends on this variable. However, it is a useful variable for branching within shell scripts.

- CALENDAR sets the path to the Calendar executables.
- CDPATH (or cdpath in the C shell) sets a variable used by the cd command. If the target directory of the cd command is specified as a relative path name, the cd command first looks for the target directory in the current directory (.). If the target is not found, the path names listed in the CDPATH variable are searched consecutively until the target directory is found and the directory change is completed.
- DESKSET sets the path to the DeskSet executables.
- history sets history for the C shell.
- LD_LIBRARY_PATH sets the search path for dynamically linked libraries.
- LPDEST sets the user's default printer.
- MAIL tells the shell where to look for new mail.
- MANPATH sets the hierarchies of the available manual pages.
- MANSECTS sets the available sections of manual pages.
- OPENWINHOME sets the path to the OpenWindows executables.
- prompt defines the shell prompt for the C shell.
- SHELL sets the default shell used by make, vi, and other tools.
- TERM (or term in the C shell) sets the terminal definition. This variable should be reset in /etc/profile or /etc/.login. When the user invokes an editor, the system looks for a file with the same name as the definition of this environment variable. The system searches the directory referenced by TERMINFO to determine the terminal characteristics.
- TERMINFO specifies the path name for an unsupported terminal that has been added to the terminfo file. Use the TERMINFO variable in /etc/profile or /etc/.login.
- TZ sets the time zone.

Users and system administrators can define additional variables for their own use. When you define an environment variable from a shell command, the variable remains in effect while you are working in the shell. When you exit the shell, the environment variable is not retained. Store "permanent" environment variables that are likely to be used during each login session in the .profile, .login, or .cshrc file. The syntax for defining environment variables depends on the shell and is described in Chapter 3, "Understanding Shells," and later in this chapter.

CDE Environment Variables

The Common Desktop Environment (CDE) has its own set of environment variables. Desktop search paths are created at login by the desktop command `dtsearchpath`. The `dtsearchpath` command uses a combination of environment variables and built-in locations to create the search paths.

The environment variables that `dtsearchpath` reads are called *input variables*. These are variables set by the system administrator or end user. The input variables use the naming convention `DTSP*`, which is an abbreviation for desktop search path.

When `dtsearchpath` runs at login, it assembles the values assigned to these variables, adds built-in locations, and creates values for output variables. Each search path has an output variable, as shown in Table 18.

Table 18 CDE Search Path Environment Variables

Search Path	Output Environment Variable	Systemwide Input Variable	Personal Input Variable
Applications	`DTAPPSEARCHPATH`	`DTSPSYSAPPHOSTS`	`DTSPUSERAPPHOSTS`
Database: actions, data types, and front panel definitions	`DTDATABASESEARCHPATH`	`DTSPSYSDATABASEHOSTS`	`DTSPUSERDATABASEHOSTS`
Icons	`XMICONSEARCHPATH`, `XMICONBMSEARCPATH`	`DTSPSYSICON`	`DTSPUSERICON`
Help data	`DTHELPSEARCHPATH`	`DTSPSYSHELP`	`DTSPUSERHELP`

CDE components use the values of the output variables. For example, Application Manager uses the value of the application search path (`DTAPPSEARCHPATH`) to locate application groups. For more information about CDE, refer to *Solaris Common Desktop Environment: Advanced User's and System Administrator's Guide*.

Defining Bourne and Korn Shell Environment Variables

To define an environment variable for the Bourne and Korn shells, type ***VARIABLE*=value;export *VARIABLE*** and press Return. The following example uses the PS1 environment variable to define a shell prompt.

```
$ PS1=oak$;export PS1
$
```

Defining C Shell Environment Variables

To define an environment variable for the C shell, type **setenv *VARIABLE* *value*** and press Return. The following example sets the DISPLAY environment variable to rogue:0.

```
% setenv DISPLAY rogue:0
%
```

Displaying Environment Variable Settings (env)

Each shell maintains an environment with a set of specifications that it gets from the user's initialization files (.profile for the Bourne and Korn shells or .cshrc and .login for the C shell) or from environment variables set interactively from a shell. These environment variables can specify information such as the user's home directory, login name, default printer, location for e-mail messages, and path for accessing the OpenWindows environment.

To display a list of the current environment variable settings, type **env** and press Return.

The following example shows all the environment variables for a system running CDE.

```
paperbark% env
MANPATH=/usr/dt/man:/usr/man:/usr/openwin/share/man
DTDATABASESEARCHPATH=/export/home/winsor/.dt/types,/etc/dt/appconfig/types/%L,
  /etc/dt/appconfig/types/C,/usr/dt/appconfig/types/%L,/usr/dt/appconfig/types
  /C
DTXSERVERLOCATION=local
LANG=C
HELPPATH=/usr/openwin/lib/locale:/usr/openwin/lib/help
DTSOURCEPROFILE=true
PATH=/usr/openwin/bin:/usr/dt/bin:/export/home/opt/SUNWadm/bin:/bin:/usr/bin:/
  usr/sbin:/usr/ucb:/etc:/usr/proc/bin:/usr/ccs/bin:/opt/hpnp/bin:/opt/NSCPcom
  :/usr/local/games:.
AB_CARDCATALOG=/usr/dt/share/answerbooks/C/ab_cardcatalog
DTUSERSESSION=winsor-paperbark-0
```

```
XMICONBMSEARCHPATH=/export/home/winsor/.dt/icons/%B%M.bm:/export/home/winsor/.
  dt/icons/%B%M.pm:/export/home/winsor/.dt/icons/%B:/etc/dt/appconfig/icons/%L
  /%B%M.bm:/etc/dt/appconfig/icons/%L/%B%M.pm:/etc/dt/appconfig/icons/%L/%B:/e
  tc/dt/appconfig/icons/C/%B%M.bm:/etc/dt/appconfig/icons/C/%B%M.pm:/etc/dt/ap
  pconfig/icons/C/%B:/usr/dt/appconfig/icons/%L/%B%M.bm:/usr/dt/appconfig/icon
  s/%L/%B%M.pm:/usr/dt/appconfig/icons/%L/%B:/usr/dt/appconfig/icons/C/%B%M.bm
  :/usr/dt/appconfig/icons/C/%B%M.pm:/usr/dt/appconfig/icons/C/%B
SESSION_SVR=paperbark
OPENWINHOME=/usr/openwin
EDITOR=/usr/dt/bin/dtpad
LOGNAME=winsor
DTSCREENSAVERLIST=StartDtscreenSwarm StartDtscreenQix     StartDtscreenFlame
  StartDtscreenHop StartDtscreenImage StartDtscreenLife     StartDtscreenRotor
  StartDtscreenPyro StartDtscreenWorm StartDtscreenBlank
MAIL=/var/mail/winsor
USER=winsor
DISPLAY=:0.0
SHELL=/bin/csh
DTAPPSEARCHPATH=/export/home/winsor/.dt/appmanager:/etc/dt/appconfig/appmanage
  r/%L:/etc/dt/appconfig/appmanager/C:/usr/dt/appconfig/appmanager/%L:/usr/dt/
  appconfig/appmanager/C
HOME=/export/home/winsor
XFILESEARCHPATH=/usr/openwin/lib/locale/%L/%T/%N%S:/usr/openwin/lib/%T/%N%S
XMICONSEARCHPATH=/export/home/winsor/.dt/icons/%B%M.pm:/export/home/winsor/.dt
  /icons/%B%M.bm:/export/home/winsor/.dt/icons/%B:/etc/dt/appconfig/icons/%L/%
  B%M.pm:/etc/dt/appconfig/icons/%L/%B%M.bm:/etc/dt/appconfig/icons/%L/%B:/etc
  /dt/appconfig/icons/C/%B%M.pm:/etc/dt/appconfig/icons/C/%B%M.bm:/etc/dt/appc
  onfig/icons/C/%B:/usr/dt/appconfig/icons/%L/%B%M.pm:/usr/dt/appconfig/icons/
  %L/%B%M.bm:/usr/dt/appconfig/icons/%L/%B:/usr/dt/appconfig/icons/C/%B%M.pm:/
  usr/dt/appconfig/icons/C/%B%M.bm:/usr/dt/appconfig/icons/C/%B
TERM=dtterm
dtstart_sessionlogfile=/dev/null
TZ=Australia/West
DTHELPSEARCHPATH=/export/home/winsor/.dt/help/winsor-paperbark-0/%H:/export/ho
  me/winsor/.dt/help/winsor-paperbark-0/%H.sdl:/export/home/winsor/.dt/help/wi
  nsor-paperbark-0/%H.hv:/export/home/winsor/.dt/help/%H:/export/home/winsor/.
  dt/help/%H.sdl:/export/home/winsor/.dt/help/%H.hv:/etc/dt/appconfig/help/%L/
  %H:/etc/dt/appconfig/help/%L/%H.sdl:/etc/dt/appconfig/help/%L/%H.hv:/usr/dt/
  appconfig/help/%L/%H:/usr/dt/appconfig/help/%L/%H.sdl:/usr/dt/appconfig/help
  /%L/%H.hv:/usr/dt/appconfig/help/C/%H:/usr/dt/appconfig/help/C/%H.sdl:/usr/d
  t/appconfig/help/C/%H.hv
XMBINDDIR=/usr/dt/lib/bindings
WINDOWID=96469001
TERMINAL_EMULATOR=dtterm
PWD=/export/home/winsor
paperbark%
```

Using the PATH Variable

The PATH environment variable is very important. When the user executes a command and uses the full path name, the shell finds the command by using that path name. However, when the user specifies only a command name, the shell searches the directories for the command in the order specified by the PATH variable. If the command is found in one of the directories, the shell executes it.

A default su path (/sbin:/usr/sbin:/usr/bin:/etc) is set by the system, but most users modify it to add additional command directories. Many user problems related to setting up the environment and accessing the right version of a command or a tool can be traced to incorrectly defined paths.

CAUTION. Including . *in the path to search the current directory is a potential security problem. If security is an issue at your site, do not include* . *as part of a user's path. Never use* . *as part of the root path.*

Setting the Path for Bourne and Korn Shells

The path for the Bourne and Korn shells is specified in the user's `$HOME/.profile` file as shown in the following example.

```
PATH=/usr/bin:/$HOME/bin:.
```

Setting the Path for the C Shell

The path for the C shell is specified in the user's `$HOME/.cshrc` file (with the `set path` environment variable) as shown in the following example.

```
set path = (/usr/bin $home/bin .)
```

See the appropriate manual pages for an in-depth description of these commands and Chapter 11, "Recognizing File Access Problems," for more information about troubleshooting problems with paths.

Using Admintool

Admintool is a graphical user interface that you can use to administer local systems. You can use Admintool for the following categories.

- User accounts
- Groups
- Hosts
- Printers
- Serial ports
- Software packages

The next section describes how to start Admintool.

Starting Admintool

When using Admintool, you must be a member of the sysadmin UNIX group (GID 14) to run Admintool using your own UID, not as root. Anyone with root permissions on a local system can use Admintool to modify, create, or delete information in the local `/etc` files for that system. Use the following steps to start Admintool.

New!

NOTE. If you access Admintool through the Solaris Management Console, you must log in as root or as a member of a role that grants you superuser permissions to run Admintool. Only then can you use Admintool to edit local password databases. See "Using AdminSuite 3.0 to Grant Access Rights to Users" on page 190 for more information.The Solaris Management Console does not recognize membership in GID 14.

1. Start Admintool from a command line by typing ***admintool&*** and pressing Return. The Admintool window is displayed.
2. Choose the Admintool view that you want to use from the Browse menu, shown in Figure 1.

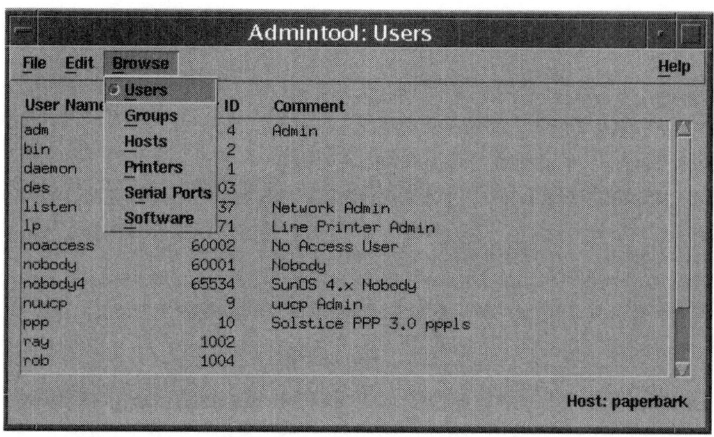

Figure 1 The Admintool Browse Menu

New!

Introducing the Solaris 8 Admin Pack

The Solaris Easy Access Server product is an extension to the Solaris Operating Environment that provides increased interoperability, security, and workgroup functionality. With the Solaris 8 Operating Environment, you no longer need Solaris Easy Access Server 3.0. The functionality previously available only in Solaris Easy Access Server is now included in the Solaris 8 Operating Environment and in the Solaris 8 Admin Pack, which is available as a free download from the Solaris System Administrator Portal at the following URL.

`www.sun.com/bigadmin/content/adminPack`

The Admin Pack includes the following tools.

- Solaris Web Start 2.02.
- Solaris Management console 1.02.
- Solaris Administration Wizards 1.0.
- Solaris AdminSuite 3.0.
- Solstice PPP 3.0.1.
- Sun Enterprise Authentication Mechanism 1.0.

The Solaris 8 base platform now includes the following tools.

- Solaris WBEM Services 1.0.
- Solaris Print Manager 1.0.
- Solstice DiskSuite 4.2

Introducing Tools in the Solaris Management Console

New!

The Solaris Management Console (SMC) is your access point for system administration tools available in the Solaris 8 Admin Pack. One of the tools is Solaris AdminSuite 3.0, which is a replacement for Solstice AdminSuite 2.3. The functionality and organization of the tools in the Solaris Management Console and in AdminSuite 3.0 are quite different from the old version of the AdminSuite tool.

Table 19 compares the functionality of AdminSuite 2.3 and AdminSuite 3.0. The descriptions apply to the AdminSuite 3.0 functionality.

Table 19 Solaris SMC and AdminSuite Tools

AdminSuite 2.3	AdminSuite 3.0	Description
Host Manager	Computer/ Networks	Manage system information and server support, excluding management of different clients such as AutoClient and stand-alone systems, diskless and dataless clients, and JavaStations that were previously provided by the AdminSuite 2.3 Host Manager.
Aliases	Users: Mailing Lists	Manage the `Aliases` database.
Auto_Home	Users: User Accounts	Manage the `Auto_home` database.
Bootparams	No current equivalent tool.	Manage the `Bootparams` database.

Table 19 Solaris SMC and AdminSuite Tools (Continued)

AdminSuite 2.3	AdminSuite 3.0	Description
Ethers	Computer/ Networks	Manage the `Ethers` database.
Hosts	Computer/ Networks	Manage the `Hosts` database.
Locale	No current equivalent tool.	Manage the `Locale` database.
Netgroup	No current equivalent tool.	Manage the `Netgroup` database.
Netmasks	Computer/ Networks	Manage the `Netmasks` database.
Networks	Computer/ Networks	Manage the `Networks` database.
Passwd	Users: User Accounts	Manage the `Passwd` database.
Protocols	No current equivalent tool.	Manage the `Protocols` database.
RPC	No current equivalent tool.	Manage the `RPC` database.
Services	No current equivalent tool.	Manage the `Services` database.
Timezone	No current equivalent tool.	Manage the `Timezone` database.
Group Manager	Users: Groups	Manage UNIX group information.
User Manager	Users: User Accounts	Manage user account information. New functionality enables you to manage the Role-Based Access Control (RBAC) functionality (Roles, Rights).
Serial Port Manager	Serial Ports	Manage serial port software for terminals and modems.
Printer Manager	N/A	Integrated with the Solaris 8 Operating Environment. Use to manage printer software for print servers and clients.

Table 19 Solaris SMC and AdminSuite Tools (Continued)

AdminSuite 2.3	AdminSuite 3.0	Description
Database Manager	Users: Mailing Lists	Manage only aliases files. The old Database manager provided more functionality.
Storage Manager (comprising Disk Manager and File System Manager)	Mounts and Shares, Disks	Manage disk slices and `fdisk` partitions on a single disk or a group of equivalent disks (Disks) and file systems for a server or for a group of clients on a server (Mounts and Shares).

Accessing Solaris AdminSuite 3.0

This section describes how to access the AdminSuite 3.0 tools.

1. From the CDE Application Manager, System_Admin folder, double-click on the Solaris Management Console icon.

   The SMC Login window is displayed, as shown in Figure 2.

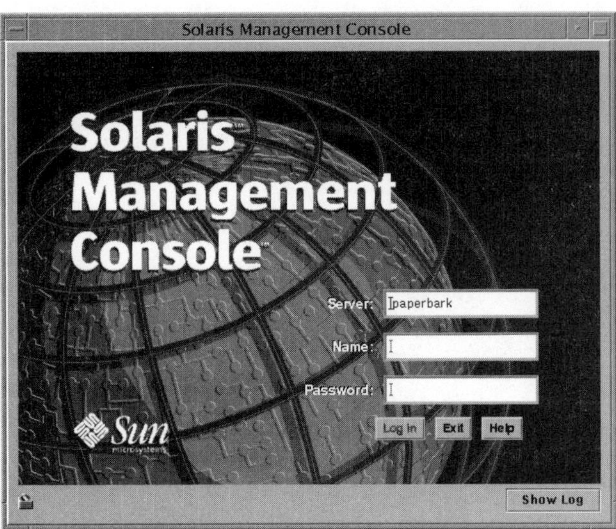

Figure 2 The SMC Login Window

2. Type your login name and password, and click on the Log in button.

   The Solaris Management Console window is displayed, as shown in Figure 3.

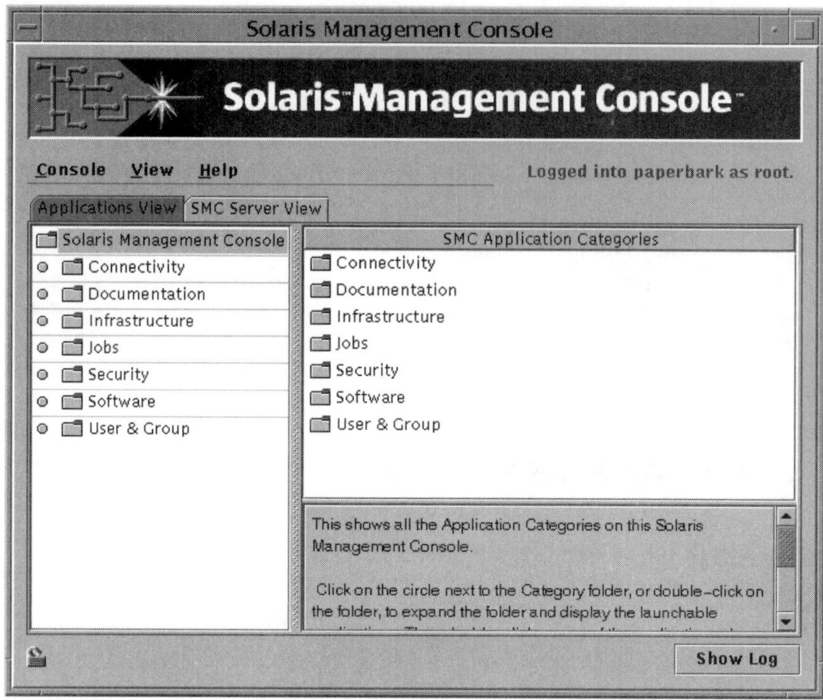

Figure 3 The Solaris Management Console Window

You can click on the dot to the left of each item to show the contents of a folder in the left pane. Figure 4 shows the top-level contents of all of the SMC folders.

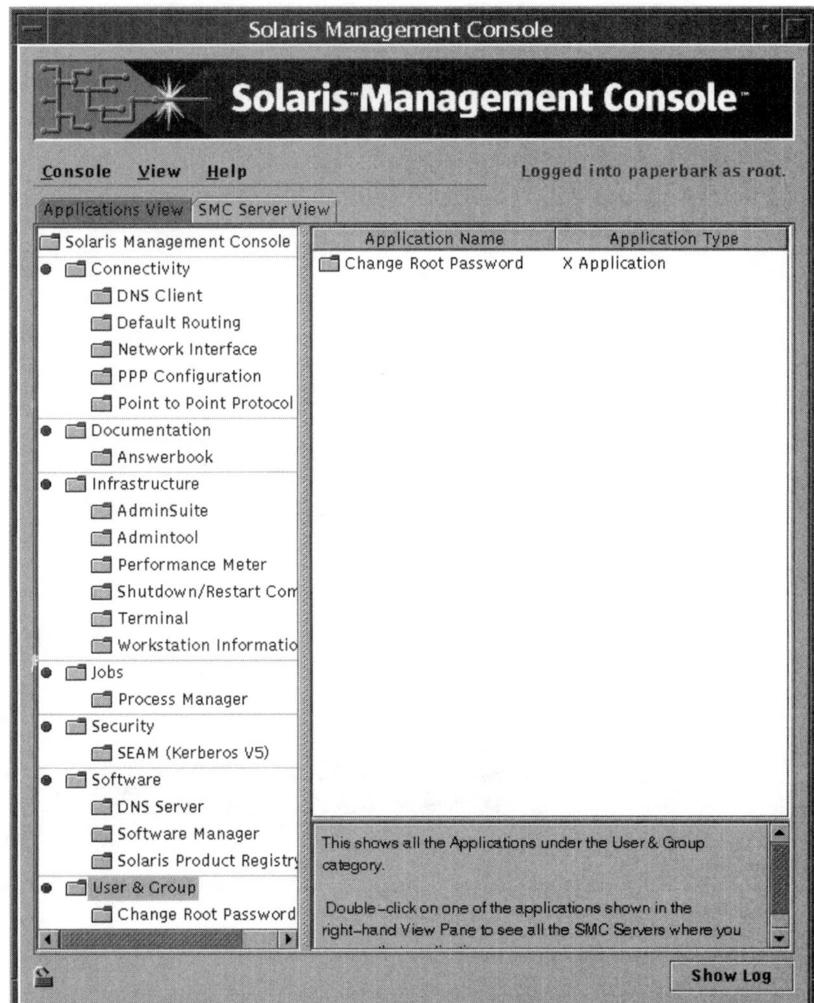

Figure 4 All Contents of the Solaris Management Console Window

3. Click on the Infrastructure folder or the word Infrastructure in the left pane.

   The contents of the Infrastructure folder are displayed in the right pane, as shown in Figure 5.

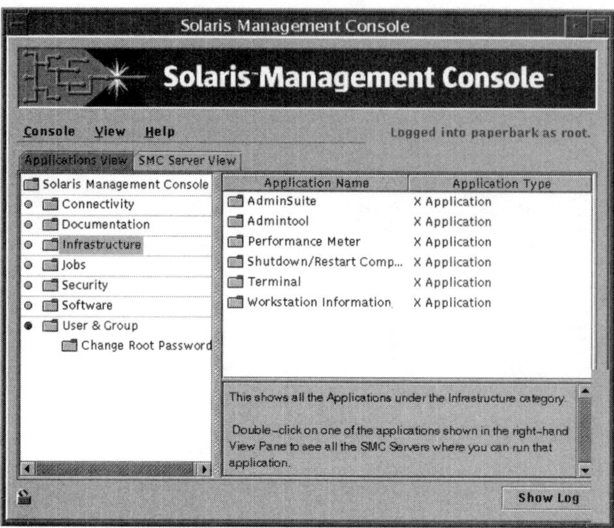

Figure 5 Contents of the Infrastructure Folder

Alternatively, you can click on the circle to the left of the folder to display the contents in the left pane, as shown in Figure 6.

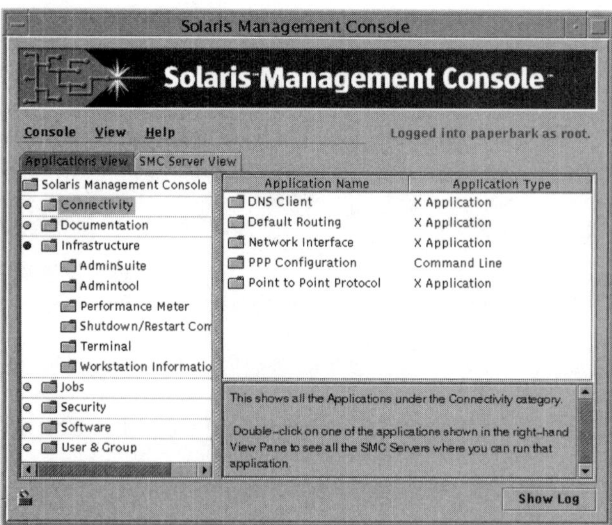

Figure 6 Another View of the Contents of the Infrastructure Folder

4. Double-click on the AdminSuite folder in either pane.

   The AdminSuite application icon is displayed in the right pane.

5. Double-click on the AdminSuite icon.

   The AdminSuite Log On window is displayed, as shown in Figure 7.

Figure 7 AdminSuite Log On Window

   If you are a member of a role that grants you access to superuser privileges for a specific set of tasks, you can log in by using the role name and password. See Chapter 5, “Administering Roles,” for more information on roles.

6. Log in, type the password, and click on the OK button.

   The AdminSuite window is displayed, as shown in Figure 8.

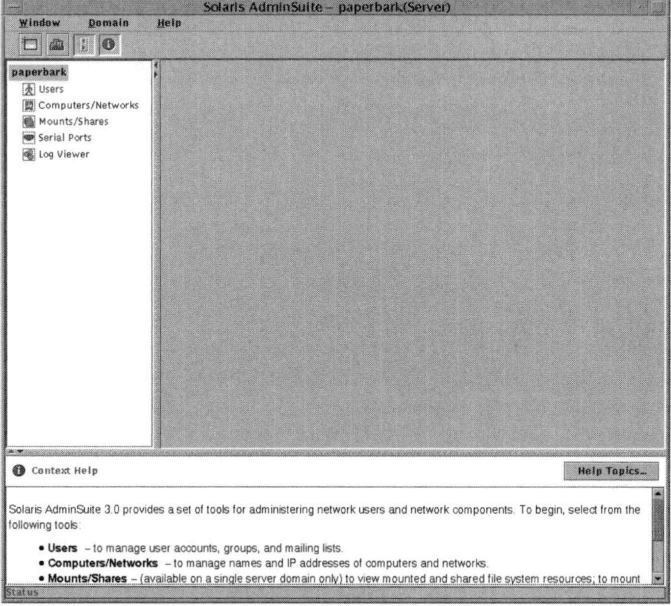

Figure 8 AdminSuite Window

Figure 9 shows the top-level contents of the AdminSuite tools in the left pane.

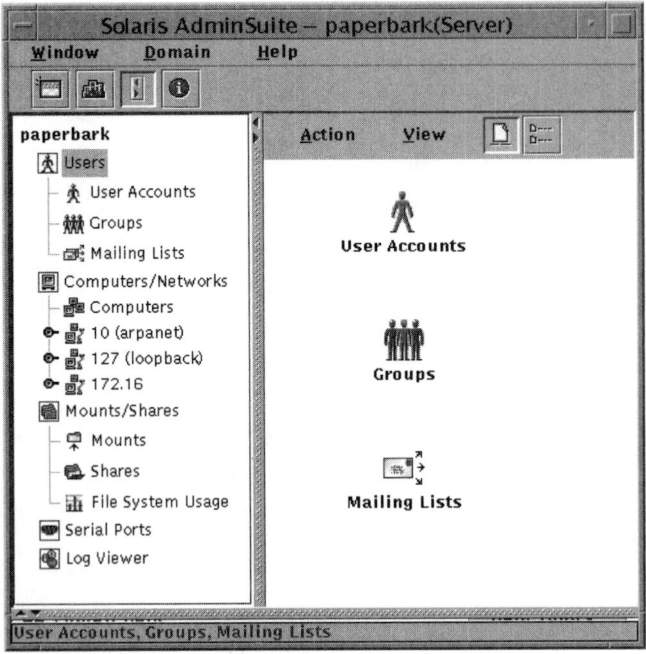

Figure 9 Top-Level Contents of AdminSuite Folders

2

USING BASIC OS COMMANDS

This chapter explains some basic operating system commands that help you find information about users and the system environment. It also describes several ways to create and edit files, combine commands and redirect output, display manual pages, and locate basic disk information.

Finding User Information

When administering systems, you often need to find out who is using the system and what they are doing. This section describes the commands—`w`, `who`, `finger`, `rusers -l`, `whodo`, `id`—that you can use to find information about users.

Determining Who Is Logged In to a System (w, who, finger, rusers -l, whodo)

You can use any one of the following commands (`w`, `who`, `finger`, `rusers -l`, or `whodo`) to find out who is logged in to a system. Each command gives you different information.

Using the w Command

New!

The `w` command displays a summary of the current activity on the system, including what each user is doing. The header line shows the current time, the length of time the system has been up, the number of users logged into the system, and the average number of jobs in the run queue over the last 1, 5, and 15 minutes. w is a combination of who, uptime, and ps -a.

The following example shows the output of the w command on the system paperbark.

```
paperbark% w
  3:29pm  up  1:45,  1 user,  load average: 0.00, 0.00, 0.01
User     tty           login@  idle   JCPU   PCPU  what
winsor   console       1:46pm  1:43                /usr/dt/bin/sdt_shell -c
 unseten
winsor   pts/4         1:46pm  1:42                /bin/csh
winsor   pts/5         1:46pm  1:42                /bin/csh
winsor   pts/6         1:46pm  1:42                /bin/csh
winsor   pts/7         1:46pm  1:22                w
paperbark%
```

Using the who Command

The who command displays a list of the users logged in to a system, with the login TTY port and the date and time. When a user is logged in remotely, the remote system name for that user is also displayed. To use the who command, type **who** and press Return.

In the following example, irving is logged in remotely (as shown by the system name in parentheses), and ignatz is logged in locally to the system oak.

```
oak% who
irving pts/1   Oct 31 14:33 (elm)
ignatz console Oct 31 12:22
oak%
```

Using the finger Command

The finger command displays a list of the login names of users logged in to a system, along with the complete name of the user (from the Information field of their /etc/password entry), the TTY port, the day of the week, the login time, and the remote system name if the user is logged in remotely. To use the finger command, type **finger** and press Return.

In the following example, user winsor is logged in remotely from castle.

```
oak% rlogin drusilla
drusilla% finger
Login  Name          TTY   Idle When      Where
winsor Janice Winsor pts/0 11   Thu 09:59 castle
drusilla%
```

Using the rusers -l Command

The `rusers -l` (remote users, login) command displays a list of login names of users who are logged in on remote systems, along with the name of the system a user is logged in to, the TTY port, the month, date, login time, and idle time. If the host is not idle, no time is displayed in the last field. To use the `rusers -l` command, type **rusers -l** and press Return.

The following example shows six users logged in to the console and two users logged in to TTY ports.

```
cinderella% rusers -l
Sending broadcast for rusersd protocol version 3...
Sending broadcast for rusersd protocol version 2...
jah       caps:console              Mar  3 13:03   22:03
amber     facehole:console          Mar  2 07:40
sebree    ondine:console            Mar  2 10:35      14
tut       cairo:console             Mar  2 10:48
jrt       cairo:ttyp5               Mar  2 16:20   47:54 (gap)
ramseyis mowthelawn:console         Mar  2 16:33      28
ramseyis mowthelawn:ttyp6           Mar  3 14:20   25:14 (:0.0)
(More logins not shown)
cinderella%
```

Using the whodo Command

The `whodo` command displays the date, time, and system name. For each user logged in, the device name, UID, and login time are shown, followed by a list of active processes associated with the UID. The list includes the device name, PID, CPU minutes and seconds used, and process name.

To find out who is logged in and doing what, type **whodo** and press Return.

The following example shows that user `winsor` is running a number of CDE applications and Netscape Navigator.

```
paperbark% whodo
Wed May  3 15:34:41 WST 2000paperbark

console        winsor    13:46
      ?             376     0:00 Xsession
    pts/3           422     0:00 sdt_shell
    pts/3           488     0:00 dtfile
    pts/3           485     0:00 dtfile
    pts/3           484     0:00 sh
    pts/3           462     0:00 dtpad
    pts/3           460     0:00 sh
    pts/3           440     0:00 ttsession
    pts/3           441     0:00 dtsession
      ?             448     0:02 dtwm
      ?             452     0:00 sdtperfmeter
      ?             451     0:00 dtterm
    pts/6           472     0:00 csh
    pts/5           469     0:00 csh
    pts/4           466     0:00 csh
    pts/4           536     0:00 ftp
      ?             449     0:00 netscape
      ?             463     0:00 netscape
      ?             461     0:06 .netscape.bin
      ?             477     0:00 .netscape.bin
    pts/3           424     0:00 csh
```

```
       ?           386     0:00 fbconsole
       ?           425     0:00 dsdm

pts/4          winsor   13:46

pts/5          winsor   13:46

pts/6          winsor   13:46

pts/7          winsor   13:46
    pts/7          475     0:00 csh
    pts/7          539     0:00 whodo
paperbark%
```

Finding User UID and GID Settings (id)

Use the `id` command to display the user ID and group ID number for a user who is logged in. This information can be helpful for troubleshooting problems when users cannot access files they think they own or when users want to find out which group they belong to. To use the `id` command, have the user log in, type **id**, and press Return. If the UID or GID does not match those for the troublesome file, you may need to change the ownership or group on the file or add the user to the appropriate group. See "Changing File Ownership or Permissions (chown, chmod, chgrp)" on page 67 and "Setting Up and Administering Groups" on page 151 for more information.

The following example shows the UID for user `winsor` is `6693` and the GID is `10`. For superuser, the UID is `0` and the GID is `0`.

```
anastasia% id
uid=6693(winsor) gid=10(staff)
anastasia% su
Password:
# id
uid=0(root) gid=1(other)
#
```

Creating and Editing Files (cat, touch, cp, mv, vi)

This section describes how to create and edit files with the `cat`, `touch`, `cp`, `mv`, Text Editor, and `vi` commands.

Using the cat Command

Use the `cat` command to create short files or to append a small amount of text to an existing file. Use the following steps to create files with the `cat` command.

1. Type **cat >** ***filename*** and press Return.
2. Type the text into the new file.
3. Press Return.
4. Press Control-D.

   The text is saved and the shell prompt is redisplayed.

Use the following steps to append text to an existing file.

1. Type **cat >>** ***filename*** and press Return.
2. Type the text to be appended to the file.
3. Press Return.
4. Press Control-D.

   The text is saved and the shell prompt is redisplayed.

To view the contents of the file, type **cat** ***filename*** and press Return. The contents of the file are displayed. If the file is too long to fit in the terminal window, it flies by and shows you the lines at the end of the file that fit in the window or on the screen.

The following example creates a file named `kookaburra` with the first verse of the kookaburra song, displays the contents of the file, appends the second verse to the file, and displays the contents again.

```
castle% cat > kookaburra
Kookaburra sits in the old gum tree
Merry merry king of the bush is he
Laugh kookaburra, laugh kookaburra
Gay your life must be.
^D
castle% cat kookaburra
Kookaburra sits in the old gum tree
Merry merry king of the bush is he
Laugh kookaburra, laugh kookaburra
Gay your life must be.

castle% cat >> kookaburra
Kookaburra sits in the old gum tree
Eating all the gumdrops he can see
Stop kookaburra, stop kookaburra
Leave some there for me.
^D
castle% cat kookaburra
Kookaburra sits in the old gum tree
Merry merry king of the bush is he
Laugh kookaburra, laugh kookaburra
Gay your life must be.

Kookaburra sits in the old gum tree
Eating all the gumdrops he can see
Stop kookaburra, stop kookaburra
Leave some there for me.
castle%
```

Using the touch Command

The `touch` command sets the access and modification times for each file to the current time. If a file does not exist, an empty one is created. You can use the `touch` command to create an empty file to check the default permissions and ownership or to create a file to which you add text at a later time.

To create an empty file, type **`touch`** ***`filename`*** and press Return. A new, empty file is created. If the file exists, then its modification time is updated to the current date and time.

The following example uses the `ls` command to determine that there is not a file named `junk`, creates the file, and uses the `ls` command to verify that the empty file is created.

```
oak% ls -l junk
junk:  No such file or directory
oak% touch junk
oak% ls -l junk
-rw-r--r--   1 irving     staff 0 Sep 11 15:06 junk
oak%
```

Copying (cp) or Renaming (mv) an Existing File

You can create a new file by copying or renaming an existing file.

To copy an existing file, type **`cp`** ***`old-filename new-filename`*** and press Return. You have made a copy of the file, retaining the original one.

```
oak% cp quest oldquest
oak%
```

To move (and rename) an existing file, type **`mv`** ***`old-filename new-filename`*** and press Return. You have changed the name of the file.

```
oak% mv quest /tmp/quest.old
oak%
```

Using Text Editor

You can use the OpenWindows Text Editor to create and edit files. You may, however, have problems using Text Editor to edit files that have root permissions.

To start Text Editor from the OpenWindows workspace from the Workspace menu, choose Programs. Then, choose Text Editor from the Programs menu. To start Text Editor from a command line, type

/usr/openwin/bin/textedit & and press Return. A Text Editor window is displayed. Use the commands from the Edit menu or the Cut, Copy, Paste, and Undo keys from the keyboard to make editing changes.

If you are running CDE, you can use the CDE Text Editor to create and edit files. To start Text Editor from the CDE front panel, click on the Personal Applications menu and click on Text Editor. To start the CDE Text Editor from the command line, type **/usr/dt/bin/dtpad&** and press Return. A Text Editor window is displayed. Use the commands from the Edit menu or the Cut, Copy, Paste, and Undo keys from the keyboard to make editing changes.

Using vi

The visual editor, vi, is commonly used by system administrators to edit text files. Whole books have been written about using vi. This section provides only a quick-reference table with some of the most commonly used editing commands.

To start vi, type **vi *filename*** and press Return. If the file does not exist, a new file is opened. The new file is created when you save changes made to it. If the file exists, the beginning of the file is displayed.

Table 20 shows a few of the many vi editing commands.

Table 20 Some Basic vi Commands

Task	Command
How to save/quit a file.	
Quit without saving changes.	:q!
Write changes.	:w
Write changes and quit.	:wq
Write changes and quit.	ZZ
How to move around in a file.	
Move cursor one character left.	h
Move cursor one character right.	l
Move cursor up one line.	k
Move cursor down one line.	j
Go to end of the file.	G
How to add text.	
Insert text (insert mode).	i *text* Esc

Table 20 Some Basic vi Commands (Continued)

Task	Command
Append text at cursor location.	`a` *`text`* `Esc`
Append text at end of the line.	`A` *`text`* `Esc`
How to exit to command mode.	`Esc`
How to make changes to a file.	
Delete line.	`dd`
Delete character.	`x`
Delete word.	`dw`
Open new line above.	`O` *`text`* `Esc`
Open new line below.	`o` *`text`* `Esc`
Yank/copy line.	`Y`
Put before.	`P`
Put after.	`p`

Combining Commands and Redirecting Output

The Solaris Operating Environment enables you to combine commands. This section describes the three ways by which you can combine commands.

Typing Several Commands on the Same Command Line (;)

You can type more than one command on a single command line by typing a semicolon (`;`) between the commands.

For example, you can change to a directory and list the commands by typing **`cd /usr/bin;ls`** and pressing Return. The following example sets an environment variable for the Bourne shell and then exports the variable.

```
$ PATH=/usr/bin:$HOME/bin:.;export PATH
$
```

Redirecting Output (<>)

Unless you indicate otherwise, commands normally display their results on the screen. You can, however, redirect the output of a command by using the redirect symbols < and >. For example, to save the output to a file instead of displaying it on the screen, use the > redirect symbol to tell the shell to put the contents into a file. In the following example, the output of the date command is redirected to a new file called `date.file`.

```
$ date > date.file
$
```

The following example shows the contents of `date.file`.

```
paperbark% more date.file
Wed May  3 15:59:50 WST 2000
paperbark%
```

You can also redirect input in the other direction. For example, to mail the contents of a file to user `ignatz@oak`, type **`mail ignatz@oak < report.file`** and press Return. The file called `report.file` is sent by e-mail to `ignatz@oak`.

Combining Commands (|)

You can use the pipe (|) operator to connect two or more commands, using the output from one command as the input to the next one. This section provides two examples of the many ways you can combine commands in a pipeline.

To print the `cat`(1) manual page, type **`man cat | lp`** and press Return. The manual page is not displayed on the screen. Instead, the output is sent to the `lp` command, which prints it on the default printer.

You can search the process list for a particular command by piping the output of `ps -e` to the `grep` command. The output is displayed on the screen. The following example displays process information for OpenWindows.

```
cinderella% ps -e | grep openwin
   260 ?        0:00 openwin
cinderella%
```

If you want to print the information, you can add an additional pipe command (`| lp`) to the end of the sequence and send it to the printer, as shown in the following example.

```
anastasia% ps -e | grep openwin | lp
request id is castle-51 (request id is castle-51 (standard input)
anastasia%
```

Using Manual Pages

Manual pages are on-line technical references for each Solaris command. Manual pages are grouped into sections, with similar types of commands within the same section. For example, most user commands are in section (1), and system administration commands are in section (1M). Manual pages may be installed on a local system or NFS-mounted from a server. This section tells you how to display manual pages and how to find out the section numbers for an individual command.

Displaying a Manual Page (man)

To display a manual page, type **man** ***command-name*** and press Return. The manual page is displayed. The following example shows the beginning of the `grep`(1) manual page.

```
cinderella% man grep

grep(1)    USER COMMANDS    grep(1)

NAME
  grep - search a file for a pattern

SYNOPSIS
     grep   [   -bchilnsvw   ]  limited-regular-expression    [
(Additional lines deleted from this example)
```

Finding the Section Number for a Manual Page (whatis, man)

Some commands are listed in more than one section. You can find the section number(s) for a manual page by using the `whatis` command.

> *NOTE. The* `whatis` *command works only if you have first used the* `catman` *command to set up your manual pages. To use the* `catman` *command to set up manual pages, become superuser and type*

catman ***n*** *and press Return, where* n *is the number of the section you want to set up.*

Use the following steps to find the section number for a manual page.

1. Type **whatis** ***command-name*** and press Return.

   The first line of the manual page for the command is displayed. Use the section number to display the manual page in the next step.

2. Type **man -s*section-number* *command-name*** and press Return.

   The manual page is displayed.

The following example shows the four different chown manual pages and displays the manual page for the chown(2) command.

```
oak% whatis chown
chown    chown (1)     - change owner of file
chown    chown (1b)    - change owner
chown    chown (1m)    - change owner
chown    chown (2)     - change owner and group of a file
oak% man -s2 chown
chown(2)                 SYSTEM CALLS                chown(2)

NAME
 chown, lchown, fchown - change owner and group of a file

SYNOPSIS
 #include <unistd.h>
 #include <sys/types.h>

int chown(const char *path, uid_t owner, gid_t group);

int lchown(const char *path, uid_t owner, gid_t group);

int fchown(int fildes, uid_towner, gid_t group);

DESCRIPTION
chown() sets the owner ID and group ID of the file specified by path or
  referenced by the open file descriptor fields to owner and group
  respectively. If owner or group is specified as -1, chown() does not change
  the corresponding ID of the file.
(Additional lines deleted from this example)
```

Finding Disk Information

Use the df and du commands described in the following sections to show disk use information and to tell if a file system is local (UFS) or remote (NFS).

Displaying Used Disk Space in Kilobytes and Percentage of Capacity (df -k)

Use the -k option of the df command to display disk information in the table format used with SunOS 4.x system software. Type **df -k** and press Return.

The file system, total kilobytes, used kilobytes, available kilobytes, percentage of capacity used, and mount point for local disk partitions are displayed, as shown in the following example.

```
paperbark% df -k
Filesystem            kbytes    used   avail capacity  Mounted on
/dev/dsk/c0t0d0s0    1388215  920657  412030    70%    /
/proc                      0       0       0     0%    /proc
fd                         0       0       0     0%    /dev/fd
mnttab                     0       0       0     0%    /etc/mnttab
swap                  529832       0  529832     0%    /var/run
swap                  530136     304  529832     1%    /tmp
/dev/dsk/c0t0d0s7     112783   25289   76216    25%    /export/home
/dev/dsk/c0t1d0s7    2012390       9 1952010     1%    /export/home0
paperbark%
```

Determining Whether File Systems Are Local or NFS Mounted (df)

To find out whether file systems are local or NFS mounted, type **df *filesystem*** and press Return. Disk formatting information (including disk location or mount point) for the file system you specify is displayed.

In the following example, the file system is NFS mounted.

```
oak% df /home/ignatz
bigriver:/export/home/ignatz
     538980  399435  85647   82%     /tmp_mnt/home/ignatz
oak%
```

In the following example, the file system is on a local disk.

```
# df /
/dev/dsk/c0t0d0s0  30383    11885  15468     43%     /
#
```

Finding All Mounted File Systems of a Specific Type (df -F)

If you want to display all the mounted file systems of one file system type, use the `-F` option followed by the file system type. The most common file system types are `ufs` for local file systems and `nfs` for network file systems. To find all mounted file systems of a specific type, type **df -F *filesystem-type*** and press Return.

In the following example, the mounted NFS file systems are displayed.

```
cinderella% df -F nfs
/net   (cinderella:(pid153)):          0 blocks          -1 files
/usr/dist cinderella:(pid153)):        1276248 blocks    -1 files
/home   (cinderella:(pid153)):         0 blocks          -1 files
/usr/man      (oak:/export/man):       272934 blocks     -1 files
cinderella%
```

In the following example, the mounted UFS (local) file systems are displayed.

```
cinderella% df -F ufs

 (/dev/dsk/c0t0d0s0): 36992    blocks   13558 files
/usr   (/dev/dsk/c0t0d0s6):  274346 blocks   94403 files
/export/home/cinderella (/dev/dsk/c0t3d0s7):379670 blocks     96046 files
cinderella%
```

In the following example, information about the mounted temporary file system is displayed.

```
cinderella% df -F tmpfs
/tmp                (swap              ):    88528 blocks    3156 files
cinderella%
```

NOTE. You cannot use the `df` *command to display SWAPFS file systems because they are never mounted.*

3

UNDERSTANDING SHELLS

The Solaris 8 Operating Environment provides six shells for use as command interpreters. The three basic shells are the Bourne shell (the default), the C shell, and the Korn shell. In addition, the Solaris 8 Operating Environment includes three freeware shells: The Bourne-Again shell (`bash`), the TC shell (`tcsh`), and the Z shell (`zsh`). One shell is defined as the default shell for each user, but users can start a new shell from the command line. This chapter describes elements that are common to all shells and then provides a section for each shell that describes some of the prevalent shell features. New!

Table 21 lists the basic shell features and shows which shells provide each feature.

Table 21 Basic Features of Bourne, Bourne-Again, Z, C, TC, and Korn Shells New!

Feature	Bourne	bash	zsh	C	tcsh	Korn
Aliases.	Yes	Yes	Yes	Yes	Yes	Yes
Command-line editing.	No	Yes	Yes	Yes	Yes	Yes
Enhanced `cd`.	No	Yes	Yes	Yes	Yes	Yes
History list.	No	Yes	Yes	Yes	Yes	Yes
Ignore CTRL-D (`ignoreeof`).	No	Yes	Yes	Yes	Yes	Yes
Initialization file separate from `.profile`.	No	Yes	Yes	Yes	Yes	Yes

Table 21 Basic Features of Bourne, Bourne-Again, Z, C, TC, and Korn Shells (Continued)

Feature	Bourne	bash	zsh	C	tcsh	Korn
Job control.	Yes	Yes	Yes	Yes	Yes	Yes
Logout file.	No	Yes	Yes	Yes	Yes	No
Protect files from overwriting (`noclobber`).	No	Yes	Yes	Yes	Yes	Yes
Syntax compatible with Bourne shell.	Yes	Yes	Yes	No	No	Yes

Commands Common to All Shells

The following sections describe commands that can be used with any shell.

Setting a Default Shell

The user's login shell is set in the last field of the user's entry in the `Passwd` database or `/etc/passwd` file. Use the AdminSuite User Accounts tool to edit the `Passwd` database in a networked environment. Use Admintool: Users to edit the local `/etc/passwd` file. To run Admintool on a local system, you must be a member of the `sysadmin` group (GID 14).

NOTE. If you access Admintool through the Solaris Management Console, you must log in as root or as a member of a role that grants you superuser permissions to run Admintool. Only then can you use Admintool to edit local password databases. See "Using AdminSuite 3.0 to Grant Access Rights to Users" on page 190 for more information.The Solaris Management Console does not recognize membership in GID 14.

Use the following steps to change the default shell with Admintool.

1. Type **`admintool&`** and press Return to start Admintool (if necessary).
2. Click on the user account you want to change.

   The user account is highlighted.
3. From the Edit menu, choose Modify.

   The Admintool: Modify User window is displayed.
4. Choose the new login shell from the Login Shell menu.
5. Click on the OK button.

The next time the user logs out and logs in again, the new shell is used.

Use the following steps to change the default shell in a networked environment with AdminSuite 3.0. See "Administering User Accounts with AdminSuite 3.0" on page 157 for detailed instructions on administering user accounts.

1. From the CDE Application Manager, System_Admin folder, double-click on the Solaris Management Console icon.

   The SMC Login window is displayed.
2. Type your login name and password, and click on the Log in button.

   The Solaris Management Console window is displayed.
3. Click on the Infrastructure folder or the word Infrastructure in the left pane.

   The contents of the Infrastructure folder are displayed in the right pane.
4. Double-click on the AdminSuite folder in either pane.

   The AdminSuite application icon is displayed in the right pane.
5. Double-click on the AdminSuite icon.

   The AdminSuite Log On window is displayed.
6. Log in, type the password, and click on the OK button.

   The AdminSuite window is displayed.
7. Click on the Users folder in the navigation pane.

   The contents of the Users folder are displayed in the right pane.
8. Double-click on the User Accounts icon.

   The Set Initial View window is displayed the first time you enter the User Accounts tool.
9. Use the Set Initial View window to filter the amount of information displayed in the User Accounts tool. Choose the filtering you want and click on the OK button.

   The user accounts are displayed in the right pane.
10. Double-click on the icon for the user account you want to edit.

    The User Properties window is displayed.
11. Choose the shell for the user account from the Logon Shell menu as shown in Figure 10.

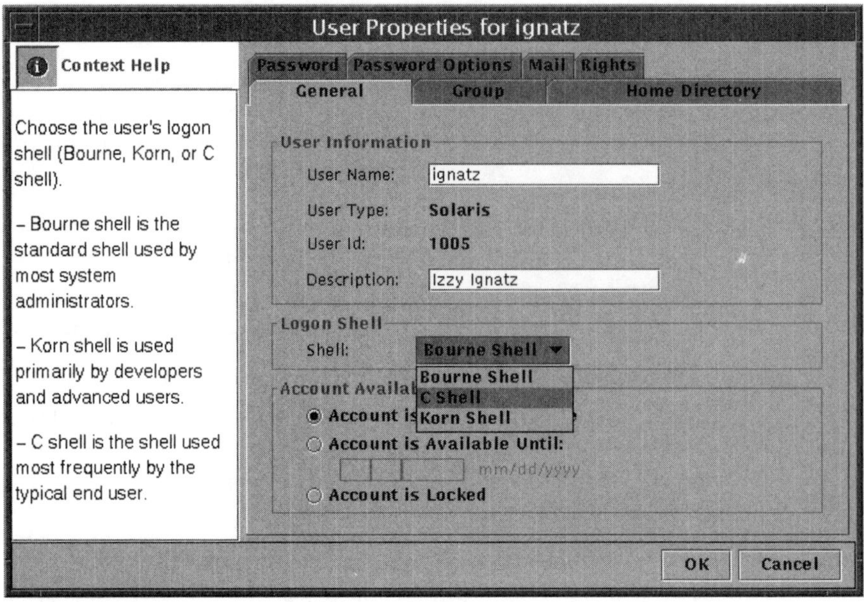

Figure 10 Logon Shell Menu

12. Click on the OK button.

    The default shell for that user is changed.

New!

Changing Shells from a Command Line (csh, ksh, sh, bash, tcsh)

If you want to use another shell without modifying the `Passwd` database, you can change shells at a command-line prompt by simply typing the name of the shell you want to use.

To change to the C shell, type **csh** and press Return. The default C shell prompt is the system name followed by a percent sign (`%`).

```
$ csh
paperbark%
```

To change to the Korn shell, type **ksh** and press Return. The default Korn shell prompt is a dollar sign (`$`).

```
paperbark% ksh
$
```

To change to the Bourne shell, type **sh** and press Return. The Bourne shell prompt also is a dollar sign ($).

```
$ sh
$
```

To change to the Bourne-Again shell, type bash and press Return. The Bourne-Again shell prompt is bash-2.03$. **New!**

```
paperbark% bash
bash-2.03$
```

To change to tcsh, type tcsh and press Return. The tcsh prompt is >. **New!**

```
paperbark% tcsh
>
```

To change to the Z shell, type zsh and press Return. With no startup files, the prompt does not change.

Quitting from a Shell (exit)

If you start a new shell from the command line, you can quit it and return to the old shell. To quit from a shell, type **exit** and press Return. If you have started (layered) another shell, you are returned to the original shell prompt.

```
$ exit
oak%
```

Clearing a Shell Window (clear)

You can clear the contents of a shell window and redisplay the prompt to the top of the window. To clear the contents of a shell window, type **clear** and press Return.

```
oak% which openwin
no openwin in . /home/ignatz /usr/deskset/bin /usr/bin
/home/ignatz/bin /bin /home/bin /etc/usr/etc/usr/ucb
oak% clear
```

The window is cleared and the prompt is redisplayed at the top.

The Bourne Shell

The default shell for the Solaris Operating Environment is the Bourne shell, developed by Steve Bourne when he was at AT&T Bell Laboratories. The Bourne shell is a small shell for general-purpose use. It also provides a full-scale scripting language that is used to develop shell scripts to capture frequently performed commands and procedures. Describing how to write shell scripts is beyond the scope of this book.

Reviewing the Bourne Shell Initialization File

The Bourne shell uses one initialization file, `.profile`, in the user's home directory to set the user's environment. When the user logs in or starts a Bourne shell from the command line, the `.profile` file is read. Use this file to set the user's path and any environment variables.

Defining Bourne Shell Environment Variables

The syntax for defining an environment variable is the same for both the Bourne and Korn shells; type ***VARIABLE=value*;export *VARIABLE*** and press Return.

```
$ PS1=oak$;export PS1
$
```

Creating Aliases as Functions for the Bourne Shell

In the Bourne shell, you can use functions to define aliases in the `.profile` file. The syntax for creating an alias function is shown below.

```
alias-name() {
     command-sequence
}
```

For example, if you frequently use the `ftp` command to send batches of files and don't want to be prompted for each file, you can create an alias for the `ftp -i` command to turn off interactive prompting. When you add the following line to your `.profile` file, `ftp` is started with interactive prompting turned off.

```
ftp() {
     ftp -i
}
```

After you have made changes to a `.profile` file, the changes are not recognized unless you source the `.profile` file by typing **`. .profile`** or until you log off and log in again. When you source the `.profile` file in a window, the changes are recognized only in the current window.

The C Shell

The C shell, written by Bill Joy when he was at UC Berkeley, is popular with many users of Berkeley UNIX. The C shell is completely different from the Bourne and Korn shells and has its own syntax. The most important advantages of the C shell are command history, command editing, and aliases. *Command history* stores a record of the most recent commands that you have used. You can display these commands and reuse them as originally issued. You can also change a command by editing it. *Aliases* let you type short names for frequently used commands. You can also combine sequences of frequently used commands and provide an alias for the sequence.

Reviewing C Shell Initialization Files

The C shell uses two initialization files in the user's home directory to set the user's environment: `.login` and `.cshrc` (C shell run control).

When you log in, the `.login` file is read, and then the `.cshrc` file. When you start the C shell from a command line, only the `.cshrc` file is read. Because the `.login` file is not always read, you should set environment variables and the path in the `.cshrc` file.

Defining C Shell Environment Variables

To define an environment variable for the C shell, type **`setenv`** ***`VARIABLE value`*** and press Return.

```
oak% setenv DISPLAY rogue:0
oak%
```

Creating Aliases for the C Shell

Define any aliases for the user in the `.cshrc` file. The syntax for creating an alias is **`alias`** ***`alias-name command-sequence`***. For example, if you frequently use the `ftp` command to send batches of files and don't want to be prompted for each file, you can create an alias for the `ftp -i` command to turn off interactive prompting. When you add the following line to your `.cshrc` file, `ftp` is started with interactive prompting turned off.

```
alias ftp "ftp -i"
```

The following example shows aliases from a `.cshrc` file. Note that if the command contains spaces, you enclose the entire command in quotes. Both double and single quotes are used in the following examples.

```
alias a alias
a h history
a c clear
a lf ls -F
a ll "ls -l | more"
a la ls -a
a s "source .cshrc"
a f 'find ~ -name core -print'
a copytotape "tar cvf /dev/rmt/0 *"
a ftp "ftp -i"
```

After you have made changes to a `.cshrc` file, the changes are not recognized unless you source the `.cshrc` file by typing `source .cshrc` or until you log off and log in again. When you source the `.cshrc` file in a window, the changes are recognized only in the current window.

Setting history for the C Shell

To set `history` for the C shell, on a command line type **`set history=`*`n`*** and press Return. `history` is set to the number of lines you specify.

```
oak% set history=10
oak%
```

You can set `history` temporarily for a shell window or set it "permanently" so that the same history setting is available at each login session. Enter the command as a line in your `.cshrc` file.

Using history for the C Shell

To display the history for the C shell, on a command line type **history** and press Return. The last *n* commands that you had set for the history are displayed.

```
oak% history
     26  pwd
     27  kermit
     28  cd Howto
     29  tar xvf /dev/rmt/0
     30  ls -l howto*
     31  cd
     32  cd Config/Art
     33  ls -l
     34  tar cvf /dev/rmt/0
     35  history
oak%
```

To repeat the previous command in a C shell, type **!!** and press Return. The previous command is executed again.

```
oak% history
     26  pwd
     27  kermit
     28  cd Howto
     29  tar xvf /dev/rmt/0
     30  ls -l howto*
     31  cd
     32  cd Config/Art
     33  ls -l
     34  tar xvf /dev/rmt/0
     35  history
oak% !!
history
     27  kermit
     28  cd Howto
     29  tar xvf /dev/rmt/0
     30  ls -l howto*
     31  cd
     32  cd Config/Art
     33  ls -l
     34  tar xvf /dev/rmt/0
     35  history
     36  history
oak%
```

To repeat the last word of the previous command in a C shell, type **!$** and press Return. The last word from the previous command is used as part of the command-line argument.

For example, you might list the complete path name of a file, and then use the path name as the argument to edit the file with `vi` or to print it.

```
oak% ls -l /home/ignatz/quest
-rw-r--r--    1 ignatz   staff          24 Jul 16 15:07 quest
oak% lp !$
lp /home/ignatz/quest
oak%
```

You can use the `!$` command anywhere within the command line. In the following example, the file /home/ignatz/quest is copied to the /tmp directory.

```
oak% ls -l /home/ignatz/quest
-rw-r--r--   1 ignatz   staff          24 Jul 16 15:07 quest
oak% cp !$ /tmp
cp /home/ignatz/quest /tmp
oak%
```

To repeat a numbered command in a C shell, type **!*n*** and press Return. The number in the shell prompt is *n*. The command is executed again.

```
oak% history
29  tar xvf /dev/rmt/0
30  ls -l howto*
31  cd
32  cd Config/Art
33  ls -l
34  tar xvf /dev/rmt/0
35  ls -l
36  cd
37  lp howto*
38  history
oak% !32
cd Config/Art
oak%
```

Setting the Backspace Key for the C Shell (stty erase)

If you want to change the erase key from Delete to Backspace, type **stty erase**, then press Control and Shift together, and then type **H** and press Return. The Backspace key is set as the erase key.

```
oak% stty erase ^H
oak%
```

Incorporating a New Command for the C Shell (rehash)

The C shell builds an internal table of commands—called a hash table—named with the path variable. When you add a new command to a directory, the command is not part of the internal table and the shell cannot execute it because it cannot find it. To incorporate a new command into the search path internal table, type **rehash** and press Return. Any new commands are incorporated into your command search path.

```
oak% newcommand
newcommand: Command not found
oak% rehash
oak% newcommand
oak%
```

Editing C Shell History Commands

You can edit commands retrieved from the history list by using the `s/`*`oldstring`*`/`*`newstring`*`/` form to substitute in the command as retrieved. In the following example, an incorrectly typed command from the history list is corrected.

```
oak% history
    31  cd
    32  ls
    33  cd /home/frame3.1
    34  ls
    35  cd ..
    36  tar cvf /dev/rmt/0 frame3.1
    37  lp questionnaire
    38  lpstat -t
    39  echo $PaTH
    40  history
oak% !39:s/a/A/
echo $PATH
.:/home/winsor:/usr/openwin/bin:/usr/deskset/bin:/home/
 winsor/bin:/bin:/home/bin:/etc:/usr/etc:/usr/bin:/home/ frame3.1/bin
oak%
```

The Korn Shell

The Korn shell, developed by David Korn of AT&T Bell Laboratories, is a superset of the Bourne shell. That is, the Korn shell uses the same syntax as the Bourne shell, but the Korn shell has more built-in functions that can be defined directly from the shell. The Korn shell provides a more sophisticated form of command editing than does the C shell. The Korn shell also provides a command history and aliases.

The Korn shell provides a complete command and scripting language. The following sections provide a brief introduction to some of the most basic features of the Korn shell.

Reviewing Korn Shell Initialization Files

The Korn shell uses two initialization files in the user's home directory to set the user's environment: `.profile` and `.`*`ksh-env`*, which is a file with any name you choose that controls the user's environment. You might want to name the file .kshrc, because its function is similar to that of the C shell .cshrc file.

When the user logs in, the .profile file is read and then the *.ksh-env* file. The *.ksh-env* file lets you configure the Korn shell session to your needs. Many of the commands that you would include in the *.ksh-env* file can be executed only by the Korn shell and cannot be included in the .profile file.

You must set the ENV environment variable to point to the *.ksh-env* file. The syntax for setting environment variables in the Korn shell is the same as for the Bourne shell: *VARIABLE=value*;export *VARIABLE*. As in the Bourne shell, you must export the variable to make it available to the shell. The following example sets the environment variable for a .kshrc file.

```
$ ENV=$HOME/.kshrc;export ENV
$
```

You must set this environment variable in the .profile file; otherwise, the .kshrc file is not found when you log in. The ENV variable has no default setting. Unless you set it, the feature is not used. The *.ksh-env* file is read each time you start the Korn shell from a command line.

Using Korn Shell Options

The Korn shell has a number of options that specify the user's environment and control execution of commands. To display the current option settings, type **set -o** and press Return. In the following example, the default options for the Korn shell for Solaris Operating Environment are displayed.

```
$ set -o
Current option settings
allexport        off
bgnice           on
emacs            off
errexit          off
gmacs            off
ignoreeof        off
interactive      on
keyword          off
markdirs         off
monitor          on
noexec           off
noclobber        off
noglob           off
nolog            off
nounset          off
privileged       off
restricted       off
trackall         off
verbose          off
vi               off
viraw            off
xtrace           off
$
```

The default options are described in Table 22. Customarily, you set these options in the `.ksh-env` file.

Table 22 Korn Shell Options

Option	Default	Description
allexport	off	Automatically export variables when defined.
bgnice	on	Execute all background jobs at a lower priority.
emacs	off	Set emacs/gmacs as the in-line editor.
errexit	off	If a command returns the value False, the shell executes the ERR trap (if set) and immediately exits.
gmacs	off	Set gmacs as the in-line editor.
ignoreeof	off	When the interactive option is also set, the shell does not exit at end-of-file. Type **exit** to quit the shell.
interactive	on	The shell automatically turns the interactive option on so that shell prompts are displayed.
keyword	off	The shell puts each word with the syntax of a variable assignment in the variable assignment list.
markdirs	off	Display a / following the names of all directories resulting from path name expansion.
monitor	on	Enable job control.
noclobber	off	Do not overwrite an existing file when the redirect operator (>) is used.
noexec	off	Read commands but do not execute them. You can use this option to debug shell script syntax errors.
noglob	off	Disable file name expansion.
nolog	off	Do not store function definitions in the history file.
nounset	off	Display an error message when the shell tries to expand a variable that is not set.
privileged	off	When this option is off, the real UID and GID are used. When this option is on, the UID and GID are set to the values that were in effect when you started the shell.

Table 22 Korn Shell Options (Continued)

Option	Default	Description
`restricted`	`off`	Set a restricted shell.
`trackall`	`off`	Make command-tracked aliases when they are first encountered.
`verbose`	`off`	Display the input as it is read.
`vi`	`off`	Set `vi` as the in-line editor.
`viraw`	`off`	Specify character-at-a-time input from `vi`.
`xtrace`	`off`	Display commands and arguments as they are executed.

To enable an option, type **`set -o`** ***`option-name`*** and press Return. To disable an option, type **`set +o`** ***`option-name`*** and press Return.

For example, entering this line in the user's *`.ksh-env`* file sets the in-line editor to `vi`.

```
set -o vi
```

The following example turns off `vi` as the in-line editor.

```
set +o vi
```

You can also set these options from a command line, using the same syntax.

Creating Korn Shell Aliases

The syntax for creating aliases for the Korn shell is `alias` *`name=value`*. The following example creates an alias for the `alias` command.

```
$ alias a=alias
$
```

The following example aliases the `history` command to the letter `h`.

```
$ a h=history
$
```

The Korn shell comes with a default set of predefined aliases. To display the list, type **alias** and press Return.

```
$ alias
autoload=typeset -fu
false=let 0
functions=typeset -f
hash=alias -t -
history=fc -l
integer=typeset -i
nohup=nohup
r=fc -e -
stop=kill -STOP
suspend=kill -STOP $$
true=:
type=whence -v
$
```

The default aliases are described in Table 23.

Table 23 Korn Shell Preset Aliases

Alias	Value	Definition
autoload	typeset -fu	Define an autoloading function.
false	let -0	Return a non-zero status. Often used to generate infinite until loops.
functions	typeset -f	Display a list of functions.
hash	alias -t -	Display a list of tracked aliases.
history	fc -l	List commands from the history file.
integer	typeset -i	Declare integer variable.
nohup	nohup	Keep jobs running even if you log out.
r	fc -e -	Execute the previous command again.
stop	kill -STOP	Suspend job.
suspend	kill -STOP $$	Suspend job.
true	:	Return a 0 exit status.
type	whence -v	Display information about commands.

Editing Commands with the Korn Shell In-line Editor

You can use the Korn shell in-line editor to edit the current command before you execute it. You can choose one of three in-line editors: emacs, gmacs, or vi. You specify the in-line editor by using the set -o *editor* option or by setting either the EDITOR or VISUAL environment variable. This section describes how to use the vi in-line editor to edit commands.

The vi in-line editor is a modified subset of the vi program; it lacks some of the features of vi. The vi in-line editor is automatically in insert mode. You can type commands and execute them by pressing Return without using the vi in-line editor. If you want to edit a command, press Escape to enter command mode. You can move along the command line with the standard cursor movement commands and use standard vi editing commands to edit the contents of the line. When the command is edited, press Return to execute it or press Escape to return to input mode.

If you want to edit the command line in a vi file, type **v** to open a vi file containing the contents of the command line. When you leave vi, the command is executed. Refer to Table 20 on page 91 for a quick-reference to common vi commands.

Setting History for the Korn Shell

The Korn shell stores history commands in a file specified by the HISTFILE variable. If the variable is not set, the files are stored in $HOME/.sh_history. You can specify the number of commands stored, using the HISTSIZE variable. If the variable is not set, the most recent 128 commands are saved. When the history list contains the maximum number of commands, as new commands are entered, the oldest commands become unavailable.

To set a different history size, type **HISTSIZE=*n*;export HISTSIZE** and press Return. History is set to the number of lines you specify.

The following example sets the history size to 200.

```
$ HISTSIZE=200;export HISTSIZE
$
```

You can set the history temporarily for a shell window or set it "permanently" by entering the command as a line in the .profile or *.ksh-env* file.

Displaying Korn Shell History Commands

You can use two commands to show the commands from the history list: fc and history. Because history is aliased to fc -l as one of the default aliases, you can use the commands interchangeably. If you do not specify a range with either the history or fc -l command, the last 16 commands are displayed.

To display the last 16 commands in the history list, type **history** and press Return. The last 16 commands in the history list are displayed.

```
$ history
    16  pwd
    17  ps -el
    18  ps -el | grep openwin
    19  cd
    20  more questionnaire
    21  su
    22  lp /etc/passwd
    23  lpstat -t
    24  man ksh
    25  du
    26  maker &
    27  tip -2400 5551212
    28  alias h=history
    29  find / -name ksh -print
    30  df -k
    31  history
$
```

An alternative way to display the same information is to type **fc -l** and press Return.

The `history` and `fc` commands take additional arguments that let you specify a range, display the last *n* number of commands, and display the commands in reverse order. See the `ksh`(1) manual page for more information.

Using Korn Shell History Commands

To use a command from the history list, type **r *n*** to reuse a command by number. The following example reuses command `27`.

```
$ r 27
tip -2400 5551212
(Connection messages are displayed)
```

To repeat the last command in the history list, type **r** and press Return.

Editing Korn Shell History Commands

You can display individual history commands and edit them by using the `fc` command with the following syntax.

```
fc [-e editor] [-r] [range]
```

The following syntax also works.

```
fc -e - [old=new] [command]
```

You use the -e option to specify an editor. If no editor is specified, the FCEDIT environment variable value is used. If no value is set, the default editor is /bin/ed. The -r option reverses the order of the commands, displaying the most recent commands at the top of the list. If you specify no range, the last command is edited.

For example, to use vi to edit the last command in a history list, type **fc -e vi** and press Return. A vi file is created containing the last entry from the history list. When you edit the command and save the changes, the command is executed.

New! The Bourne-Again Shell

The Bourne-Again shell, bash, is a Bourne-shell-compatible language interpreter that executes commands read from the standard input or from a file. bash incorporates useful features from the Korn and C shells. bash is a conformant implementation of the IEEE POSIX Shell and Tools specification (IEEE Working Group 1003.2).

Reviewing Bourne-Again Shell Initialization Files

When you invoke bash as an interactive login shell or as a non-interactive shell with the --login option, bash first reads and executes commands from the /etc/profile file if that file exists. After reading /etc/profile, bash looks for ~/.bash_profile, ~/.bash-login, and ~/.profile, in that order. It reads and executes commands from the first file that exists and is readable. To prevent the shell from reading these files, you can invoke bash with the --noprofile option.

When a login shell exists, bash reads and executes commands from the ~/.bash_logout file if it exists.

When you start an interactive shell that is not a login shell, bash reads and executes commands from ~/.bashrc if it exists. You can inhibit this behavior by using the --norc option when you start the interactive shell. Alternatively, you can force bash to read and execute commands from another file by specifying the --rcfile *file* option.

When you start bash interactively, for example to run a shell script, it looks for the BASH_ENV environment variable, expands its value, and uses the expanded value as the name of a file to read and execute. bash behaves as if you executed the following command, but the value of the PATH variable is not used in the search for the file name.

```
if [ -n "$BASH_ENV" ]; then . "$BASH_ENV"; fi
```

Refer to the bash(1) manual page for complete information.

The TC Shell

The tcsh shell is an enhanced and completely compatible variation of the Berkeley UNIX C shell, csh(1). You can use tcsh as an interactive login shell and a shell script command processor. It includes a command-line editor, programmable word completion, spelling correction, a history mechanism, job control, and a C-like syntax.

Reviewing TC Shell Initialization Files

When you invoke tcsh as an interactive login shell, it executes commands from the /etc/csh.cshrc and /etc/csh.login system files. It then executes commands from files in the user's home directory, in the following order.

- ~/.tshrc
- ~/.cshrc (if /.tshrc is not found)
- ~/.history (or the value of the histfile shell variable)
- ~/.login
- ~/.cshdirs (or the value of the dirsfile shell variable)

Depending on how the shell is compiled, it may read /etc/csh.login before instead of after /etc/csh.cshrc, and ~/.login before instead of after ~/.tshrc or ~/.cshrc and ~/.history.

When you start an interactive shell that is not a login shell, only /etc/csh.cshrc and ~/.tshrc or ~/.cshrc are read on startup.

Refer to the tcsh(1) manual page for complete information.

New! The Z Shell

The Z shell (zsh) is a UNIX command interpreter that you can use as an interactive login shell and as a shell script command processor. The Z shell most closely resembles the Korn shell with enhancements. The Z shell provides command-line editing, built-in spelling correction, programmable command completions, shell functions (with autoloading), a history mechanism, and a host of other features.

Reviewing Z Shell Initialization Files

The Z shell first reads files from the /etc/zshenv file. If the RCS option is not set in /etc/zshsenv, all other initialization files are skipped. Otherwise, commands are read from $ZDOTDIR/.zshenv. If ZDOTDIR is not set, HOME is used instead. If the first character of argument zero passed to the shell is - or if you use the -l option, then the shell is assumed to be a login shell and commands are read from /etc/zprofile and then $ZDOTDIR/.zprofile. Then, if the shell is interactive, commands are read from /etc/zshrc and then $ZDOTDIR/.zshrc. Finally, if the shell is a login shell, /etc/zlogin and $ZDOTDIR/.zlogin are read.

Refer to the zsh(1) manual page for complete information.

4

ADMINISTERING USER ACCOUNTS AND GROUPS

This chapter describes how to set up and administer user accounts and groups with Admintool and AdminSuite. You can use Admintool to edit only files in the local `/etc` directory. You can edit network accounts with AdminSuite.

> *NOTE. The Solaris Operating Environment provides the following SVR4 useradd commands:* `useradd`, `userdel`, `usermod`, `groupadd`, `groupmod`, *and* `groupdel`. *Because these commands are only minimally network-aware, they are not described in this chapter. If you want to use these commands to administer user accounts on stand-alone systems, refer to the appropriate manual pages.*

New!

The Solaris 8 Operating Environment provides role-based access control (RBAC). See Chapter 5, "Administering Roles," for information on how to grant users selected superuser permissions. The `useradd`, `userdel`, and `usermod` commands have been modified to enable you to create, modify, and delete role accounts on a local system.

Tools for Adding and Administering User Accounts

Table 24 lists the recommended tools for adding and administering user accounts on systems with a graphics monitor running an X Window System such as CDE or OpenWindows.

Table 24 Recommended Tools for Administering User Accounts

New!

Environment	Recommended Tool	Availability/ Documentation
Remote or local systems in a networked, nameservice (NIS, NIS+) environment.	User Accounts and Groups (graphical user interface) from AdminSuite 3.0.	Available as a free download from `www.sun.com`. Instructions provided in this chapter.
Local system.	Admintool (graphical user interface).	Provided with the Solaris 8 Operating Environment. Instructions provided in this chapter.
Command line.	Terminal window (CDE Environment) or shell tool or command tool (OpenWindows Environment).	Provided with the Solaris 8 Operating Environment. See Table 25 for a list of available commands. Refer to the appropriate manual pages.

You can add and administer user accounts from the command line if you choose not to use Admintool or AdminSuite. Table 25 lists the Solaris commands you can use to administer user accounts.

Table 25 Solaris Commands Used to Administer User Accounts

Task	Name Service	Commands
Add a user account.	NIS +	`nistbladm` `nisclient`
	NIS	`useradd` `make`
	None	`useradd`
Modify a user account.	NIS+	`nistbladm`
	NIS	`usermod` `make`
	None	`usermod`

Table 25 Solaris Commands Used to Administer User Accounts (Continued)

Task	Name Service	Commands
Delete a user account.	NIS+	`nistbladm` `nisclient`
	NIS	`userdel` `make`
	None	`userdel`
Set up user account defaults.	NIS+	`not available`
	NIS	`useradd -D` `make`
	None	`useradd -D`
Disable a user account.	NIS+	`nistbladm`
	NIS	`passwd -r nis -l` `make`
	None	`passwd -r files -l`
Change a user's password.	NIS+	`passwd -r nisplus`
	NIS	`passwd -r nis`
	None	`passwd -r files`
Sort user accounts.	NIS+	`niscat` `sort`
	NIS	`ypcat` `sort`
	None	`awk` `sort`
Find a user account.	NIS+	`nismatch`
	NIS	`ypmatch`
	None	`grep`
Add a group.	NIS+	`nistbladm`
	NIS	`groupadd` `make`
	None	`groupadd`

Table 25 Solaris Commands Used to Administer User Accounts (Continued)

Task	Name Service	Commands
Modify users in a group.	NIS+	`nistbladm`
	NIS	`groupmod` `make`
	None	`groupmod`
Delete a group.	NIS+	`nistbladm`
	NIS	`groupdel` `make`
	None	`groupdel`

The following sections describe how to use Admintool and AdminSuite 3.0 to add and delete user accounts.

You may find it useful to create a form from the following checklist to ensure that you have all the needed information about a user account before you create it.

- User name.
- UID.
- Primary group.
- Secondary groups.
- Comment.
- Default shell.
- Password status and aging.
- Home directory server name.
- Home directory path name.
- Mounting method.
- Permissions on home directory.
- Mail server.
- Department name.
- Department administrator.
- Manager.
- Employee name.
- Employee title.
- Employee status.

- Employee number.
- Start date.
- Mail aliases to add account to.
- Desktop system name.

Adding User Accounts

Before you add users to the network, the users' systems must be installed and configured. When appropriate, NIS+ or NIS software should be installed and running on the network.

Adding users so that they can log in and start working has two parts: setting up the user account and providing the user with a working environment.

When you set up a user account, you perform the following tasks.

- Edit the `/etc/passwd` file.
- Define the user's group(s).
- Create a home directory.
- Define the user's environment.
- Create a password.

The next sections provide background information and describe how to do these tasks.

Editing the /etc/passwd File

You must be root or a member of the `sysadmin` group (GID 14) before you can use Admintool to edit the local `/etc/passwd` file.

New!

NOTE. If you access Admintool through the Solaris Management Console, you must log in as root or as a member of a role that grants you superuser permissions to run Admintool. Only then can you use Admintool to edit local password databases. See "Using AdminSuite 3.0 to Grant Access Rights to Users" on page 190 for more information.The Solaris Management Console does not recognize membership in GID 14.

You need the following information for each user you plan to add.

- Login name.
- User ID (UID).

- Primary group ID (GID).
- Identifying information (name, office, extension, home phone).
- Home directory.
- Login shell.

User ID Number

A UID is always associated with each user name and is used by systems to identify the owners of files and directories and to identify the user at login. If you create user accounts for a single individual on more than one system, always use the same user name and UID. In that way, the user can easily move and copy files between systems without ownership problems.

A UID must be a whole number less than or equal to 2147483647. The maximum UID was increased from 60000 to 2147483647 starting with the Solaris 2.5.1 release.

UIDs are required for both regular user accounts and special system accounts. Table 26 lists the UIDs that are reserved for user accounts and system accounts.

Table 26 Reserved UIDs

UIDs	Login Accounts	Description
0	root	Root account.
1	daemon	Daemon account.
2	bin	Pseudouser bin account.
3-99	sys, uucp logins, who, tty, and ttytype	System accounts.
100-60000	Regular users	General-purpose accounts.
60001	nobody	Unauthenticated users.
60002	noaccess	Compatibility with previous Solaris and SVR4 releases.
60003-2147483647	Regular users	General-purpose accounts.

CAUTION. Be careful when using UIDs in the 60000 to 2147483647 range. These numbers do not have full functionality and are incompatible with many Solaris features. See Table 27 for more information.

Even though UIDs 0 through 99 are reserved for use by system accounts, you can add a user with one of these UIDs. You should not, however, use these UIDs for regular user accounts. Use the numbers 0 through 99 to assign system accounts, `uucp` logins, and pseudouser logins.

Large User IDs and Group IDs

Previous Solaris Operating Environments used 32-bit data types to contain UIDs and GIDs. UIDs and GIDs were constrained to a maximum useful value of 60000. The limit on UID and GID values has been raised to the maximum value of a signed integer, or 2147483647 starting with the Solaris 2.5.1 release. Table 27 lists the interoperability issues with the Solaris Operating Environment products and commands.

Table 27 Interoperability Issues for UIDs and GIDs over 60000 New!

Category	Product/Command	Issues/Cautions
NFS Interoperability.	SunOS 4.x NFS software.	SunOS 4.x NFS server and client code truncates large UIDs and GIDs to 16 bits. This truncation can create security problems if SunOS 4.x systems are used in an environment where large UIDs and GIDs are being used. SunOS 4.x and compatible systems require a patch.
Name Service Interoperability.	NIS name service File-based name service.	Users with UIDs above 60000 can log in and use the `su` command on systems running the Solaris 2.5 Operating Environment and compatible versions; however, their UIDs and GIDs are set to 60001 (`nobody`).
	NIS+ name service.	Users with UIDs above 60000 are denied access on systems running the Solaris 2.5 Operating Environment, compatible versions, and the NIS+ name service.
Printed UIDs/GIDs.	OpenWindows File Manager.	Large UIDs and GIDs are not displayed correctly if the OpenWindows File Manager is used with the extended file listing display option.

Table 28 summarizes the limitations of using large UIDs and GIDs.

New!

Table 28 Limitations of Using UIDs and GIDs over 60000

UID/GID Number	Limitation
60003 or greater.	A UID and GID of `nobody` are assigned to users who log in to systems running the Solaris 2.5 Operating Environment and compatible releases and the NIS or `files` name service.
65536 or greater.	Solaris 2.5 Operating Environment and compatible release systems running the NFS version 2 software truncate UIDs in this category to 16 bits, creating possible security problems.
	Using the `cpio` command with the default archive format to copy files displays an error message for each file, and the UID and GID are set to `nobody` in the archive.
	SPARC-based systems: Systems running the SunOS 4.0 Operating Environment and compatible applications display `EOVERFLOW` messages from some system calls, and the UID and GID are set to `nobody`.
	IA-based systems: SVR3-compatible applications on an IA system are likely to display `EOVERFLOW` messages from system calls.
	IA-based systems: If users create a file or directory on a mounted System V file system, the System V file system returns an `EOVERFLOW` error.
100000 or greater.	The `ps -l` command displays a maximum five-digit UID, so the printed column is not aligned when it includes a UID or GID greater than 99999.
2622144 or greater.	Using the `cpio` command with `-H odc` format or the `pax -x cpio` command to copy files returns an error message for each file, and the UIDs and GIDs are set to `nobody` in the archive.
10000000 or greater.	Using the `ar` command sets UIDs and GIDs to `nobody` in the archive.
2097152 or greater.	UIDs and GIDs are set to `nobody` when the `tar` command, the `cpio -H ustar` command, or the `pax -x tar` command is used.

Creating a Home Directory

The *home directory* is that portion of a file system that is allocated to an individual user for storing private files. The amount of space you allocate for a home directory may vary, depending on the kinds of files the users create and the type of work they do. You should probably allocate at least 15 Mbytes of disk space for each user's home directory.

A user's home directory can be either on the local system or on a remote file server. In either case, by convention the home directory is created as `/export/home/`*`login-name`*. Note that this convention is new with the Solaris Operating Environment. The server name is no longer included as part of the user's home directory path. On a large server that supports a number of users' home directories, there may be a number of directories under `/export`—such as `home1`, `home2`, `home3`, and so on—with directories for different users under them. Regardless of where their home directory is located, users access their home directory through a mount point named `/home/`*`login-name`*.

Always refer to the home directory as `$HOME`, not as `/export/home/username`. In addition, use relative paths to create any symbolic links in a user's home directory (for example, `../../../x/y/x`), so that the links are valid no matter where the home directory is mounted.

This section describes the default procedure for the Solaris Operating Environment; the procedure assumes that the user's system is on a network and that AutoFS is used to make the home directory accessible. Whether the home directory originates on a server or on the local system, you need to make it accessible to other systems by using the `share` command to export the file system so that the user can access the home directory from other systems on the network.

In addition, you must define how the home directory is mounted. Use one of the following ways.

- Add an entry to the `NIS+ Auto_home` database, `NIS auto.home map`, or local `/etc/auto_home` files so that the home directory is automatically mounted. This method is preferred.
- Add an entry in the `/etc/vfstab` file on the user's system to NFS-mount the home directory.

To support automatic mounting of home directories, the Solaris Operating Environment includes the following entry in the `/etc/auto_master` file.

```
/home          auto_home          -nobrowse
```

New!

This entry tells AutoFS to mount the directories specified in the `auto_home` database onto the `/home` mount point on the local system. The entries in `auto_home` use the following format.

```
login-name     system-name:/export/home/login-name
```

When a user logs in with *`login-name`*, AutoFS mounts the specified directory (`/export/home/`*`login-name`*) from the specified system (*`system-name`*) onto the `/home` mount point on the system to which the user is logged in.

This method works even when the home directory is stored on the same system to which the user has logged in. But more importantly, the user can log in to any other system and have his or her home directory mounted on `/home` on that system.

NOTE. When AutoFS is used to mount home directories, you are not permitted to create any directories under the `/home` *mount point on the user's system. The system recognizes the special status of* `/home` *when AutoFS is active.*

To create a home directory, you must already have created the user's account. You need the following information.

- User's login name and UID.
- The name of the system on which to create the home directory. If the home directory is accessed over the network, the home directory system should be on the same network segment as the user's local system.

  Use the `df` command to check the servers to make sure there is enough space for a new home directory.
- The name of the directory where you will create the user's account.

  By convention, the home directory is named `/export/home`. However, on a large file server you may have multiple directories—`/export/home1`, `/export/home2`, and so on. Under each directory, different subdirectories are created for different users (for example, `/export/home/`*`login-namea`*, `/export/home/`*`login-nameb`* `...` `/export/home1/`*`login-namey`* `...` `/export/home2/`*`login-namez`*, and so forth).

All the following steps apply regardless of whether the home directory is created on the local system or on a remote file server.

1. Become superuser on the system where you want to create the home directory.
2. Type **`cd /export/`*`home-dir`*** and press Return.

The *home-dir* is the name of the directory where you want to create the user's home directory. The following example changes to the directory /export/home1.

```
# cd /export/home1
```

3. Type **mkdir *login-name*** and press Return.

   login-name is the login name of the user. You have created a directory that matches the login name of the user. The following example creates a directory for a user with a login name of ignatz.

```
# mkdir ignatz
```

4. Type **chown *login-name login-name*** and press Return.

   The user now owns the home directory. The following example changes the ownership for user ignatz.

```
# chown ignatz ignatz
```

5. Type **chgrp *primary-GID login-name*** and press Return.

   The user is assigned to the primary group you specified in the Passwd database for the user account. The following example changes the primary group for user ignatz to the staff group.

```
# chgrp staff ignatz
#
```

6. Type **chmod 755 /export/*home-dir/login-name*** and press Return.

   The user's home directory permissions are set to rwx for owner, r-x for group, and r-x for other. The following example changes home directory permissions for user ignatz.

```
# chmod 755 /export/home1/ignatz
#
```

The following steps describe how to share a home directory from a Solaris server. The procedure for sharing home directories from a SunOS 4.x server uses the export command.

1. Type **share** and press Return to find out whether the home directory has already been shared.

If the home directory is listed, information that looks like the following example is displayed.

```
oak% su
Password:
# share
-              /export/home        rw     ""
#
```

If the home directory is not listed, perform the following steps to set it up so that it can be shared by other systems. You perform these steps once for each /export/*home-dir* directory. By convention, these directories are named /export/home, /export/home1, /export/home2, and so on.

2. Edit the file /etc/dfs/dfstab and add the following line.

```
share -F nfs /export/home-dir
```

3. Type **shareall -F nfs** and press Return.

   All the share commands in the /etc/dfs/dfstab file are executed so that you do not need to reboot the system. If you reboot the system, the shareall command is automatically run.

4. Type **ps -ef | grep mountd** and press Return.

   If the daemon mountd is running, the procedure is complete. The following example shows that mountd is not running. If mountd is not running, follow the next step.

```
# ps -ef | grep mountd
    root     221     218  16  18:07:25 pts/1   0:00 grep mountd
#
```

5. Type **/etc/init.d/nfs.server start** and press Return.

   The daemons required for sharing file directories are started.

NOTE. If your network is not running NIS or NIS+, you need to add the home directory server's Internet Protocol (IP) address and system name to the /etc/hosts *file on the user's system. You can use the Admintool: Hosts window to edit the local* /etc/hosts *file.*

If you use disk quotas, set up a disk quota for the user.

After you have created the user's home directory, you must make it available. You make the home directory available either by adding it to the Auto_home database (the preferred method) for use by AutoFS, or by adding an entry to the /etc/vfstab file on the user's system for NFS mounting.

NFS-Mounting the Home Directory

If the directory (disk space) for a user's home directory is located on another system and AutoFS is not being used to make that space available, use the following steps to NFS-mount the home directory.

1. Become superuser on the user's system.
2. Edit the `/etc/vfstab` file and create an entry for the user's home directory.

   For example, to create an entry for user `ignatz` with a home directory on server `oak`, you would add the following line to the file.

```
oak:/export/home1/ignatz - /home/ignatz nfs - yes rw,intr
```

3. To create the mount point on the user's system, type **`mkdir /home/`*`login-name`*** and press Return.

NOTE. The home directory does not have the same name on the user's system as it does on the server. For example, `/export/home/ignatz` *on the server is mounted as* `/home/ignatz` *on the user's system.*

1. Type **`chown`** ***`login-name`*** **`/home/`*`login-name`*** and press Return.

   The user now owns the home directory.
2. Type **`chgrp`** ***`primary-GID`*** **`/home/`*`login-name`*** and press Return.

   The user's primary group has permission to access the user's home directory.
3. Type **`mountall`** and press Return.

   All entries in the current `vfstab` file (whose `automnt` fields are set to `Yes`) are mounted.
4. To verify that all entries are mounted, type **`mount`** and press Return.

   The file systems that are mounted are displayed.

Defining the User's Environment

To completely set up the user account, you must also perform the following tasks.

- Define default initialization files.
- Set up a mail account.
- Set up a printer.

Defining Initialization Files

When a user logs in, the `login` program sets a number of variables, such as `HOME`, `LOGNAME`, and `TZ`. Then, a file called the *system profile (initialization file)* is run to set systemwide defaults such as `PATH`, message of the day, and `umask`. Finally, the user profile initialization file (or files) that sets variables specific to the user is run. For example, the user profile can modify the `PATH` to include applications run by only that user. Each shell has its own initialization file (or files), as shown in Table 29.

Table 29 Shell User Initialization Files

Shell	Initialization File	Purpose
C	`$HOME/.login`	Define user's environment at login.
	`$HOME/.cshrc`	Define user's environment for all C shells invoked after login shell.
Bourne	`$HOME/.profile`	Define user's environment at login.
Korn	`$HOME/.profile`	Define user's environment at login.
	`$HOME/ksh-env`	Define user's environment at login in the file specified by the *`ksh-env`* environment variable.

The Solaris 8 Operating Environment provides default user initialization files for each shell in the `/etc/skel` directory, as shown in Table 30.

Table 30 Default Home Directory Initialization Files

Shell	File Name
C	`/etc/skel/local.login`
C	`/etc/skel/local.cshrc`
Bourne or Korn	`/etc/skel/local.profile`

The default `/etc/skel/local.login` file is shown below.

New!

```
# @(#)local.login 1.5     98/10/03 SMI
stty -istrip
# setenv TERM `tset -Q -`

#
# if possible, start the windows system.  Give user a chance to bail out
#
if ( "`tty`" == "/dev/console" ) then

    if ( "$TERM" == "sun" || "$TERM" == "sun-color" || "$TERM" == "AT386" )
 then

        if ( ${?OPENWINHOME} == 0 ) then
```

```
            setenv OPENWINHOME /usr/openwin
        endif

        echo ""
        echo -n "Starting OpenWindows in 5 seconds (type Control-C to
 interrupt)"
        sleep 5
        echo ""
        $OPENWINHOME/bin/openwin
        clear           # get rid of annoying cursor rectangle
        logout          # logout after leaving windows system

    endif

endif
```

The default `/etc/skel/local.cshrc` file is shown below.

```
# @(#)cshrc 1.11 89/11/29 SMI
umask 022
set path=(/bin /usr/bin /usr/ucb /etc .)
if ( $?prompt ) then
        set history=32
endif
```

The default `/etc/skel/local.profile` file is shown below.

New!

```
# @(#)local.profile 1.8     99/03/26 SMI
stty istrip
PATH=/usr/bin:/usr/ucb:/etc:.
export PATH

#
# If possible, start the windows system
#
if [ "`tty`" = "/dev/console" ] ; then
    if [ "$TERM" = "sun" -o "$TERM" = "sun-color" -o "$TERM" = "AT386" ]
    then

        if [ ${OPENWINHOME:-""} = "" ] ; then
            OPENWINHOME=/usr/openwin
            export OPENWINHOME
        fi

        echo ""
        echo "Starting OpenWindows in 5 seconds (type Control-C to
 interrupt)"
        sleep 5
        echo ""
        $OPENWINHOME/bin/openwin

        clear           # get rid of annoying cursor rectangle
        exit            # logout after leaving windows system

    fi
fi
```

As you can see, these files define a minimal environment. To minimize the need to edit the customization files for each user, you can customize the files in `/etc/skel` to set as many systemwide default variables as you can. You need to edit individual user's customization files to set the user's path.

Creating Site Initialization Files

It is important that both the administrator and the user are able to customize the user initialization files. You can create site initialization files by locating the initialization files centrally and distributing them globally. With site initialization files, you can continue to introduce new functionality to the user's work environment and also enable the user to customize individual user initialization files.

You create a site initialization file and add a reference to it in the user's initialization file. When you reference a site initialization file in a user initialization file, all updates to the site initialization file are automatically reflected when the user logs in to the system or when a user starts a new shell.

You can do any customization in a site initialization file that you can do in a user initialization file. Site initialization files typically reside on a server or a set of servers and appear as the first statement in a user initialization file. Each site initialization file must be the same type of shell script as the user initialization file that references it.

To reference a site initialization file for a C shell user initialization file, put a line similar to the following example at the beginning of the user initialization file.

```
source /net/machine-name/export/site-files/site-init-file
```

To reference a site initialization file in a Bourne or Korn shell user initialization file, put a line similar to the following example at the beginning of the user initialization file.

```
. /net/machine-name/export/site-files/site-init-file
```

Example of a Site Initialization File The following example shows a C shell site initialization file named `site.login` in which a user can choose a particular version of an application.

```
# @(#)site.login
main:
echo "Application Environment Selection"
echo ""
echo "1. Application, Version 1"
echo "2. Application, Version 2"
echo ""
echo -n "Type 1 or 2 and press Return to set your
application environment: "
set choice = $<
if ( $choice !~ [1-2] ) then
goto main
endif
switch ($choice)
case "1":
```

```
setenv APPHOME /opt/app-v.1
breaksw
case "2":
setenv APPHOME /opt/app-v.2
endsw
```

You would reference the `site.login` site initialization file located on a server named `server2` in a user's `.cshrc` file (C shell users only) with the following line. The automounter must be running on the user's system.

```
source /net/server2/site-init-files/site.login
```

Avoiding Local System References in Site Initialization Files Do not add specific references to the local system in the user's initialization file. Instructions in a user initialization file should be valid regardless of the system to which the user logs in. New!

To make a user's home directory available anywhere on the network, always refer to the home directory with the variable `$HOME`. For example, use `$HOME/bin` instead of `/export/home/`*`username`*`/bin`. `$HOME` automounts the user's home directory when the user logs in to another system.

To access files on a local disk, use global path names such as `/net/`*`machine-name`*`/`*`directory-name`*. Any directory referenced by `/net/`*`machine-name`* can be mounted automatically on any system to which the user logs in, assuming the system is running AutoFS.

Setting Up User Initialization Files

To set up user initialization files, you must already have created the user's home directory and know which shell (C, Bourne, or Korn) is set in the user's account entry in the `Passwd` database. Use the following steps to set up the user's initialization files.

1. Become superuser on the system with the user's home directory.
2. Type **`cd /home-dir/login-name`** and press Return.

   You are in the user's home directory. The following example changes to user `ignatz's` directory, which is in `/export/home1`.

```
# cd /export/home1/ignatz
#
```

3. Type **`cp /etc/skel/local.* .`** and press Return.

   You have copied all of the default user initialization files to the user's home directory.

4. Type **`chmod 744 local.*`** and press Return.

Permissions are set for the initialization files.

5. Type **chown *login-name* *** and press Return.

   The user now owns the initialization files.

```
# chown ignatz *
#
```

6. Type **chgrp *primary-GID* local.*** and press Return.

   The files are assigned to the primary group (for example, `staff`) you specified in the `Passwd` database for the user account.

```
# chgrp 10 local.*
#
```

7. Rename the shell initialization files. If the user's shell is the C shell, type **mv local.login .login; mv local.cshrc .cshrc** and press Return. If the user's shell is the Korn or Bourne shell, type **mv local.profile .profile** and press Return.
8. Type **rm local.*** and press Return.

   You have removed the unused shell initialization files.
9. Mount the user's home directory.
10. On the user's system, log in as the user.
11. Assign the user an interim password.

    See "Creating a Password" on page 140 for information on how to create passwords.
12. Check to make sure the user's environment is set up correctly.
13. Edit the user's initialization file (or files) and make changes as needed.

Use the following steps to edit the user's initialization file (or files).

1. Set the user's default path to include the home directory and directories or mount points for the user's windowing environment and applications.

   To change the path setting, add or modify the line for `PATH` as follows. For the C shell, type **set path =(*/dirname1 /dirname2 /dirname3...* .)**. For example, enter a line like the following in the user's `$HOME/.cshrc` file.

```
set path=(/usr/openwin/bin /usr/dt/bin /usr/bin /$home/bin /lib /usr/lib .)
```

For the C shell, type **source .cshrc** to source the `.cshrc` file so that the new path is recognized by the shell.

For the Bourne or Korn shell, type **PATH=*/dirname1:/dirname2:/dirname3...*:.;export PATH**. For example, enter a line such as the following in the user's `$HOME/.profile` file.

```
PATH=/usr/openwin/bin:/usr/dt/bin:/usr/bin:/$HOME/bin:/lib:/usr/lib:.; export
 PATH
```

2. To check that the `PATH` environment variable is set correctly, type **echo $PATH** and press Return.

   Note that the variables shown are in Bourne or Korn shell syntax, even if the user's shell is the C shell.

```
paperbark% echo $PATH
/usr/openwin/bin:/usr/dt/bin:/export/home/winsor/bin:/lib:/usr/lib:.
paperbark%
```

3. Add or change the settings of environment variables. For the C shell, type **setenv *VARIABLE value*** (or **set *variable=value*** for the path and term variables).

   The following example sets the history to the last 100 commands.

```
setenv HISTORY 100
```

For the Bourne or Korn shell, type ***VARIABLE=value*;export *VARIABLE*.**

The following example sets the user's default mail directory.

```
MAIL=/var/mail/ignatz;export MAIL
```

4. Check the `umask` setting. If you need to change it, type **umask *nnn*** and press Return. You can either include or omit leading zeros.

For example, to set file permissions to 644, type **umask 022** and press Return. Table 31 shows the file permissions that are created for each of the octal values of umask.

Table 31 Permissions for umask Values

Octal Value	File Permissions
0	rwx
1	rw-
2	r-x
3	r--
4	-wx
5	-w-
6	--x
7	--- (none)

The LANG variable and LC environment variables determine the locale-specific conversions and conventions the shell uses. These conversions and conventions include time zones, collation orders, and formats of dates, time, currency, and numbers. If necessary, set these variables in the user's initialization file. LANG sets all possible conversions and conventions for a given locale. If you have special needs, you can set various aspects of localization separately by using the LC variables LC_COLLATE, LC_CTYPE, LC_MESSAGES, and LC_NUMERIC. Table 32 shows the values for several locales.

Table 32 Values for LANG and LC Variables

Value	Locale
de:	German
fr:	French
iso_8895_1	English and European
it	Italian
japanese	Japanese
korean	Korean
sv	Swedish
tchinese	Taiwanese

If the system needs to support multibyte characters (for example, Japanese), add the following command to the system initialization file (`/etc/profile` or `/etc/.login`).

```
stty cs8 defeucw
```

When the initialization files are complete, log out of the user's account.

Setting Up a User's Mail Account

Each user has a mailbox either on a local system or on a mail server and a mail alias in the `/etc/mail/aliases` file that points to the location of the mailbox. Use the following steps to set up a mail client with a mailbox on a mail server.

1. Become superuser on the mail client's system.
2. Create a `/var/mail` mount point on the mail client's system.
3. Edit the `/etc/vfstab` file and add an entry for the `/var/mail` directory on the mail server, mounting it on the local `/var/mail` directory. Use the `actimeo=0` option, as shown in the following example, or locking of the mailbox files fails. **New!**

```
server:/var/mail - /var/mail nfs - no rw,hard,actimeo=0
```

   The client's mailbox is automatically mounted any time the system is rebooted.

4. Type **`mount -a`** to mount the mailbox.

   The client's mailbox is mounted.

5. Use Admintool to edit the `/etc/hosts` file and add an entry for the mail server.

NOTE. The `sendmail` *program automatically creates mailboxes in the* `/var/mail` *directory the first time a message is delivered. You do not need to create individual mailboxes for your mail clients.*

If you are using NIS+, use the following steps to set up mail aliases for the user.

1. Compile a list of each of your mail clients, the locations of their mailboxes, and the names of the mail server systems.
2. Become superuser on any system.
3. For each alias, type **`aliasadm -a`** ***`alias expanded-alias`*** **`[`*`options comments`*`]`** and press Return.

The alias is added to the NIS+ aliases table. The following example adds an alias for user `iggy.ignatz`.

```
# aliasadm -a iggy iggy.ignatz@oak "Iggy Ignatz"
#
```

4. Type **aliasadm -m *alias*** and press Return.

   The entry you created is displayed.
5. Check the entry to be sure it is correct.

Alternatively, you can use AdminSuite to edit network mail aliases. The Mailing Lists tool is in the Users folder in the AdminSuite Infrastructure folder. See "Administering User Accounts with AdminSuite 3.0" on page 157 for instructions on how to access the Users folder.

Setting Up a User's Printer

After adding users to a system, make sure they have access to a printer. See Chapter 10, "Administering Printing," for information on how to set up printing services.

Creating a Password

Passwords are an important part of system security. Each user account should be assigned a password of 6 to 10 characters as a combination of letters and numbers. See the `passwd(1)`, `yppasswd(1)`, or `nispasswd(1)` manual pages for information about changing passwords and password attributes.

In the SunOS 4.x system, encrypted passwords are stored in the `/etc/passwd` file along with the rest of the information about the user. In the Solaris 8 Operating Environment, the encrypted password and associated password aging information are stored in the `Shadow` field of the NIS+ `Passwd` database (or in the local `/etc/shadow` file). Permissions on the `Shadow` field are restricted. Permissions for the `/etc/shadow` file are `-r--------`. Only root can read the `/etc/shadow` file, and only the `passwd`, `yppasswd`, and `nispasswd` commands can write to the file.

The following example shows the contents of an `/etc/shadow` file.

```
root:4ZfnV.kupl.SA:11081::::::
daemon:NP:6445::::::
bin:NP:6445::::::
sys:NP:6445::::::
adm:NP:6445::::::
lp:NP:6445::::::
uucp:NP:6445::::::
nuucp:NP:6445::::::
listen:*LK*:::::::
```

```
nobody:NP:6445::::::
noaccess:NP:6445::::::
nobody4:NP:6445::::::
winsor:OVHZsESoDAEwk:11081::::::
ray:::::::
des:::::::
rob::11080:::::
ppp:*LK*::::::
ignatz::::::::
```

To create or modify passwords, use one of the following commands.

- `/usr/bin/passwd` (for no naming service).
- `/usr/bin/nispasswd` (for the NIS+ naming service).
- `/usr/bin/yppasswd` (for the NIS naming service).

Users can create or change their own passwords at any time. You must be root to create the initial password for any other user. In addition, to create an NIS+ password, you must have the appropriate NIS+ privileges and you must have established the necessary networkwide credentials. (See the `nispasswd`(1) manual page.)

Use the following steps to create an NIS+ password.

1. Become superuser on the NIS+ server.
2. Type **`nispasswd`** ***`login-name`*** and press Return.

   The message `New NIS+ password`: is displayed.
3. Type the new password and press Return.

   The prompt `Retype new NIS+ password`: is displayed.
4. Retype the password and press Return.

   The password is assigned and added to the NIS+ database.

The following example assigns a new password for the user `ignatz`.

```
oak% su
Password:
# nispasswd ignatz
New NIS+ password:
Retype new NIS+ password:
#
```

Use the following steps to change an NIS+ password.

1. Become superuser on the NIS+ server.
2. Type **`nispasswd`** ***`login-name`*** and press Return.

   The prompt `Old password`: is displayed.
3. Type the old password and press Return.

   The prompt `New password`: is displayed.
4. Type the new password and press Return.

The prompt `Re-enter new password`: is displayed.

5. Retype the password and press Return.

   The password is assigned and added to the `/etc/shadow` file.

The following example changes the password for user `ignatz`.

```
oak% su
Password:
# nispasswd ignatz
Old password:
New password:
Re-enter new password:
#
```

NOTE. You can also use `nispasswd` *to define, change, and view password attributes, such as password aging. See the* `nispasswd`*(1) manual page for more information.*

Use the following steps to create an NIS password.

1. Become superuser on any system in the NIS domain.
2. Type **`yppasswd`** ***`login-name`*** and press Return.

   The message `Changing NIS password for` *`login-name`* and the prompt `New password`: are displayed.
3. Type the new password and press Return.

   The prompt `Retype new password`: is displayed.
4. Retype the password and press Return.

   The password is assigned and added to the NIS master file.

The following example changes the NIS password for user `yaya`.

```
oak% su
Password:
# yppasswd yaya
Changing NIS password for yaya
New password:
Retype new password:
NIS entry changed on eucalyptus
#
```

Changing an NIS password is similar to changing an NIS+ password. When prompted to do so, type the old password, and then type the new password two times, as prompted.

Use the following steps to create a local password.

1. Become superuser on the local system.
2. Type **`passwd`** ***`login-name`*** and press Return.

   The prompt `New password`: is displayed.

3. Type the new password and press Return.

   The prompt `Re-enter new password:` is displayed.

4. Retype the password and press Return.

   The password is assigned, as shown in the following example, and added to the `/etc/shadow` file.

```
oak% su
# passwd smallberries
New password:
Re-enter new password:
#
```

NOTE. You can also use `passwd` *to define, change, and view password attributes, such as password aging. See the* `passwd(1)` *manual page for more information.*

Changing a local password is similar to changing an NIS+ password. When prompted to do so, type the old password, and then type the new password two times, as prompted.

Administering User Accounts with Admintool

You can use the Admintool: Users window to add, modify, and delete user accounts on a local system. The following sections describe how to administer local user accounts with Admintool. You can administer network user accounts with AdminSuite 3.0. See "Administering User Accounts with AdminSuite 3.0" on page 157 for more information.

Always run Admintool with your own UID, not as root. You must be a member of the `sysadmin` group (GID 14). If the network is running NIS+, you also need create and delete permissions on the NIS+ databases.

NOTE. If you access Admintool through the Solaris Management Console, you must log in as root or as a member of a role that grants you superuser permissions to run Admintool. Only then can you use Admintool to edit local password databases. See "Using AdminSuite 3.0 to Grant Access Rights to Users" on page 190 for more information.The Solaris Management Console does not recognize membership in GID 14. New!

Adding a User Account with Admintool

Use the following steps to add a user account to a local system with the Admintool: Users window.

1. From the CDE Application Manager, System_Admin folder, double-click on the Admintool icon. Or, in a terminal window, type **admintool&** and press Return.

   The Admintool: Users window is displayed, as shown in Figure 11.

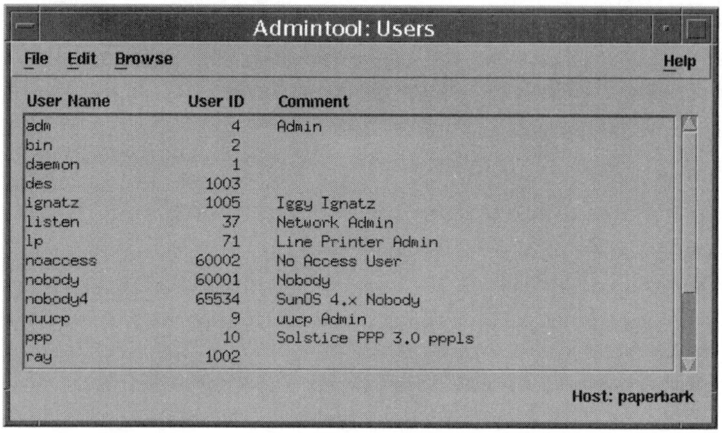
Admintool: Users
File Edit Browse
Help
User Name User ID Comment
adm 4 Admin
bin 2
daemon 1
des 1003
ignatz 1005 Iggy Ignatz
listen 37 Network Admin
lp 71 Line Printer Admin
noaccess 60002 No Access User
nobody 60001 Nobody
nobody4 65534 SunOS 4.x Nobody
nuucp 9 uucp Admin
ppp 10 Solstice PPP 3.0 pppls
ray 1002
Host: paperbark

Figure 11 The Admintool: Users Window

2. From the Browse menu, choose Users (if necessary), as shown in Figure 12.

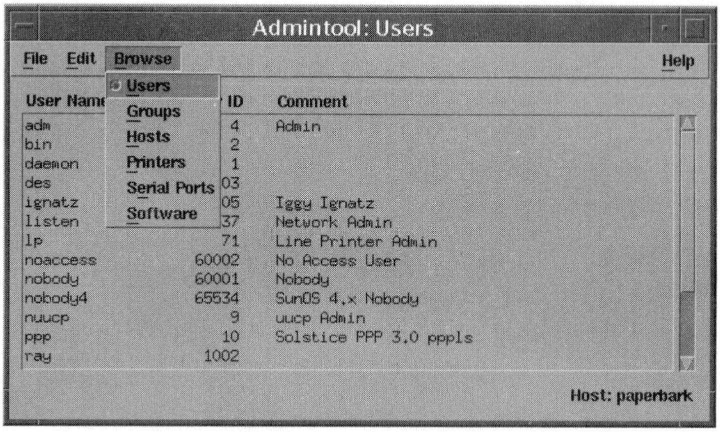
Admintool: Users
File Edit Browse
Help
Users
Groups
Hosts
Printers
Serial Ports
Software
Comment
Admin
Iggy Ignatz
Network Admin
Line Printer Admin
No Access User
Nobody
SunOS 4.x Nobody
uucp Admin
Solstice PPP 3.0 pppls
Host: paperbark

Figure 12 The Users Browse Menu

The Admintool: Users window is displayed.

3. From the Edit menu, choose Add, as shown in Figure 13.

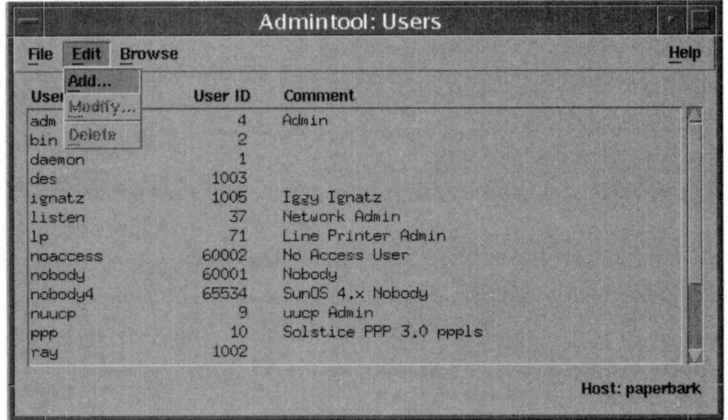

Figure 13 The Users: Edit Menu

The Admintool: Add User window is displayed, as shown in Figure 14.

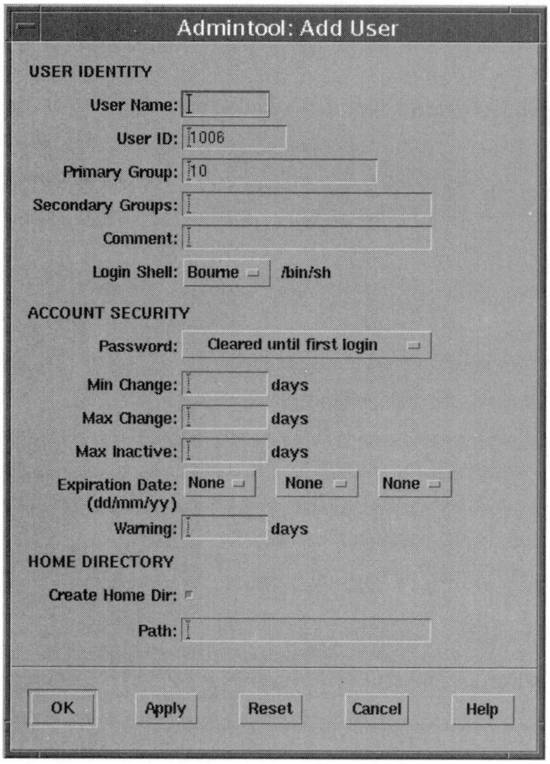

Figure 14 The Admintool: Add User Window

4. Type the user's login name in the User Name text field.

   Choose a login name unique to your organization with two to eight lowercase characters and digits (excluding colons).

5. Type the UID number in the User ID text field.

   Choose a number between 100 and 60000 or between 60003 and 2147483647 that is unique to your organization. By default the Admintool: Add User window assigns a default UID number, sequentially starting with 1001.

6. Type the user's group name or group number in the Primary Group field.

   The default primary group number is 10.

7. If the user is assigned to any secondary groups, type the names or numbers of the additional groups in the Secondary Groups text field.

8. Type identifying information about the user in the Comment text field.

9. Choose a default login shell for the user from the Login Shell menu. If you choose Other, you can specify bash, tcsh, or zsh as the login shell. See Chapter 3, "Understanding Shells," for more information. New!
10. Choose a password status from the Password menu.
11. If you want additional password aging information, set it in the appropriate text fields.
12. If you want to automatically create the user's home directory, click SELECT on the Create Home Dir checkbox.
13. Type the path of the home directory to be entered in the Passwd database in the Path text field. If you checked the Create Home Dir box, the home directory is created.
14. When you have filled in all the information, click on the OK button.

    The information is added to the /etc/passwd, /etc/shadow, and /etc/group files. If specified, the user's home directory is created with the proper ownership.
15. Set up the user initialization files manually, as described in "Defining the User's Environment" on page 131.

Modifying User Accounts with Admintool

When information about the user changes, use the Admintool: Users window to edit the information in the /etc/passwd file. Unless you define a user (login) name or UID that conflicts with existing ones, you probably do not need to modify a user account's login name or UID.

In a network environment, you may need to change the Auto_home database for the user's home directory when users move from one system to another, and from one server to another.

If you need to modify user passwords, use the passwd (no naming service), yppasswd (NIS), and nispasswd (NIS+) commands.

To modify a user account with Admintool, you must be a member of the sysadmin group (GID 14). If you want to change a user's home directory, create the new directory (mkdir) before making changes by using the Admintool: Users window.

NOTE. If you access Admintool through the Solaris Management Console, you must log in as root or as a member of a role that grants you superuser permissions to run Admintool. Only then can you use Admintool to edit local password databases. See "Using AdminSuite 3.0 to Grant Access Rights to Users" on page 190 for more information.The Solaris Management Console does not recognize membership in GID 14.

Use the following steps to modify a user account.

1. In the Admintool: Users window, click on the user account you want to modify, as shown in Figure 15.

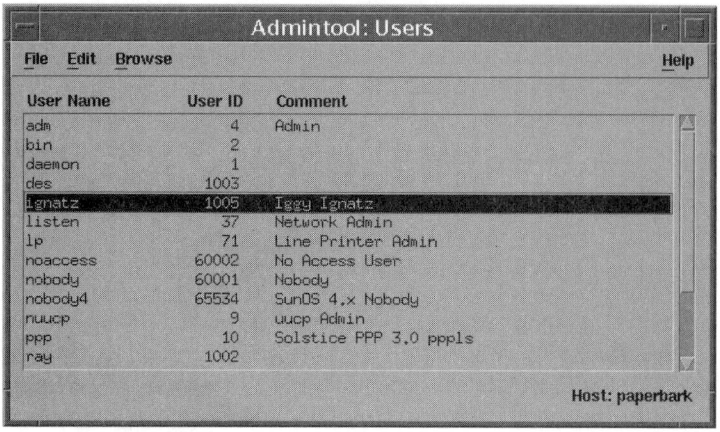

Figure 15 Highlighting a User Account

2. From the Edit menu, choose Modify, as shown in Figure 16.

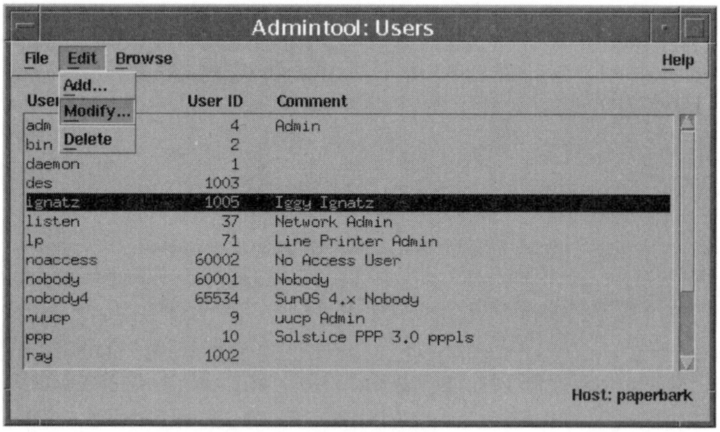

Figure 16 Choosing Modify from the Edit Menu

The Admintool: Modify User window is displayed, as shown in Figure 17.

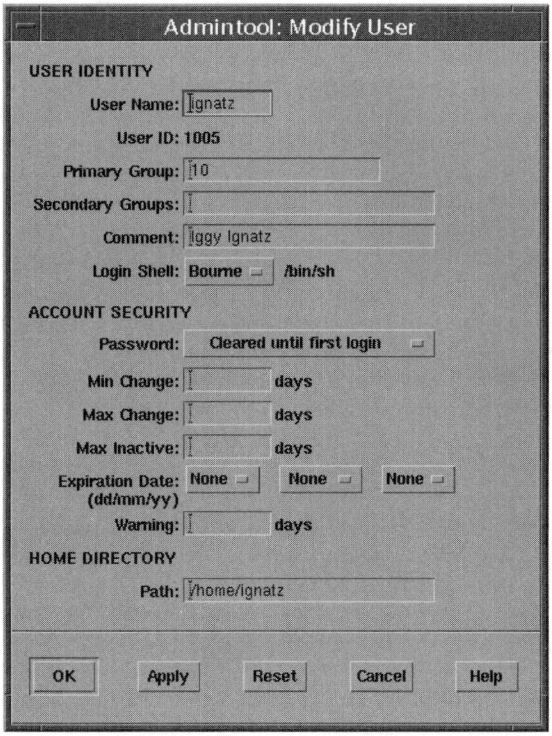

Figure 17 The Admintool: Modify User Window

3. Make the modifications to the user account.
4. When the changes are complete, click on the OK button.

   The changes are made to the user account.

Deleting User Accounts

Use the following checklist for deleting a user account.

- Delete the user's entry from the NIS+ `Passwd` database, NIS map, or `/etc/passwd` files.
- Remove the user's name from entries in the NIS+ Group database, NIS map, or `/etc/group` files.
- Remove the user from any printer access or deny lists.
- Decide whether you want to delete or archive all of the user's files.
- Delete the user's mail file.
- Remove the user from the `Auto_home` database.

- Remove the user from any aliases.
- If this is the last user on the client system, remove the `/var/mail` mount point.

Deleting a User Account with Admintool

To delete a user account with Admintool, you must be a member of the `sysadmin` group (GID 14).

Use the following steps to delete a user account.

1. From the Admintool: Users window, click on the user account you want to delete.

   The user account is highlighted.
2. From the Edit menu, choose Delete.

   An alert window is displayed, as shown in Figure 18, asking you to confirm or cancel the action.

Figure 18 Alert Window

3. If you want to delete the home directory along with the user account, click on the Delete Home Directory check box.
4. Click on the Delete button to delete the user account.

   The user account is deleted and removed from the list in the Admintool: Users list. If you checked the Delete Home Directory check box, the home directory is also deleted. If you want to retain the account, click on the Cancel button to dismiss the window.

Disabling User Accounts

Occasionally, you may need to temporarily or permanently disable a login account. You should have good reason for taking such action. For example, the user may be on leave of absence or you may have strong evidence that the account is being misused or security is being violated.

The easiest way to disable a login account is to lock the password for an account. To lock the password on a local system, modify the user account and choose Account is Locked from the Password menu in the Admintool: Modify User window, as shown in Figure 19.

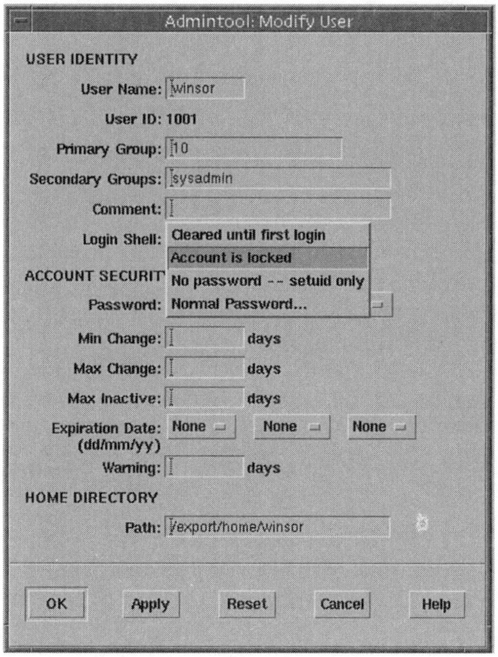

Figure 19 The Admintool: Modify User Password Menu

On a local system, you can control access to a user's account by requiring password aging, by setting an expiration date for the login account, or by requiring that a user access the account at regular intervals. Another way that you can disable a login is to temporarily change the password.

Setting Up and Administering Groups

The *Group database* (NIS maps, NIS+ tables, or local `/etc/group` file) stores information about user groups, traditionally called *UNIX groups*. A *user group* is a collection of users who can share files and other system resources. For example, a set of users who are working on the same project could be formed into a user group.

Each group has a GID, which identifies it internally to the system. A group should have a name and a list of user names. User groups can be defined in two ways.

- Implicitly, by the GID for the user's primary group, which is defined in the user account. Whenever a new GID appears in the `Group` field of the `Passwd` database, a new group is defined.
- Explicitly, by name, GID, and user list, as entered into the `Group` database.

NOTE. It's best to explicitly define all groups so every group has a name.

All users belong to at least one group—their primary group—which is indicated by the `Group` field of their user account. Although it is not required by the operating system, you should add the user to the member list of the group you've designated as his or her primary group. Optionally, users can belong to up to 16 secondary groups. To belong to a secondary group, the user must be added to the group's member list.

The `groups` command shows the groups to which a user belongs. For any user, only one group at a time can be considered the primary group. However, users can temporarily change the primary group (with the `newgrp` command) to any other group they belong to.

Some applications, such as the file system, look at the user's primary group only. For example, ownership of files created and accounting data recorded reflect only the primary group. Other applications may take into account a user's membership across groups. For example, a user has to be a member of the `sysadmin` group to use Admintool to make changes to a database, but it doesn't matter if `sysadmin` is the current primary group.

User groups are probably best known as the groups referred to by the read-write-execute permissions for the user, group, and other on files and directories. These permissions are a cornerstone of security. You cannot access others' files (if they do not allow world access) unless your primary or a secondary group has permission to access the files. For example, a group called `techwrite` could be created for technical writers, and a central directory of document files could be set up with write permission for the `techwrite` group. That way, only writers would be able to change the files.

User groups can be local to a workstation or used across a network. Across the network, user groups allow a set of users on the network to access a set of files on a workstation or file server without making those files available to everyone.

NOTE. NIS+ supports another, unrelated, kind of group, called an NIS+ group, which assigns access rights to NIS+ objects. These groups have nothing to do with using NIS+ to maintain a database of user groups.

Setting Up Fields in the Group Database

The `Group` database (NIS maps, NIS+ tables, or local `/etc/group` file) has the following fields.

- Group Name.
- Group ID.
- User (Member) List.

An additional Group Password field is rarely used. The Group Password field is a relic of earlier versions of UNIX. It is usually left empty or filled with an asterisk. If a group has a password, the `newgrp` command prompts users to enter it. However, there is no command to set the password.

Setting Up a Group Name Field

The Group Name field contains the name assigned to the group. For example, members of the chemistry department in a university may be called `chem`. Group names can have a maximum of nine characters.

Setting Up a Group ID Field

The Group ID field contains the group's numerical ID. It must be unique from all other group IDs on a system and should be unique across the entire organization. Each GID must be a whole number between 0 and 60002, but customarily you use numbers from 100 to 60000. (Numbers 60001 and 60002 are assigned to `nobody` and `noaccess`, respectively, and numbers under 100 are reserved for system default group accounts.) When you use Admintool to add user accounts, you must specify the user's primary group; otherwise, the default primary group is root with a GID of `0`. For security reasons, you do not want users to have a group of `root`.

Starting with the Solaris 2.5.1 release, you can also assign GID numbers between 6003 and 2147483647. If you use GID numbers in this range, refer to Table 27 on page 125 and Table 28 on page 126 for information about interoperability issues and limitations on large GID numbers.

Setting Up a User (Member) List Field

The User List field contains a list of the users in the group. User names are separated by commas. These names must be the official login names defined in the `Passwd` database. As already noted, each user can belong to a maximum of 17 groups.

Identifying Default UNIX User Groups

By default, all Solaris workstations and servers have the following groups.

```
root::0:root
other::1:
bin::2:root,bin,daemon
sys::3:root,bin,sys,adm
adm::4:root,adm,daemon
uucp::5:root,uucp
mail::6:root
tty::7:root,tty,adm
lp::8:root,lp,adm
nuucp::9:root,nuucp
staff::10:
daemon::12:root,daemon
sysadmin::14:
nobody::60001:
noaccess::60002:
nogroup::65534
```

NOTE. The `sysadmin` *group with a GID of 14 is part of the default set of groups. This group specifies the users who have access to all functions of Admintool.*

Creating New Groups with Admintool

As a system administrator, you frequently may create new group accounts. You must create a group and assign it a GID before you can assign users to it.

Use Admintool to create and maintain local groups. You must be a member of the `sysadmin` group (GID 14) before you can use Admintool to create or edit group accounts.

NOTE. If you access Admintool through the Solaris Management Console, you must log in as root or as a member of a role that grants you superuser permissions to run Admintool. Only then can you use Admintool to edit local password databases. *See "Using AdminSuite 3.0 to Grant Access Rights to Users" on page 190 for more information.**The Solaris Management Console does not recognize membership in GID 14.*

You need the following information to create a new group.

- Login names of users who will belong to the group.
- UIDs of users who will belong to the group.
- Group name.
- GID.

Use the following steps to add groups to a local `/etc/group` file.

1. Start Admintool (if necessary) by typing **`admintool&`** and pressing Return.
2. From the Browse menu, choose Groups. The Admintool: Groups window is displayed, as shown in Figure 20.

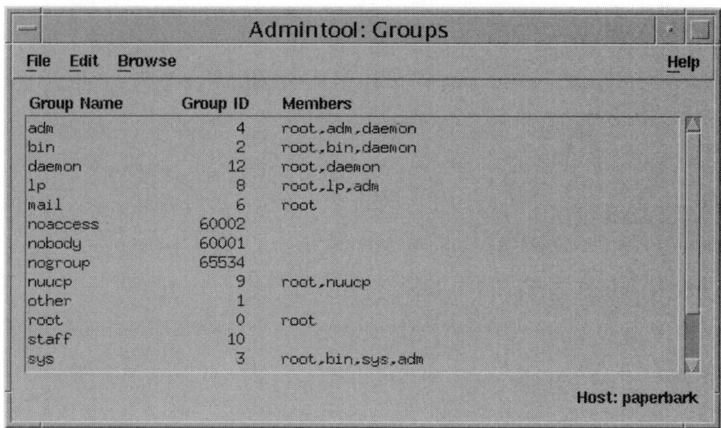

Figure 20 The Admintool: Groups Window

3. From the Edit menu, choose Add.

   The Admintool: Add Group window is displayed, as shown in Figure 21.

Figure 21 The Admintool: Add Group Window

4. Type the name of the group, the new group number, and the members of the group.

   Members of a group are defined as a comma-separated list of login names. Spaces are not allowed. If you need help in determining the format for any of the fields, click on the Help button. A help window is displayed, as shown in Figure 22.

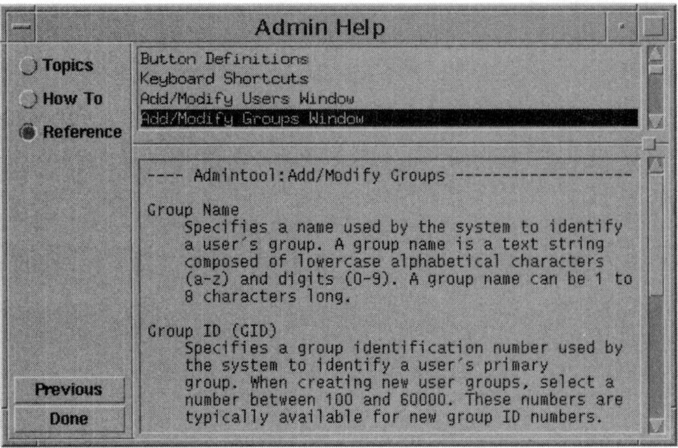

Figure 22 The Admintool: Help Window

5. When the information is complete, click on the OK button.

   The group is created and added to the local `/etc/group` file.

Modifying or Deleting Groups with Admintool

Membership in group accounts can change frequently as new employees are hired and other employees change job responsibilities. Consequently, you have to modify existing group accounts to add or remove users. If you choose to have a user belong to secondary groups, you have to modify those groups to add the user to the user lists. When adding groups, you may make a mistake. The ability to modify or delete groups helps you correct such mistakes.

> *NOTE. When projects finish, groups set up for them may no longer be needed, and you can delete these groups. Be careful to avoid conflicts if you reuse the GIDs from deleted groups.*

Modifying a Group

Use the following steps to modify a group entry.

1. Start Admintool (if necessary).
2. From the Browse menu, choose Groups.

   The Admintool: Groups window is displayed.
3. Click on the group you want to modify.

   The item is highlighted.
4. From the Edit menu, choose Modify.

   The Admintool: Modify Group window is displayed.

5. Make the changes to the group.
6. When the changes are complete, click on the OK button. The changes are made to the local `/etc/group` file.

Deleting a Group

If a group account is no longer needed, you can delete it. Use the following steps to delete a group:

1. Click on the group you want to delete.

   The item is highlighted.
2. From the Edit menu, choose Delete.

   An alert window is displayed, asking if you want to delete the group.
3. Click on the Delete button.

   The group is deleted from the `/etc/group` file and is removed from the list in the Admintool: Groups window. If you want to retain the group, click on the Cancel button.

Administering User Accounts with AdminSuite 3.0 New!

You can use the AdminSuite 3.0 User Accounts window to add, modify, and delete one or multiple accounts in a networked environment You can switch domains, add or delete domains, and set security policies. You can view detailed information about each user account. You can also assign a subset of superuser rights to individual users for AdminSuite-defined authorizations. See "Using AdminSuite 3.0 to Grant Access Rights to Users" on page 190 for more information.

AdminSuite 3.0 is available as a free download from `www.sun.com/bigadmin/content/adminPack` as part of the Solaris 8 Admin Pack.

You access AdminSuite 3.0 from the Solaris Management Console (SMC). The SMC resides in the System_Admin folder of the CDE Application Manager.

NOTE. The Solstice Launcher is not supported in the Solaris 8 release.

For a discussion of the tasks involved in adding user accounts, refer to "Adding User Accounts" on page 123.

Adding a Single User Account with AdminSuite

Use the following steps to add a user account to a networked environment with the AdminSuite User Accounts window.

1. Refer to "Accessing Solaris AdminSuite 3.0" on page 79 for instructions on how to access the AdminSuite 3.0 window shown in Figure 23.

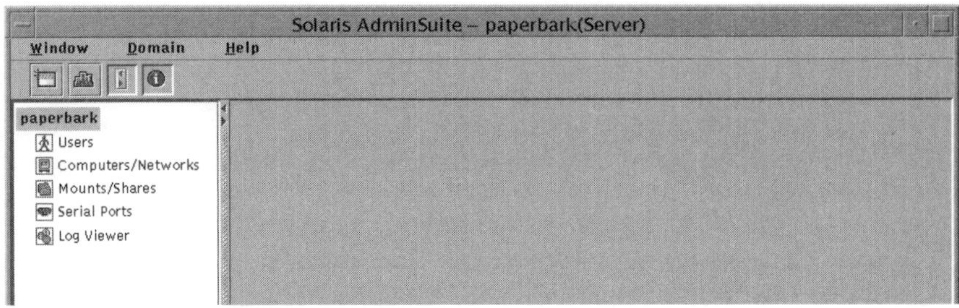

Figure 23 AdminSuite Window

2. Click on the Users folder in the navigation pane.

   The contents of the Users folder are displayed in the right pane, as shown in Figure 24.

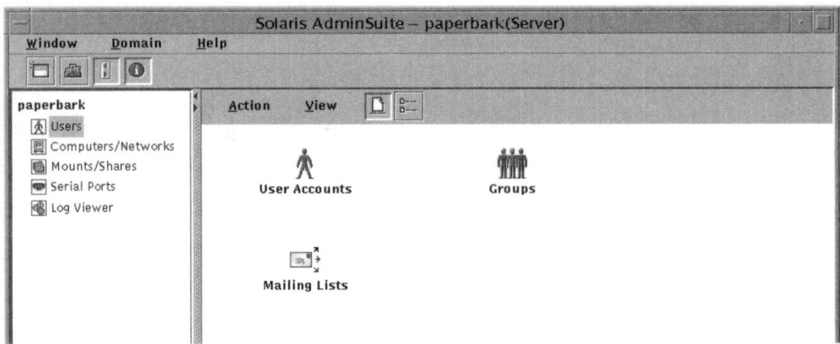

Figure 24 Contents of the Users Folder

   You can hide the navigation pane by choosing Hide Navigation Pane from the Window menu. You can hide the Help pane by choosing Hide Context Help Pane from the Help menu. The rest of the examples in this section have both panes hidden.

3. Double-click on the User Accounts icon.

   The Set Initial View window is displayed the first time you enter the User Accounts tool, as shown in Figure 25.

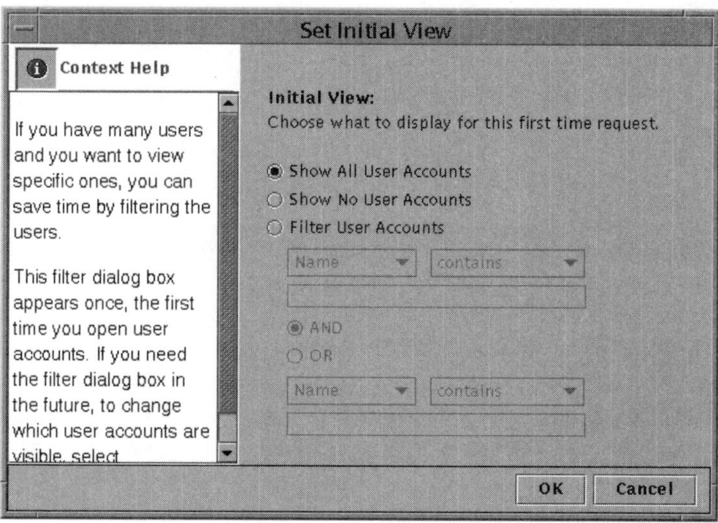

Figure 25 Set Initial View Window

4. Use the Set Initial View window to filter the amount of information displayed in the User Accounts tool. Choose the filtering you want and click on the OK button.

   If you have many users, you may want to display only a partial set of your user list. If you want to filter subsequent views, choose Filter from the View menu. All users on the system `paperbark` are displayed in Figure 26.

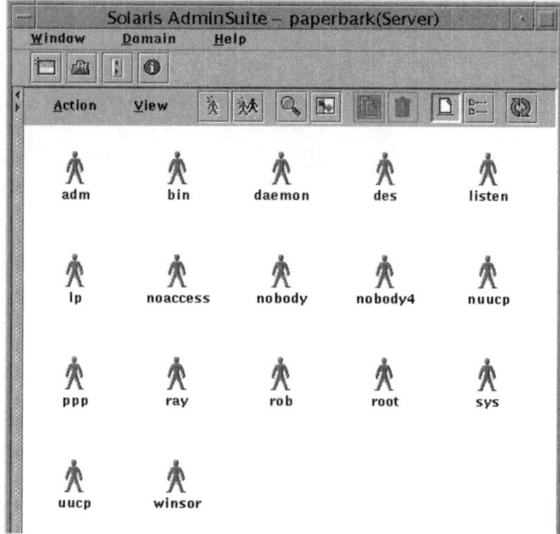

Figure 26 User Accounts

You can use the items from the View menu to display user accounts as large icons or to show the details for each user. The default is to display large icons. If you choose Details, the View menu has a Sort By option that you can use to sort the details by Name, Description, User ID, or Type.

5. Choose Add User from the Action menu, as shown in Figure 27.

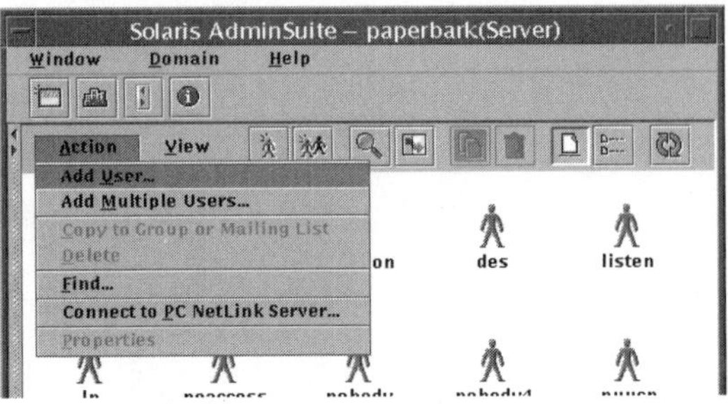

Figure 27 Action Menu

The Add User Wizard window is displayed, as shown in Figure 28.

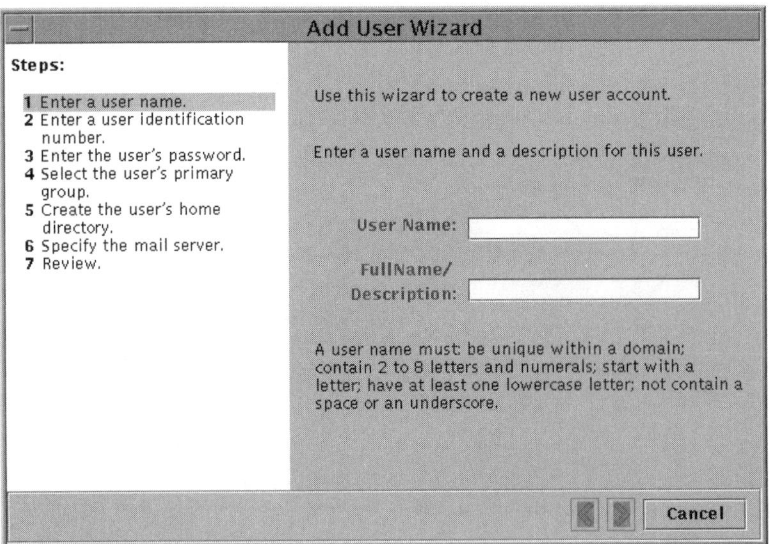

Figure 28 Add User Wizard Window

The Add User Wizard displays the steps in the left pane and guides you through filling out the forms on each screen.

6. Fill in each screen and click on the right arrow key at the bottom of the window to go to the next screen.

When you have filled in all of the information for the user, the last step is to review the information, as shown in Figure 29.

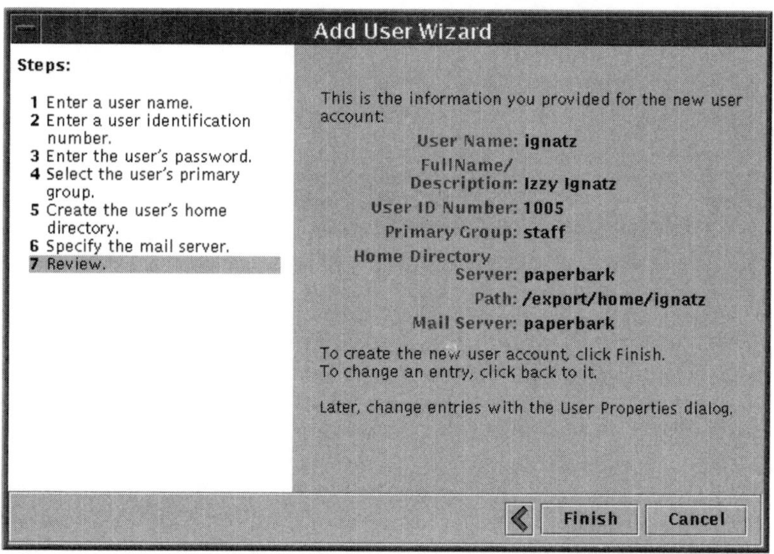

Figure 29 Review the Information

7. Click on the left arrow at the bottom of the window to go back to any screen and revise the information. When you are done, return to the Review task and click on the Finish button.

   The user is added to the Add Users window and highlighted, as shown in Figure 30.

Figure 30 User Accounts Window with New User Highlighted

Adding Multiple User Accounts with AdminSuite

You can add multiple users to a single server with the AdminSuite User Account Manager.

NOTE. The home directory server must be running AdminSuite 3.0.

1. Choose Add Multiple Users from the Action window, as shown in Figure 31.

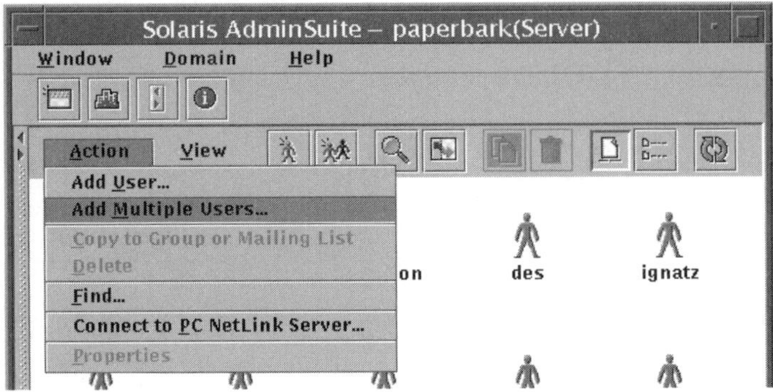

Figure 31 Add Multiple Users Item

The Add Multiple Users Wizard window is displayed as shown in Figure 32.

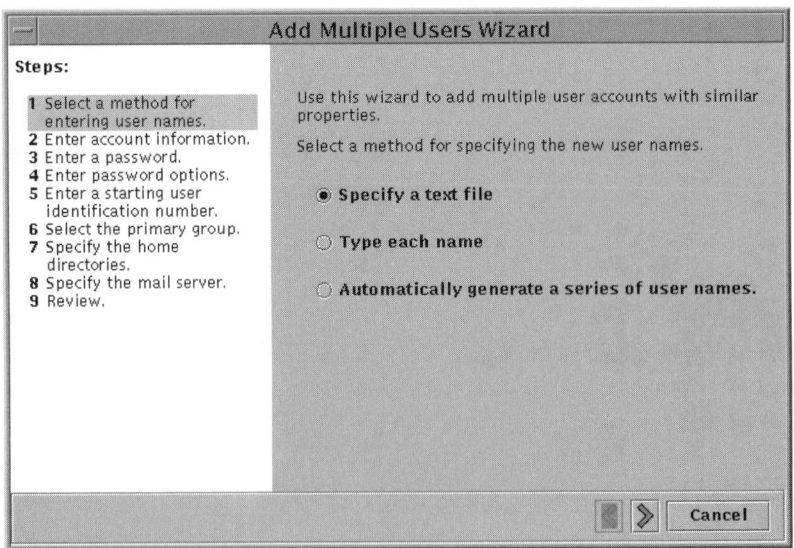

Figure 32 Add Multiple Users Wizard Window

2. Specify a method for generating user names.

   You can specify the names as entries, one per line, in a file; type each name or automatically generate a series of user names with a common prefix followed by a series of numbers.

3. Follow the rest of the steps in the Add Multiple Users Wizard, review the information, and click on Finish.

   The set of users is added to the home directory server that you specified.

Modifying User Accounts with AdminSuite

You can show detailed information about each user account by double-clicking on the icon for the individual user.

Figure 33 shows the window that is displayed when you double-click on a user account icon. You can use this window to view or modify most of the properties of any existing user account. Simply click on the tab to display the relevant information, make the changes you want, and click on the OK button.

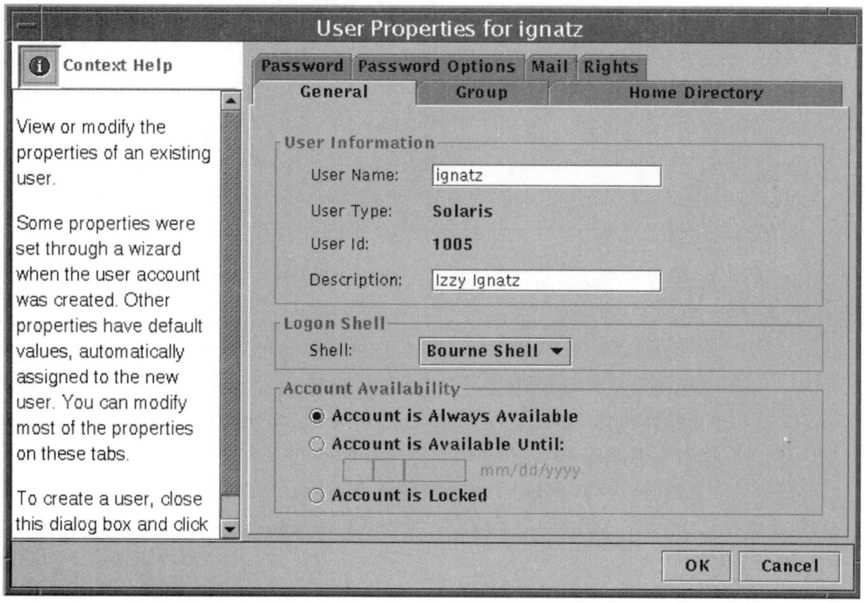

Figure 33 User Properties Window

Deleting User Accounts with the AdminSuite User Account Manager

The AdminSuite User Account manager handles the following duties when you delete a user account.

- Removes all entries in the directory services databases.
- Removes the user name from all groups.
- Does not remove the home directory.
- Does not remove the user's mailbox.

Use the following steps to delete a user account with the AdminSuite User Account Manager.

1. From the AdminSuite User Accounts window, click on the user account you want to delete.
2. From the Actions menu, choose Delete.

   An alert window is displayed, as shown in Figure 34, asking you to confirm or cancel the action.

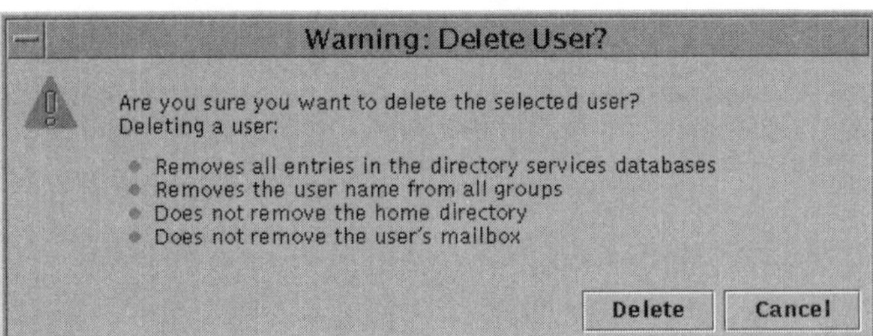

Figure 34 Alert Window

3. Click on the Delete button to delete the user account.

   The user account is deleted and removed from the list in the User Manager window. All entries are removed from the directory services database, and the user name is removed from all groups.
4. Manually delete the home directory.
5. Manually delete the user's mailbox.

Administering Groups with the AdminSuite Groups Tool

Refer to "Setting Up and Administering Groups" on page 151 for a description of groups.

Creating New Groups with AdminSuite

Use the following steps to add groups to a local system or in a networked environment.

1. Start AdminSuite (if necessary). From the CDE Application Manager, System_Admin folder, double-click on the Solaris Management Console icon.
2. Type your login name and password, and click on the Log in button.
3. Click on the Infrastructure folder or the word Infrastructure in the left pane.
4. Double-click on the AdminSuite folder.
5. Double-click on the AdminSuite icon.
6. Log in, type the password, and click on the OK button.
7. Click on the Users folder in the navigation pane.

   The contents of the Users folder are displayed in the right pane, as shown in Figure 35.

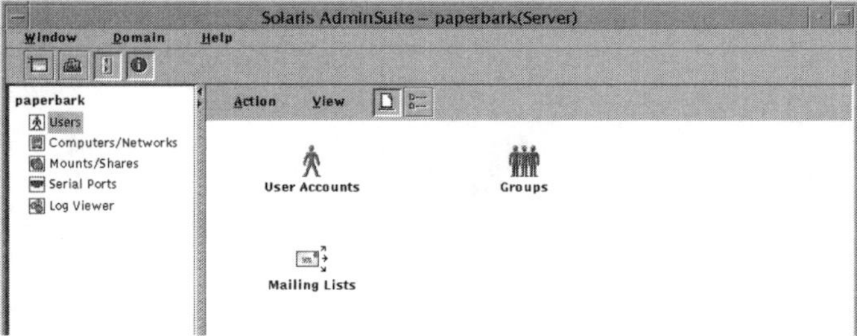

Figure 35 Contents of the Users Folder

8. Double-click on the Groups icon.
9. The Filter Grous window is displayed the first time you enter the User Accounts tool, as shown in Figure 36.

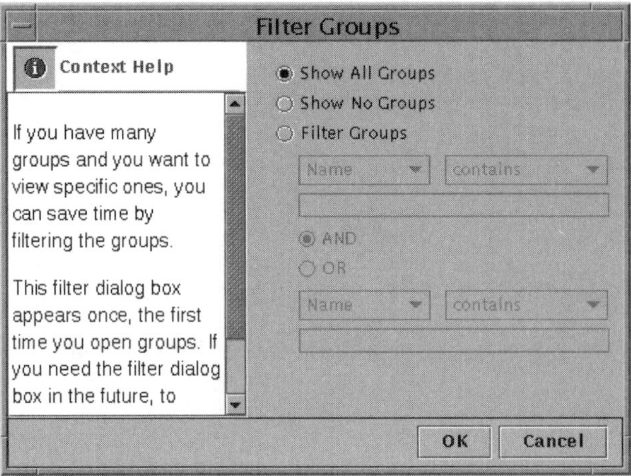

Figure 36 Filter Groups Window

10. Use the Filter Groups window to filter the amount of information displayed in the Groups tool. Choose the filtering you want and click on the OK button.

    If you have many groups, you may want to display only a partial set of your group list. If you want to filter subsequent views, choose Filter from the View menu. All groups on the system `paperbark` are displayed in Figure 37.

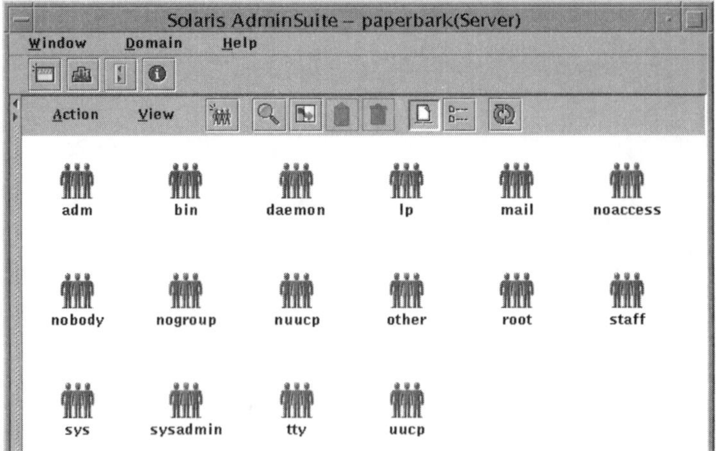

Figure 37 Groups

You can use the items from the View menu to display Groups as large icons or to show the details for each user. The default is to display large icons. If you choose Details, the View menu has a Sort By option that you can use to sort the details by Group Name or by Group ID.

11. Choose Add Group from the Action menu, as shown in Figure 38.

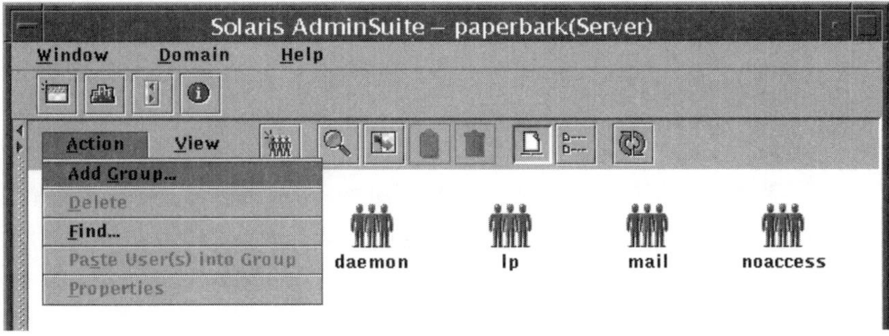

Figure 38 Action Menu

The Add Group Wizard window is displayed, as shown in Figure 39.

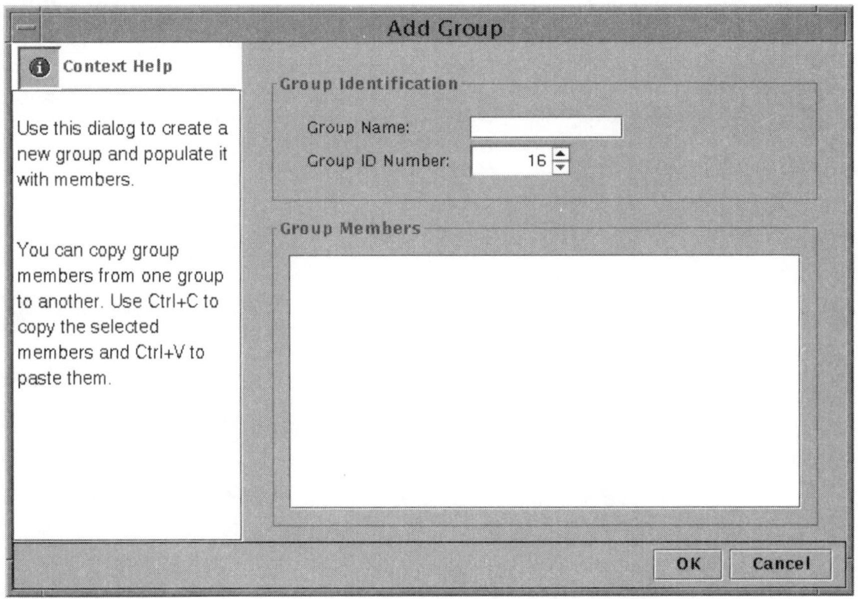

Figure 39 Add Group Window

The Add Groups Wizard displays the steps in the left pane and guides you through filling out the forms on each screen.

12. Type the name of the group, the new group number, and the members of the group.

Members of a group are defined as a comma-separated list of login names. Spaces are not allowed.

13. When you are done creating the group and assigning members, click on the OK button.

Adding a Large Number of User Accounts to a Group with AdminSuite

Use the following steps to add a large number of users to a group.

NOTE. Before you use the following procedure, if you have hidden the Navigation Pane, choose Show Navigation Pane from the Window menu.

Refer to "Creating New Groups with AdminSuite" on page 165 for instructions on how to display the Add Group window.

1. In the Add Group window, create the group name and number and then click on the OK button to close the Add Group window.
2. In the AdminSuite Users window, double-click on the User Accounts icon.
3. Select the user accounts you want to add to the group. Click SELECT on the first icon to select it, then press Control and click SELECT to add another user account to the selection.
4. From the Action menu of the User Accounts window, choose Copy to Group or Mailing List, as shown in Figure 40.

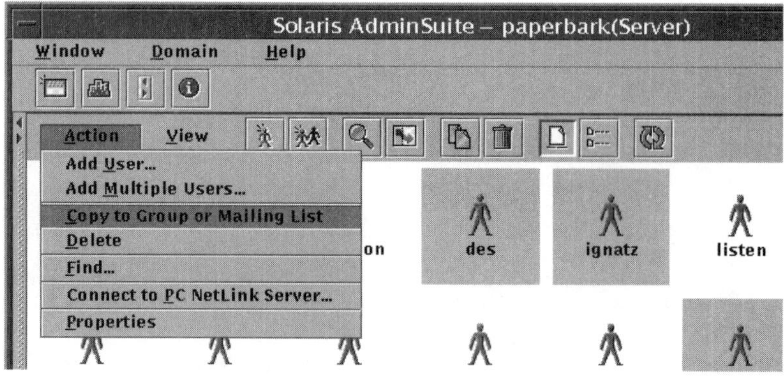

Figure 40 Choose Copy to Group or Mailing List from the Action Menu

5. Click on the Groups icon, then click on the group or groups to which you want to add the user accounts. To add a group to the selection, press Control and click SELECT.

6. From the Action menu, Choose Paste User(s) into Group, as shown in Figure 41.

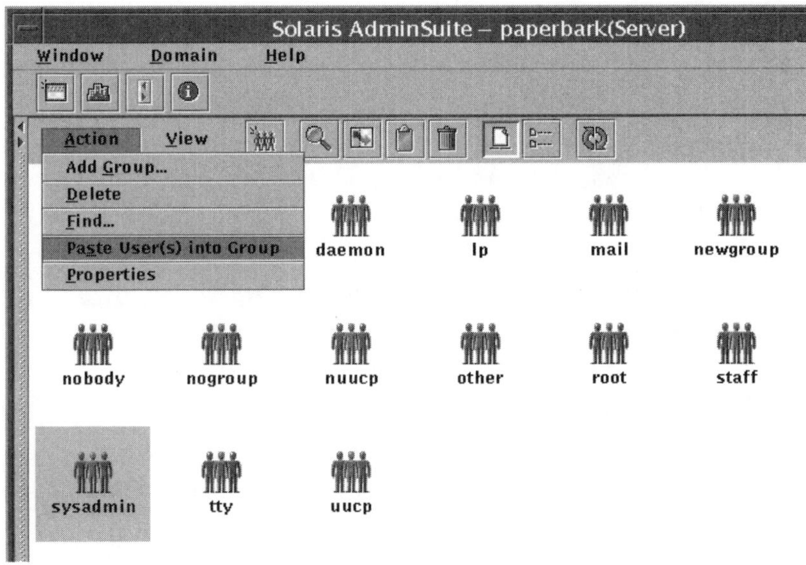

Figure 41 Choose Paste User(s) into Group from the Action Menu

7. If you want to confirm that the users have been added, double-click on the icon for the group.

   The Group Properties window shows the information about the group, as shown in Figure 42.

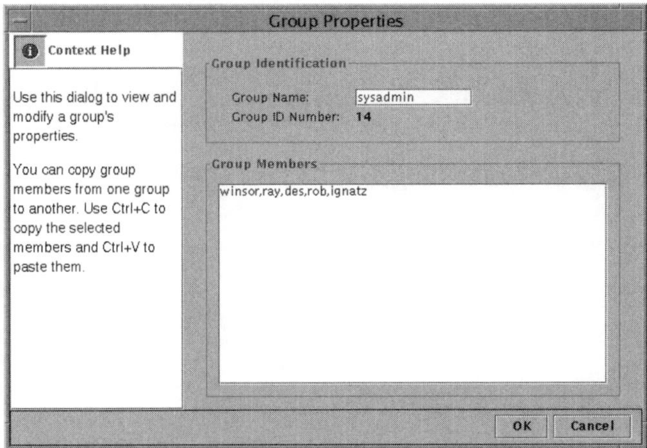

Figure 42 Group Properties Window

Modifying Groups with AdminSuite

Use the following steps to modify a group entry.

1. Start AdminSuite (if necessary). From the CDE Application Manager, System_Admin folder, double-click on the Solaris Management Console icon.
2. Type your login name and password, and click on the Log in button.
3. Click on the Infrastructure folder or the word Infrastructure in the left pane.
4. Double-click on the AdminSuite folder.
5. Double-click on the AdminSuite icon.
6. Log in, type the password, and click on the OK button.
7. Click on the Users folder in the navigation pane.
8. Double-click on the Groups icon.
9. Double-click on the group you want to modify.

   The Group Properties window shows the information about the group, as shown in Figure 43.

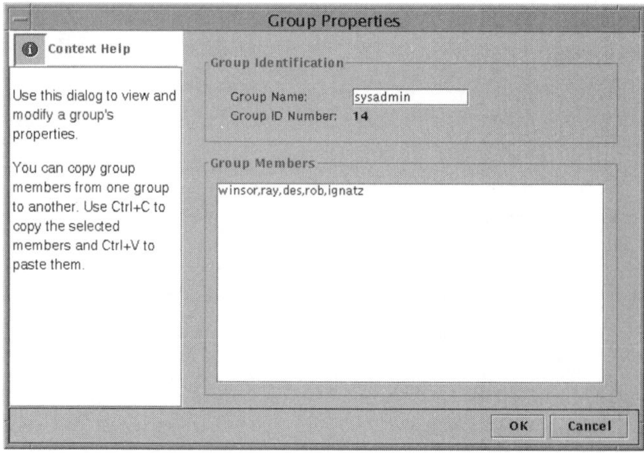

Figure 43 Group Properties Window

10. Make the changes and click on the OK button.

    The group properties are modified.

Deleting a Group with AdminSuite

If a group account is no longer needed, you can delete it. The Groups tool performs the following tasks for a deleted group.

- Removes the entry in the group directory service database.
- Finds all user accounts with this group as their primary group and changes the primary group to `staff`.

Use the following steps to delete a group.

1. Click on the Groups icon.
2. Click on the group or groups you want to delete.

   The item is highlighted.
3. From the Actions menu, choose Delete.

   The Warning: Delete Group? alert is displayed, as shown in Figure 44.

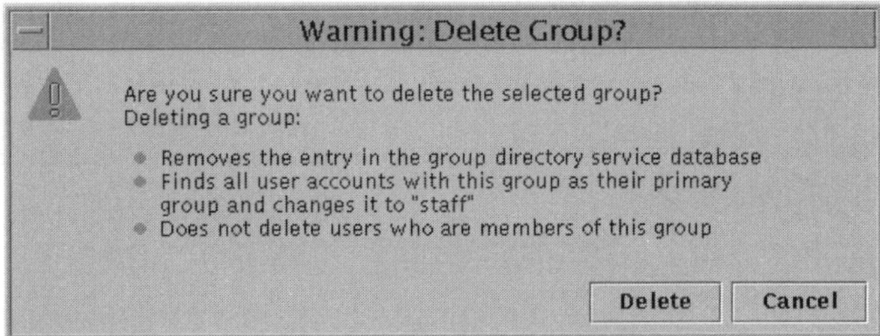

Figure 44 Warning: Delete Group? Window

4. Click on the Delete button.

   The group is deleted from the Groups window and from the group directory service database, and the primary group of any user accounts that have this group is changed to `staff`.

Solaris User Registration

Solaris User Registration is a tool for gathering information about new Solaris releases, upgrade offers, and promotions. This tool automatically starts when a user first logs in to the desktop. The Solaris User Registration tool enables a user to register now, later, or never. The registration process provides Sun with the user's Solaris version, survey type, platform, hardware, and locale.

NOTE. Solaris User Registration is not started when a user is logged in as root or superuser.

If the user chooses to register, a copy of the completed form is stored in `$HOME/.solregis/uprops`. If the user chooses to never register, he can always start User Registration in one of the following ways.

- By typing **`solregis&`** at any command-line prompt.
- By clicking on the Registration icon in the Application Manager's desktop tools folder in the CDE environment.

For more information, refer to the `solregis(1)` manual page.

Accessing Solaris Solve

When users complete the Solaris User Registration process, they can access Solaris Solve, an exclusive Web site that offers valuable Solaris product information and solutions in one convenient location. Solaris Solve provides a quick and easy way for users to get the most recent information on what is happening with the latest Solaris release. Solaris Solve also provides a preview of additional Sun contract and service opportunities.

To complete the Solaris User Registration form and access Solaris, users can follow the steps below.

1. Fill in the electronic Solaris User Registration profile.
2. Submit the profile by e-mail or print the profile to fax or mail.
3. Create a login ID and password to access the Solaris Solve site.

   Even if users do not access the Solaris Solve site immediately, we recommend that users create a Solaris Solve login ID and password during the Solaris User Registration process. A Solaris Solve ID and password should contain 6 to 8 alphanumeric characters without spaces or colons.
4. Access the Solaris Solve site.

Error Conditions

Table 33 suggests ways to resolve user problems with registration.

Table 33 Registration Errors

Problem	Solution
Registration form failed to initialize: Web page window is displayed, requesting that user see the system administrator to resolve the problem.	Check for missing registration files.
Form could not be e-mailed: Dialog box is displayed requesting that user see the system administrator to resolve problem.	Check whether e-mail is configured correctly. Also ensure that CDE is available on the user system because it must be present before the completed registration form can be e-mailed. Alternatively, users can print the form and fax or mail it.
Form could not be printed: Dialog box is displayed requesting that the user see the system administrator to resolve problem.	Check whether the printer is configured correctly. Alternatively, user can e-mail form.
Form could not be saved: Dialog box is displayed, verifying that registration succeeded; however, the registration information cannot be recalled when updating registration.	Check user's home directory. Required action depends on the system configuration.

Restarting Solaris User Registration

New!

Use the following steps to restart the Solaris User Registration process.

1. Type **`cd $HOME/.solregis`** and press Return.
   Focus is in the `.solregis` directory.
2. Type **`rm uprops`** and press Return.
   You have removed the `uprops` file that contains the previous registration information.
3. Type **`/usr/dt/bin/solregis&`** and press Return.
   The Solaris User Registration form is redisplayed.

4. Fill in the form and click on the appropriate button at the bottom of the window to either register by e-mail or print a copy to fax or mail.

Disabling User Registration

If system administrators register for your organization, you may want to disable individual user registration as part of setting up user accounts. You can disable User Registration either before or after installing Solaris software. Before Solaris software is installed, you can disable User Registration in the following ways.

- Deselect the `SUNWsregu` package (interactive installation).
- Modify a custom JumpStart profile to not install the `SUNWsregu` package.
- Create and run a finish script that creates a file named `solregis` that contains the line: `DISABLE=1` in the `/etc/default` directory on one or more systems.

After Solaris software is installed, you can disable User Registration in the following ways.

- Use the `pkgrm` command to remove the `SUNWsregu` package.
- Create a `solregis` file that contains the line `DISABLE=1` in the `/etc/default` directory.

5

ADMINISTERING ROLES

The Solaris 8 Operating Environment provides role-based access control (RBAC). RBAC is new security feature that provides a flexible way to package certain superuser privileges for assignment to user accounts. You no longer need to give users all superuser privileges to enable them to perform a set of tasks that require superuser privileges. New!

With traditional security models, superuser has full superuser privileges and other users do not have enough power to fix their own problems. With role-based access control (RBAC), you now have an alternative to the traditional all-or-nothing security model.

With RBAC, you can divide superuser capabilities into several packages and assign them separately to individuals sharing administrative responsibilities. When you separate superuser privileges with RBAC, users can have a variable degree of access and you can control delegation of privileged operations to other users.

RBAC includes the following features.

- Authorization—A right used to grant access to a restricted function.
- Execution profile (or just profile)—A bundling mechanism for grouping authorizations and commands with special attributes; for example, user and group IDs.
- Role—A special type of user account that can be used to perform a set of administrative tasks.

In addition to RBAC, AdminSuite 3.0 tool uses the `auth_attr` and `user_attr` databases (described below) to enable you to assign authorizations defined by AdminSuite to individual users. These rights act independently of roles and RBAC. See "Using AdminSuite 3.0 to Grant Access Rights to Users" on page 190 for more information.

This chapter first describes the elements of RBAC and the files used to administer it. Then, the chapter provides an example of how to create a role and assign it to a user. The chapter also describes how to use AdminSuite 3.0 to grant access rights to users.

The RBAC Databases

Four RBAC databases provide users access to privileged operations.

- `/etc/user_attr` (extended user attributes database)—Associates users and roles with authorizations and execution profiles.
- `/etc/security/auth_attr` (authorization attributes database)—Defines authorizations and their attributes and identifies the associated help file.
- `/etc/security/prof_attr` (execution profile attributes database)—Defines profiles, lists the profile's assigned authorizations, and identifies the associated help file.
- `/etc/security/exec_attr` (profile execution attributes database)—Defines the privileged operations assigned to a profile.

The `user_attr` database is the only database that is required. Use of the other databases depends on which security features are implemented.

You can directly assign authorizations and profiles to users in the `user_attr` database. You can also assign the user to a role to give the user access to any privileged operations associated with that role.

Profiles are defined in the `prof_attr` database and can include authorizations defined in `auth_attr` and commands with attributes defined for that profile in `exec_attr`.

The `pfexec`(1) command is used to execute commands with the attributes specified by the user profiles in the `exec_attr`(4) database. Commands that are assigned to profiles are run in special shells called *profile shells.*

- `pfsh` corresponds to the Bourne shell (`sh`).
- `pfcsh` corresponds to the C shell (`csh`).
- `pfksh` corresponds to the Korn (`ksh`) shell.

See the pfexec(1) manual page for more information.

Extended User Attributes Database (user_attr)

The /etc/user_attr database supplements the passwd and shadow databases. It contains extended user attributes such as authorizations and execution profiles. It also enables you to assign roles to a user.

A role is a special type of user account that enables a user to perform a set of administrative tasks. It is similar to a normal user account except that you do not access the role through the login window. Instead, users access their roles only with the su command by typing ***su rolename*** and pressing Return.

From a role account, a user can access commands with special attributes, typically root user ID, that are not available to users in normal accounts.

When you have created appropriate roles by using the AdminSuite-defined authorizations starting with solaris.admin and have assigned users to them, the users can also use the role name and role password to log in to system administration tools such as Admintool and AdminSuite 3.0 and perform the tasks to which they have been granted access.

Syntax of the user_attr Database

The default /etc/user_attr database is shown below.

```
# Copyright (c) 1999 by Sun Microsystems, Inc. All rights reserved.
#
# /etc/user_attr
#
# user attributes. see user_attr(4)
#
#pragma ident     "@(#)user_attr     1.2     99/07/14 SMI"
#
root::::type=normal;auths=solaris.*,solaris.grant;profiles=All
```

Each entry consists of a single line with five fields separated by colons (:). You can continue lines by using the backslash character (\). Each entry has the following form.

```
user:qualifier:res1:res2:attr
```

The fields are described in Table 34.

Table 34 Fields in the user_attr Database

user	The name of the user as specified in the passwd(4) database.	
qualifier	Reserved for future use.	
res1	Reserved for future use.	
res2	Reserved for future use.	
attr	An optional list of semicolon-separated (;) key-value pairs that describe the security attributes to apply to the object when it is executed. You can specify zero or more keys. The four valid keys are auths, profiles, roles, and type.	
	auths	Specify a comma-separated list of authorization names chosen from the names defined in the auth_attr(4) database. You can specify authorization names by using the asterisk (*) character as a wildcard. For example, solaris.printer.* grants all Sun printer authorizations.
	profiles	Specify an ordered, comma-separated list of profile names chosen from prof_attr(4). A profile determines which commands a user can execute and which command attributes can be specified. At a minimum, each user in user_attr should have the All profile, which makes all commands available but without any attributes.
		The order of profiles is important; it works similarly to UNIX search paths. The first profile in the list that contains the command to be executed defines which (if any) attributes are applied to the command. Profiles are enforced by the profile shells (see pfexec(1)). If no profiles are assigned, the profile shells do not permit the user to execute any commands.

Table 34 Fields in the user_attr Database (Continued)

	`roles`	Specify an optional, comma-separated list of role names from the set of user accounts in this database whose `type` field indicates the account is a role. If the role's key value is not specified, the user cannot assume any role. You cannot assign roles to other roles.
	`type`	Specify either `normal` to indicate that this account is for a normal user, or `role` to indicate that this account is for a role. A user can assume a role only after logging in.

NOTE. Because the list of legal keys is likely to expand, any code that parses this database must be written to ignore unknown key-value pairs without error. When you create new keywords, prefix the names with a unique string, such as the company's stock symbol, to avoid potential naming conflict. All of the Solaris keys except those in the `user_attr` *database are prefixed with the string* `solaris`.

Examples of user_attr Database Entries

The entry in the default `user_attr` database is shown below.

```
root::::type=normal;auths=solaris.*,solaris.grant;profiles=All
```

This entry assigns to root the `All` profile, which enables root to use all commands in the system. It also assigns two authorizations. The `solaris.*` wildcard authorization grants root all of the `solaris` authorizations. The `solaris.grant` authorization grants root the right to grant to others any `solaris` authorizations that root has. This combination of authorizations enables root to grant to others any or all `solaris` authorizations.

Use the `roleadd`(1M) command to define a role. See "How to Create a Role" on page 188 for information on using `roleadd` to create roles. Use the `useradd -R` option to assign a role to a user's account. The following example shows the entry in the `auth_attr` database to add the `sysadmin` role and assign user `winsor` to that role.

```
sysadmin::::type=role;profiles=Device Management,Machine Administration, Users
  Groups & Mailing Lists,All
winsor::::type=normal;auths=solaris.system.date;roles=sysadmin;profiles=All
```

When assuming the `sysadmin` role, `winsor` has access to the `Device Management`, `Machine Administration`, and the `All` profiles.

Authorizations Database (auth_attr)

An authorization is a user right that grants access to a restricted function. It is a unique string that identifies what is being authorized and who created the authorization.

Certain privileged programs check authorizations to determine whether users can execute restricted functionality. For example, the `solaris.jobs.admin` authorization is required for one user to edit the `crontab` file of another user.

All authorizations are stored in the `/etc/security/auth_attr` database. When you assign authorizations directly to users or roles, the authorizations are entered in the `user_attr` database. You can also assign authorizations to execution profiles, which in turn are then assigned to users.

Syntax of the auth_attr Database

The default `/etc/security/auth_attr` database is shown below.

```
#
# Copyright (c) 1999 by Sun Microsystems, Inc. All rights reserved.
#
# /etc/security/auth_attr
#
# authorizations. see auth_attr(4)
#
#pragma ident     "@(#)auth_attr     1.2     99/08/16 SMI"
#
solaris.*:::Solaris Primary Administrator::help=PriAdmin.html
solaris.grant:::Grant All Solaris Rights::help=PriAdmin.html
#
solaris.audit.:::Audit Management::help=AuditHeader.html
solaris.audit.config:::Configure Auditing::help=AuditConfig.html
solaris.audit.read:::Read Audit Trail::help=AuditRead.html
#
solaris.device.:::Device Allocation::help=DevAllocHeader.html
solaris.device.allocate:::Allocate Device::help=DevAllocate.html
solaris.device.config:::Configure Device Attributes::help=DevConfig.html
solaris.device.grant:::Delegate Device Administration::help=DevGrant.html
solaris.device.revoke:::Revoke or Reclaim Device::help=DevRevoke.html
#
solaris.jobs.:::Cron and At Jobs::help=JobHeader.html
solaris.jobs.admin:::Cron & At Administrator::help=JobsAdmin.html
solaris.jobs.grant:::Delegate Cron & At Administration::help=JobsGrant.html
solaris.jobs.user:::Create at or cron jobs::help=JobsUser.html
#
solaris.login.:::Login Control::help=LoginHeader.html
solaris.login.enable:::Enable Logins::help=LoginEnable.html
solaris.login.remote:::Remote Login::help=LoginRemote.html
#
solaris.profmgr.:::Execution Profile Management::help=ProfmgrHeader.html
solaris.profmgr.assign:::Assign Profiles to Users or Roles::help=ProfmgrAssign.html
solaris.profmgr.write:::Create, Modify, Delete Profiles::help=ProfmgrWrite.html
#
solaris.role.:::Role Management::help=RoleHeader.html
solaris.role.assign:::Assign Roles to Users::help=RoleAssign.html
```

```
solaris.role.write:::Add, Modify, Delete Roles::help=RoleWrite.html
#
solaris.system.:::Machine Administration::help=SysHeader.html
solaris.system.date:::Set Date & Time::help=SysDate.html
solaris.system.shutdown:::Shutdown the System::help=SysShutdown.html
```

When you install AdminSuite, the following AdminSuite-defined authorizations are added to the `auth_attr` database.

```
solaris.admin.serialmgr.:::Serial Ports::help=SerialPortMgrHeader.html
solaris.admin.logsvc.write:::Change Log Settings::help=LogSvcWrite.html
solaris.admin.hostmgr.:::Computers/Networks::help=HostMgrHeader.html
solaris.admin.fsmgr.write:::Mount/Share File Systems::help=FsMgrWrite.html
solaris.admin.serialmgr.delete:::Delete Serial Ports::help=SerialMgrDelete.html
solaris.admin.usermgr.pswd:::Change User Passwords::help=UserMgrPswd.html
solaris.admin.usermgr.write:::Add, Modify & Delete::help=UserMgrWrite.html
solaris.admin.serialmgr.modify:::Modify Serial Port
  information::help=SerialMgrModify.html
solaris.admin.logsvc.:::Log Viewer::help=LogSvcHeader.html
solaris.admin.usermgr.:::Users, Groups & Mailing Lists::help=UserMgrHeader.html
solaris.admin.hostmgr.write:::Write Computer & Network
  Information::help=HostMgrWrite.html
solaris.admin.logsvc.purge:::Backup & Delete Log Files::help=LogSvcPurge.html
solaris.admin.fsmgr.:::File Systems::help=FsMgrHeader.html
```

Each entry consists of a single line with six fields separated by colons (:). You can continue lines by using the backslash character (\). Each entry has the following form.

```
authname:res1:res2:short_desc:long_desc:attr
```

The fields are described in Table 35.

Table 35 Fields in the auth_attr Database

authname	The name of the authorization as a unique string in the format *prefix*.[*suffix*]. Authorizations for the Solaris Operating Environment use `solaris.` as the prefix. All other authorizations should use a prefix that begins with the reverse-order Internet domain name of the organization that creates the authorization (for example, `com.wellard`). The suffix indicates what is being authorized, which is typically the functional area and operation.
	When *authname* has no suffix (that is, the name consists of a prefix and functional area and ends with a period), the *authname* serves as a heading for use by applications in their GUIs instead of as an authorization. `solaris.printmgr.` is an example of a heading.

Table 35 Fields in the auth_attr Database (Continued)

	When *authname* ends with the word grant, the *authname* serves as a grant authorization and lets the user delegate related authorizations to other users—that is, authorizations with the same prefix and functional area. solaris.printmgr.grant is an example of a grant authorization. It gives the user the right to delegate such authorizations as solaris.printmgr.admin and solaris.printmgr.nobanner to other users.
res1	Reserved for future use.
res2	Reserved for future use.
short_desc	A short name for the authorization that is suitable for display in user interfaces such as in a scrolling list in a GUI.
long_desc	A long description that identifies the purpose of the authorization, the applications in which it is used, and the type of user interested in using it. The long description can be displayed in the help text of an application.
attr	An optional list of semicolon-separated (;) key-value pairs that describe the attributes of an authorization. You can specify zero or more keys. You can use the help= keyword to identify an HTML help file. A Web browser can read the help file with the following URL. file:/usr/lib/help/auths/locale/C/index.html

Examples of auth_attr Database Entries

The following example shows a portion of the default auth_attr database.

```
solaris.admin.usermgr.:::Users, Groups & Mailing
 Lists::help=UserMgrHeader.html
```

When the authorization is defined in the auth_attr database, you can then assign it to a user in the user_attr database. The following example assigns the authorization solaris.admin.usermgr. to user winsor.

```
winsor:::type=normal;auths=solaris.admin.usermgr.;roles=sysadmin;profiles=All
```

Execution Profiles (prof_attr)

With execution profiles, you can group authorizations and commands with special attributes and assign them to users or roles. The special attributes include real and effective UIDs and GIDs. The most common attribute is to set the real or effective UID to root. Definitions of execution profiles are stored in the `prof_attr` database.

`/etc/security/prof_attr` is a local source for execution profile names, descriptions, and other attributes of execution profiles. You can use `prof_attr` with other profile sources, including the `prof_attr` NIS map and NIS+ table.

Syntax of the prof_attr Database

The default `/etc/security/prof_attr` database is shown below.

```
#
# Copyright (c) 1999 by Sun Microsystems, Inc. All rights reserved.
#
# /etc/security/prof_attr
#
# profiles attributes. see prof_attr(4)
#
#pragma ident     "@(#)prof_attr     1.2     99/07/12 SMI"
#
All:::Standard Solaris user:help=All.html
Audit Control:::Administer the audit
 subsystem:auths=solaris.audit.config,solaris.jobs.admin;help=AuditControl.ht
 ml
Audit Review:::View the audit
 trail:auths=solaris.audit.read;help=AuditReview.html
Device Management:::Control Access to Removable
 Media:auths=solaris.device.*;help=DevMgmt.html
Printer Management:::Control Access to Printer:help=PrinterMgmt.html
```

Each entry consists of a single line with five fields separated by colons (:). You can continue lines by using the backslash character (\). Each entry has the following form.

```
profname:res1:res2:desc:attr
```

The fields are described in Table 36.

Table 36 Fields in the prof_attr Database

profname	The name of the profile. Profile names are case sensitive.
res1	Reserved for future use.
res2	Reserved for future use.

Table 36 Fields in the prof_attr Database (Continued)

desc	A long description that explains the purpose of the profile, including what type of user would be interested in using it. The long description should be suitable for display in the help text of an application.	
attr	An optional list of semicolon-separated(;) key-value pairs that describe the security attributes to apply to the object when it is executed. You can specify zero or more keys. The two valid keys are `help` and `auths`.	
	`help`	Assign the name of a file ending in `.htm` or `.html`.
	`auths`	Specify a comma-separated list of authorization names chosen from those names defined in the `auth_attr`(4) database. You can specify authorization names with the asterisk (`*`) character as a wildcard. For example, `solaris.printer.*` means all Sun authorizations for printing.

Examples of prof_attr Database Entries

The following example shows the Device Management portion of the default `prof_attr` database. All authorizations beginning with the `solaris.device` string are assigned to it.

```
Device Management:::Control Access to Removable
 Media:auths=solaris.device.*;help=DevMgmt.html
```

The Device Management profile, which is defined in the `prof_attr` database, is assigned to the `sysadmin` role in the `user_attr` database, as shown below.

```
root::::type=normal;auths=solaris.*,solaris.grant;profiles=All
advanced::::type=role;profiles=Device Management,Printer Management
```

These authorizations are defined in the auth_attr database, as shown in the extract below.

```
#
solaris.device.:::Device Allocation::help=DevAllocHeader.html
solaris.device.allocate:::Allocate Device::help=DevAllocate.html
solaris.device.config:::Configure Device Attributes::help=DevConfig.html
solaris.device.grant:::Delegate Device Administration::help=DevGrant.html
solaris.device.revoke:::Revoke or Reclaim Device::help=DevRevoke.html
```

Execution Attributes (exec_attr)

An execution attribute associated with a profile is a command with any special security attributes that can be run by those users or roles to whom the profile is assigned. Special security attributes refer to such attributes as UID, EUID, GID, and EGID that can be added to a process when the command is run.

Syntax of the exec_attr Database

Definitions of executions attributes are stored in the /etc/security/exec_attr database. The default exec_attr database is shown below.

```
#
# Copyright (c) 1999 by Sun Microsystems, Inc. All rights reserved.
#
# /etc/security/exec_attr
#
# execution attributes for profiles. see exec_attr(4)
#
#pragma ident     "@(#)exec_attr     1.2     99/07/12 SMI"
#
#
All:suser:cmd:::*:
Audit Control:suser:cmd:::/etc/init.d/audit:euid=0;egid=3
Audit Control:suser:cmd:::/etc/security/bsmconv:uid=0
Audit Control:suser:cmd:::/etc/security/bsmunconv:uid=0
Audit Control:suser:cmd:::/usr/sbin/audit:euid=0
Audit Control:suser:cmd:::/usr/sbin/auditconfig:euid=0
Audit Control:suser:cmd:::/usr/sbin/auditd:uid=0
Audit Review:suser:cmd:::/usr/sbin/auditreduce:euid=0
Audit Review:suser:cmd:::/usr/sbin/praudit:euid=0
Audit Review:suser:cmd:::/usr/sbin/auditstat:euid=0
Printer Management:suser:cmd:::/etc/init.d/lp:euid=0
Printer Management:suser:cmd:::/usr/bin/cancel:euid=0
Printer Management:suser:cmd:::/usr/bin/lpset:egid=14
Printer Management:suser:cmd:::/usr/bin/enable:euid=lp
Printer Management:suser:cmd:::/usr/bin/disable:euid=lp
Printer Management:suser:cmd:::/usr/sbin/accept:euid=lp
Printer Management:suser:cmd:::/usr/sbin/reject:euid=lp
Printer Management:suser:cmd:::/usr/sbin/lpadmin:egid=14
Printer Management:suser:cmd:::/usr/sbin/lpfilter:euid=lp
Printer Management:suser:cmd:::/usr/sbin/lpforms:euid=lp
Printer Management:suser:cmd:::/usr/sbin/lpmove:euid=lp
Printer Management:suser:cmd:::/usr/sbin/lpshut:euid=lp
Printer Management:suser:cmd:::/usr/sbin/lpusers:euid=lp
```

Each entry consists of a single line with seven fields separated by colons (:). You can continue lines by using the backslash character (\). Each entry has the following form.

```
name:policy:type:res1:res2:id:attr
```

The fields are described in Table 37.

Table 37 Fields in the exec_attr Database

name	The name of the profile. Profile names are case sensitive.
policy	The security policy associated with this entry. Currently, `suser`—the superuser policy model—is the only valid policy entry.
type	The type of entry whose attributes are specified. Currently, `cmd`—command—is the only valid type.
res1	Reserved for future use.
res2	Reserved for future use.
id	A string identifying the entity. You can use the asterisk wildcard character. Commands should have the full path or a path with a wildcard character, To specify arguments, write a script with the arguments and point *id* to the script.
attr	An optional list of semicolon-separated (;) key-value pairs that describe the security attributes to apply to the entity when it is executed. You can specify zero or more keys. The list of valid keywords depends on the policy being enforced. `euid`, `uid`, `egid`, and `gid` are the four valid keys.
	`euid` and `uid` contain a single user name or a numeric user ID. Commands designated with `euid` run with the effective UID indicated, which is similar to setting the setuid bit on an executable file. Commands designated with `uid` run with both the real and effective UIDs.
	`egid` and `gid` contain a single group name or numeric group ID. Commands designated with `egid` run with the effective GID indicated, which is similar to setting the setgid bit on an executable file. Commands designated with `gid` run with both the real and effective GIDs.

Examples of exec_attr Database Entries

The following example shows the Printer Management profile defined in the prof_attr database.

```
Printer Management:::Control Access to Printer:help=PrinterMgmt.html
```

The Printer Management profile has 13 execution attributes with the appropriate security attributes assigned to it in the exec_attr database, as shown below.

```
Printer Management:suser:cmd:::/etc/init.d/lp:euid=0
Printer Management:suser:cmd:::/usr/bin/cancel:euid=0
Printer Management:suser:cmd:::/usr/bin/lpset:egid=14
Printer Management:suser:cmd:::/usr/bin/enable:euid=lp
Printer Management:suser:cmd:::/usr/bin/disable:euid=lp
Printer Management:suser:cmd:::/usr/sbin/accept:euid=lp
Printer Management:suser:cmd:::/usr/sbin/reject:euid=lp
Printer Management:suser:cmd:::/usr/sbin/lpadmin:egid=14
Printer Management:suser:cmd:::/usr/sbin/lpfilter:euid=lp
Printer Management:suser:cmd:::/usr/sbin/lpforms:euid=lp
Printer Management:suser:cmd:::/usr/sbin/lpmove:euid=lp
Printer Management:suser:cmd:::/usr/sbin/lpshut:euid=lp
Printer Management:suser:cmd:::/usr/sbin/lpusers:euid=lp
```

Commands for Managing Role-Based Access Control

Direct editing of the databases is not recommended. Instead, you can use the commands listed in Table 38 to manage role-based access control.

Table 38 Commands for Managing Role-Based Access Control

Command	Description
auths(1)	Display authorizations for a user.
makedbm(1M)	Make a dbm file.
ncsd(1M)	Nameservice cache daemon. This daemon is useful for caching the user_attr, prof_attr, and exec_attr databases.
pam_roles(5)	Role account management module for PAM. Checks for the authorization to assume a role.

Table 38 Commands for Managing Role-Based Access Control (Continued)

Command	Description
pfexec(1) pfsh(1) pfcsh(1) pfksh(1)	Profile shells, used to execute commands with attributes specified in the exec_attr database.
policy.conf(4)	Configuration file for security policy. Lists granted authorizations.
profiles(1)	Display profiles for a specified user.
roles(1)	Display roles granted to a user.
roleadd(1M)	Add a role account on the system.
roledel(1M)	Delete a role's account from the system.
rolemod(1M)	Modify a role's account information on the system.
useradd(1M)	Add a user account on the system. The -P option assigns a policy, the -R option assigns a role, the -A option assigns an authorization.
userdel(1M)	Delete a user's login from the system.
usermod(1M)	Modify a user's account information on the system. The -P option modifies a policy, the -R option modifies a role, the -A option modifies an authorization.

How to Create a Role

Use the following steps to create a role. The example creates a role named `usracct` that grants authorization to administer user accounts for the `solaris.admin.usermgr*` profiles.

NOTE. For this example to work, you must have AdminSuite 3.0 installed on your system. The `solaris.admin` *authorizations are added when AdminSuite 3.0 is installed as part of the Solaris Management Console.*

1. Become superuser.
2. Type **`roleadd -D`** and press Return.

   The default settings for the `roleadd` command are displayed, as shown in the following example.

```
# roleadd -D
group=other,1  basedir=/home  skel=/etc/skel
shell=/bin/pfsh  inactive=0  expire=  auths=
profiles=All
#
```

3. Use **`roleadd -d`** with any or all of the `-g`, `-b`, `-f`, or `-e` options to change the default values.

   Any subsequent roles that you create in this session with the `roleadd` command use these values.
4. Look in the `/etc/security/auth_attr` file and write down the authorization(s) that you want to assign to this role.

   This example grants authorization to the `solaris.admin.usermgr.pswd` and `solaris.admin.usermgr.write` profiles.
5. Look in the `/etc/security/prof_attr` file and write down the profiles that you want to assign to this role.
6. Type **`roleadd -c "comment" -s`** ***`shell`*** **`-A`** ***`authorization`*** **`-P`** ***`profile role`*** and press Return.

   The following example creates the `usracct` role and sets `/bin/pfcsh` as the default shell.

```
# roleadd -c "User Account Management" -s /bin/pfcsh  -A
 solaris.admin.usermgr.pswd,solaris.admin.usermgr.write -P "User Account
 Management" usracct
#
```

The following entry is added to the `/etc/passwd` file.

```
usracct:x:1007:1:User Account Management:/home/usracct:/bin/pfcsh
```

The following entry is added to the `/etc/shadow` file.

```
usracct:*LK*:::::::
```

The following entry is added to the /etc/user_attr file.

```
usracct::::type=role;auths=solaris.admin.usermgr.pswd,solaris.admin.usermgr.wr
  ite;profiles=User Account Management
```

7. Type **passwd *role*** and press Return. Type a password for the role two times, as prompted.

   The password is assigned to the role. The following example sets a password for the usracct role.

```
# passwd usracct
New password:
Re-enter new password:
passwd (SYSTEM): passwd successfully changed for usracct
#
```

   At this point, any user who knows the usracct password can log in to AdminSuite by using the usracct role name and password and can create and modify user accounts.

8. Edit /etc/user_attr and add the following line.

```
username::::type=normal;auths=authorization;roles=role;profiles=prof
```

   The following example assigns the usracct role to user winsor.

```
winsor::::type=normal;auths=solaris.admin.usermgr.pswd,solaris.admin.usermgr.w
  rite;roles=usracct;profiles=All
```

Using AdminSuite 3.0 to Grant Access Rights to Users

AdminSuite 3.0 enables you to assign a subset of superuser rights to individual users with the Users: User Accounts tool. You can grant or deny individual rights, enable all rights, or disable all rights. When rights are granted, users have superuser access to the commands and tools associated with the set of rights that you grant. See “Accessing Solaris AdminSuite 3.0” on page 79 for instructions on the download URL and how to access AdminSuite.

The list of rights you can grant are listed below.

- Audit Management
    - Configure Auditing
    - Read Audit Trail
- Device Allocation
    - Allocate Device
    - Configure Device Attributes
    - Delegate Device Administration
    - Revoke or Reclaim Device
- Cron and At Jobs
    - Cron & At Administrator
    - Delegate Cron & At Administration
    - Create At or Cron Jobs
- Login Control
    - Enable Logins
    - Remote Login
- Execution Profile Management
    - Assign Profiles to Users or Roles
    - Create, Modify, Delete Profiles
- Role Management
    - Assign Roles to Users
    - Add, Modify, Delete Roles
- Machine Administration
    - Set Date and Time
    - Shut Down the System
- File Systems
    - Mount/Share File Systems
- Computers/Networks
    - Write Computer & Network Information
- Log Viewer
    - Back Up & Delete Log Files
    - Change Log Settings
- Serial Ports
    - Delete Serial Ports
    - Modify Serial Port Information

- Users, Groups, & Mailing Lists
    - Change User Passwords
    - Add, Modify, & Delete

Use the following steps to grant access rights to users.

NOTE. You must log in as root, as a role login that grants all access rights or as a user who has been given the `grant` *authorization to be able to grant access rights to user accounts.*

Use the following steps to grant user rights with the AdminSuite User Accounts window.

1. Refer to "Accessing Solaris AdminSuite 3.0" on page 79 for instructions on how to access the AdminSuite 3.0 window shown in Figure 45.

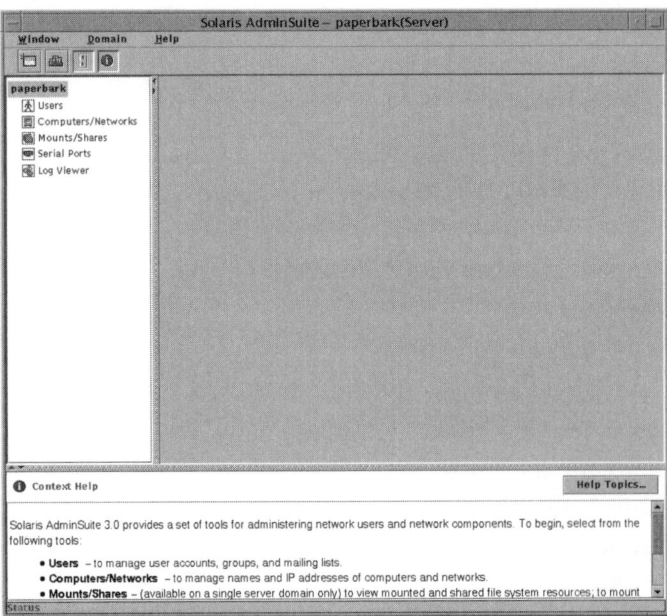

Figure 45 AdminSuite Window

2. Click on the Users folder in the navigation pane.

    The contents of the Users folder are displayed in the right pane, as shown in Figure 46.

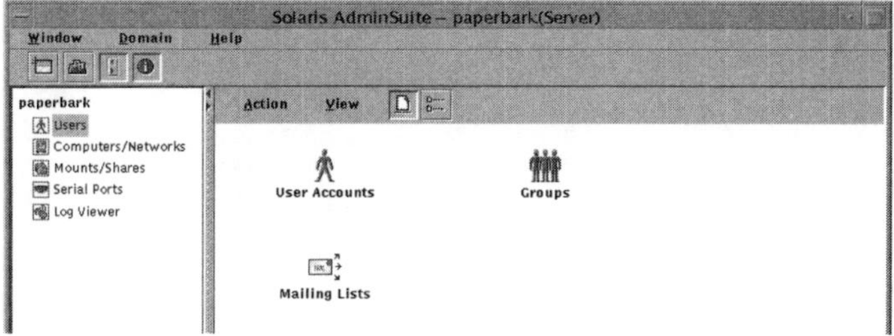

Figure 46 Contents of the Users Folder

3. Double-click on the User Accounts icon.

   The Set Initial View window is displayed the first time you enter the User Accounts tool, as shown in Figure 47.

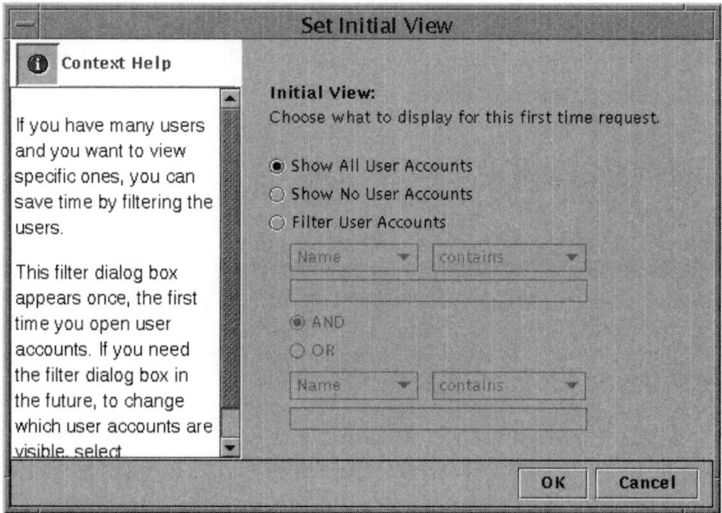

Figure 47 Set Initial View Window

4. Use the Set Initial View window to filter the amount of information displayed in the User Accounts tool. Choose the filtering you want and click on the OK button.

   If you have many users, you may want to display only a partial set of your user list. If you want to filter subsequent views, choose Filter from the View menu. All users on the system `paperbark` are displayed in Figure 48.

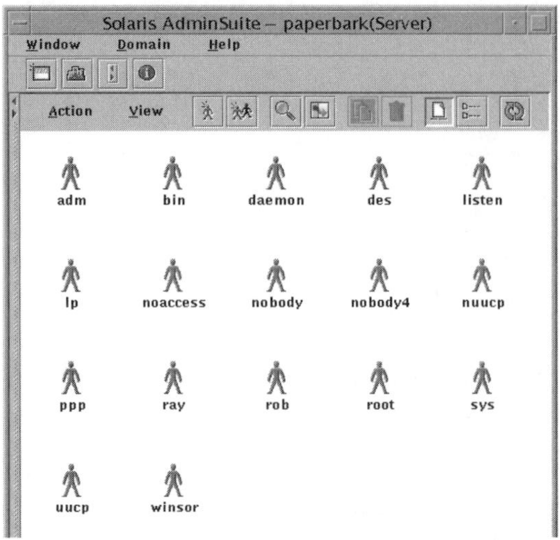

Figure 48 User Accounts

5. Double-click on the icon for a user account.

   The user properties for that user are displayed, as shown in Figure 49.

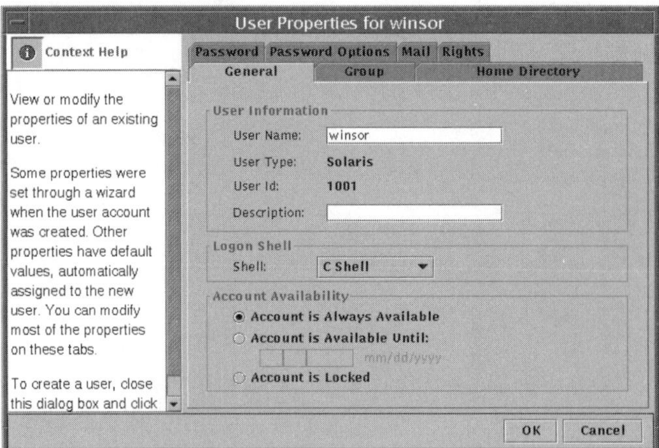

Figure 49 User Properties for User winsor

6. Click on the Rights tab at the right of the top row of tabs.

   The list of rights is displayed, as shown in Figure 50.

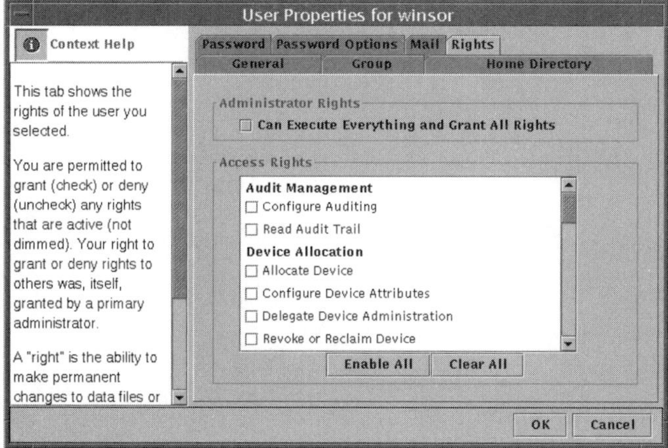

Figure 50 User Properties for User winsor

7. Scroll through the list and click on the check box to assign individual rights. Alternatively, you can click on the Enable All button at the bottom of the scrolling list to assign all rights to the user. To remove rights, click on the Clear All button.
8. When you have chosen the rights to assign to the user, click on the OK button.

   The User Properties window is closed, and the rights you checked are assigned to the user.

6

Administering File Systems

A file system is a structure of directories used to locate and store files. The term *file system* is used in several different ways.

- To describe the entire file tree from the root directory downward.
- To describe a particular type of file system: disk-based, network-based, or virtual.
- To describe the data structure of a disk slice or other media storage device.
- To describe a portion of a file tree structure that is attached to a mount point on the main file tree so that a portion is accessible.

Usually, you can tell from context which meaning is intended.

The Solaris system software uses the *virtual file system (VFS)* architecture, which provides a standard interface for different file-system types. The *kernel* handles basic operations—such as reading, writing, and listing files—without requiring the user or program to know about the underlying file-system type.

The file-system administrative commands provide a common interface that enables you to maintain file systems of different types. These commands have two components: a generic component and a component specific to each type of file system. The generic commands apply to most types of file systems; the specific commands apply to only one type of file system.

Administering the Solaris file system is one of your most important system administration tasks. The file-system story is a complex one, and understanding it can help you more effectively administer file systems. This chapter describes the following topics.

- The types of file systems.
- The default Solaris file system.
- The virtual file-system table (/etc/vfstab).
- The file-system administrative commands.
- Making local and remote files available to users.
- Backing up and restoring file systems.

New! What's New in File Systems in the Solaris 7 Release

The Solaris 7 release provides two new file-system features.

- UFS logging.
- A new `mount` command option to ignore access time updates on files.

See "Understanding Mounting and Unmounting" on page 216 for more information.

New! What's New in File Systems in the Solaris 8 Release

The Solaris 8 release provides the following new file-system features.

- The TMPFS file system provides a /var/run repository for temporary system files. See "The Temporary File System (TMPFS)" on page 201 for more information.
- The /etc/mnttab file is no longer a text-based file. Instead, it is an MNTFS file system that provides read-only information directly from the kernel about mounted file system for the local system. See "The /etc/mnttab File System (MNTFS)" on page 204 for more information.
- The UDF file system, the industry-standard format for storing information on optical media technology called Digital Versatile Disc or Digital Video Disc (DVD), is included in this release. See "Disk-Based File Systems" on page 199 for more information.
- The `-F xmemfs` option to the `mount` command is new in the Solaris 8 release. XMEMFS is an IA-platform extended-memory file system that provides file-system semantics to manage and access large amounts of physical memory that can exceed 4 Gbytes in size. See "Understanding Mounting and Unmounting" on page 216 for more information.

Types of File Systems

The Solaris Operating Environment supports three types of file systems.

- Disk-based.
- Network-based.
- Virtual (previously called pseudo).

Disk-Based File Systems

Disk-based file systems are stored on physical media such as hard disks, CD-ROMs, diskettes, and DVD discs. Disk-based file systems can be written in different formats. The following list describes the available formats. New!

- UFS—UNIX file system (based on the BSD Fat Fast File system that was provided in the 4.3 Tahoe release). The default disk-based file system in Solaris system software is UFS. Before you can create a file system on a disk, the disk must be formatted and divided into slices (partitions).
- S5FS—IA UNIX file system (based on the BSD Fat Fast File system that was provided in the 4.3 Tahoe release). The default disk-based file system in Solaris IA system software is S5FS.
- HSFS—High Sierra and ISO 9660 file system. High Sierra is the first CD-ROM file system; ISO 9660 is the official standard. The HSFS file system is used on CD-ROM and is a read-only file system. The Solaris HSFS supports Rock Ridge extensions to ISO 9660, which provide all UFS file-system semantics and file types except for writeability and hard links.
- PCFS—The PC file system allows read/write access to data and programs on DOS-formatted diskettes written for DOS-based personal computers.
- UDFS—Universal Disk Format file system, new in the Solaris 8 release, is the industry-standard format for storing information on the optical media technology called DVD (Digital Versatile Disc or Digital Video Disc). See “Using DVD-ROM Devices” on page 244 for more information. New!

  UDFS support is provided in the following new packages.

  - `SUNWudfr`—32-bit kernel component.
  - `SUNWudfrx`—64-bit kernel component.
  - `SUNWudf`—`/usr` component.

  The Solaris UDF file system provides the following features.

- Access to industry-standard CD-ROM and DVD-ROM media when they contain a UDF file system.
- Flexibility in exchanging information across platforms and operating systems.
- A mechanism for implementing, according to the DVD video specification based on the UDF format, new applications that offer broadcast-quality video, high-quality sound, and interactivity.

This UDF release does not contain the following features.

- Support for write-once media, CD-RW, and DVD-RAM, with either the sequential disk-at-once and incremental recording.
- UFS components such as quotas, ACLs, transaction logging, file-system locking, and file-system threads. These components are not part of the UDF 1.50 specification.

The System V (S5) file system traditionally provided with System V releases is not included in the Solaris Operating Environment because of significant limitations, such as a maximum of 64,000 files in a file system, a restriction of 14 characters for file names, and lack of a quota facility.

Each type of disk-based file system is customarily associated with a particular media device.

- UFS and S5FS with hard disk and any other media (tape, CD-ROM, diskette).
- HSFS with CD-ROM.
- PCFS with diskette.
- New! UDF with DVD.

These associations are not, however, restrictive. For example, CD-ROMs and diskettes can have UFS file systems installed on them.

Network-Based File Systems

Network-based file systems are file systems that are accessed over the network. Typically, network-based file systems are file systems that reside on one system and are accessed by other systems across the network. The available network-based file systems is the NFS network, or distributed file system.

With NFS you can administer distributed resources (files or directories) by sharing them (exporting them from a server) and mounting them on individual systems. See “Making File Systems Available” on page 215 for more information.

NOTE. Support for the RFS—remote file sharing—file-system type has been removed in the Solaris 8 release. New!

Virtual File Systems

Virtual file systems (previously called pseudo file systems) are virtual or memory-based file systems that provide access to special kernel information and facilities. Most virtual file systems do not use file-system disk space. Some virtual file systems, such as the temporary file system, may, however, use the swap space on a physical disk. Cache file systems use a file system on the disk to contain the cache.

The Cache File System (CacheFS)

You can use the Cache File System to improve performance of remote file systems or slow devices such as CD-ROM drives. When a file system is cached, the data read from the remote file system or CD-ROM is stored in a cache on the local system. See "Cache File Systems" on page 235 for more information.

The Temporary File System (TMPFS)

The TMPFS file system uses local memory for disk reads and writes. Access to files in a TMPFS file system is typically much faster than access to files in a UFS file system. Files in the TMPFS file system are not permanent. They are deleted when the file system is unmounted and when the system is shut down or rebooted.

TMPFS is the default file-system type for the `/tmp` directory in the Solaris Operating Environment. You can copy or move files into or out of the `/tmp` directory, just as you would in a UFS `/tmp` file system.

TMPFS file systems can improve system performance by saving the cost of reading and writing temporary files to a local disk or across the network. For example, temporary files are created when you compile a program. The operating system generates a lot of disk or network input and output activity while manipulating these files. Using TMPFS file systems to hold these temporary files can significantly speed up their creation, manipulation, and deletion.

The TMPFS file system uses swap space as a temporary storage area. If a system with a TMPFS file system does not have adequate swap space, two problems can occur.

- The TMPFS file system can run out of space, just as a regular file system can fill up.

- Because TMPFS allocates swap space to save file data (if necessary), some programs may not be able to execute because there is not enough swap space.

See Chapter 8, "Administering Systems," for information about increasing swap space.

The Loopback File System (LOFS)

The LOFS file system lets you create a new virtual file system. You can access files through an alternative path name. For example, you can create a loopback mount of / onto `/tmp/newroot`. The entire file-system hierarchy looks like it is duplicated under `/tmp/newroot`, including any file systems that were mounted from NFS servers. All files are accessible either with a path name starting from / or with a path name starting from `/tmp/newroot` until a different file system is mounted in `/tmp/newroot` or any of its subdirectories.

The Process File System (PROCFS)

The PROCFS file system resides in memory. It contains a list of active processes, by number, in the `/proc` directory. Information in the `/proc` directory is used by commands such as `ps`. Debuggers and other development tools can also access the address space of the processes by using file-system calls. The following example shows a listing of the contents of the `/proc` directory.

```
paperbark% ls -l /proc
total 128
dr-x--x--x   5 root      root          736 May 11 08:45 0
dr-x--x--x   5 root      root          736 May 11 08:45 1
dr-x--x--x   5 root      root          736 May 11 08:46 108
dr-x--x--x   5 root      root          736 May 11 08:46 125
dr-x--x--x   5 root      root          736 May 11 08:46 155
dr-x--x--x   5 root      root          736 May 11 08:46 161
dr-x--x--x   5 daemon    daemon        736 May 11 08:46 165
dr-x--x--x   5 root      root          736 May 11 08:46 168
dr-x--x--x   5 root      root          736 May 11 08:46 179
dr-x--x--x   5 root      root          736 May 11 08:46 185
dr-x--x--x   5 root      root          736 May 11 08:46 195
dr-x--x--x   5 root      root          736 May 11 08:45 2
dr-x--x--x   5 root      root          736 May 11 08:46 200
dr-x--x--x   5 root      root          736 May 11 08:46 213
dr-x--x--x   5 root      root          736 May 11 08:46 222
dr-x--x--x   5 root      root          736 May 11 08:46 225
dr-x--x--x   5 root      root          736 May 11 08:46 227
dr-x--x--x   5 daemon    other         736 May 11 08:46 241
dr-x--x--x   5 daemon    other         736 May 11 08:46 242
dr-x--x--x   5 root      root          736 May 11 08:46 275
dr-x--x--x   5 root      root          736 May 11 08:45 3
dr-x--x--x   5 root      root          736 May 11 08:46 304
dr-x--x--x   5 root      root          736 May 11 08:46 317
dr-x--x--x   5 root      root          736 May 11 08:46 323
dr-x--x--x   5 root      root          736 May 11 08:46 324
dr-x--x--x   5 root      root          736 May 11 08:46 333
dr-x--x--x   5 root      root          736 May 11 08:46 336
dr-x--x--x   5 root      root          736 May 11 08:46 337
dr-x--x--x   5 root      staff         736 May 11 08:46 340
dr-x--x--x   5 root      root          736 May 11 08:46 346
dr-x--x--x   5 root      root          736 May 11 08:46 349
dr-x--x--x   5 root      root          736 May 11 08:46 350
```

```
dr-x--x--x   5 root      root        736 May 11 08:46 357
dr-x--x--x   5 root      root        736 May 11 08:47 370
dr-x--x--x   5 winsor    staff       736 May 11 08:47 375
dr-x--x--x   5 winsor    staff       736 May 11 08:47 385
dr-x--x--x   5 winsor    staff       736 May 11 08:47 389
dr-x--x--x   5 winsor    staff       736 May 11 08:47 421
dr-x--x--x   5 winsor    staff       736 May 11 08:47 422
dr-x--x--x   5 winsor    staff       736 May 11 08:47 424
dr-x--x--x   5 winsor    staff       736 May 11 08:47 439
dr-x--x--x   5 root      root        736 May 11 08:45 44
dr-x--x--x   5 winsor    staff       736 May 11 08:47 440
dr-x--x--x   5 root      root        736 May 11 08:47 441
dr-x--x--x   5 winsor    staff       736 May 11 08:47 447
dr-x--x--x   5 winsor    staff       736 May 11 08:47 449
dr-x--x--x   5 winsor    staff       736 May 11 08:47 450
dr-x--x--x   5 winsor    staff       736 May 11 08:47 451
dr-x--x--x   5 winsor    staff       736 May 11 08:47 452
dr-x--x--x   5 winsor    staff       736 May 11 08:47 453
dr-x--x--x   5 winsor    staff       736 May 11 08:47 455
dr-x--x--x   5 root      root        736 May 11 08:45 46
dr-x--x--x   5 winsor    staff       736 May 11 08:48 461
dr-x--x--x   5 winsor    staff       736 May 11 08:48 462
dr-x--x--x   5 winsor    staff       736 May 11 08:48 463
dr-x--x--x   5 winsor    staff       736 May 11 08:48 464
dr-x--x--x   5 winsor    staff       736 May 11 08:48 466
dr-x--x--x   5 root      root        736 May 11 08:48 468
dr-x--x--x   5 winsor    staff       736 May 11 08:48 470
dr-x--x--x   5 winsor    staff       736 May 11 08:48 473
dr-x--x--x   5 winsor    staff       736 May 11 08:48 476
dr-x--x--x   5 winsor    staff       736 May 11 08:48 483
dr-x--x--x   5 winsor    staff       736 May 11 08:48 486
dr-x--x--x   5 winsor    staff       736 May 11 09:36 521
paperbark%
```

CAUTION. Do not delete the files in the `/proc` *directory. Deleting processes from the* `/proc` *directory is not the recommended way to kill them. See Chapter 1, "Introducing Solaris System Administration," for information on how to kill a process. Remember,* `/proc` *files do not use disk space, so there is little reason to delete files from this directory.*

The `/proc` directory does not require any system administration.

Enhancements to the /proc File System and Watchpoints Starting with the Solaris 2.6 release, the flat `/proc` file system is restructured into a directory hierarchy that contains additional subdirectories for state information and control functions. It also provides a watchpoint facility that remaps read/write permissions on the individual pages of the address space of a process. This facility has no restrictions and is multithread (MT) safe.

The new `/proc` file structure provides complete binary compatibility with the old `/proc` interface except that the new watchpoint facility cannot be used with the old interface. Debugging tools have been modified to use the new `/proc` watchpoint facility, which means the entire watchpoint process is faster.

The following restrictions no longer apply to setting watchpoints with the `dbx` debugging tool.

- Setting watchpoints on local variables on the stack because of SPARC register windows.
- Setting watchpoints on multithreaded processes.

For more information, refer to the `proc`(4), `core`(4), and `adb`(4) manual pages.

The `/proc` directory does not require system administration.

New!

The /etc/mnttab File System (MNTFS)

The system modifies the `/etc/mnttab` (mount table) whenever you mount or unmount a file system. In previous Solaris releases, the `/etc/mnttab` mount table was a text-based file that stored information about mounted file systems. This file could get out of sync with the state of mounted file systems.

In the Solaris 8 release, `/etc/mnttab` is a MNTFS file system that provides read-only information directly from the kernel about mounted file systems for the local system.

Because of this structural difference, the following `mnttab` behavior is changed.

- Programs or scripts cannot write to `/etc/mnttab`.
- The `mount -m` option for faking `mnttab` entries no longer works.

MNTFS requires no administration. See `mnttab`(4) for more information.

You can display the contents of the `/etc/mnttab` file with the `cat` or `more` commands, but you cannot edit it. The following example shows an `/etc/mnttab` file. You can use the `grep` command to search for specific entries in the `/etc/mnttab` file.

```
paperbark% more /etc/mnttab
/dev/dsk/c0t0d0s0       /       ufs
  rw,intr,largefiles,onerror=panic,suid,de
v=800000        958013089
/proc   /proc   proc    dev=2d80000     958013088
fd      /dev/fd fd      rw,suid,dev=2e40000     958013090
mnttab  /etc/mnttab     mntfs   dev=2f40000     958013092
swap    /var/run        tmpfs   dev=1   958013092
swap    /tmp    tmpfs   dev=2   958013094
/dev/dsk/c0t0d0s7       /export/home    ufs
  rw,intr,largefiles,onerror=panic
,suid,dev=800007        958013094
/dev/dsk/c0t1d0s7       /export/home0   ufs
  rw,intr,largefiles,onerror=panic
,suid,dev=80000f        958013094
-hosts  /net    autofs  indirect,nosuid,ignore,nobrowse,dev=3000001
  95801311
8
auto_home       /home   autofs  indirect,ignore,nobrowse,dev=3000002
  95801311
8
-xfn    /xfn    autofs  indirect,ignore,dev=3000003     958013118
paperbark:vold(pid228)  /vol    nfs     ignore,dev=2fc0001      958013123
paperbark%
```

Additional Virtual File Systems

The following additional types of virtual file systems are listed for your information. They do not require administration.

- FIFOS (first-in first-out)—Named pipe files that give processes common access to data.
- FDFS (file descriptors)—Provides explicit names for opening files using file descriptors.
- NAMEFS—Used mostly by STREAMS for dynamic mounts of file descriptors on top of files.
- SPECFS (special)—Provides access to special character and block devices.
- SWAPFS—File system used by the kernel when you create additional swap space with the `mkfile` and `swap` commands.

The Default Solaris File System

The Solaris file system is hierarchical, starting with the root directory (/) and continuing downward through a number of directories. The Solaris Operating Environment installs a default set of directories and uses a set of conventions to group similar types of files together. Table 39 describes the default Solaris file system and shows the type of each file system.

Table 39 The Default Solaris File System

Directory	File-System Type	Description
`/`	`ufs`	The top of the hierarchical file tree. The root directory contains the directories and files critical for system operation, such as the kernel (`/kernel/unix`), the device drivers, and the programs used to start (boot) the system. It also contains the mount point directories where local and remote file systems can be attached to the file tree.
`/etc/mnttab`	`mntfs`	Read-only information provided directly from the kernel about mounted file systems for the local system. New in the Solaris 8 Operating Environment.

New!

Table 39 The Default Solaris File System (Continued)

Directory	File-System Type	Description
`/usr`	`ufs`	System files and directories that can be shared with other users. Files that run only on certain types of systems are in the `/usr` directory (for example, SPARC executables). Files (such as manual pages) that can be used on all types of systems are in `/usr/share`.
`/export/home` or `/home`	`NFS, ufs`	The mount point for the users' home directories, which store users' work files. By default, `/home` is an automounted file system. On stand-alone systems, `/home` may be a UFS file system on a local disk slice.
`/var`	`ufs`	System files and directories that are likely to change or grow over the life of the local system. These include system logs, `vi` and `ex` backup files, `uucp` files, and mail and calendar files.
`/opt`	`NFS, ufs`	Mount point for optional, third-party software. On some systems, `/opt` can be a `ufs` file system on a local disk slice.
`/tmp`	`tmpfs`	Temporary files, cleared each time the system is booted or unmounted.
`/proc`	`procfs`	A list of active system processes, by number.

The root (`/`) and `/usr` file systems are both needed to run a system. Some of the most basic commands from the `/usr` file system (such as `mount`) are included in the root file system so that they are available when the system boots or is in single-user mode.

The Virtual File-System Table (/etc/vfstab)

Each system has a virtual file-system table, `/etc/vfstab`, that lists all the disk slices and file systems available to the system. The file-system table also specifies the mount point and options for each file system. In the SunOS 4.x system software, the file-system table is called /etc/fstab. The /etc/vfstab file replaces /etc/fstab and functions in a similar manner. The default file-system configuration table (the /etc/vfstab file) depends on the selections made for each system when system software was installed. You should edit the /etc/vfstab file for each system to automatically mount local UFS file systems, essential NFS file systems, and any other appropriate file systems.

This section describes the contents of the /etc/vfstab file and provides information on how to edit and use the file. The file-system table is an ASCII file. Comment lines begin with #. The following example shows an /etc/vfstab file for a system with two disks.

```
castle% more /etc/vfstab
#device         device          mount           FS      fsck    mount   mount
#to mount       to fsck         point           type    pass    at boot options
#
#/dev/dsk/c1d0s2 /dev/rdsk/c1d0s2 /usr          ufs     1       yes     -
fd      -       /dev/fd fd      -       no      -
/proc   -       /proc   proc    -       no      -
/dev/dsk/c0t3d0s1       -       -       swap    -       no      -
/dev/dsk/c0t3d0s0       /dev/rdsk/c0t3d0s0      /       ufs     1       no      -
swap    -       /tmp    tmpfs   -       yes     -
castle%
```

Refer to "Disk-Naming Conventions" on page 287 for information on disk device naming conventions.

Note that, for / and /usr, the automount field value is specified as no because these file systems are mounted as part of the boot sequence before the mountall command is run. If the automount field value is specified as yes, the mountall program redundantly (and unnecessarily) tries to mount these already mounted file systems.

The file-system table has seven fields, each separated by a Tab, as described in Table 40.

Table 40 Fields in the /etc/vfstab File

Field	Description
device to mount	The device to mount can be one of the following.
	The block special device for local ufs file systems (for example, /dev/dsk/c0t0d0s0).
	The resource name for remote file systems (for example, myserver:/export/home for an NFS file system).
	The name of the slice on which to swap (for example, /dev/dsk/c0t3d0s1).

Table 40 Fields in the /etc/vfstab File (Continued)

Field	Description
	The `/proc` directory and proc file-system type.
	`CD-ROM` as HSFS file-system type.
	`/dev/diskette` as PCFS or UFS file-system type. This field is also used to specify swap file systems.
`device to fsck`	The raw (character) special device that corresponds to the file system identified by the *`special`* field (for example, `/dev/rdsk/c0t0d0s0`). This field determines the raw interface that is used by `fsck`. Use a dash (`-`) when there is no applicable device, such as for a read-only file system or a network-based file system.
`mount point`	The default mount point directory (for example, `/usr` for `/dev/dsk/c0t0d0s6`).
`FS type`	The type of file system identified by the *`special`* field.
`fsck pass*`	The `pass` number used by `fsck` to decide whether to check a file system. When the field contains a dash (`-`), the file system is not checked. When the field contains a value of 1 or more, the file system is checked; non-`ufs` file systems with a zero `fsck` pass are checked. For `ufs` file systems only, when the field contains a zero (`0`), the file system is not checked. When `fsck` is run on multiple `ufs` file systems that have `fsck` pass values greater than 1 and the `preen` option (`-o p`) is used, `fsck` automatically checks the file systems on different disks in parallel to maximize efficiency. When the field contains a value of `1`, the file system is checked sequentially. Otherwise, the value of the pass number has no effect.
`mount at boot`	Indicate `yes` or `no` for whether the file system should be automatically mounted by `mountall` when the system is booted. Note that this field has nothing to do with the automounter software.
`mount options`	A list of comma-separated options (with no spaces) that are used in mounting the file system. Use a dash (`-`) to show no options. See the `mount_`*`file-system-type`*(1M) manual page for a list of the available options.

* In the Solaris Operating Environment, `fsck pass` does not explicitly specify the order in which file systems are checked as it did with SunOS 4.x system software.

NOTE. You must have an entry in each field in the `/etc/vfstab` *file. If there is no value for the field, be sure to enter a dash (–).*

NFS Client Failover

Client *failover*, introduced in the Solaris 2.6 release, provides a high level of availability of read-only file systems by enabling a client to automatically mount the file system from another server if the first server becomes unavailable.

The file system can become unavailable if the server crashes, if the server is overloaded, or if a network faults. The failover in these conditions can occur at any time without disrupting the processes running on the client.

Failover file systems must be mounted read-only. The file systems must be identical for failover to succeed. You cannot use file systems mounted by CacheFS with failover because extra information stored for each CacheFS file system cannot be updated during failover.

When using client failover, you specify additional hosts from which to mount a file system in case the first host cannot be reached. You can specify alternative failover servers in the `/etc/vfstab` file, through the automounter, or from the command line.

The following example shows an `/etc/vfstab` client failover entry.

```
paperbark,castle:/export/share/local  -  /usr/local  nfs  -  no  -o  ro
```

NOTE. You cannot mix servers running different versions of the NFS protocol by using a command line or in an `/etc/vfstab` *entry. You can mix servers supporting NFS V2 and V3 protocols only with* `autofs`*. In this case, client failover uses the best subset of version 2 or version 3 servers.*

The following example uses the `mount` command with client failover.

```
# mount -F nfs -r paperbark,castle:/export/share/man /usr/man
#
```

Creation of an Entry in the File-System Table

Use the following steps to create an entry in the file-system table.

1. Become superuser.
2. Edit the `/etc/vfstab` file using an editor such as `vi`.

3. Add the entry, separating each field with white space (a space or a Tab). If a field has no entry, enter a dash (-).
4. Save the changes.
5. Check to be sure the mount point directory is present. If it's not, create the mount point by changing to the directory where you want to create it, typing **mkdir *directory-name***, and pressing Return.
6. Type **mount *mount-point*** and press Return.

   The entry is mounted.

The following example mounts the disk slice /dev/dsk/c0t3d0s7 as a ufs file system attached to the mount point directory /files1 with the default mount options (read/write). It specifies the raw character device /dev/rdsk/c0t3d0s7 as the device to check with fsck. The fsck pass value of 2 means that the file system is checked, but not sequentially.

```
#device           device              mount    FS    fsck  mount    mount
#to mount         to fsck             point    type  pass  at boot  options
#
/dev/dsk/c0t3d0s7 /dev/rdsk/c0t3d0s7 /files1  ufs   2     yes      -
```

The following example mounts the directory /export/man from the system oak as an nfs file system on mount point /usr/man. You do not specify a device to fsck or a fsck pass for NFS file systems. In the following example, mount options are ro (read-only) and soft. For greater reliability, for read/write NFS file systems, specify the hard mount option (rw,hard).

```
#device           device       mount          FS       fsck     mount     mount
#to mount         to fsck      point          type     pass     at boot   options
oak:/export/man    -           /usr/man       nfs      -        yes      ro,soft
```

The following example mounts a CD-ROM drive on a mount point named /hsfiles. CD-ROM files typically are read-only, so you specify ro for the mount options. Specify no for mount at boot because you are most likely to mount and unmount a CD-ROM from the command line or by using volume management. Because hsfs is read-only, specify no device to fsck and no fsck pass number.

```
#device           device       mount          FS       fsck     mount     mount
#to mount         to fsck      point          type     pass     at boot   options
/dev/dsk/c0t6d0s2 -            /hsfiles       hsfs     -        no        ro
```

The following example mounts the diskette drive on a mount point named /pcfiles. Specify no for mount at boot because you are most likely to mount and unmount a diskette from the command line or by using volume management. Specify no to fsck or fsck pass, because the pcfs file system does not support fsck.

```
#device          device      mount           FS      fsck    mount     mount
#to mount        to fsck     point           type    pass    at boot   options
/dev/diskette    -           /pcfiles        pcfs    -       no        rw
```

The following example mounts the root file system on a loopback mount point named /etc/newroot. Specify yes for automount, no device to fsck, and no fsck pass number. Loopback file systems must always be mounted after the file systems used to make up the loopback file system. Be sure that the loopback entry is the last entry in the /etc/vfstab file so that it follows the entries that depend on it.

```
#device          device      mount           FS      fsck    mount     mount
#to mount        to fsck     point           type    pass    at boot   options
/                -           /tmp/newroot    lofs    -       yes       -
```

File-System Administrative Commands

This section lists the file-system administrative commands and describes the syntax.

Most file-system administrative commands have a generic and a file-system-specific component. Use the generic commands, which use the file-system-specific component. Table 41 lists the generic file-system administrative commands, which are located in the /usr/sbin directory. Most of these commands also have file-system-specific counterparts.

Table 41 Generic File-System Administrative Commands

Command	Description
clri(1M)	Clear inodes.
df(1M)	Report the number of free disk blocks and files.
ff(1M)	List file names and statistics for a file system.
fsck(1M)	Check the integrity of a file system and repair any damage found.
fsdb(1M)	File-system debugger.
fstyp(1M)	Determine the file-system type.
labelit(1M)	List or provide labels for file systems when copied to tape (for use by the volcopy command only).

Table 41 Generic File-System Administrative Commands (Continued)

Command	Description
`mkfs(1M)`	Make a new file system.
`mount(1M)`	Mount file systems and remote resources.
`mountall(1M)`	Mount all file systems specified in a file-system table.
`ncheck(1M)`	Generate a list of path names with their i-numbers.
`umount(1M)`	Unmount file systems and remote resources.
`umountall(1M)`	Unmount all file systems specified in a file-system table.
`volcopy(1M)`	Make an image copy of a file system.

CAUTION. Do not use the file-system–specific commands directly. If you specify an operation on a file system that does not support it, the generic command displays the error message `command: Operation not applicable for FSType type.`

Syntax of Generic Commands

Most of the generic file-system commands use the following syntax.

```
command [-F FStype] [-V][generic-options][-o specific-options]
   [special|mount-point] [operands]
```

The options and arguments to the generic commands are shown in Table 42.

Table 42 Generic File-System Command Syntax

Option	Description
`-F FStype`	Specify the type of file system. If you do not use this option, the command looks for an entry that matches the special, raw device, or mount point field in the `/etc/vfstab` file. Otherwise, the default is taken from the file `/etc/default/fs` for local file systems and from the file `/etc/dfs/fstypes` for remote file systems.
`-V`	Echo the completed command line. The echoed line may include additional information derived from `/etc/vfstab`. Use this option to verify and validate the command line. It does not execute the command.

Table 42 Generic File-System Command Syntax

Option	Description
generic-options	
	Options common to different types of file systems.
-o *specific-options*	
	A list of options specific to the type of file system. The list must have the following format: -o followed by a space, followed by a series of *keyword* [=*value*] pairs separated by commas with no intervening spaces.
special | *mount-point*	
	Identify the file system. Name either the *mount-point* or the *special* device file for the slice holding the file system. For some commands, the *special* file must be the raw (character) device, and for other commands it must be the block device. See Chapter 7, "Administering Devices," for more information about disk device names. In some cases, this argument is used as a key to search the /etc/vfstab file for a matching entry from which to obtain other information. In most cases, this argument is required and must come immediately after *specific-options*. However, it is not required when you want a command to act on all the file systems (optionally limited by type) listed in the /etc/vfstab file.
operands	Arguments specific to a type of file system. See the specific manual page of the command (for example, mkfs_ufs) for a detailed description.

Manual Pages for Generic and Specific Commands

Both the generic and specific commands have manual pages. The specific manual page is a continuation of the generic manual page. To look at a specific manual page, append an underscore and the file-system type abbreviation to the generic command name. For example, to see the specific manual page for mounting an HSFS file system, type **man mount_hsfs** and press Return. LOFS, PCFS, and PROCFS do not have specific manual pages for the mount command.

How File-System Commands Determine File-System Type

The generic file-system commands determine the file-system type with the following sequence.

1. From `-F`, if supplied.
2. By matching a special device with an entry in `/etc/vfstab` (if *`special`* is supplied). For example, `fsck` first looks for a match against the `fsck device` field; if no match is found, it then checks against the *`special`* device field.
3. By using the default specified in `/etc/default/fs` for local file systems and in `/etc/dfs/fstypes` for remote file systems.

Types of File Systems

If you want to determine the type of a file system, you can obtain the information from the same files that the generic commands use.

- The `FS type` field in the file-system table (`/etc/vfstab`).
- The `/etc/default/fs` file for local file systems.
- The `/etc/dfs/fstypes` file for remote file systems.

To find a file system's type in the `/etc/vfstab` file, type **`grep`** ***`mount-point`*** **`/etc/vfstab`** and press Return. Information for the mount point is displayed, as shown in the following example.

```
drusilla% grep /tmp /etc/vfstab
swap            -               /tmp            tmpfs   -       yes     -
drusilla%
```

If `vfstab` does not have an entry for a file system, use one of the following procedures to determine the file system's type.

To identify a mounted file system's type, type **`grep`** ***`mount-point`*** **`/etc/mnttab`** and press Return. Information on the mount point is displayed, as shown in the following example.

```
drusilla% grep /home /etc/mnttab
drusilla:(pid129)   /home nfs
   ro,ignore,map=/etc/auto_home,indirect,dev=21c0004 693606637
bigriver:/export/home/bigriver  /tmp_mnt/home/bigriver  nfs     rw,dev=21c0005
   695409833
drusilla%
```

NOTE. Although the `/etc/mnttab` *file is no longer a text file in the Solaris 8 release, you can still use the* `grep` *command to search it for specific entries.*

Or, type **mount** and press Return. A list of the mounted file systems is displayed, as shown in the following example.

```
drusilla% mount
/ on /dev/dsk/c0t3d0s0 read/write on Tue Dec 24 12:29:22 1999
/usr on /dev/dsk/c0t1d0s6 read/write on Tue Dec 24 12:29:22 1999
/proc on /proc read/write on Tue Dec 24 12:29:22 1999
/usr/man on swsvr4-50:/export/svr4/man read/write/remote on Mon Dec 30
   12:49:11 1999
/usr/openwin on swsvr4-50:/export/svr4/openwinV3 read/write/remote on Mon Dec
   30 \  13:50:54 1999
/tmp on swap o on Wed Jan  8 13:38:45 1992
/mnt on swsvr4-50:/export/svr4 read/write/remote on Fri Jan 10 15:51:23 1992
/tmp_mnt/home on bigriver:/export/home read/write/remote on Tue Jan 14 \
   09:23:53 1992
drusilla%
```

Or, use the following steps.

1. Type **devnm** ***mount-point*** and press Return.

   The raw device name is displayed.
2. Become superuser.
3. Type **fstyp /dev/rdsk/c*n*t*n*d*n*s*n*** and press Return.

   The type of the file system is displayed, as shown in the following example.

```
drusilla% devnm /usr
/dev/dsk/c0t1d0s6 /usr
drusilla% su
Password:
# fstyp /dev/rdsk/c0t3d0s0
ufs
#
```

Making File Systems Available

When you have created a file system, you need to make it available; you do this by mounting it. A mounted file system is attached to the system directory tree at the specified mount point and becomes available to the system. The root file system is always mounted. Any other file system can be connected or disconnected from the root file system.

You can mount a local file system in the following ways.

- By creating an entry in the /etc/vfstab (virtual file-system table) file. The /etc/vfstab file contains a list of file systems that are automatically mounted when the system is booted in multiuser state. See "The Virtual File-System Table (/etc/vfstab)" on page 206 for a description of the /etc/vfstab file.
- From a command line by using the mount command.

File systems on disk slices must always be mounted on the server system and shared (exported) before other systems can access them. See "Sharing Files from a Server" on page 224 for information about sharing file systems. When file systems are shared from a server, a client can mount them as NFS file systems in any of the following three ways.

- By adding an entry to the /etc/vfstab file so that the file system is automatically mounted when the system is booted in multiuser state.
- By using the automount program to automatically mount or unmount the file system when a user changes into (mount) or out of (umount) the automounting directory.
- By using the mount command at a command line.

Understanding Mounting and Unmounting

File systems can be attached to the hierarchy of directories available on a system. This process is called *mounting*. To mount a file system you need the following things.

- To be superuser.
- A mount point on the local system. The mount point is a directory to which the mounted file system is attached.
- The resource name of the file system to be mounted (for example, /usr).

As a general rule, local disk slices should always be included in the /etc/vfstab file. Any software from servers, such as CDE, OpenWindows, or manual pages, and home directories from a server can either be included in the /etc/vfstab file or be automounted, depending on the policy at your site.

When you mount a file system, any files or directories that might be present in the mount point directory are unavailable as long as the file system is mounted. These files are not permanently affected by the mounting process and become available again when the file system is unmounted. However, mount directories usually are empty because you usually do not want to obscure existing files.

The system tracks the mounted file systems in the /etc/mnttab (mount table) file. Whenever you mount or unmount a file system, the /etc/mnttab file is modified to show the list of currently mounted file systems. You can display the contents of the mount table with the cat or more command, but you cannot edit the mount table as you would the /etc/vfstab file. The following example shows a mount table file.

```
drusilla% more /etc/mnttab
/dev/dsk/c0t3d0s0       /       ufs     rw,suid 693186371
/dev/dsk/c0t1d0s6       /usr    ufs     rw,suid 693186371
/proc   /proc   proc    rw,suid 693186371
swap    /tmp    tmpfs   ,dev=0 693186373
swsvr4-50:/export/svr4/openwinV3 /usr/openwin    nfs     rw,dev=21c0000
   693186443
swsvr4-50:/export/svr4/man       /usr/man        nfs     rw,dev=21c0001
   693186447
drusilla:(pid127)     /nse  nfs
   ro,ignore,map=/etc/auto.nse,indirect,dev=21c0002 693186449
drusilla:(pid127)    /net    nfs     ro,ignore,map=-hosts,indirect,dev=21c0003
   693186449
drusilla:(pid127)        /home   nfs
   ro,ignore,map=/etc/auto_home,indirect,dev=21c0004       693186449
bigriver:/export/home/bigriver  /tmp_mnt/home/bigriver  nfs    rw,dev=21c0005
   693186673
drusilla%
```

Using Mount and Unmount File-System Commands

Table 43 lists the commands in the /usr/sbin directory that you use to mount and unmount file systems.

Table 43 Commands for Mounting and Unmounting File Systems

Command	Description
mount(1M)	Mount file systems and remote resources.
mountall(1M)	Mount all file systems specified in a file-system table.
umount(1M)	Unmount file systems and remote resources.
umountall(1M)	Unmount all file systems specified in a file-system table.

The mount command does not mount a read/write file system that has inconsistencies. If you receive an error message from the mount or mountall command, you may need to check the file system.

The umount command does not unmount a file system that is busy. A file system is considered busy if a user is in a directory in the file system or if a program has a file open in that file system.

Table 44 describes the general mount options that you can specify with the -o option of the mount command. If you specify multiple options, separate them with commas (no spaces). For example, -o ro,nosuid.

Table 44 Commands for Mounting and Unmounting File Systems

<table>
<tr><th></th><th>Option</th><th>File System</th><th>Description</th></tr>
<tr><td>New!</td><td>rw | ro</td><td>CacheFS, NFS, PCFS, UFS, S5FS, UDFS</td><td>Specify read/write or read-only. If you do not specify this option, the default is read/write.</td></tr>
<tr><td>New!</td><td>nosuid</td><td>HSFS, NFS, UFS, UDFS</td><td>Prevent setuid execution and prevent devices on the file system from being opened. The default is to enable setuid execution and enable devices to be opened.</td></tr>
<tr><td>New!</td><td>remount</td><td>NFS, UFS, S5FS, UDFS</td><td>With rw, remount a file system with read/write access.</td></tr>
<tr><td>New!</td><td>f</td><td>None</td><td>Because of the structural change in the /etc/mnttab file in the Solaris 8 release, you can no longer use the -f option to force an entry in the /etc/mnttab file</td></tr>
<tr><td></td><td>m</td><td>UFS, S5FS</td><td>Mount the file system without making an entry in /etc/mnttab.</td></tr>
<tr><td>New!</td><td colspan="3">logging | nologging</td></tr>
<tr><td></td><td></td><td>UFS</td><td>Enable or disable UFS logging. See “UFS Logging” on page 219 for more information.</td></tr>
<tr><td></td><td>bg | fg</td><td>NFS</td><td>If the first attempt fails, retry in the background (bg) or in the foreground (fg). The default is fg.</td></tr>
<tr><td></td><td colspan="3">soft | hard</td></tr>
<tr><td></td><td></td><td>NFS</td><td>Specify the procedure if the server does not respond. soft indicates that an error is returned. hard indicates that the retry request is continued until the server responds. The default is hard.</td></tr>
<tr><td></td><td colspan="3">intr | nointr</td></tr>
<tr><td></td><td></td><td>NFS</td><td>Specify whether keyboard interrupts can be used to kill a process hung while waiting for a response on hard-mounted file</td></tr>
</table>

Table 44 Commands for Mounting and Unmounting File Systems (Continued)

Option	File System	Description
		systems. The default is `intr` (interrupts allowed).
`retry=n`	NFS	Retry the mount operations when it fails.
`largefiles`		
	NFS	A file system mounted using this option may contain files larger than 2 Gbytes, but it is not a requirement. This option is the default.
`nolargefiles`		
	NFS	Disable the `-largefiles` mount option to provide backward compatibility with previous file-system behavior and enforcing the 2-Gbyte maximum file size limit.
`index` *`filename`*		
	NFS URL	Automatically load a file matching *`filename`* if it is found in a directory referenced by an NFS URL.
`public`	NFS URL	Reset the `public` file handle to the current directory to enable you to access an NFS URL even if the file system cannot be mounted in the usual way.
`size=`*`sz`*	XMEMFS	Specify the size of the XMEMFS file system. This option is required. New!
`largebsize`	XMEMFS	Specify the large memory page size as the file-system block size. New!

UFS Logging

New!

UFS logging, new in the Solaris 7 Operating Environment, is the process of storing the changes that make up a complete UFS operation in a log file before the transactions are applied to the UFS file system. Once a transaction is stored, you can apply it to the file system later.

UFS logging is not enabled by default. To enable UFS logging, specify the `-o logging` option with the `mount` command when mounting a file system.

If you specify `logging`, then logging is enabled for the duration of the mounted file system. Logging is the process of storing transactions (changes that make up a complete UFS operation) in a log before the transactions are applied to the file system. Once a transaction is stored, the transaction can later be applied to the file system. This option prevents file systems from becoming inconsistent, thereby eliminating the need to run `fsck`. And, because you can bypass `fsck`, logging reduces the time required to reboot a system if it crashes or after an unclean halt. The default behavior is `nologging`.

The log is allocated from free blocks on the file system and sized at approximately 1 megabyte per 1 gigabyte of file system up to a maximum of 64 megabytes. You can enable logging on any UFS file system, including root (`/`). The log created by UFS logging is continually flushed as it fills up. The log is totally flushed when the file system is unmounted or by the `lockfs -f` command.

The `fsdb` command has been updated with new debugging options to support UFS logging.

Finding the Mounted File Systems

To display a list of mounted file systems, type **mount** and press Return. All the file systems currently mounted are displayed, as shown in the following example.

```
oak% mount
/ on /dev/dsk/c0t0d0s0 read/write/setuid on Wed Oct 23 10:08:50 1999

/usr on /dev/dsk/c0t0d0s6 read/write/setuid on Wed Oct 23 10:08:50 1999

/proc on /proc read/write/setuid on Wed Oct 23 10:08:50 1999

/tmp on swap on Wed Oct 23 10:08:52 1999

/usr/openwin on cheers:/export/openwin hard/remote on Wed Oct 23
10:11:08 1999

/home on blowup:(pid136) read only/intr/map=auto.home/indirect on Wed Oct 23
   10:11:10 1999

/vol on blowup:(pid136) read only/intr/map=auto.vol/indirect on Wed Oct 23
   10:11:10 1999

/nse on blowup:(pid136) read only/intr/map=/etc/auto.nse /indirect on Wed Oct
   23 10:11:10 1999
oak%
```

Mounting All File Systems in the /etc/vfstab File

Use the following steps to mount all file systems in the `/etc/vfstab` file.

1. Become superuser.
2. Type **mountall** and press Return.

All the file systems in the local `/etc/vfstab` file are mounted, as shown in the following example.

```
oak% su
Password:
# mountall
oak#
```

Mounting All File Systems of a Specific Type

Use the following steps to mount all file systems of a specific type that are in the `/etc/vfstab` file. The most common file system types are `ufs` for local disk slices and `nfs` for network file systems. See "Types of File Systems" on page 214 for a complete list of file system types.

1. Become superuser.
2. Type **`mountall -F`** ***`filesystem-type`*** and press Return.

   All the file systems of the type you specify that are in the local `/etc/vfstab` file are mounted.

The following example mounts all NFS file systems.

```
oak% su
Password:
# mountall -F nfs
#
```

Starting with the Solaris 2.6 release, the `-largefiles` mount option is used as the default for mounting UFS file systems. If you want to prevent users from mounting file systems that contain files larger than 2 Gbytes, you must explicitly use the `nolargefiles` mount option to disable the default behavior.

Mounting a Single File System (mount)

Use the following steps to mount a single file system that has an entry in the `/etc/vfstab` file.

1. Become superuser.
2. Type **`mount`** ***`mount-point`*** and press Return.

   The file system is mounted, as shown in the following example.

```
oak% su
Password:
# mount /opt
#
```

Remounting a UFS File System Without Large Files (mount)

After you mount a file system with the default `largefiles` mount option and large files have been created, you cannot remount the file system with the `nolargefiles` option until you remove any large files and run `fsck` to reset the state to `nolargefiles`.

The `nolargefiles` mount option provides total compatibility with previous file system behavior and enforces the 2-Gbyte maximum file size limit.

Use the following steps to remount a UFS file system without large files.

1. Become superuser.
2. Type **`cd /`*`filesystem`*** and press Return.
3. Type **`find . -xdev -size +2000000 -exec ls -l {} \;`** and press Return.
4. Remove any large files listed as the result of the **`find`** command.
5. Type **`umount /`*`filesystem`*** and press Return.
6. Type **`fsck /dev/rdsk/`*`device-name`*** and press Return.
7. Type **`mount -o nolargefiles /dev/rdsk/`*`device-name`*** and press Return.

   The file system is mounted.

In the following example, the directory `/files1` is searched for large files, unmounted, `fsck` is run, and the directory is mounted again with the `nolargefiles` option.

```
oak% su
Password:
# cd /files1
# find . -xdev -size +2000000 -exec ls -l {} \;
# umount /files1
# fsck /dev/rdsk/c0t3dos7 /files1
# mount -o nolargefiles /dev/dsk/c0t3d0s7 /files1
#
```

Unmounting All Remote File Systems (umountall -F nfs)

Follow these steps to unmount all remote file systems.

1. Become superuser.
2. Type **`umountall -F nfs`** and press Return.

   All the remote file systems in the local`/etc/vfstab` file are unmounted, as shown in the following example.

```
oak% su
Password:
# umountall -F nfs
#
```

CAUTION. If you unmount all file systems (by using `umountall` *without any arguments), the system may be unusable and you may need to reboot it.*

Unmounting Individual File Systems (umount)

You cannot unmount a directory that is being used. If you want to unmount a directory that is being used, all users must close any open files and change out of the directory.

1. Become superuser.
2. If necessary, have users change out of the directory you want to unmount.
3. Type **`umount`** ***`mount-point`*** and press Return.

   The file system you specify is unmounted.

In the following example, the `mount` command is used first to find the mount point for the file system to be unmounted.

```
oak% mount
/ on /dev/dsk/c0t0d0s0 read/write/setuid on Wed Oct 23 10:08:50 1999

/usr on /dev/dsk/c0t0d0s6 read/write/setuid on Wed Oct 23 10:08:50 1999

/proc on /proc read/write/setuid on Wed Oct 23 10:08:50 1999

/tmp on swap on Wed Oct 23 10:08:52 1999

/usr/openwin on cheers:/export/openwin hard/remote on Wed Oct 23
10:11:08 1999

/home on blowup:(pid136) read only/intr/map=auto.home/indirect on Wed Oct 23
   10:11:10 1999

/vol on blowup:(pid136) read only/intr/map=auto.vol/indirect on Wed Oct 23 10:11:10
   1999

/nse on blowup:(pid136) read only/intr/map=/etc/auto.nse /indirect on Wed Oct 23
10:11:10 1999
[41]oak% su
Password:
# cd /
# umount /home
#
```

Automounting Directories

You can mount file systems shared through NFS by using a method called *automounting*. The AutoFS program runs in the background and mounts and unmounts remote directories as they are needed. Whenever a user on a client system running AutoFS accesses a remote file or directory available through the automounter, AutoFS mounts the file system on the user's system. The remote file system remains mounted as long as the user remains in the directory and has one or more files open. If the remote file system is not accessed for a certain period of time, it is automatically unmounted. AutoFS mounts and unmounts file systems as required without any intervention on the part of the user other than changing into or out of a directory.

You can mount some file hierarchies with AutoFS, and you can change others by using the `/etc/vfstab` file and the `mount` command. A diskless machine *must* have entries for `/` (root), `/usr`, and `/usr/kvm` in the `/etc/vfstab` file.

CAUTION. Because shared file systems should always remain available, do not use AutoFS to mount `/usr/share`.

AutoFS works with the file systems specified in maps. These maps can be maintained as NIS, NIS+, or local files. The AutoFS maps can specify several remote locations for a particular file. This way, if one of the servers is down, the automounter can try to mount from another machine.

You can specify which servers are preferred for each resource in the maps by assigning each server a weighting factor. AutoFS starts automatically when a system enters run level 3. You can also start it from a command line. (Describing how to set up and administer the automounter is beyond the scope of this book.) By default, the Solaris Operating Environment automounts `/home`.

Sharing Files from a Server

NFS is a distributed file system that can be used to share files or directories from one system to other systems across a network. Computers that are running different operating systems can also share files. For example, systems running DOS can share files with systems running UNIX.

NFS makes the actual physical location of the file system irrelevant to the user. You can use NFS to enable users to see all the relevant files, regardless of location. Instead of placing copies of commonly used files on every system, NFS enables you to place one copy on one system's disk and let all other systems access it across the network. Under NFS, remote file systems are virtually indistinguishable from local ones.

A system becomes an NFS server if it has file systems to share or export over the network. A server keeps a list of currently exported file systems and their access restrictions (such as read/write or read-only).

You may want to share resources, such as files, directories, or devices from one system on the network (typically, a server) with other systems. For example, you might want to share third-party applications or source files with users on other systems.

When you share a resource, you make it available for mounting by remote systems. You can share a resource in the following ways.

- Using the `share` or `shareall` command.
- Adding an entry to the `/etc/dfs/dfstab` (distributed file-system table) file.

The default `/etc/dfs/dfstab` file shows the syntax and an example of entries.

```
paperbark% more /etc/dfs/dfstab

#       Place share(1M) commands here for automatic execution
#       on entering init state 3.
#
#       Issue the command '/etc/init.d/nfs.server start' to run the NFS
#       daemon processes and the share commands, after adding the very
#       first entry to this file.
#
#       share [-F fstype] [ -o options] [-d "<text>"] <pathname> [resource]
#       .e.g,
#       share  -F nfs  -o rw=engineering  -d "home dirs"  /export/home2

paperbark%
```

Checking the Data Consistency of a File System (fsck)

The UFS file system relies on an internal set of tables to keep track of *inodes*—structures the kernel uses to maintain information about each file—and used and available blocks. When these internal tables are not properly synchronized with data on a disk, inconsistencies result and file systems need to be repaired.

File systems can be damaged or become inconsistent because of abrupt termination of the operating system in the following ways.

- Power failure.
- The system halted by either the `halt` or `uadmin` command.
- The system turned off without proper shutdown procedure.

- A software error in the kernel.

File-system corruption, though serious, is not common. When a system is booted, a file-system consistency check is done automatically. Most of the time, this file-system check repairs problems it encounters.

Check file systems with the `fsck` (file-system check) command. The `fsck` command puts files and directories that are allocated but unreferenced in the `lost+found` directory in that file system. The inode number of each file is assigned to the name of the recovered file. If the `lost+found` directory does not exist, `fsck` creates it. If there is not enough space in the `lost+found` directory, `fsck` increases its size.

You may need to interactively check file systems in the following cases.

- When you cannot mount them.
- When they develop problems while in use.

NOTE. When an in-use file system develops inconsistencies, strange error messages may be displayed in the console window, or the system may crash. Before using `fsck`*, you may want to refer to the* `fsck`*(1M) manual page for more information.*

Finding Out Whether a File System Needs Checking

Use the following steps to determine whether a file system needs to be checked.

1. Become superuser.
2. Unmount the file system if it is mounted.
3. Type **`fsck -m /dev/rdsk/cntndnsn`** and press Return.

The state flag in the superblock of the file system you specify is checked to determine whether the file system is clean or requires checking.

If you omit the device argument in the `fsck` command, all the UFS file systems listed in `/etc/vfstab` with a `fsck` pass value greater than 0 are checked. In the following example, the first file system needs to be checked; the second file system does not.

```
paperbark% su
Password:
# umount /dev/rdsk/c0t0d0s6
# fsck -m /dev/rdsk/cØtØdØs6
** /dev/rdsk/c0t0d0s6
ufs fsck: sanity check: /dev/rdsk/c0t0d0s6 needs checking
# umount /dev/rdsk/c0t0d0s7
# fsck -m /dev/rdsk/cØtØdØs7
** /dev/rdsk/c0t0d0s7
ufs fsck: sanity check: /dev/rdsk/c0t0d0s7 okay
#
```

Checking File Systems Interactively

Use the following steps to check all file systems interactively.

1. Become superuser.
2. Unmount the file system.
3. Type **fsck** and press Return.

   All file systems in the `/etc/vfstab` file with entries in the `fsck pass` field greater than 0 are checked. You can also specify the mount point directory or `/dev/rdsk/cntndnsn` as arguments to `fsck`. Any inconsistency messages are displayed.

In the following example, `/dev/rdsk/c0t0d0s6` is checked and the incorrect block count is corrected.

```
paperbark% su
Password:
# umount /dev/rdsk/c0t0d0s6
# fsck /dev/rdsk/c0t0d0s6
checkfilesys: /dev/rdsk/c0t0d0s6
** Phase 1 - Check Block and Sizes
INCORRECT BLOCK COUNT I=2529 (6 should be 2)
CORRECT? y

** Phase 2 - Check Pathnames
** Phase 3 - Check Connectivity
** Phase 4 - Check Reference Counts
** Phase 5 - Cylinder Groups
Dynamic 4.3 FFFS
929 files, 8928 used, 2851 free (75 frags, 347 blocks, 0.6% fragmentation)
/dev/rdsk/c0t0d0s6 FILE SYSTEM STATE SET TO OKAY

***** FILE SYSTEM WAS MODIFIED *****
```

Backing Up and Restoring File Systems

Backing up files means making copies of them, usually on removable media, as a safeguard in case the originals get lost or damaged. Backup tapes are convenient for restoring accidentally deleted files, but they are essential in case of serious hardware failures or other disasters.

Backing up files is one of the most crucial system administration functions. You must plan and carry out a procedure for regularly scheduled backups of your file systems for three major reasons.

- To ensure file-system integrity against a possible system crash.
- To protect user files against accidental deletion.
- To act as an important safeguard before reinstalling or upgrading a system.

When you back up file systems as scheduled, you have the assurance that you can restore any files to a reasonably recent state. In addition, you may want to back up file systems to transport them from one system to another or to *archive* them—saving files on a transportable media—so that you can remove or alter the files that remain on the system.

When you plan a backup schedule, you need to consider the following factors.

- Which command to use to back up the file systems.
- What media to use.
- What backup schedule to use.
- Which file systems to back up.
- Which files are critical to users on this system.
- Where the files are located—are they in a single file system?
- How often these files change.
- How quickly you would need to restore these files in the event of damage or loss.
- How often the relevant file systems can be unmounted so that they are available for backup.

Outlining possible backup strategies is beyond the scope of this book. See the `ufsdump`(1M) manual page for a suggested dump schedule. The discussions that follow describe how to use the `ufsdump` command to make backups and how to retrieve files using the `ufsrestore` command.

Table 45 lists the commands that you can use to back up and restore individual files and file systems.

Table 45 Commands for Backing Up and Restoring Files and File Systems

Task	Command
Back up and restore complete or individual file systems to a local or remote tape device.	`ufsdump` and `ufsrestore`.
Back up complete file systems for all systems on a network from a server.	Solstice Backup software. Refer to the *Solstice Backup 5.1 Administration Guide.*
Back up and restore an NIS+ master server.	`nisbackup` and `nisrestore`. Refer to the `nisbackup` and `nisrestore` manual pages.

Specifying Tape Characteristics

The `ufsdump` command uses a set of defaults when you do not specify any tape characteristics. You can specify tape cartridge (`-c`), density (`-d`), size (`-s`), and number of tracks (`-t`). Note that you can specify the options in any order as long as the arguments that follow match the order of the options. Table 46 describes some typical media for backing up file systems.

Table 46 Tape Capacity Arguments to the ufsdump Command

Medium	Capacity
1/2-inch reel tape	140 Mbytes (6,250 bpi)
2.5-Gbyte 1/4-inch cartridge (QIC) tape	2.5 Gbytes
DDS3 4-mm cartridge tape (DAT)	12–24 Gbytes
14-Gbyte 8-mm cartridge tape	14 Gbytes
DLT 7000 1/2-inch cartridge tape	35–70 Gbytes

New!

Backing Up a File System With QIC-150 Cartridge Tapes (ufsdump)

To do a full backup on a file system, be sure all users are logged out. Then bring the system to single-user mode. (See "Tape Device-Naming Conventions" on page 248 if you need information about tape device names.)

You can dump or restore files from a remote drive by adding ***remote-host:*** to the front of the tape device name with the following syntax.

```
remote-host:/dev/rmt/unit
```

For example, the device name for a remote tape drive `/dev/rmt/0`, on the system `oak`, would be `oak:/dev/rmt/0`.

Use the following steps to do a level 0 (full) backup of a file system.

1. Type **`telinit s`** and press Return.
   The system is brought to single-user mode, which ensures that no users can change the file systems you are backing up.
2. Insert a tape cartridge in the QIC-150 tape drive.

3. Type **ufsdump 0cuf /dev/rmt/*unit* cntndnsn** and press Return.

   The 0 option specifies a level 0 (complete) dump. The c option specifies cartridge tape. The u option updates the dump record. The f option followed by the device name specifies the device file. Type the raw disk slice for the file system you want to back up, for example, c0t0d0s7 for /files1.

   The following example does a level 0 dump of the c0todos7 slice.

```
oak% su
Password:
# telinit s
# ufsdump Øcuf /dev/rmt/Ø cØtØdØs7
  DUMP: Date of this level 0 dump: Wed Mar 11 10:16:53 1992
  DUMP: Date of last level 0 dump: the epoch
  DUMP: Dumping /dev/rdsk/c0t3d0s7 (/export/home) to /dev/rmt/0
  DUMP: mapping (Pass I) [regular files]
  DUMP: mapping (Pass II) [directories]
  DUMP: estimated 956 blocks (478KB)
  DUMP: Writing 63 Kilobyte records
  DUMP: dumping (Pass III) [directories]
  DUMP: dumping (Pass IV) [regular files]
  DUMP: level 0 dump on Wed Mar 11 10:16:53 1992
  DUMP: 956 blocks (478KB) on 1 volume
  DUMP: DUMP IS DONE
#
```

4. If the dump requires more than one tape, the ufsdump command tells you when to change to a new tape.
5. Label the tape with the command, file system, and date so that you can easily find the backup tape if you need to restore files.

Performing Incremental Backups

You can specify different backup levels with the ufsdump command, making it possible to back up only those files that were changed since a previous backup at a lower level. Use the following steps to back up incremental changes since the last complete dump.

1. Bring the system to single-user mode.
2. Become superuser.
3. Put a tape into the tape drive.
4. All on one line, type **ufsdump [*1-9*]ucf /dev/rmt/*unit* /dev/rdsk/cntndnsn** and press Return. Type the level of the backup at the beginning of the ufsdump arguments. For example, for a level 9 backup, type **9ucf** as the first argument.
5. Remove the tape from the tape drive and label it.

Restoring a Backed-Up File System (ufsrestore)

The `ufsrestore` command copies files from backups created by the `ufsdump` command into the current working directory. You can use `ufsrestore` to reload an entire file-system hierarchy from a level 0 dump and incremental dumps that follow it or to restore one or more single files from any dump tape. Files are restored with their original owner, last modification time, and mode (permissions).

Before you start to restore files or file systems, you need the following information.

- Which tapes you need.
- The raw device name for the file systems you want to restore.
- The type of tape drive you will use.
- The device name (local or remote) for the tape drive.

Determining Which Tapes to Use

Before you can begin restoring file systems or files, you must determine which backup tapes you need. When restoring an entire file system, you always need the most recent level 0 backup tape. You also need the most recent incremental backup tapes made at each of the higher levels. Refer to the backup plan that you are using to determine the levels and number of tapes you need. For example, if you make level 0 and level 9 backups, you need the most recent level 0 and level 9 backup tapes.

Use the following steps to determine which tapes to use to restore individual files or file systems.

1. Ask the user the date when the file or file system was lost or the approximate date of the files to be recovered.
2. Refer to your backup plan to find the date of the last backup that would have the file or file system on it.

   Note that you do not necessarily use the most recently backed up version of the file. To retrieve the most recent version of a file, work backward through the incremental backups from highest to lowest level and most recent to least recent.
3. If you have on-line archive files created by the `ufsdump -a` option, type **`ufsrestore ta`** ***`archive-name`*** **`/path/`*****`filename(s)`*** and press Return. Be sure to use the complete path for the *`filename`*(s).

   A list of the files and the media they are stored on is displayed.
4. Retrieve the media containing the backups.

Be aware of the storage organization of backup media at your site so that you can locate media that are months or years old.

5. Insert media in the drive and type **ufsrestore tf *device-name /path/filename***(s) and press Return. Be sure to use the complete path for the *filename(s)*.

   If a file is in the backup, its name and inode number are listed. Otherwise, a message says it is not on the volume.

6. If you have multiple dump files on the same tape, you can use the `-s` *n* option to position the tape at the dump you want to use.

   For example, type **ufsrestore xfs /dev/rmt0 5** and press Return to position the tape at the fifth dump and restore it.

Restoring a Full Backup

Use the following steps to restore a full backup of a file system on a QIC-150 cartridge tape.

CAUTION. This procedure completely destroys any data already in the file system by creating a new file system on the slice.

1. Become superuser.
2. Type **telinit s** and press Return.

   The system is brought to single-user mode, which ensures that no one is using the file system you are restoring.

3. Type **umount *mount-point*** and press Return.

   The mount point you specify (for example, `/files1`) is unmounted.

4. Type **newfs /dev/rdsk/c*n*t*n*d*n*s*n*** and press Return.

   The raw device file for the disk slice (for example, `/dev/rdsk/c0t0d0s7` for the `/home` slice) is wiped clean and the file system is rebuilt.

5. Type **mount /dev/dsk/c*n*t*n*d*n*s*n*** and press Return.

   The file system, specified as the block file device (for example, `/dev/dsk/c0t0d0s7` for `/files1`), is remounted at the mount point you specify.

6. Type **cd *mount-point*** and press Return.

   You are in the directory you want to restore.

7. Insert the tape cartridge in the QIC-150 tape drive.
8. Type **ufsrestore rvf /dev/rmt/0h** and press Return.

   The file system is restored.

In the following example, the /files1 slice c0t0d0s7 is restored.

```
oak% su
Password:
# telinit s
# umount /files1
# newfs /dev/rdsk/c0t0d0s7
# mount /dev/dsk/c0t0d0s7 /files1
# cd /files1
# ufsrestore rvf /dev/rmt/0h
#
```

Restoring Files Interactively

When restoring individual files and directories, it is a good idea to restore them to a temporary directory such as /var/tmp. After you verify them, you can move the files to their proper locations. You can restore individual files and directories to their original locations. If you do so, be sure you are not overwriting newer files with older versions from the backup tape.

Use the following steps to restore files interactively.

1. Become superuser.
2. Write-protect the tape for safety.
3. Put the backup tape in the tape drive.
4. Type **cd /var/tmp** and press Return.

   If you want to restore the files to a different directory, substitute the directory name for /var/tmp in this step.
5. Type **ufsrestore if /dev/rmt/*unit*** and press Return.

   Some informational messages and the restore> prompt are displayed.
6. Create a list of files to be restored.
   - To list the contents of a directory, type **ls** and press Return.
   - To change directories, type **cd *directory-name*** and press Return.
   - To add a directory or file name to the list of files to be restored, type **add *filename*** and press Return.
   - To remove a directory or file name from the list of files to be restored, type **delete *filename*** and press Return.
   - To keep the mode of the current directory unchanged, type **setmodes** and press Return. Then type **n** and press Return.
7. When the list is complete, type **extract** and press Return. Then, ufsrestore asks you which volume number to use.
8. Type the volume number and press Return. If you have only one volume, type **1** and press Return.

The files and directories in the list are extracted and restored to the current working directory.

9. Type **quit** and press Return.

   The shell prompt is displayed.

10. Use the `ls -l` command to list the restored files and directories.

    A list of files and directories is displayed.

11. Check the list to be sure all the files and directories you specified in the list have been restored.

12. Use the `mv` command to move the files to the proper directories.

The following example restores the files `backup.examples` and `junk` from the `pubs` directory.

```
# cd /var/tmp
# ufsrestore if /dev/rmt/0
ufsrestore > ls
.:
 lost+found/   pubs/

ufsrestore > cd pubs
ufsrestore > ls
 ./pubs:
 .Xauthority          .login               .profile             backup.examples%
 .Xdefaults           .mtdeletelog         .wastebasket/        core
 .cshrc               .openwin-init        Junk/                dead.letter
 .desksetdefaults     .openwin-init.BAK    backup.examples      junk

ufsrestore > add backup.examples
ufsrestore > add junk
ufsrestore > setmodes
set owner/mode for '.'? [yn] n
ufsrestore > extract
You have not read any volumes yet.
Unless you know which volume your file(s) are on you should start
with the last volume and work towards the first.
Specify next volume #: 1
set owner/mode for '.'? [yn] n
ufsrestore > quit
# ls -l
total 6
drwxrwxrwt   3 sys      sys         512 Mar 11 10:36 ./
drwxrwxr-x  18 root     sys         512 Mar 10 16:43 ../
drwxr-xr-x   2 pubs     staff       512 Mar 11 10:11 pubs/
# pwd
/var/tmp
# cd pubs
# ls
./                ../                backup.examples   junk
#
```

Restoring a Single File from a Backup Tape (ufsrestore)

Use the following steps to restore a single file from a backup tape.

1. Become superuser.
2. Put the backup tape in the tape drive.
3. Type **cd /var/tmp** and press Return.

If you want to restore the files to a different directory, substitute the directory name for `/var/tmp` in this step.

4. Type **`ufsrestore xf /dev/rmt/`*`unit filename`*** and press Return.

   The `x` option tells `ufsrestore` to copy specific files or directories in the *`filename`* argument. The message `set owner/mode for '.'? [yn]` is displayed.

5. Type **`n`** and press Return.

   Directory modes remain unchanged.

6. Type the volume number where files are located and press Return. If there is only one volume, type **`1`** and press Return.

   The file is restored to the current working directory.

7. Type **`ls -l`** ***`filename`*** and press Return.

   A listing for the file is displayed.

8. Use the `mv` command to move the file to the proper directory.

Cache File Systems

You can use the Cache File System (CacheFS) to improve NFS server performance and scalability by reducing server and network load. CacheFS is designed as a layered file system that enables the system to cache one file system on another. In an NFS environment, CacheFS increases the client per server ratio, reduces server and network loads, and improves performance for clients on slow links such as Point-to-Point Protocol (PPP).

Understanding CacheFS

With CacheFS you can enable a client system to cache a file system from a server. Initial access to the file system may seem slow, but subsequent uses of the same file by the user are faster. Typically, you would cache an NFS or HSFS file system. You create cache file systems individually on each client system that needs improved NFS performance.

NOTE. CacheFS does not support caching of the root (/) and `/usr` *file systems. To find out how to cache these file systems, you must purchase the Solstice AutoClient 2.1 Administration Guide.* New!

1. On the client system, use the `cfsadmin`(1M) command to create a cache so that file systems you specify to be mounted in the cache can be accessed by the user locally instead of across the network. To prevent conflicts within the CacheFS software, after you have created

the cache you should not perform any operations within the cache directory on the client system.

2. On the client, create a mount point where the file system from the server—called the *back file system*—is mounted.
3. New! Note the name of the server and path to the back file system you want to cache. The format is `server:front-filesystem`.
4. Mount a file system in a cache by using the `mount` command on the client, adding an entry to the client's `/etc/vfstab` file, or using AutoFS to automount the file system.

After you have completed the setup of the CacheFS, files are dynamically placed in the cache as the user accesses them.

NOTE. You can mount only file systems that are shared. Refer to the `share`*(1M) manual page for more information or see "Sharing Files from a Server" on page 224.*

Creating a Cache

Use the following steps on a client system to create a cache.

1. Decide what name you want to use for the cache directory.
2. On the client system, become superuser.
3. Type **`cfsadmin -c`** ***`cache-directory`*** and press Return.

In the following example, a cache file system named `cachefile` is created in the `/local` directory.

```
oak% su
# cfsadmin -c /local/cachefile
#
```

Specifying a File System to Be Mounted in the Cache

You can specify file systems to be mounted in the cache so that users can locally access files in the cache file system you create. You can specify the file systems to be cached in three ways.

- Using the `mount`(1M) command on the client system. When you use the `mount` command, the files must be mounted from the command line every time the system is rebooted.
- Editing the `/etc/vfstab` file on the client system. When you add an entry to the `/etc/vfstab` file, the specified files are available for caching even when the system is rebooted.
- Using AutoFS. When you modify AutoFS maps, the specified files are available for caching even when the system is rebooted.

Creating a Mount Point

Regardless of the mechanism you choose to mount the file system, you need to create a mount point on the client system where CacheFS mounts the files. The mounted files are then cached in the cache directory that you created.

Type **mkdir** ***cache-directory*** and press Return. In the following example, a mount point named /cachemount is created.

```
# mkdir /cachemount
#
```

Specifying a File System (mount) You provide the following parameters for the mount command.

- The file-system type of the back file system on the server: **backfstype=*fstype***. The value for *fstype* can be either nfs or hsfs.
- The name of the cache directory on the client system: **cachedir=*cache-directory***.
- The name of the back file system on the server: ***server*:*back-filesystem***.
- The mount point on the client system: ***mount-point***.

Use the following steps to mount a cache file system from a command line.

1. On the client system, become superuser.
2. All on one line, type **mount -F cachefs -o backfstype=*fstype*,cachedir=*cache-directory* [,*options*] *back-file-system mount-point*** and press Return.
3. Type **cachefsstat *mount-point*** and press Return.

   The output from this command verifies that the cache you created was mounted.

The following example creates a cache file named /local/cachefile, creates a mount point named /cachemount, and mounts the NFS file system castle:/docs as a cached file system named /cachemount in the cache named /local/cachefile.

```
paperbark% su
Password:
# mkdir /local
# cfsadmin -c /local/cachefile
# mkdir /cachemount
# mount -F cachefs -o backfstype=nfs,cachedir=/local/cachefile castle:/docs /cachemount
# cachefsstat /cachemount

    /cachemount
                    cache hit rate:   100% (0 hits, 0 misses)
```

```
        consistency checks:      0 (0 pass, 0 fail)
                  modifies:      0
        garbage collection:      0
#
```

If the file system was not mounted in the cache, an error message similar to the following is displayed.

```
# cachefsstat /docs-cachemount
cachefsstat: /docs-cachemount not a cachefs mountpoint
#
```

Specifying a File System (*/etc/vfstab file*) When you add a cache file system to the `/etc/vfstab` file on the client system, the back file system remains available to users as a cached file system.

Use the following steps to mount a cache file system from the `/etc/vfstab` file.

1. On the client system, become superuser.
2. Using an editor, add the following line to the `/etc/vfstab` file.

```
/dev/dsk/device-name  /dev/rdsk/device-name /mount-point cachefs 2 yes  -
```

3. Type **`mount`** ***`mount-point`*** and press Return or reboot the system to mount the file system.

The following example mounts the `/usr/local` directory in the cache directory.

```
/dev/disk/c0t1d0s0  /dev/rdsk/c0t1d0s0  /cache  ufs  2  yes  -
```

Specifying a File System (AutoFS Map) You add a cache file system to the `auto_direct` AutoFS map by specifying the `-fstype=cachefs` mount option. Note that you also specify the CacheFS mount options (for example, `backfstype` and `cachedir`). Refer to the `automount`(1M) manual page for more information about automount maps or to the *Solaris Advanced System Administrator's Guide,* available from Sun Microsystems Press.

Use the following steps to specify a cache file system in the AutoFS map.

1. Become superuser.
2. Using an editor, add the following line to the `auto_direct` map.

```
/mount-point -fstype=cachefs,cachedir=/directory, backfstype=nfs
   server:/file-system
```

3. Reboot the system.
4. Type **cd *files-system*** and press Return.
5. Type **ls *files-system*** and press Return.

   Review the output of the `ls` command to verify that the entry was made correctly.

Maintaining Caches

After you set up cache file systems, you can perform the following maintenance tasks on them.

- Modify file systems in the cache by unmounting, deleting, re-creating, and remounting the cache.
- Display cache information.
- Check cache consistency.
- Delete a file system from the cache.
- Check cached file-system integrity.

If you are using the `/etc/vfstab` file to mount file systems, you modify the cache by editing the file-system options in the `/etc/vfstab` file. If you are using AutoFS, you modify the cache by editing the file-system options in the AutoFS maps.

Table 47 lists the commands that you can use to perform cache maintenance. Refer to the appropriate manual page for more details.

Table 47 Commands for Maintaining Cache File Systems

Command	Description
`cfsadmin`	Display information about cached file systems, delete a cached file system from a specified cache, and specify consistency checking on demand. See the `cfsadmin`(1M) manual page for more information.

Table 47 Commands for Maintaining Cache File Systems (Continued)

Command	Description
`cachefspack`	Create packing lists that specify individual files and directories that you want packed in the cache. A packing list contains files or directories to be packed in the cache. If a directory is in the packing list, all its subdirectories and files are also packed. See the `cachefspack`(1M) manual page for more information.
`cachefslog`	Specify the location of a CacheFS log file. This command also displays where statistics are currently being logged and enables you to halt logging. See the `cachefslog`(1M) manual page for more information.
`cachefswssize`	Interpret the log file to give a recommended cache size. See the `cachefsswsize`(1M) manual page for more information.
`cachefsstat`	Display statistical information about a specific file system or all cached file systems. The information provided in the output of this command is taken directly from the cache. See the `cachefsstat`(1M) manual page for more information.
`fsck -F cachefs {-m} {-o noclean}` *`cache-directory`*	
	Check the integrity of cached file systems and automatically correct problems without requiring user interaction. See the `fsck_cachefs`(1M) manual page for more information.

7

ADMINISTERING DEVICES

New!

Device management in the Solaris Operating Environment continues to evolve. This chapter describes what's new in device management in the Solaris 8 release and introduces some new device management commands.

This chapter explains disk device names and commands used for administering disks, describes how to use DVD devices, how to use tapes and diskettes to copy files, and how to use volume management to access diskettes and CD-ROMs. This chapter also introduces the Service Access Facility (SAF)—which you must use to administer terminals, modems, and other network devices with the Solaris Operating Environment—provides steps for setting up port monitors for print servers and print clients, and provides steps for adding a bidirectional modem to a system.

See Chapter 6, "Administering File Systems," for information about how to back up and restore complete file systems. See Chapter 10, "Administering Printing," for information about administering printers.

Automatic Configuration of Devices

The Solaris kernel is configured automatically. A kernel module is a software component that performs a specific task on the system. An example of a loadable kernel module is a device driver that is loaded when the device is accessed.

The system determines what devices are attached to it at boot time. Then, the kernel configures itself dynamically, loading needed modules into memory. Device drivers are loaded when devices such as disk and tape devices are accessed for the first time. This process is called *autoconfiguration* because all kernel modules are loaded automatically as they are needed.

With autoconfiguration, main memory is used more efficiently because modules are loaded as they are needed. Also, you do not need to reconfigure the kernel when new devices are added to the system.

You can customize the way kernel modules are loaded by modifying the `/etc/system` file. See `system`(4) for more information.

New!

Improved Device Configuration (defvsadm)

In previous Solaris releases, the `drvconfig` command handled device configuration to manage the physical device entries in the `/devices` directory. Five link generators—`devlinks`, `disks`, `tapes`, `ports`, and `audlinks`—managed the logical links in the `/dev` directory. These commands were not aware of hot-pluggable devices nor were they flexible enough for devices with multiple instances. For compatibility, in the Solaris 8 release, these commands are symbolic links to the new `devfsadm` command.

In the Solaris 8 release, the `devfsadm` command manages the special device files in the `/dev` and `/devices` directories. By default, `devfsadm` tries to load every driver in the system and attach to all possible device instances. Then, it creates the device files in the `/devices` directory and the logical links in the `/dev` directory. In addition, `devfsadm` also maintains the `path_to_inst`(4) database.

`devfsadmd`, the `devfsadm` daemon, handles both reconfiguration boot processing and updating the `/dev` and `/devices` directories in response to dynamic reconfiguration events. This daemon is started from the `/etc/rcS.d/S50devfsadm` script when a system is booted.

Because `devfsadmd` automatically detects device configuration changes generated by any reconfiguration event, you do not need to run `devfsadm` interactively.

Displaying Device Configuration Information

New!

Use the commands in Table 48 to display system and device configuration information.

Table 48 Device Configuration Commands

`prtconf`(1M)	Display system configuration information, including total amount of memory and the device configuration as described by the device hierarchy of the system.
`sysdef`(1M)	Display device configuration information, including system hardware, pseudodevices, loadable modules, and selected kernel parameters.
`dmesg`(1M)	Display system diagnostic messages as well as a list of devices attached to the system since the last reboot.

See Chapter 8, "Administering Systems," for examples of these commands.

SCSI and PCI Hot-Plugging

New!

Hot-plugging is the capability to physically add, remove, or replace system components while a system is running. *Dynamic reconfiguration*, available on certain SPARC servers, enables a service provider to remove and replace hot-pluggable system I/O boards in a running system, thereby eliminating the time lost in rebooting. Also, if a replacement board is not immediately available, the system administrator can use dynamic reconfiguration to shut down a failing board while the system continues to operate.

With the Solaris 8 release, you can use the `cfgadm` command to hot-plug SCSI devices on SPARC- and IA-based platforms and PCI adapter cards on IA-based systems. The `cfgadm` command enables you to perform the following tasks.

- Display system component status.
- Test system components.
- Change component configurations.
- Display configuration help messages.

With the `cfgadm` command you can reconfigure system components while the system is running. The `cfgadm` command guides you through the steps needed to add, remove, or replace system components. See `cfgadm`(1M) for more information.

NOTE. Not all SCSI and PCI controllers support hot-plugging with the `cfgadm` *command.*

New! Device-Naming Conventions

You need to know how to specify device names when using commands to manage disks, file systems, and other devices. In most cases, you use logical device names to represent devices connected to the system. Both logical and physical device names are represented on the system by logical and physical device files.

When a system is booted for the first time, the kernel creates a device hierarchy to represent all of the devices connected to the system. The kernel uses the device hierarchy information to associate drivers with their appropriate devices and provides a set of pointers to the drivers that perform specific operations.

You reference devices in the following three ways in the Solaris Operating Environment.

- Physical device name—The full device path name in the device information hierarchy. You find physical device files in the `/devices` directory.
- Instance name—The abbreviation name the kernel uses for every possible device on the system. For example, `sd0` and `sd1` represent the instance names of two disk devices. Instance names are mapped in the `/etc/path_to_inst` file.
- Logical device name—You use logical device names with most file system commands to refer to devices. Logical device files in the `/dev` directory are symbolically linked to physical device files in the `/devices` directory.

See "Tape Device-Naming Conventions" on page 248 for information on tape device-naming conventions. See "Disk-Naming Conventions" on page 287 for information on disk-naming conventions.

New! Using DVD-ROM Devices

The Solaris 8 Operating Environment includes support for the Universal Disk Format (UDFS) file system, which is the industry-standard format for storing information on the optical media technology called DVD (Digital Versatile Disc or Digital Video Disc).

UDFS is provided as dynamically loadable 32-bit and 64-bit modules, with system administration commands that you can use to create, mount, and check the file system on both SPARC and IA platforms. The Solaris UDFS works with supported ATAPI and SCSI DVD drives, CD-ROM devices, and disk and diskette drives. In addition, the Solaris UDFS is fully compliant with the UDF 1.50 specification. See "Disk-Based File Systems" on page 199 for more information.

Hardware and Software Requirements

The UDF file system requires the following components.

- The Solaris 7 11/99 or Solaris 8 Operating Environment.
- Supported SPARC or Intel platforms.
- Supported CD-ROM or DVD-ROM device.

UDF Compatibility Issues

This first Solaris UDF file-system implementation provides support for industry-standard read-write UDF version 1.50 and fully internationalized file-system commands.

Connecting a DVD-ROM Device

Use the following steps to connect a DVD-ROM device.

1. Become superuser.
2. Type **`touch /reconfigure`** and press Return.

   The `/reconfigure` file is created.
3. Type **`telinit 0`** and press Return to shut down the system and turn off power.
4. Connect the DVD-ROM device.
5. Turn on power to the system.

Accessing Files on a DVD-ROM Device

Use the following steps to access files on a DVD-ROM device.

NOTE. If a system has both a CD-ROM and a DVD-ROM device, the CD-ROM might be named `/cdrom/cdrom0` *and the DVD-ROM might be named* `/cdrom/cdrom1`. *If the system has only a DVD-ROM device, try using* `/cdrom/cdrom0`.

1. Type **ls /cdrom** and press Return.

   The contents of the /cdrom directory are displayed.

2. Type **ls /cdrom/cdrom1** (or **ls /cdrom/cdrom0** if the system has no CD-ROM device) and press Return.

   The following example displays the contents of a DVD-ROM device.

```
$ ls /cdrom/cdrom1
Copyright  install.sh  product.gz
$
```

Automatic display with the CDE file manager is not yet implemented. You can use all other CDE file manager functions, such as drag and drop for copying and imagetool features.

Displaying UDF File System Parameters

Use the -F udfs option of the mkfs command to display UDF file system parameters.

1. Become superuser.
2. Type **mkfs -F udfs -m /dev/rdsk/*device-name*** and press Return.

   See mkfs_udfs(1M) for more information.

Creating a UDF File System

Use the -F udfs option of the mkfs command to create a UDF file system.

1. Become superuser.
2. Type **mkfs -F udfs /dev/rdsk/*device-name*** and press Return.

   See mkfs_udfs(1M) for more information.

3. Verify the UDF file system is created by mounting it.

   See "Mounting a UDF File System" on page 247 for more information.

Determining Whether a File System Is a UDF File System

Use the fstyp command to determine whether a file system is a UDF file system.

1. Become superuser.
2. Type **fstyp -v /dev/rdsk/*device-name*** and press Return.

Checking a UDF File System

Use the `-F udfs` option of the `fsck` command to check the integrity of a UDF file system.

1. Become superuser.
2. Type **`fsck -F udfs /dev/rdsk/`*`device-name`*** and press Return.

   See `fsck_udfs`(1M) for more information.

Mounting a UDF File System

Use the `-F udfs` option of the `mount` command to mount UDF file systems.

1. Become superuser.
2. Type **`mount -F udfs /dev/rdsk/`*`device-name /mountpoint`*** and press Return.
3. Type **`ls`** ***`/mountpoint`*** and press Return to verify that the UDF file system is mounted.

   See `mount_udfs`(1M) for more information.

Unmounting a UDF File System

Use the `umount` command to unmount UDF file systems.

1. Become superuser.
2. Type **`umount /dev/rdsk/`*`device-name`*** and press Return.

Labeling a Device with a UDF File System and Volume Name

Use the `-F udfs` option of the `labelit` command to create a file system and volume name for a UDF file system.

1. Become superuser.
2. Type **`labelit -F udfs /dev/rdsk/`*`device-name fsname volume`*** and press Return.

   See `labelit_udfs`(1M) for more information.

Using Tapes

This section describes tape device–naming conventions, useful commands for streaming tape cartridges, and how to use the tar, cpio, and pax commands to archive and retrieve files from tapes.

You can use the tar, cpio, and pax commands to copy files and file systems to tape. The command you choose depends on how much flexibility and precision you require for the copy.

Use tar to copy files and directory subtrees to a single tape. Note that the Solaris tar command can archive special files (block and character devices, fifos), but the SunOS 4.x tar command cannot extract them. The cpio command provides better portability between different versions of the UNIX operating system.

Use cpio to copy arbitrary sets of files, special files, or file systems that require multiple tape volumes, or to copy files from Solaris systems to SunOS 4.x systems. The cpio command packs data onto tape more efficiently than does tar and skips over any bad spots in a tape when restoring. The cpio command also provides options for writing files with different header formats (tar, ustar, crc, odc, bar) for portability between systems of different types.

Use pax to copy files, special files, or file systems that require multiple tape volumes or when you want to copy files to and from POSIX-compliant systems.

Because tar, cpio, and pax use the raw tape device, you do not need to format or make a file system on tapes before you use them. The tape drive and device name you use depend on the hardware and configuration for each system.

Tape Device-Naming Conventions

Tape device-naming conventions use a logical—not a physical—device name. Logical tape device files are located in the /dev/rmt subdirectory as symbolic links from the /devices directory. In general, you specify a tape drive device as shown in Figure 51.

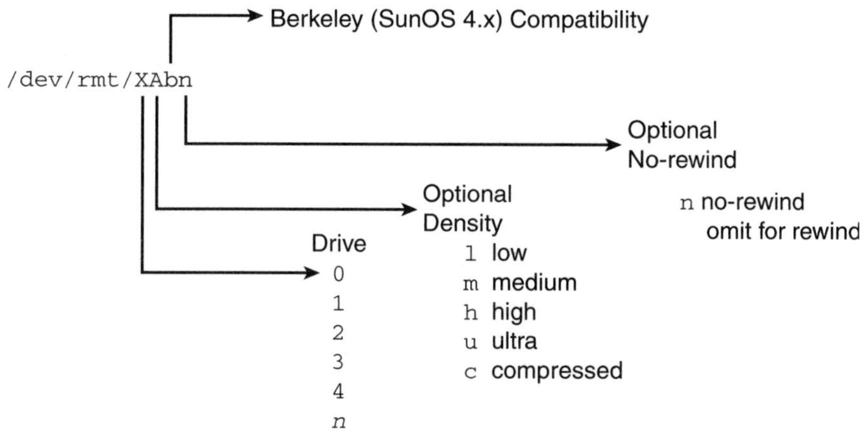

Figure 51 Tape Drive Device Names

Device 0 is the first tape device connected to the system (`/dev/rmt/0`). The tape device could be a QIC-11, QIC-24, QIC-150, 4mm, 8mm, or DAT drive.

Specifying the Drive Number by the Default Density

Normally, you specify a tape drive by its *logical unit number*, which is a number from 0 to *n*. If you do not specify a density, the drive writes at its "preferred" density, which is usually the highest density the tape supports.

You can attach a maximum of seven SCSI tape drives to a SCSI controller. **New!**

To specify the first drive, use the following device name.

```
/dev/rmt/0
```

To specify the second drive, use the following device name.

```
/dev/rmt/1
```

NOTE. Most device names start their numbering sequence with zero (0). Consequently, when you talk about the first disk or target, its number is 0, not 1.

Specifying Different Densities for a Tape Drive

You may want to transport a tape to a system whose tape drive supports only a certain density. In that case, specify a device name that writes at the desired density. Use the following naming convention.

```
/dev/rmt/XA
```

To determine the different densities that are supported for a drive, look at the `/dev/rmt` subdirectory, which includes the set of tape device files that support different output densities for each tape.

The unit and density characters are shown in Table 49. For example, to specify a raw magnetic tape device on the first (0) drive with medium density, use the following device name.

```
/dev/rmt/0m
```

Table 49 Unit and Density Characters in Tape Device Names

Device Name	= /dev/rmt/*XA*
X	Tape drive number (digit) from 0 to *n*, regardless of controller type.
A	Density (character), depending on controller and drive type.
`null`	Default, preferred (highest) density.
`l`	Low.
`m`	Medium.
`h`	High.
`u`	Ultra.
`c`	Compressed.

Specifying the No-Rewind Option

After the command is executed, the tape is automatically rewound unless you specify the no-rewind option as part of the device name. To specify no rewinding, type **n** at the end of the device name.

For example, to specify a raw magnetic tape device on the first (0) drive with medium density and no rewind, use the following device name.

```
/dev/rmt/0mn
```

Understanding Device Abbreviations for Different Tape Controllers and Media

You can have both SCSI and non-SCSI tape drives on the same system. A SCSI controller can have a maximum of seven SCSI tape drives, and a non-SCSI controller can have a maximum of four tape drives. For each drive number (*X*), the density character depends on the controller and drive type, as described in the following paragraphs.

Table 50 shows the device abbreviations for different tape controllers/units and media. Note that the first character in the device abbreviation for drive number does not have to be 0 as shown, but could be 1, 2, or 3, and so on, depending on how many tape drives are attached to the system.

Table 50 Device Abbreviations for Tape Controllers/Units and Media

Con-troller	Drive Unit	Size	Type	Format	Tracks	Device Abbreviation
Xylogics 472	Fujitsu M2444	1/2-inch	Reel	1600 bpi	9	`/dev/rmt/0m`
		1/2-inch	Reel	6250 bpi	9	`/dev/rmt/0h`
SCSI front-loaded	HP	1/2-inch	Reel	800 bpi	9	`/dev/rmt/0m`
				6250 bpi	9	`/dev/rmt/0h`
SCSI	Sysgen	1/4-inch	Cartridge	QIC-11	4	`/dev/rmt/01`
				QIC-24	4	`/dev/rmt/0m`
				QIC-11	9	`/dev/rmt/01`
				QIC-24	9	`/dev/rmt/0m`
	Emulex MT-02	1/4-inch	Cartridge	QIC-11	4	`/dev/rmt/01`
				QIC-24	4	`/dev/rmt/0m`
				QIC-11	9	`/dev/rmt/01`
				QIC-24	9	`/dev/rmt/0m`
	Archive QIC-150	1/4-inch	Cartridge	QIC-15	18	`/dev/rmt/0h`

Table 50 Device Abbreviations for Tape Controllers/Units and Media (Continued)

Con-troller	Drive Unit	Size	Type	Format	Tracks	Device Abbreviation
	Wangtek QIC-150	1/4-inch	Cartridge	QIC-15	18	`/dev/rmt/0h`
	Desktop Backup Pack	1/4-inch	Cartridge	QIC-15	18	`/dev/rmt/0h`
	Exabyte 8200 (2.3 Gb)	8 mm	Cartridge	8 mm	Helical scan	`/dev/rmt/0m`
	Exabyte 8500 (2.3 Gb)	8 mm	Cartridge	8 mm	Helical scan	`/dev/rmt/0l`
	Exabyte 8500 (5 Gb)	8 mm	Cartridge	8 mm	Helical scan	`/dev/rmt/0m`
	Archive Python	4 mm	Cartridge	4 mm	Helical scan	`/dev/rmt/0`

Using Rack-Mounted Non-SCSI 1/2 -Inch Reel Drives

For 1/2-inch rack-mounted tape drives with either a Tapemaster or Xylogics 472 controller, substitute the density from Table 51 for the *A* variable in the device name (`/dev/rmt/XA`).

Table 51 Designating Density for Rack-Mounted 1/2 -Inch Tape Drives

Character	Density
`null`	Default "preferred" (highest) density (usually 6250 bpi uncompressed).
`l`	800 bpi.
`m`	1600 bpi.
`h`	6250 bpi.
`u`	6250 bpi compressed.

If you omit the density character, the tape is usually written at its highest density, not compressed.

Using SCSI ¼-Inch Cartridge and ½-Inch Front-Loaded Reel Drives

For SCSI ¼-inch cartridge and ½-inch front-loaded reel drives, substitute the density from Table 52 for the *A* variable in the device name (`/dev/rmt/XA`).

Table 52 Designating Format or Density for SCSI Tape Drives

Character	Density, ¼ -Inch Cartridge	Density, ½-Inch Front-Loaded Reel-to-Reel
`null`	Default, preferred (highest) density.	Default, preferred (highest) density.
`l`	QIC-11 format.	800 bpi.
`m`	QIC-24 format.	1600 bpi.
`h`	QIC-150.	6250 bpi.
`u`	Reserved.	Reserved.

For ¼-inch cartridges, density is specified by the format in which the data is written: the QIC format. The QIC-11 and QIC-24 formats write approximately 1000 bpi on each track. The density for QIC-150 is somewhat higher. The preferred density for a 60-Mbyte ¼-inch cartridge drive is QIC-24 and for a 150-Mbyte ¼-inch cartridge drive is QIC-150.

A 150-Mbyte drive can write only QIC-150; it cannot be switched to write QIC-24 or QIC-11. Format selection is useful only for drives that can write both QIC-24 and QIC-11.

Specifying Helical Scan Drives

Helical scan drives (for example, Exabyte 8mm or Wang/DAT 4mm) are a special case of SCSI drives. They write only at the preferred density. Consequently, you always specify them using only the drive number, for example, `/dev/rmt/0`. You can also specify the no-rewind option.

Useful Commands for Streaming Tapes

The following sections contain a few commands for use with streaming tapes.

Retensioning a Magnetic Tape

If errors occur when a tape is read, retension the tape, clean the tape drive, and then try again. Type **`mt -f /dev/rmt/`*`n`*` retension`** and press Return. The tape in the tape drive you specify is retensioned.

The following example retensions the tape in drive /dev/rmt/1.

```
oak% mt -f /dev/rmt/1 retension
oak%
```

Rewinding a Magnetic Tape

To rewind a magnetic tape, type **mt -f /dev/rmt/*n* rewind** and press Return. The tape in the tape drive you specify by the device number *n* is rewound.

The following example rewinds the tape in drive /dev/rmt/1.

```
oak% mt -f /dev/rmt/1 rewind
oak%
```

Showing the Status of a Magnetic Tape Drive

To show the status of a magnetic tape drive, type **mt -f /dev/rmt/*n* status** and press Return. Status for the tape drive you specify is displayed.

The following example shows that no tape is in drive /dev/rmt/1.

```
oak% mt -f /dev/rmt/1 status
/dev/rmt/1: no tape loaded or drive offline
oak%
```

The following example shows status for the tape in drive /dev/rmt/1.

```
oak% mt -f /dev/rmt/1 status
Archive QIC-150 tape drive:
   sense key(0x6)= unit attention   residual= 0   retries= 0
   file no= 0   block no= 0
oak%
```

The tar Command

Use the tar command to copy files and directory subtrees to a single tape. The advantages of the tar command are that it is available on most UNIX operating systems and that public domain versions are readily available. The disadvantages of the tar command are that tar is not aware of file system boundaries, full path-name length cannot exceed 255 characters, it does not copy empty directories or special files such as device files, and it cannot be used to create multiple tape volumes.

The following sections describe how to use the `tar` command to copy files to a tape, list the files, append the files, and retrieve the files.

Copying Files to a Tape (tar)

Use the following steps to copy files to a tape.

1. Change to the directory that contains the file you want to copy.
2. Insert a write-enabled tape into the tape drive.

CAUTION. Copying files to a tape with the `c` *option to* `tar` *destroys any files already on the tape. If you want to preserve the files already on the tape, use the* `r` *option described in "Appending Files to a Tape (tar)" on page 256.*

3. Type **`tar cvf /dev/rmt/`*`n filename filename filename`* `...`** and press Return.

   The `c` (copy) option copies the files you specify, the `v` (verbose) option displays information about the files as they are copied, and the `f` (files) option followed by the tape device name specifies where the `tar` files are to be written. The file names you specify are copied to the tape, overwriting any existing files on the tape.

NOTE. You can use metacharacters (`?` *and* `*`*) as part of the file names you specify. For example, to copy all documents with a* `.doc` *suffix, type* **`*.doc`** *as the file name argument. If you specify a directory name as the file name, the directory and all its subdirectories are recursively copied to the tape.*

4. Remove the tape from the drive and write the names of the files on the tape label.

The following example copies two files to a tape in tape drive 0.

```
oak% cd /home/winsor
oak% ls evaluation*
evaluation.doc   evaluation.doc.backup
oak% tar cvf /dev/rmt/0 evaluation*
a evaluation.doc 86 blocks
a evaluation.doc.backup 84 blocks
oak%
```

Listing the Files on a Tape (tar)

Use the following steps to list the files on a tape.

1. Insert a tape into the tape drive.
2. Type **`tar tvf /dev/rmt/`*`n`*** and press Return.

The `t` (table) option lists the files you specify, the `v` (verbose) option displays complete information about the files as they are listed in a form similar to the `ls -l` command, and the `f` (files) option followed by the tape device name specifies the device where the `tar` files are located.

In the following example, the table of contents for the tape in drive 0 contains two files.

```
oak% tar tvf /dev/rmt/0
rw-rw-rw-6693/10  44032 Apr 23 14:54 2000 evaluation.doc
rw-rw-rw-6693/10  43008 Apr 23 14:47 2000 evaluation.doc.backup
oak%
```

Reading from left to right, the first column shows the permissions for the file; the second column shows the UID and GID file ownership; the third column shows the number of characters (bytes) in the file; the fourth, fifth, sixth, and seventh columns contain the month, day, date, and year the file was last modified, and the final column contains the name of the file.

Appending Files to a Tape (tar)

Use the following steps to append files without overwriting files already on the tape.

1. Change to the directory that contains the file you want to copy.
2. Insert a tape that is not write-protected into the tape drive.
3. Type **`tar rvf /dev/rmt/`*`n filename filename filename ...`*** and press Return.

   The file names you specify are appended to the files already on the tape in the drive you specify.

NOTE. You can use metacharacters (`?` and `*`) as part of the file names you specify. For example, to copy all documents with a `.doc` suffix, type **`*.doc`** *as the file-name argument.*

4. Remove the tape from the drive and write the names of the files on the tape label.

The following example appends one file to the files already on the tape in drive 0.

```
oak% cd /home/winsor
oak% tar cvf /dev/rmt/0 junk
a junk 1 blocks
oak% tar rvf /dev/rmt/0
rw-rw-rw-6693/10  44032 Apr 23 14:54 2000 evaluation.doc
rw-rw-rw-6693/10  43008 Apr 23 14:47 2000 evaluation.doc.backup
rw-rw-rw-6693/10     18 Dec 10 11:36 2000 junk
oak%
```

You can put more than one set of `tar` files on a tape if you use the `n` (no-rewind) option as part of the tape device name. For example, type **`tar cvf /dev/rmt/nn filename`**. The tape is not rewound after the files are copied, and the next time you use the tape, the files are written after the end of the previous set of files.

Retrieving Files and Directories from a Tape (tar)

Use the following steps to retrieve files from a tape.

1. Change to the directory where you want to put the files.
2. Insert the tape into the tape drive.
3. Type **`tar xvf /dev/rmt/n`** and press Return.

   All the files on the tape in the drive you specify are copied to the current directory.

The following example copies all files from the tape in drive 0.

```
oak% cd /home/winsor/Evaluations
oak% tar xvf /dev/rmt/0
x evaluation.doc, 44032 bytes, 86 tape blocks
x evaluation.doc.backup, 43008 bytes, 84 tape blocks
oak%
```

To retrieve individual files from a tape, type **`tar xvf /dev/rmt/n filename filename filename...`** and press Return. The file names you specify are extracted from the tape and placed in the current working directory. The following example copies files with the prefix `evaluation` from the tape in drive 0.

```
oak% cd /home/winsor/Evaluations
oak% tar xvf /dev/rmt/0 evaluation*
x evaluation.doc, 44032 bytes, 86 tape blocks
x evaluation.doc.backup, 43008 bytes, 84 tape blocks
oak%
```

Use the following steps to retrieve directories and subdirectories recursively from a tape.

1. Change to the parent directory where you want to copy the files.

   If the directory already exists, be sure you are in the parent directory and that it is okay to overwrite the contents of the directory before you copy the files from the tape. For example, to restore the contents of a directory named `Book` that is in `/home/winsor/Book`, you would change to `/home/winsor` and type **`tar xvf /dev/rmt/n Book`** and press Return. If you are in the directory `/home/winsor/Book`, the files are restored as `/home/winsor/Book/Book`.
2. Type **`tar xvf /dev/rmt/n directory-name`** and press Return.

The directory and all its subdirectories are recursively copied from the tape.

NOTE. The names of the files extracted from the tape exactly match the names of the files stored on the archive. If you have any doubts about the names or paths of the files, first list the files on the tape. See "Listing the Files on a Tape (tar)" on page 255 for instructions and the `tar(1)` *manual page for more information.*

The cpio Command

The `cpio` command copies files, special files (files used to represent peripheral devices attached to a system), and file systems that require multiple tape volumes, and provides compatibility for copying files from Solaris systems to SunOS 4.x systems. Advantages of using the `cpio` command are that it packs data onto tape more efficiently than does the `tar` command, skips over any bad spots in a tape when restoring files, provides options for writing files with different header formats (`tar`, `ustar`, `crc`, `odc`, `bar`) for portability between different system types, and creates multiple tape volumes.

When you use the `cpio` command to create an archive, the command takes a list of files or path names from standard input and writes to standard output. You redirect the output to either a file or a device. The following sections describe how to use the `cpio` command to copy files to a cartridge tape, list the files, retrieve all files, and retrieve a subset of the files from a cartridge tape.

Copying All Files in a Directory to a Tape (cpio)

Use the following steps to copy all files in a directory to a tape.

1. Insert a write-enabled tape into the tape drive.
2. Type **`ls | cpio -oc > /dev/rmt/`*`n`*** and press Return.

   The `o` option copies the files. The `c` option writes header information in ASCII character form for portability. All the files in the directory are copied to the tape in the drive you specify, overwriting any existing files on the tape, and the total number of blocks copied is displayed.
3. Remove the tape from the drive and write the names of the files on the tape label.

In the following example, all the files in the directory /home/winsor/TOI are copied to the tape in tape drive 0.

```
oak% cd /home/winsor/TOI
oak% ls | cpio -oc > /dev/rmt/0
31 blocks
oak%
```

Listing the Files on a Tape (cpio)

Use the following steps to list files on a tape.

1. Insert a tape into the tape drive.
2. Type **cpio -civt < /dev/rmt/*n*** and press Return. The i option reads in the contents of the tape. The v option displays the output in a format similar to the output from the ls -l command. The t option lists the table of contents for the files on the tape in the tape drive you specify.

NOTE. Listing the table of contents takes as long as it does to read the archive file because the cpio *command must process the entire archive.*

In the following example, the table of contents for the tape in drive 0 contains four files.

```
oak% cpio -civt < /dev/rmt/0
100666 winsor   3895  Feb 24 15:13:02 2000  Boot.chapter
100666 winsor   3895  Feb 24 15:13:23 2000  Directory.chapter
100666 winsor   6491  Feb 24 15:13:52 2000  Install.chapter
100666 winsor   1299  Feb 24 15:14:00 2000  Intro.chapter
31 blocks
oak%
```

The first column shows permissions in octal format; the second column shows the owner of the file; the third column displays the number of characters (bytes) in the file; the fourth, fifth, sixth, and seventh columns show the month, date, time, and year the file was last modified; and the final column shows the name of the file.

Retrieving All Files from a Tape (cpio)

If the archive was created with relative path names, the input files are built as a directory within the current directory. If, however, the archive was created with absolute path names, the same absolute paths are used to re-create the file.

CAUTION. Using absolute path names can be dangerous because you can overwrite the original files and you cannot choose to restore files to a different location.

Use the following steps to retrieve all files from a tape.

1. Change to the directory where you want to put the files.
2. Insert the tape into the tape drive.
3. Type **cpio -icv < /dev/rmt/*n*** and press Return.

   All the files on the tape in the drive you specify are copied to the current directory.

The following example copies all files from the tape in drive 0.

```
oak% cpio -icv < /dev/rmt/0
Boot.chapter
Directory.chapter
Install.chapter
Intro.chapter
31 blocks
oak%
```

Retrieving a Subset of Files from a Tape (cpio)

You can retrieve a subset of the files from the archive by specifying a pattern to match and using shell wildcard characters enclosed in quotation marks after the options.

1. Change to the directory where you want to put the files.
2. Insert the tape into the tape drive.
3. Type **cpio -icv "**file*" < /dev/rmt/*n*** and press Return.

   All the files that match the pattern "**file*" are copied to the current directory. You can specify multiple patterns, but each must be enclosed in quotation marks.

The following example copies all files that end in the suffix chapter from the tape in drive 0.

```
oak% cd /home/winsor/Book
oak% cpio -icv "*chapter" < /dev/rmt/0
Boot.chapter
Directory.chapter
Install.chapter
Intro.chapter
31 blocks
oak%
```

See the cpio(1) manual page for more information.

The pax Command

Starting with the Solaris 2.5 release, the pax command, which stands for *portable archive interchange,* is provided. The pax command provides better portability than do the tar or cpio commands for POSIX-compliant systems.

Use the pax command to copy files, special files, or file systems that require multiple tape volumes or when you want to copy files to and from POSIX-compliant systems. Disadvantages of the pax command are that it is not aware of file system boundaries and the full path-name length cannot exceed 255 characters.

Copying All Files in a Directory to a Tape (pax)

Use the following steps to use the pax command to copy all the files in the current directory to a tape.

1. Change to the directory that contains the files you want to copy.
2. Insert a write-enabled tape into the tape drive.
3. Type **pax -w -f < /dev/rmt/*n* .** and press Return.

   The -w option writes the current directory contents to tape. The -f option identifies the tape drive. The dot (.) at the end of the command specifies the current directory. The pax command does not list the files as they are copied.
4. Type **pax -l -f < /dev/rmt/*n*** and press Return.

   The -l option lists the files on the tape to verify that the files are copied.
5. Remove the tape from the drive and write the names of the files on the tape label.

The following example copies all files from the tape in drive 0.

```
castle% pax -w -f /dev/rmt/0 .
castle% pax -l -f /dev/rmt/0
.
./addusr-1.rs
./addusr-2.rs
./at-addmn.rs
./at-base.rs
./at-menu.rs
castle%
```

See the pax(1) manual page for more information.

NOTE. When you use the pax *command to copy files to a single-volume tape, you can also list and retrieve files from that tape with the* tar *command.*

Retrieving All Files on a Tape (pax)

Use the following steps to use the pax command to copy all the files on a tape into the current directory.

1. Change to the directory where you want to copy the files.
2. Insert a write-enabled tape into the tape drive.
3. Type **pax -r -f < /dev/rmt/*n* .** and press Return.

   The -r option reads the contents of the tape to the current directory. The -f option identifies the tape drive. The dot (**.**) at the end of the command specifies the current directory. The pax command does not list the files as they are copied.
4. Type **ls -l** and press Return.

   The ls -l command lists the files in the current directory and shows their permissions to verify that the files are copied.
5. Remove the tape from the drive and write the names of the files on the tape label.

The following example copies all files from the tape in drive 0.

```
castle% pax -r -f /dev/rmt/0 .
pax: . :not owner
castle% ls -l
-rw-rw-rw-   1 winsor   staff     245660 Sep 12 11:52 addusr-1.rs
-rw-rw-rw-   1 winsor   staff     245660 Sep 12 10:31 addusr-2.rs
-rw-rw-rw-   1 winsor   staff     181315 Sep 12 10:29 at-addmn.rs
-rw-rw-rw-   1 winsor   staff     181309 Sep 12 10:27 at-base.rs
-rw-rw-rw-   1 winsor   staff     181315 Sep 12 10:28 at-menu.rs
castle%
```

Volume Management

Starting with the Solaris 2.2 system software, volume management automates mounting of CD-ROMs and diskettes; users no longer need to have superuser permissions to mount a CD-ROM or a diskette.

CAUTION. The Solaris 2.0 and 2.1 procedures for mounting CD-ROMs and diskettes do not work for Solaris 2.2 and later releases. Volume management controls the /dev/dsk/c0t6d0s0 *path to a CD-ROM drive and the* /dev/diskette *path to the diskette drive. If you try to access a CD-ROM or diskette and specify these paths, an error message is displayed.*

Volume management provides users with a standard interface for dealing with diskettes and CD-ROMs. Volume management provides three major benefits.

- Automatically mounting diskettes and CDs simplifies their use.
- Users can access diskettes and CDs without having to become superuser.

- Users on the network can gain automatic access to diskettes and CDs mounted on remote systems.

Mounting devices manually requires the following steps.

1. Insert media.
2. Become superuser.
3. Determine the location of the media device.
4. Create a mount point.
5. Make sure the focus is in the mount point directory.
6. Mount the device using the proper mount options.
7. Exit the superuser account.
8. Work with files on media.
9. Become superuser.
10. Unmount the media device.
11. Eject media.
12. Exit the superuser account.

Using volume management requires the following steps.

1. Insert media.
2. For diskettes, use the `volcheck` command.
3. Work with files on media.
4. Eject media.

Volume Management Files

Volume management consists of the `/usr/sbin/vold` volume management daemon, the `/etc/vold.conf` configuration file used by the `vold` daemon to determine which devices to manage, the `/etc/rmmount.conf` file used to configure removable media mounts, and actions in `/usr/lib/rmmount`. The volume daemon logs messages in the `/var/adm/vold.log` file.

The default `/etc/vold.conf` file is shown below. **New!**

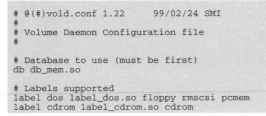

```
# @(#)vold.conf 1.22     99/02/24 SMI
#
# Volume Daemon Configuration file
#

# Database to use (must be first)
db db_mem.so

# Labels supported
label dos label_dos.so floppy rmscsi pcmem
label cdrom label_cdrom.so cdrom
```

```
label sun label_sun.so floppy rmscsi pcmem

# Devices to use
use cdrom drive /dev/rdsk/c*s2 dev_cdrom.so cdrom%d
use floppy drive /dev/rdiskette[0-9] dev_floppy.so floppy%d
use pcmem drive /dev/rdsk/c*s2 dev_pcmem.so pcmem%d forceload=true
# use rmscsi drive /dev/rdsk/c*s2 dev_rmscsi.so rmscsi%d

# Actions
insert dev/diskette[0-9]/* user=root /usr/sbin/rmmount
insert dev/dsk/* user=root /usr/sbin/rmmount
eject dev/diskette[0-9]/* user=root /usr/sbin/rmmount
eject dev/dsk/* user=root /usr/sbin/rmmount
notify rdsk/* group=tty user=root /usr/lib/vold/volmissing -p

# List of file system types unsafe to eject
unsafe ufs hsfs pcfs udfs
```

If a system has additional diskette drives, volume management automatically creates two subdirectories in `/vol/dev` for each additional drive—one to provide access to the file systems and the other to provide access to the raw device. For a second diskette drive, volume management creates directories named `diskette1` and `rdiskette1`. For a third diskette drive, it creates directories named `diskette2` and `rdiskette2` (and so on for additional drives).

If you want additional CD-ROM drives on a system, you must edit the `/etc/vold.conf` file and add the new devices to the `Devices to use` list. The syntax for a `Devices to use` entry is shown below.

```
use device type special shared-object symname options
```

New! Volume management does not automatically mount DVD devices.

Table 53 describes each of the fields for the `Devices to use` syntax.

Table 53 Device Control Syntax Descriptions

Field	Supported Default Values	Description
device	`cdrom, floppy`	The removable media device.
type	`drive`	The type of device—multiple or single media support.
special	`/dev/dsk/c0t6` `/dev/diskette`	Path name of the device to be used in the `/dev` directory.
shared-object	`/usr/lib/vold/`*shared-object-name*	Location of the code that manages the device.

Table 53 Device Control Syntax Descriptions

Field	Supported Default Values	Description
symname	`cdrom0, floppy0`	The symbolic name that refers to this device. The *symname* is placed in the device directory: either `/cdrom` or `/floppy`).

options	`user=nobody`
	`group=nobody`
	`mode=0666`
		The user, group, and mode permissions for the inserted media.

The `/etc/rmmount.conf` file is shown below.

```
# @(#)rmmount.conf 1.8     00/01/05 SMI
#
# Removable Media Mounter configuration file.
#

# File system identification
ident hsfs ident_hsfs.so cdrom
ident ufs ident_ufs.so cdrom floppy rmscsi pcmem
ident pcfs ident_pcfs.so floppy rmscsi pcmem
ident udfs ident_udfs.so cdrom floppy

# Actions
action cdrom action_filemgr.so
action floppy action_filemgr.so
action rmscsi action_filemgr.so
```

The files in the `/usr/lib/vold` directory are listed below.

```
castle% ls -1 /usr/lib/vold
db_mem.so.1
db_nis.so.1
dev_cdrom.so.1
dev_floppy.so.1
dev_pcmem.so.1
dev_rmscsi.so.1
dev_test.so.1
eject_popup
label_cdrom.so.1
label_dos.so.1
label_sun.so.1
label_test.so.1
volcancel
volmissing
volmissing_popup
volstat
castle%
```

The files in the `/usr/lib/rmmount` directory are listed below.

```
oak% ls -1 /usr/lib/rmmount
action_filemgr.so.1
action_workman.so.1
oak%
```

If you encounter problems with volume management, check the /var/adm/vold.log file for information. An example of this file is shown below.

```
oak% more /var/adm/vold.log
Tue Jun  1 17:34:24 1999 warning: dev_use: couldn't find a driver for drive
  cdrom at /dev/dsk/c0t6
Tue Jun  1 17:39:12 1999 warning: dev_use: couldn't find a driver for drive
  cdrom at /dev/dsk/c0t6
Tue Jun  1 18:24:24 1999 warning: dev_use: couldn't find a driver for drive
  cdrom at /dev/dsk/c0t6
Wed Jun 23 15:08:47 1999 warning: check device 36.2: device not managed
Wed Jun 23 15:09:58 1999 warning: check device 36.2: device not managed
Wed Jun 23 15:11:08 1999 warning: check device 36.2: device not managed
Thu Jul 15 13:51:23 1999 warning: check device 36.2: device not managed
Thu Jul 15 13:52:53 1999 warning: check device 36.2: device not managed
Thu Jul 15 14:04:37 1999 warning: check device 36.2: device not managed
Thu Jul 15 14:05:52 1999 warning: check device 36.2: device not managed
Thu Jul 15 14:06:16 1999 warning: check device 36.2: device not managed
Wed Jul 21 16:33:33 1999 fatal: svc_tli_create: Cannot create server handle
Thu Jul 22 16:32:28 1999 warning: cdrom: /dev/rdsk/c0t6d0s2; Device busy
castle%
```

If you want to display debugging messages from the volume management daemon, you can start the daemon by typing **/usr/sbin/vold -v -L 10**. With these flags set, the volume management daemon logs quite a bit of information in /var/adm/vold.log.

Another way to gather debugging information is to run the rmmount command with the debug flag. To do so, edit /etc/vold.conf and change the lines with /usr/sbin/rmmount in them to include the -D flag, as shown in the following example.

```
insert /vol*/dev/diskette[0-9]/* user=root /usr/sbin/rmmount -D
```

Volume Management Mount Points

Volume management automatically mounts CD-ROM file systems on the /cdrom mount point when you insert the media into the drive.

When you insert a diskette in the diskette drive, you must ask the system to check the diskette drive. You can check for a diskette in any one of the following ways.

- From the command line, type **volcheck** and press Return.
- From the CDE front panel, click on the Folders menu and then click on Open Floppy.
- From the CDE File Manager File menu, choose Open Floppy.
- From the OpenWindows File Manager File menu, choose Check for Floppy.

When you use any of these methods, the files are mounted on the /floppy mount point. Table 54 describes the mount points and how volume management uses them.

Table 54 Volume Management Mount Points

Medium/Mount Point	State of Medium
Diskette	
/floppy/floppy0	Symbolic link to mounted diskette in local diskette drive.
/floppy/*floppy-name*	Mounted named diskette.
/floppy/unnamed_floppy	Mounted unnamed diskette.
CD-ROM	
/cdrom/cdrom0	Symbolic link to mounted CD-ROM in local CD-ROM drive.
/cdrom/*CD-ROM-name*	Mounted named CD-ROM.
/cdrom/*CD-ROM-name/partition*	Mounted named CD-ROM with partitioned file system.
/cdrom/unnamed_cdrom	Mounted unnamed CD-ROM.

If the medium does not contain a file system, volume management provides block and character devices in the /vol file system, as shown in Table 55.

Table 55 CD-ROM and Diskette Device Locations When No File System Is Present

Medium/Device Location	State of Medium
Diskette	
/vol/dev/diskette0/unnamed_floppy	Formatted unnamed diskette-block device access.
/vol/dev/rdiskette0/unnamed_floppy	Formatted unnamed diskette—raw device access.
/vol/dev/diskette0/unlabeled	Unlabeled diskette—block diskette-raw device access.
CD-ROM	
/vol/dev/dsk/c0t6/unnamed_cdrom	CD-ROM—block device access.

Table 55 CD-ROM and Diskette Device Locations When No File System Is Present (Continued)

Medium/Device Location	State of Medium
/vol/dev/rdsk/c0t6/unnamed_cdrom	CD-ROM—raw device access.

New!

Limitation on UFS Formats with Volume Management for CDs

UFS formats are not portable between architectures, so you must use them on the architecture for which they were formatted. For example, a UFS CD formatted for a SPARC platform cannot be recognized by an IA platform. Likewise, an IA UFS CD cannot be mounted by volume management on a SPARC platform. The same limitation applies to diskettes.

Most CDs are formatted according to the ISO 9660 standard (High Sierra File System—HSFS), which imposes no limitations on volume management.

CD-ROMs and Volume Management

The following sections describe how to access files from local and remote CD-ROM drives.

Mounting a Local CD-ROM

Use the following procedure to mount a CD-ROM from a local drive.

1. Push the button on the front of the CD-ROM drive to open the tray.
2. Place the CD-ROM into the tray so that the CD label is visible.

   The CD-ROM is automatically mounted on the `/cdrom` mount point. If File Manager is running, a window displays the contents of the CD-ROM, as shown in Figure 52.

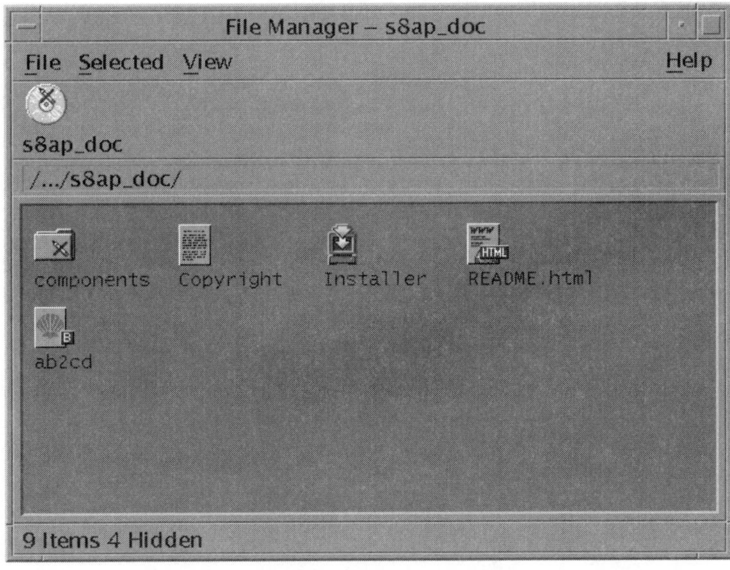

New!

Figure 52 The CDE File Manager CD-ROM Window

3. To access files on the CD-ROM from a command line, type **`cd /cdrom/cdrom0`** and press Return.
4. Type **`ls -L`** and press Return.

   The list of files in the `/cdrom/cdrom0` directory is displayed. Use the `-L` option because some of the files on the CD may be symbolic links.

You can use the File Manager CD-ROM window and the command line interchangeably. For example, you can eject a CD-ROM either from a command line by typing **`eject cdrom`** or by choosing Eject from the File menu in the File Manager CD-ROM window.

New!

Sharing Files from a Remote CD-ROM Drive

Before you can share CD-ROM files from a command line, the `mountd` daemon must be running. To check for the `mountd` daemon, on the system with the CD-ROM drive attached, type **`ps -ef | grep mountd`** and press Return.

If the `mountd` daemon is running, other systems can access shared files. If the `mountd` daemon is not running, you need to stop NFS services and restart them. Be sure to notify any users of the system that NFS services will be interrupted momentarily when you use the following procedure.

Use the following steps to start the `mountd` daemon.

1. Become superuser.
2. Type **`/etc/rc3.d/S15nfs.server stop`** and press Return.
   NFS services are stopped.
3. Type **`/etc/rc3.d/S15nfs.server start`** and press Return.
   NFS services are restarted and the CD files are exported.

The following example uses the `ps` command to verify that the `mountd` daemon is not already running, and if you are superuser it runs the `S15nfs.server` script to stop NFS services and restart them.

```
oak% ps -ef | grep mountd
    root  4571  4473  5 12:53:51 pts/3    0:00 grep mountd
oak% su
Password:
# /etc/rc3.d/S15nfs.server stop
# /etc/rc3.d/S15nfs.server start
#
```

Use the following steps to share CD files from a remote CD-ROM drive.

1. Insert the CD-ROM into the CD drive.
   The CD-ROM is mounted.
2. Become superuser on the Solaris 2.2 (or later) system with the CD-ROM drive attached.
3. Type **`share -F nfs -o ro /cdrom/cdrom0`** and press Return.
   The files on the CD are shared and accessible to other systems.

NOTE. Volume management does not recognize entries in the `/etc/dfs/dfstab` *file. With Solaris 2.3 volume management, you can set up remote CD-ROM mounts to be automatically shared by editing the* `/etc/rmmount.conf file`*. Refer to the* `rmmount.conf`*(4) manual page for more information.*

The following example shares the files on the `/cdrom/cdrom0` mount point as NFS files and uses the `ps` command to verify that the `mountd` daemon is running.

```
oak% su
Password:
# share -F nfs -o ro /cdrom/cdrom0
# ps -ef | grep mountd
    root  4655  4473  6 12:56:05 pts/3    0:00 grep mountd
    root  4649     1 47 12:55:25 ?        0:00 /usr/lib/nfs/mountd
#
```

How to Access Shared CD-ROM Files You can use the `/mnt` directory as the mount point for the CD-ROM files, or you can create another directory.

NOTE. Do not use the /cdrom *mount point to mount local files. Volume management may interfere with accessing files on the volume management* /cdrom *mount point.*

When the CD-ROM is in the remote drive and the files are shared, use the following steps to access the shared files on a local system.

1. On the local system, become superuser.
2. All on one line, type **mount** ***remote-system-name:/cdrom/cdrom0 /mount-point*** and press Return.

   The files from the remote system directory /cdrom/cdrom0 are mounted on the */mount-point* directory. The cdrom0 subdirectory is symbolically linked to the actual name of the CD-ROM that has a name assigned by the application vendor.

The following example mounts the files from the remote system castle on the /mnt mount point.

```
oak% su
Password:
# mount castle:/cdrom/cdrom0 /mnt
# cd /mnt
# ls
SUNWssser  SUNWsssra  SUNWsssrb  SUNWsssrc  SUNWsssrd  SUNWssstr
#
```

How to Unmount Shared CD-ROM Files When you are through using the CD-ROM files, use the following steps to unmount the remote CD-ROM.

1. On the local system, become superuser.
2. Type **cd** and press Return.
3. Type **umount** ***/mount-point*** and press Return.

   The files from the remote system directory /cdrom/cdrom0 are unmounted.

How to Find Out If a CD Is Still in Use If a Device busy error message is displayed when you try to unmount a CD-ROM, you can use the fuser command to find out who is currently accessing the CD.

1. Become superuser.
2. Type **fuser -u /cdrom/cdrom0** and press Return.

   The process ID and user name of those currently accessing the CD are displayed.
3. Type **fuser -u -k /cdrom/cdrom0** and press Return.

   The processes accessing the CD are killed.
4. Type **eject cdrom** and press Return, or choose Eject from the File menu in the CD File Manager window.

In the following example, user winsor is accessing the CD.

```
paperbark% eject cdrom
/vol/dev/rdsk/c0t6d0/s8ap_doc: Device busy
paperbark% su
Password:
# fuser -u /cdrom/cdrom0
/cdrom/cdrom0:       467c(winsor)
# fuser -u -k /cdrom/cdrom0
# eject cdrom
# exit
paperbark%
```

Diskettes and Volume Management

When you insert a diskette into the diskette drive, to prevent excessive reads, volume management does not mount the diskette automatically. Excessive reads can quickly wear out the diskette drive. You must use the volcheck command that checks for the presence of a diskette in the diskette drive.

New!

Limitation on UFS Formats with Volume Management for Diskettes

UFS formats are not portable between architectures, so you must use them on the architecture for which they were formatted. For example. a UFS diskette formatted for a SPARC platform cannot be recognized by an IA platform. Likewise, an IA UFS diskette cannot be mounted by volume management on a SPARC platform. The same limitation applies to CDs.

UFS incompatibility can occur more often with diskettes than with CDs because formats often can be established by the user. Be aware that if you format a UFS diskette on one architecture, you won't be able to use it on a different architecture.

Command-Line Access

Use the following steps to format a diskette from a command line.

1. Insert a diskette into the diskette drive.
2. Type **volcheck** and press Return.

   The system has access to the unformatted diskette.
3. Type **fdformat** and press Return to format a UFS file system or **fdformat -d** to format an MS-DOS file system.
4. When prompted, press Return to begin formatting the diskette.
5. For UFS file systems, you must also make a new file system on the diskette. To do so, become superuser and type

newfs /vol/dev/rdiskette0/unnamed_floppy, and press Return.

Use the following steps to access files on a formatted diskette.

1. Insert a formatted diskette in the diskette drive.
2. Type **volcheck** and press Return.

   If there is a formatted diskette in the drive, volume management mounts it on the /floppy mount point. If no diskette is in the drive, no error message is displayed. The volcheck command redisplays the prompt. When the diskette is mounted on the /floppy mount point, you can access files on it either from the command line or from the File Manager Floppy window, described in "CDE File Manager Access" on page 276.
3. Type **cd /floppy** and press Return.
4. Type **ls** and press Return.

   The name of the diskette is displayed.
5. Type **cd *diskette-name*** and press Return.
6. Type **ls** and press Return.

   The names of the files on the diskette are displayed. You can copy files to and from the diskette with the cp command.

In the following example, the diskette is not mounted, so the only directory in /floppy is ms-dos_5. After volcheck mounts the diskette, the directory with the name of the diskette is displayed. The diskette in this example contains only a lost+found directory.

```
oak% cd /floppy
oak% ls
ms-dos_5
oak% volcheck
oak% ls
ms-dos_5         unnamed_floppy
oak% cd unnamed_floppy
oak% ls
lost+found
oak% cp /home/winsor/Appx/appxA.doc .
oak% ls
appxA.doc lost+found
oak%
```

Determining If a Diskette Is Still in Use

New!

You cannot unmount a file system whose current working directory is in use. If you get the message Device busy, a process has its current working directory on the diskette. You can use the fuser command to find out who is currently accessing the diskette.

1. Become superuser.
2. Type **`fuser -u /floppy/floppy0`** and press Return.

   The process ID and user name of those currently accessing the diskette are displayed.
3. Type **`fuser -u -k /floppy/floppy0`** and press Return.

   The processes accessing the diskette are killed.
4. Type **`eject floppy0`** and press Return.

NOTE. On a SPARC platform, the diskette is physically ejected from its drive. On an IA platform, you have to eject the diskette by hand. If you are running MS-Windows, look for a message on screen that says you can now eject the diskette. If the diskette jams, eject it manually by inserting an unfolded paper clip about an inch into the small hole in the front of the drive.

Ejecting a Diskette

Use the following steps to eject the diskette.

1. Type **`cd`** and press Return.

   You have changed out of the `/floppy` directory.
2. Type **`eject`** and press Return.

   After a few seconds, the diskette is ejected from the drive.

CDE Front Panel Access

If you are running CDE, you can use the Folders menu on the front panel to display the contents of a diskette. Use the following steps to open a diskette from the front panel.

1. Insert a formatted or unformatted diskette into the diskette drive.
2. From the front panel, open the Folders menu, shown in Figure 53, and click on Open Floppy.

Figure 53 Front Panel Files Menu.

3. If the diskette is unformatted, the Format Floppy window is displayed, as shown in Figure 54.

Format Floppy

Are you sure you want to format this floppy?

Warning: Formatting will destroy any information on the floppy and is not undoable.

Format: UNIX

Disk Name:

Format | Cancel | Cancel & Eject | Help

Figure 54 Format Floppy Window

4. Choose the format, type a diskette name in the text field if you want to assign one, and click on the Format button.

   The diskette is formatted and a new file system is created. When the diskette is formatted and contains the file system, the File Manager

Floppy window displays the contents of the diskette. The floppy is mounted to /floppy and a File Manager window opens.

If the diskette is already formatted, after the light on the front panel stops flashing (about 5 to 10 seconds), the floppy is mounted to /floppy and a File Manager window opens. Figure 55 shows an example of the File Manager floppy window for a formatted diskette.

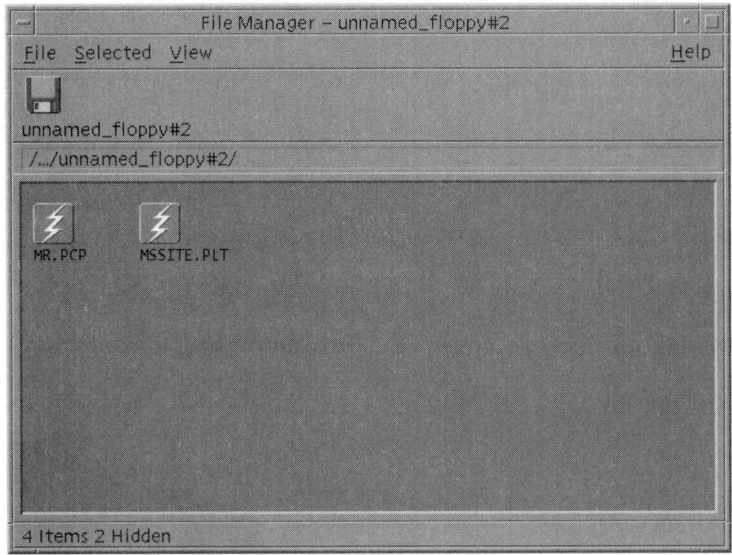

Figure 55 The CDE File Manager Floppy Window

CDE File Manager Access

If you are running CDE File Manager, you can use it to format a diskette, display the contents, and copy files to and from the diskette. Use the following steps to open a diskette from the CDE File Manager.

1. Insert a formatted or unformatted diskette into the diskette drive.
2. From the File Manager File menu, shown in Figure 56, choose Open Floppy.

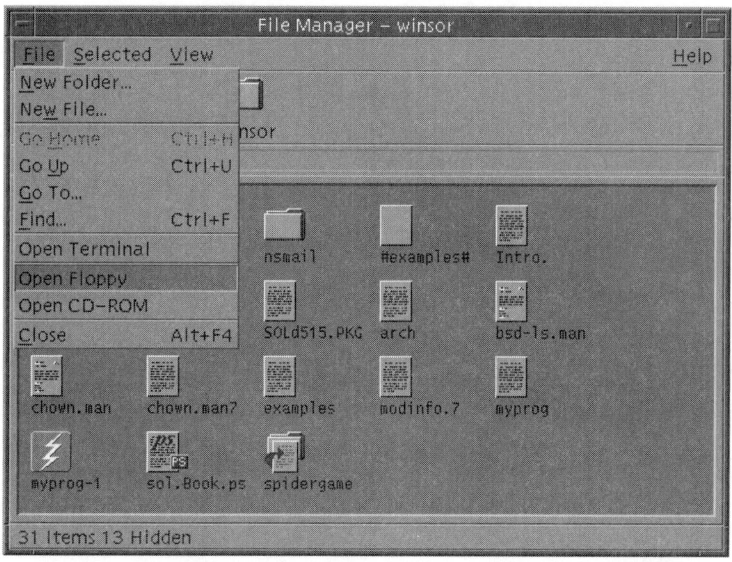

Figure 56 The CDE FIle Manager Menu

If the disk is unformatted, the Format Floppy window is displayed. If the disk is formatted, the File Manager window display shows the contents of the diskette.

3. From the File Manager File menu you can also eject, format, and rename the diskette, as shown by the menu items in Figure 57.

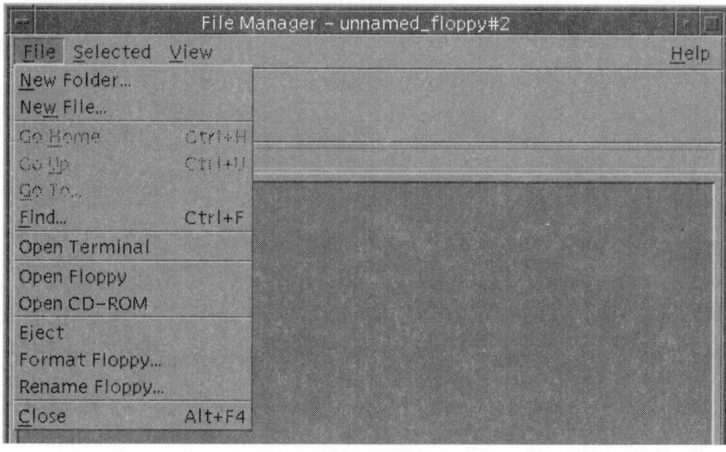

Figure 57 The CDE FIle Manager Floppy Menu

Using the tar and cpio Commands with Diskettes

If a diskette contains tar or cpio files, volume management does not mount it. You cannot access files on the diskette from the old /dev/rdiskette device name because volume management provides access to the media, not to the device.

You can access tar and cpio files on a diskette by using the symbolic link to the character device for the media that is in floppy drive 0 with the following device name.

```
/vol/dev/aliases/floppy0
```

Use the following steps to copy a file to a formatted diskette with the tar command.

1. Insert a formatted diskette into the diskette drive.
2. Type **volcheck** and press Return.
3. Type **tar cvf /vol/dev/aliases/floppy0** ***filename*** and press Return.

   The files are copied to the diskette.
4. Type **eject** and press Return.

   After a few seconds, the diskette is ejected.

Use the following steps to copy all tar files from a diskette.

1. Insert a formatted diskette into the diskette drive.
2. Change to the directory where you want to put the files.
3. Type **volcheck** and press Return.

   The diskette is mounted.
4. Type **tar xvf /vol/dev/aliases/floppy0** and press Return.

   The files are copied to the diskette.
5. Type **eject** and press Return.

   After a few seconds, the diskette is ejected.

Alternatively, with Solaris 2.2 (and later) systems, you can access tar or cpio files by using the following device name syntax.

```
/vol/dev/rfd0/media-name
```

The most common *media-name* is unlabeled.

With Solaris 2.3, the device name syntax is changed. You access `tar` or `cpio` files with the following device name syntax.

```
/vol/dev/rdiskette0/media-name
```

The most frequent *`media-name`* for media without a file system is `unlabeled`.

For example, to copy a `tar` file to a diskette, type **`tar cvf /vol/dev/rdiskette0/unlabeled`** ***`filename`*** and press Return. To retrieve all `tar` files from a diskette, type **`tar xvf /vol/dev/rdiskette0/unlabeled`** and press Return.

Volume Management Troubleshooting

From time to time, you may encounter problems with mounting diskettes (or, less frequently, a CD-ROM). If you encounter a problem, first check to find out whether volume management knows about the diskette. The best way to check is to look in `/vol/dev/rdiskette0` to see if something is there. If the files are not mounted, you may have forgotten to run the `volcheck` command or you may have a hardware problem. If references to `/vol` hang, the `/usr/sbin/vold` daemon has probably died, and you should restart it by typing **`/etc/init.d/volmgt start`** and pressing Return.

If you find a name in `/vol/dev/rdiskette0` and nothing is mounted in `/floppy/`*`media-name`*, it is likely that the data on the media is not a recognized file system. It may be a `tar`, `cpio`, or Macintosh file system. You can access these media through the block or character devices found in `/vol/dev/rdiskette0` or `/vol/dev/diskette0` and use your own tools to interpret the data on them.

Volume Management and workman

Many people use the `workman` program to play music from their CD-ROM drive. `workman` is not a Sun product, but it is in wide use. To use `workman` with volume management, add the line shown in bold to the `/etc/rmmount.conf` file. Be sure the line comes before the `cdrom action_filemgr` line.

```
# @(#)rmmount.conf 1.8     00/01/05 SMI
#
# Removable Media Mounter configuration file.
#

# File system identification
ident hsfs ident_hsfs.so cdrom
ident ufs ident_ufs.so cdrom floppy rmscsi pcmem
ident pcfs ident_pcfs.so floppy rmscsi pcmem
```

```
ident udfs ident_udfs.so cdrom floppy

# Actions
action cdrom action_workman.so pathname
action cdrom action_filemgr.so
action floppy action_filemgr.so
action rmscsi action_filemgr.so
```

A `pathname` is the name of the path where users access the `workman` program—for example, `/usr/dist/exe/workman`.

When you have made this change, audio CD-ROMs are automatically detected and the `workman` program is started when a CD-ROM is inserted into the CD-ROM drive.

NOTE. When you set up `workman` *in the way described here, you should not try to start* `workman` *from the application because volume management may get confused. In addition, with Solaris 2.2 (and later) volume management, if you are using* `workman`*, you must eject the CD-ROM from the* `workman` *application. If you eject the CD-ROM from another window,* `workman` *hangs. This problem is fixed in Solaris 2.3 and later system software.*

Disabling Volume Management

You may want to disable volume management for some users. To do so, use the following steps.

1. Become superuser.
2. Remove or rename the `/etc/rc2.d/S92volmgt` script.
3. Type **`/etc/init.d/volmgt stop`** and press Return.

You can disable part of volume management and leave other parts functional. You may, for example, want to automatically mount CD-ROMs but use the Solaris 2.0 method for accessing files on a diskette. You can do so by commenting out the lines for diskettes in the `/etc/vold.conf` file, as shown below.

New!

```
# @(#)vold.conf 1.22     99/02/24 SMI
#
# Volume Daemon Configuration file
#

# Database to use (must be first)
db db_mem.so

# Labels supported
label dos label_dos.so floppy rmscsi pcmem
label cdrom label_cdrom.so cdrom
label sun label_sun.so floppy rmscsi pcmem

# Devices to use
use cdrom drive /dev/rdsk/c*s2 dev_cdrom.so cdrom%d
```

```
# use floppy drive /dev/rdiskette[0-9] dev_floppy.so floppy%d
use pcmem drive /dev/rdsk/c*s2 dev_pcmem.so pcmem%d forceload=true
# use rmscsi drive /dev/rdsk/c*s2 dev_rmscsi.so rmscsi%d

# Actions
insert dev/diskette[0-9]/* user=root /usr/sbin/rmmount
insert dev/dsk/* user=root /usr/sbin/rmmount
eject dev/diskette[0-9]/* user=root /usr/sbin/rmmount
eject dev/dsk/* user=root /usr/sbin/rmmount
notify rdsk/* group=tty user=root /usr/lib/vold/volmissing -p

# List of file system types unsafe to eject
unsafe ufs hsfs pcfs udfs
```

Using Diskettes Without Volume Management

Use double-sided (DS), high-density (HD) 3.5-inch diskettes. Before you can copy UFS files or file systems to diskette, you must format the diskette. Use the `tar` command to copy UFS files to a single formatted diskette. Use `cpio` if you need to copy UFS files to multiple formatted diskettes. The `cpio` command recognizes end of media and prompts you to insert the next volume.

You also can make a DOS-file system on a diskette. To use a DOS-formatted diskette, you mount the diskette as a PCFS file system and use basic OS commands such as `cp` and `mv` to archive and retrieve files from the diskette.

Diskette Device Names

The device name for the diskette drive in the Solaris Operating Environment. is `/dev/diskette`. The raw device file for a diskette is `/dev/rdiskette`.

Diskettes for UFS File Systems

The following sections describe how to format diskettes for use with UFS file systems and how to copy files with the `tar` and `cpio` commands. They also describe how to retrieve files that were created with the SunOS 4.x `bar` command.

Formatting a UFS Diskette

Use the following steps to format a diskette for use with Solaris UFS file systems.

1. Check the diskette to make sure that it is not write protected.
2. Put the diskette in the drive.

CAUTION. Reformatting destroys any files already on the diskette.

3. Type **fdformat** and press Return.

   The message `Press return to start formatting floppy` is displayed.

4. Press Return.

   While the diskette is being formatted, a series of dots (. . .) is displayed. When formatting is complete, the prompt is redisplayed

```
oak% fdformat
Press return to start formatting floppy.
.........................................................................
oak%
```

Removing a Diskette from the Drive

Use the `eject` command to remove a diskette from the disk drive. You can also use the `eject` command to remove a CD-ROM disc from a CD-ROM drive. The default for the `eject` command is `/dev/diskette` when you type it with no arguments. To remove a diskette from the diskette drive, type **eject** and press Return. The diskette is ejected.

NOTE. If the drive jams, you can eject a diskette manually by inserting a straightened wire paper clip into the pinhole under the diskette slot.

To eject a CD-ROM disc from a CD-ROM drive, type **eject cdrom** and press Return.

Copying UFS Files to a Single Formatted Diskette

This section provides steps for using the `tar` command to copy files to a single formatted diskette. Note that the `tar` command does not require the raw device name, `/dev/rdiskette`. You can use either the `/dev/rdiskette` or `/dev/diskette` device name. The examples in this book use the raw device name.

Use the following steps to copy UFS files to a single formatted diskette.

1. Change to the directory that contains the file(s) you want to copy.
2. Insert a write-enabled formatted diskette into the drive.

CAUTION. Copying files to a formatted diskette with the `c` *option destroys any files already on the diskette. If you want to preserve the files already on the diskette, use the* `r` *option described in* *"Appending Files to a Formatted Diskette (tar)" on page 283.*

3. Type **tar cvf /dev/rdiskette *filename filename filename...*** and press Return.

   The file names you specify are copied to the diskette, overwriting any existing files on the diskette.

*NOTE. You can use metacharacters (? and *) as part of the file names you specify. For example, to copy all documents with a* .doc *suffix, type* ***.doc** *as the file-name argument.*

4. Type **eject** and press Return to remove the diskette from the drive.

   The diskette is ejected from the drive.
5. Write the names of the files on the diskette label.

The following example copies two files to a diskette.

```
oak% cd /home/winsor
oak% ls evaluation*
evaluation.doc    evaluation.doc.backup
oak% tar cvf /dev/rdiskette evaluation*
a evaluation.doc 86 blocks
a evaluation.doc.backup 84 blocks
oak% eject
oak%
```

Listing the Files on a Diskette (tar)

Use the following steps to list files that were copied with the tar command.

1. Insert a diskette into the drive.
2. Type **tar tvf /dev/rdiskette** and press Return.

   The t option lists the table of contents for the files on the diskette.

In the following example, the table of contents for the diskette contains two files.

```
oak% tar tvf /dev/rdiskette
rw-rw-rw-6693/10  44032 Apr 23 14:54 2000 evaluation.doc
rw-rw-rw-6693/10  43008 Apr 23 14:47 2000 evaluation.doc.backup
oak%
```

See the tar(1) manual page for more information.

If you need a multiple-volume interchange command, use cpio. The tar command is only a single-volume command.

Appending Files to a Formatted Diskette (tar)

When you copy tar files to a formatted diskette, any files already on the diskette are overwritten. If you want to add other files, but keep the files already on the diskette, use the following steps.

1. Change to the directory that contains the file you want to copy.
2. Insert a write-enabled formatted diskette into the drive.
3. Type **tar rvf /dev/rdiskette** ***filename filename filename...*** and press Return.

   The file names you specify are appended to the files already on the diskette.

*NOTE. You can use metacharacters (? and *) as part of the file names you specify. For example, to copy all documents with a* .doc *suffix, type* ***.doc** *as the file name argument.*

4. Type **eject** and press Return to remove the diskette from the drive.

   The diskette is ejected from the drive.
5. Write the names of the additional files on the diskette label.

The following example appends one file to the files already on the diskette.

```
oak% cd /home/winsor
oak% tar rvf /dev/rdiskette junk
a junk 1 blocks
oak% tar tvf /dev/rdiskette
rw-rw-rw-6693/10  44032 Apr 23 14:54 2000 evaluation.doc
rw-rw-rw-6693/10  43008 Apr 23 14:47 2000 evaluation.doc.backup
rw-rw-rw-6693/10     18 Dec 10 11:36 2000 junk
oak% eject
oak%
```

Retrieving Files from a Diskette (tar)

Use the following steps to retrieve all files from a diskette.

1. Change to the directory where you want to put the files.
2. Insert the diskette into the drive.
3. Type **tar xvf /dev/rdiskette** and press Return.

   All the files on the diskette are copied to the current directory.
4. Type **eject** and press Return to remove the diskette from the drive.

   The diskette is ejected from the drive.

The following example copies all files from the diskette.

```
oak% cd /home/winsor/Evaluations
oak% tar xvf /dev/rdiskette
x evaluation.doc, 44032 bytes, 86 tape blocks
x evaluation.doc.backup, 43008 bytes, 84 tape blocks
oak% eject
oak%
```

To retrieve individual files from a diskette, type **tar xvf /dev/rdiskette** ***filename filename filename...*** and press

Return. The file names you specify are extracted from the diskette and placed in the current working directory. The following example copies all files with the prefix `evaluation` from the diskette.

```
oak% cd /home/winsor/Evaluations
oak% tar xvf /dev/rdiskette
x evaluation.doc, 44032 bytes, 86 tape blocks
x evaluation.doc.backup, 43008 bytes, 84 tape blocks
oak% eject
oak%
```

Retrieving bar Files from Diskettes (cpio)

The SunOS 4.x `bar` command is not provided with the Solaris Operating Environment. You can retrieve files from diskettes that were archived with the SunOS 4.x `bar` command by using the `-H bar` option to `cpio`.

> *NOTE. You can use the* `-H bar` *option with* `-i` *to retrieve files only. You cannot create files with the* `bar` *header option. It is good practice to list the contents of an archive before extracting them.*

Use the following steps to retrieve `bar` files from a diskette.

1. Change to the directory where you want to put the files.
2. Insert the diskette that contains `bar` files into the drive.
3. Type **`cpio -ivH bar < /dev/diskette`** and press Return.
   All the files on the diskette are copied to the current directory.
4. Type **`eject`** and press Return to remove the diskette from the drive.

Multiple Diskettes for Archiving Files (cpio)

If you are copying large files or file systems onto diskettes, you want to be prompted to replace a full diskette with another formatted diskette. The `cpio` command provides this capability. The `cpio` options you use are the same as you would use to copy files to tape, except you would specify `/dev/rdiskette` as the device instead of the tape device name. See "The cpio Command" on page 258 for information on how to use `cpio`.

Making a UFS File System on a Diskette (newfs /dev/rdiskette)

If you want to mount a UFS diskette, you must first create a file system on it.

1. Format the diskette.
2. Become superuser.
3. Type **`newfs /dev/rdiskette`** and press Return.

A UFS file system is created on the diskette, as shown in the following example.

```
oak% fdformat
Press return to start formatting floppy.
.............................................................................
  ..
oak% su
Password:
# newfs /dev/rdiskette
#
```

Diskettes for PCFS (DOS) File Systems

You can format diskettes with the PCFS file system for use with DOS systems. The following sections describe how to format a DOS diskette and how to mount the diskette for use with the Solaris Operating Environment. See "Types of File Systems" on page 199 for a description of the PCFS file system.

Formatting a Diskette with a PCFS (DOS) File System

Use the following steps to format a diskette with the PCFS file system.

1. Put a diskette in the drive.

CAUTION. Reformatting destroys any files already on the diskette.

2. Type **fdformat -d** and press Return.

   The message `Press return to start formatting floppy` is displayed.

3. Press Return.

   While the diskette is being formatted, a series of dots (...) is displayed. When formatting is complete, the prompt is redisplayed, as shown in the following example.

```
oak% fdformat -d
Press return to start formatting floppy.
..........................................................................
oak%
```

Mounting a PCFS Diskette

You can mount a PCFS diskette that was formatted with the `fdformat -d` command, or a DOS diskette that was formatted on a DOS system. When you mount a PCFS file system, you can create, read, write, and delete files in the file system with Solaris file commands, subject to DOS naming conventions. See the `pcfs(7)` manual page for more information about the format and features of the PCFS file system.

Use the following steps to mount a PCFS file system from a diskette.

1. Insert the PCFS diskette in the drive.
2. Become superuser.
3. Type **mount -F pcfs /dev/diskette *mount-point*** and press Return.

   The file system is mounted on the *mount-point* you specify.

You can mount a PCFS file system with different mount options (for example, -o rw). See the mount_pcfs(1M) manual page for a description of the options that can be included in the list.

If you use PCFS diskettes frequently, you may want to add the following entry to your /etc/vfstab file.

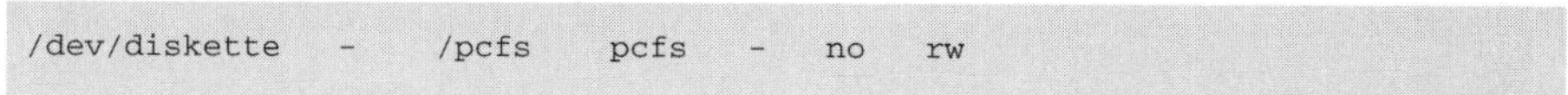

```
/dev/diskette   -   /pcfs   pcfs   -   no   rw
```

Create a directory named /pcfs to use as the mount point for the diskette. With the mount point and the entry in the /etc/vfstab file, you can mount a PCFS diskette by becoming superuser and typing **mount /pcfs** and pressing Return. Once the diskette is mounted, you can use any of the Solaris file commands such as cp or mv to copy files to and from the diskette.

Unmounting a PCFS Diskette

When you are done with the PCFS diskette, you must unmount it before you can eject it. To unmount the diskette, first make sure the focus is not in the mount point directory or any of its subdirectories. Then, type **umount *mount-point*** and press Return. To eject the diskette, type **eject** and press Return.

Administering Disks

The following sections describe the Solaris disk-naming conventions, commands for finding disk information (du, prtvtoc), and ways to repair or replace a bad disk.

Disk-Naming Conventions

Solaris disks have both block and raw (character) device files. The device name is the same, regardless of whether the command requires the block or raw device file.

Each type of device file has its own subdirectory in `/dev`: `/dev/dsk` (the block interface) or `/dev/rdsk` (the raw interface).

Some commands, such as `mount`, use the block interface device name from the `/dev/dsk` directory to specify the disk device. Other commands, such as `newfs`, require the raw interface device name from the `/dev/rdsk` directory to specify the disk device.

The device name you use to identify a specific disk with either type of interface depends on the controller type: bus-oriented (SCSI or IPI) or direct. You refer to a disk device by specifying the subdirectory to which it is symbolically linked (either `/dev/dsk` or `/dev/rdsk`) followed by a string identifying the particular controller, disk, and slice.

```
/dev/[r]dsk/cwtxdysz
```

`cw` is the controller number, `tx` is the target number, `dy` is the drive number, and `sz` is the slice identifier.

Using Disks with Bus Controllers

Figure 58 shows the device-naming convention for SPARC disks with bus controllers.

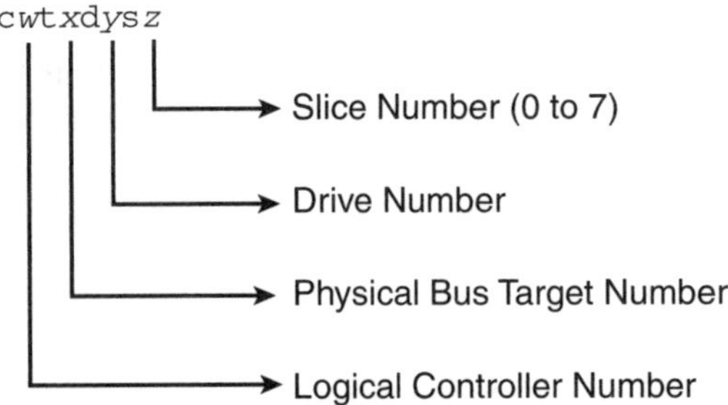

Figure 58 Naming Conventions for SPARC Disks with Bus Controllers

New! Figure 59 shows naming conventions for IA disks with SCSI controllers

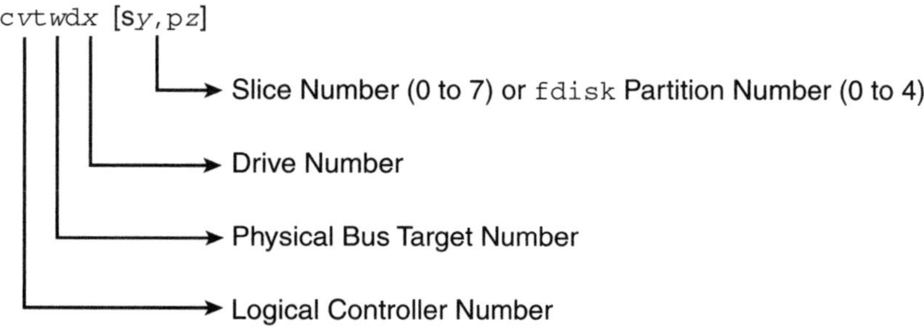

Figure 59 Naming Conventions for IA Disks with Bus Controllers

Each file system on a disk is assigned to a *slice*—a group of cylinders set aside for use by that file system. To specify a slice (partition) on a disk with a bus controller (either SCSI or IPI), use a device name with these conventions: `/dev/dsk/cWtXdYsZ` (the block interface) or `/dev/rdsk/cWtXdYsZ` (the raw interface).

NOTE. Solaris disk device names use the term slice *(and the letter* `s` *in the device name) to refer to the slice number.* Slice *is simply another name for a disk partition.*

Use the following guidelines to determine the values for the device file name.

- If you have only one controller on your system, *W* is always 0.
- For SCSI controllers, *X* is the target address set by the switch on the back of or inside the unit.
- *Y* is the number of the drive attached to the target. If the disk has an embedded controller, *Y* is always 0.
- *Z* is the slice (partition) number, with a value ranging from 0 to 7. To specify the entire disk, use slice 2. Table 56 shows conventional assignments of slice (partition) numbers for the disk on which root is found.

Table 56 Customary Assignments of Slices for Disk with Root

Slice	File System	Use
0	`root`	Operating system.
1	`swap`	Virtual memory space.
2	-	Entire disk.
3-5		Available for use according to your administrative policy.

Table 56 Customary Assignments of Slices for Disk with Root (Continued)

Slice	File System	Use
6	`/usr`	Executable programs, program libraries, and documentation.

Table 57 shows some examples of raw device names for disks with bus-oriented controllers.

Table 57 Examples of Device Names for Disks with Bus-Oriented Controllers

Device Name	Description
`/dev/rdsk/c0t0d0s0`	Raw interface to the first slice (root) on the first disk at the first SCSI target address on the first controller.
`/dev/rdsk/c0t0d0s2`	Raw interface to the third slice (which represents the whole disk) on the first disk at the first SCSI target address on the first controller.
`/dev/rdsk/c0t1d0s6`	Raw interface to seventh (`/usr`) slice on the first disk at the second SCSI target address on the first controller.

New!

NOTE. In releases before the Solaris 7 Operating Environment, SCSI support on the Intel platform was handled by the `cmdk` *driver. Starting with the Solaris 7 release, this support is handled by the* `sd` *driver. This driver is similar to the SCSI disk driver on Solaris SPARC platforms, which is also named* `sd`.

There is no change in the administration of these devices. You will see references to `sd` *instead of* `cmdk` *in the output of the* `prtconf`, `sysdef`, `dmesg`, *and* `format` *commands.*

Features and functionality are a superset of the features supplied by `cmdk`, *so applications that use logical disk names in* `/dev/dsk` *are not affected by the driver change. IA systems with IDE devices still use the* `cmdk` *driver.*

Using Disks with Direct Controllers

Disks with direct controllers do not have a target entry as part of the device name. To specify a slice (partition) on a disk with a direct controller, use a device name with the following conventions: `/dev/dsk/cXdYsZ` (the block interface) or `/dev/rdsk/cXdYsZ` (the raw interface).

Figure 60 shows the naming convention for SPARC-based disks with direct controllers. If you have only one controller on your system, *x* is always 0. Use slice 2 to specify the entire disk.

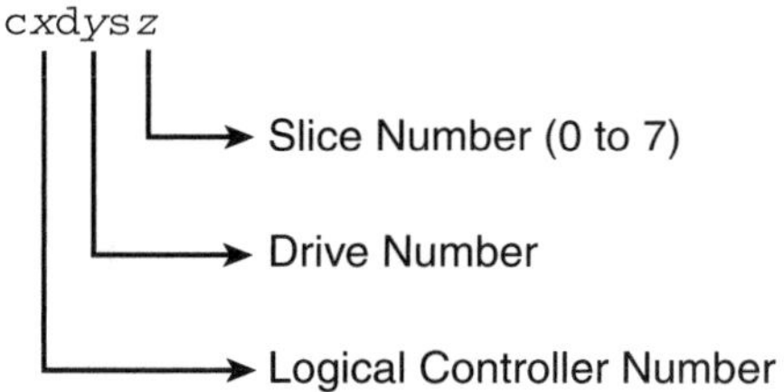

Figure 60 Naming Conventions for SPARC-Based Disks with Direct Controllers

Figure 61 shows the naming convention for IA-based disks with direct controllers.

New!

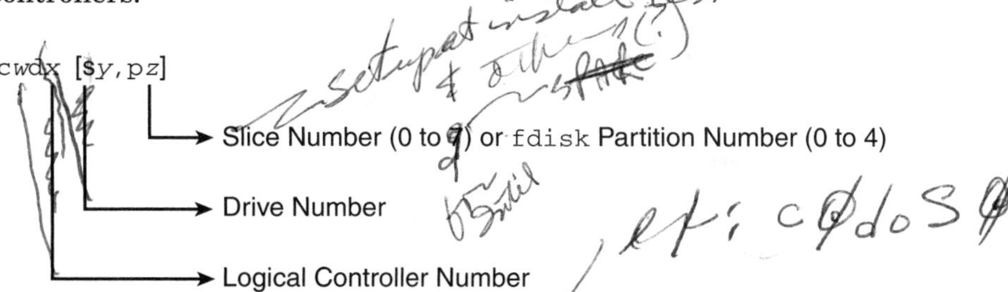

Figure 61 Naming Conventions for IA-Based Disks with Direct Controllers

Use slice 2 (`s2`) to specify the entire Solaris `fdisk` partition.

Table 58 shows some examples of raw device names for disks with direct controllers.

Table 58 Examples of Device Names for Disks with Direct Controllers

Device Name	Description
`/dev/rdsk/c0d0s0`	Raw interface to the first controller on the first disk to the first slice (root).
`/dev/rdsk/c0d0s2`	Raw interface to the first controller on the first disk to the third slice (the entire disk).
`/dev/rdsk/c0d1s6`	Raw interface to the first controller on the second disk to the seventh (`/usr`) slice. By convention, the slice numbers are assigned to specific file systems, as shown in Table 56.

Setting Up Disk Slices

Files are stored within file systems. Each disk slice is treated as a separate disk drive both by the operating system and by the system administrator. When setting up slices, be aware of the following constraints.

- Each disk slice holds only one file system.
- No file system can span multiple slices.

You set up slices differently on SPARC and IA platforms, as described in Table 59.

Table 59 Slice Differences on Platforms

SPARC Platform	IA Platform
Entire disk is used for Solaris environment.	Disk is divided into `fdisk` partitions, one per operating environment.
Disk is divided into eight slices, numbered 0–7.	The Solaris `fdisk` partition is divided into 10 slices, numbered 0–9.

SPARC Disk Slices

On SPARC-based systems, you define eight disk slices and assign each to a conventional use, as described in Table 60.

Table 60 SPARC Disk Slice Conventions

Slice	File System	Client/ Server	Description
0	`root`	Both	Hold files and directories that make up the operating system.
1	`swap`	Both	Provide virtual memory or swap space.
2	–	Both	By convention, refer to the entire disk. The entire disk is defined automatically by the `format` command and the Solaris installation programs. Do not change the size of this slice.

Table 60 SPARC Disk Slice Conventions (Continued)

Slice	File System	Client/ Server	Description
3	`/export`	Server	Hold alternative versions of the operating system that are required by client systems whose architecture differs from that of the server. Clients with the same architecture type as the server obtain executables from the `/usr` file system, usually slice 6.
4	`/export/swap`	Server	Provide virtual memory/swap space for client systems.
5	`/opt`	Both	Hold application software added to a system. If a slice is not allocated for this file system during installation, the `/opt` directory is put in slice 0.
6	`/usr`	Both	Hold operating system commands—also known as *executables*—designed to be run by users. This slice also holds documentation, system programs such as `init` and `syslogd`, and library routines.
7	`/home` or `/export/home`	Both	Hold files created by user accounts.

IA Disk Slices

On IA-based systems, you divide disks into `fdisk` partitions. Each `fdisk` partition is a section of the disk reserved for a particular operating environment. For a Solaris `fdisk` partition, you define 10 slices, numbered from 0 through 9 and assign each to a conventional use. The uses for slices 0 through 7 are the same as on Solaris systems, described in Table 60. Table 61 describes slices 8 and 9.

Table 61 IA Conventions for Slices 8 and 9

Slice	File System	Client/ Server	Description
8	—	Both	Contain the boot slice information at the beginning of the Solaris partition that enables Solaris to boot from the hard disk.
9	—	Both	Provide an area reserved for alternate disk blocks. Slice 9 is known as the alternate sector slice.

Determining Which Slices to Use

When you set up file systems for a disk, you choose not only the size of each slice but also which slices to use. Your decisions depend on the configuration of the system and the software you want to install on the disk. System types are defined by how they access the root (/) and `/usr` file systems, including the swap area. For example, stand-alone and server systems mount these file systems from a local disk; other clients mount the file system remotely.

New! In previous releases, you could set up the following five system configurations.

- Servers.
- Diskless clients.
- Stand-alone systems.
- Dataless clients.
- Solstice AutoClient systems.

With the Solaris 8 release, the system configurations are simplified to servers, stand-alone systems, and JavaStations™. The JavaStation is a client designed for zero administration. It optimizes Java™ technology and takes full advantage of the network to deliver everything from Java applications and services to complete, integrated system and network management. You do no local administration for a JavaStation. The server handles booting, administration, and data storage.

Table 62 summarizes the three system types.

Table 62 System Configurations and Slice Requirements

System Type	Local File Systems	Local Swap	Remote File Systems	Network Use
Server	root (/)	Yes	None	High
	/usr			
	/home			
	/opt			
	/export/home			
	/export/root			
Stand-alone	root (/)	Yes	None	Low
	/usr			
	/export/home			
JavaStation	None	No	/home	High

Disk Use Check (du)

To find the number of 512-byte disk blocks used per file or directory, type **du** and press Return. When directories contain subdirectories, the subdirectories and their contents are included in the block count, as shown in the following example.

```
oak% du
2913    ./3.0templates
639     ./Art
347     ./Howto
1998    ./Clipart
607     ./Newtemplates
38      ./Modemstuff
2004    ./Config/Art
6593    ./Config
13280   .
oak%
```

The output is displayed in 512-byte blocks. To convert to megabytes, divide by 2048. In the preceding example 13280/2048 = 6.48 Mbytes.

Disk Information Check (prtvtoc)

Use the `prtvtoc` (print volume table of contents) command to display information about disk partitioning. The `prtvtoc` command works only when the slice you specify has space allocated to it. Otherwise, it displays the error message No such device or address. If you use the standard slice-naming conventions, specifying slice 2 displays the contents of the entire disk.

Use the following steps to display information about disk partitioning.

1. Become superuser.
2. Type **prtvtoc /dev/rdsk/*cntndnsn*** and press Return.

   Information for the disk you specify is displayed, as shown in the following example.

```
paperbark% su
Password:
# prtvtoc /dev/rdsk/c0t0d0s2
* /dev/rdsk/c0t0d0s2 partition map
*
* Dimensions:
*      512 bytes/sector
*       80 sectors/track
*       19 tracks/cylinder
*     1520 sectors/cylinder
*     3500 cylinders
*     2733 accessible cylinders
*
* Flags:
*    1: unmountable
*   10: read-only
*
*                          First      Sector     Last
* Partition   Tag  Flags    Sector     Count      Sector   Mount Directory
       0       2    00    1048800    2865200   3913999    /
       1       3    01          0    1048800   1048799
       2       5    00          0    4154160   4154159
       7       8    00    3914000     240160   4154159    /export/home
```

Bad-Disk Repair

The following sections describe the steps for repairing a bad disk or reinstalling a new one.

Try Archiving the Files

If you can access the drive, do a ufsdump of all the file systems on the disk. See "Backing Up and Restoring File Systems" on page 227 for information on how to use the ufsdump command.

Try Copying Data from the Disk

If you cannot run ufsdump on the disk, find another disk of the same type, connect it to the system, and use either the dd or volcopy commands to copy the data from the bad disk. See the dd(1M) and volcopy(1M) manual pages for complete information on how to use these commands.

The dd command makes a literal (block) copy of a complete UFS file system to another file system or to a tape. By default, the dd command copies its standard input to its standard output.

NOTE. Do not use the dd *command with variable-length tape drives.*

You can specify a device name in place of the standard input, the standard output, or both. The following example copies contents of a diskette to a file in the /tmp directory.

```
oak% dd < /floppy/floppy0 > /tmp/output.file
2400+0 records in
2400+0 records out
oak%
```

The dd command reports on the number of blocks it reads and writes. The number after the + is a count of the partial blocks that were copied.

The dd command syntax is different from most other commands. You specify options as *keyword=value* pairs, where *keyword* is the option you want to set and *value* is the argument for that option. For example, you can replace the standard input and output with the following syntax.

```
dd if=input-file of=output-file
```

The following example uses the *keyword=value* pairs instead of the redirect symbols in the previous example.

```
oak% dd if=/floppy/floppy0 of=/tmp/output.file
```

Use the following steps to clone a disk with the dd command.

1. Make sure the source and destination disks have the same geometry.
2. Become superuser.
3. On the system with the master disk, type **touch /reconfigure** and press Return.

   The /reconfigure file is required on the system with the master disk so that it recognizes the clone disk once it is rebooted.
4. Type **init 0** and press Return to shut down the system.
5. Attach the clone disk to the system and turn on the system.
6. At the ok prompt type **boot** and press Return.
7. All on one line, type **dd if=/dev/dsk/*device-name* of=/dev/dsk/*device-name* bs=*blocksize*** and press Return.

The input file, `if`, is the master disk device. The output file, `of`, is the clone disk device.

8. Type **fsck /dev/rdsk/*device-name*** and press Return to check the new file system.
9. Type **mount /dev/rdsk/*device-name* /mnt** and press Return to mount the clone disk's root file system.
10. Edit the `/etc/vfstab` file on the clone disk to reference the correct device names.
11. Type **umount /mnt** and press Return to unmount the clone disk's root file system.
12. Type **init 0** and press Return to shut down the system.
13. Type **boot disk*n* -s** and press Return to boot the clone disk in single-user mode.
14. Type **sys-unconfig** and press Return to unconfigure the clone disk.

    The system is shut down after the disk is unconfigured.
15. Type **boot disk*n*** and press Return to boot the clone disk.
16. Provide the relevant system information such as host name, time zone, and so on.
17. Log in as root to verify the system information once the system has booted, as shown in the following example.

```
oak% su
Password
# dd < /floppy/floppy0 > /tmp/output.file
# boot
(Boot messages)
# dd if=/dev/dsk/c0t0d0s2 of=/dev/dsk/c0t2d0s2 bs=100k
# fsck /dev/rdsk/c0t2d0s2
# mount /dev/dsk/c0t2d0s2 /mnt
# cd /mnt/etc
# vi vfstab
(Modify entries for the new disk)
# cd /
# umount /mnt
# init 0
(Shutdown messages)
# boot disk2 -s
(Boot messages)
# sys-unconfig
# boot disk2
```

Try Repairing Any Bad Blocks

If the disk has bad blocks, you may be able to repair them with the `format` command. See the `format`(1M) manual page for more information.

Try Reformatting the Disk

If the disk is bad, reformatting it may fix the problem. Use the `format` command to reformat a disk. See the `format`(1M) manual page for more information.

CAUTION. Remember that formatting the disk destroys all data.

Replacing the Bad Disk

If reformatting and repairing bad blocks do not work, replace the disk. See the disk installation manual for more information.

Adding Defect List, Format, Partition, and Label Disk (format)

Use the following steps to put a defect list on a new disk, and to format, partition, and label it.

CAUTION. You must format the disk after you add the defect list. Any data on the disk is destroyed by formatting. If the disk is not new, be sure the data is backed up before you proceed. See "Backing Up and Restoring File Systems" on page 227 for complete information on how to back up and restore file systems.

1. Become superuser.
2. Type **`format`** and press Return.
3. A list of available disks is displayed, as shown in the following example.

```
paperbark% su
# format
Searching for disks...done


AVAILABLE DISK SELECTIONS:
       0. c0t0d0 <SUN2.1G cyl 2733 alt 2 hd 19 sec 80>
          /sbus@1f,0/SUNW,fas@e,8800000/sd@0,0
       1. c0t1d0 <SUN2.1G cyl 2733 alt 2 hd 19 sec 80>
          /sbus@1f,0/SUNW,fas@e,8800000/sd@1,0
Specify disk (enter its number):
```

4. Type the number of the new disk from the list that is displayed.

   The Format menu and the `format>` prompt are displayed.
5. Type **`defect`** and press Return.
6. Type **`primary`** and press Return.

The original defect list is added to the disk, as shown in the following example.

```
defect> primary
Extracting primary defect list . . . Extraction complete.
Current Defect List updated, \
total of 30 defects.
```

7. Type **quit** and press Return.

   The `format>` prompt is displayed.

8. Type **format** and press Return.

   The disk begins formatting. Formatting takes about 10 minutes for a 107-Mbyte disk, longer for bigger disks.

9. When the `format>` prompt is redisplayed, type **partition** and press Return.

10. Re-create the partitions to match the partitions on the defective disk.

11. Type **label** and press Return.

    The disk is labeled.

12. Type **quit** and press Return.

    The Format menu and `format>` prompt are redisplayed.

13. Type **quit** and press Return.

    The shell prompt is redisplayed, as shown in the following example.

```
oak% su
Password:
# format
Searching for disks...done


AVAILABLE DISK SELECTIONS:
       0. sd0 at esp0 slave 24
          sd0: <SUN0207 cyl 1254 alt 2 hd 9 sec 36>
       1. sd2 at esp0 slave 16
          sd2: <SUN0207 cyl 1254 alt 2 hd 9 sec 36>
Specify disk (enter its number): 1
selecting c0t0d0
[disk formatted]
FORMAT MENU:
        disk       - select a disk
        type       - select (define) a disk type
        partition  - select (define) a partition table
        current    - describe the current disk
        format     - format and analyze the disk
        repair     - repair a defective sector
        label      - write label to the disk
        analyze    - surface analysis
        defect     - defect list management
        backup     - search for backup labels
        verify     - read and display labels
        save       - save new disk/partition definitions
        inquiry    - show vendor, product and revision
        volname    - set 8-character volume name
        quit
format > defect
defect > primary
Extracting primary defect list . . . Extraction complete.
```

```
Current Defect List updated, total of 30 defects.
defect > quit
format > format
format> partition
PARTITION MENU:
        0      - change '0' partition
        1      - change '1' partition
        2      - change '2' partition
        3      - change '3' partition
        4      - change '4' partition
        5      - change '5' partition
        6      - change '6' partition
        7      - change '7' partition
        select - select a predefined table
        modify - modify a predefined partition table
        name   - name the current table
        print  - display the current table
        label  - write partition map and label to the disk
        quit
partition> <partition the disk>
partition> label
partition> quit
format > quit
#
```

Remaking the File Systems (newfs)

A disk must be formatted, partitioned, and labeled before you can create UFS file systems on it. If you are re-creating an existing UFS file system, unmount the file system before performing the following steps.

1. Become superuser.
2. Type **newfs /dev/rdsk/c*n*t*n*d*n*s*n*** and press Return.

   You are asked if you want to proceed.

CAUTION. Be sure you have specified the correct device name for the partition before performing the next step. If you specify the wrong partition, you will erase its contents when the new file system is created.

3. Type **y** to confirm.

   The `newfs` command uses optimized default values to create the file system.

The following example creates a file system on `/dev/rdsk/c0t3d0s7`.

```
oak% su
Password:
# newfs /dev/rdsk/cØt3dØs7
newfs: construct a new file system /dev/rdsk/c0t3d0s7 (y/n)? y
/dev/rdsk/c0t3d0s7:     163944 sectors in 506 cylinders of 9 tracks, 36
 sectors
       83.9MB in 32 cyl groups (16 c/g, 2.65MB/g, 1216 i/g)
super-block backups (for fsck -b #) at:
 32, 5264, 10496, 15728, 20960, 26192, 31424, 36656, 41888,
 47120, 52352, 57584, 62816, 68048, 73280, 78512, 82976, 88208,
 93440, 98672, 103904, 109136, 114368, 119600, 124832, 130064, 135296,
 140528, 145760, 150992, 156224, 161456,
#
```

Mounting the File System on a Temporary Mount Point (mount)

Type **mount /dev/dsk/*cntndnsn* /mnt** and press Return. The file system is mounted on the `/mnt` temporary mount point. To mount the disk, specify the block device directory (`/dev/dsk`), not the raw device directory.

Restoring Files to the File System (ufsrestore)

Restore the contents of the latest full backup, and then restore subsequent incremental backups from lowest to highest level (`ufsrestore`), by using the following steps.

1. As superuser, type **cd /mnt** and press Return.

   You have changed to the mount point directory.
2. Write-protect the tapes for safety.
3. Insert the first volume of the level 0 tape into the tape drive.
4. Type **ufsrestore rvf /dev/rmt/*unit*** and press Return.

   If this is a multivolume restore, when prompted, remove the first tape and insert the last tape in the tape drive. Follow instructions about the order of the rest of the tapes. The level 0 tape is restored.
5. Remove the tape and load the next lowest level tape in the drive.

   Always restore tapes starting with 0 and continuing until you reach the highest level.
6. Type **ufsrestore rvf /dev/rmt/*unit*** and press Return.

   The next level tape is restored.
7. Repeat steps 5 and 6 for each additional tape.
8. Type **ls** and press Return.
9. A list of files in the directory is displayed. Check the listing to verify that all the files are restored.
10. Type **rm restoresymtable** and press Return.

    The `restoresymtable` created by `ufsrestore` is removed.

Unmounting the File System from Its Temporary Mount Point (umount)

Use the following steps to unmount the file system from its temporary mount point.

1. As superuser, type **cd /** and press Return.
2. Type **umount /mnt** and press Return.

   The file system is unmounted from the temporary mount point.

Checking the File System for Inconsistencies (fsck)

Type **fsck /dev/rdsk/c*n*t*n*d*n*s*n*** and press Return. The file system is checked for consistency.

Performing a Level 0 Backup of the Restored File System (ufsdump)

You always should do an immediate backup of a newly created file system because `ufsrestore` repositions the files and changes the inode allocation.

Use the following steps to perform a level 0 backup of the restored file system.

1. Remove the last tape and insert a new write-enabled tape in the tape drive.
2. Type **ufsdump 0uf /dev/rmt/*unit* /dev/rdsk/c*n*t*n*d*n*s*n*** and press Return.

Mounting the File System at Its Permanent Mount Point (mount)

Type **mount /dev/dsk/c*n*t*n*d*n*s*n*** and press Return. The restored file system is mounted and available for use.

Understanding the Service Access Facility

The Solaris Operating Environment uses the *Service Access Facility (SAF)* to register and monitor port activity for modems, terminals, and printers. SAF is new with the Solaris Operating Environment. SAF controls the resources that let users perform the following tasks.

- Log in (either locally or remotely).
- Access printers across the network.
- Access files across the network.

SAF is a complex hierarchy of background processes and administrative commands. Explaining SAF in depth is beyond the scope of this book. The following sections provide a brief introduction to the elements of SAF. For complete information about SAF, see *Solaris Advanced System Administrator's Guide* available from Sun Microsystems Press.

Admintool GUI for SAF Functionality

Starting with the Solaris 2.3 release, Admintool provides a graphical user interface to work with printers, monitors, and modems on a local system.

Starting Admintool

Use the following steps to access the Admintool: Serial Ports windows.

1. In a terminal window, type **admintool&** and press Return.
   The Admintool: Users window is displayed.
2. From the Browse menu, choose Serial Ports, as shown in Figure 62.

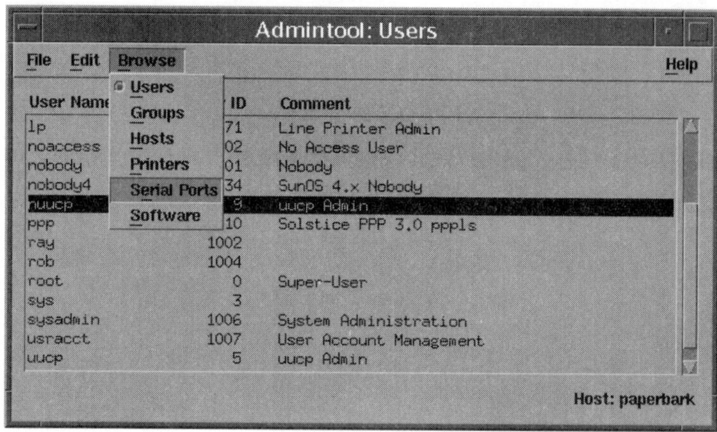

Figure 62 The Admintool Browse Menu

The Admintool: Serial Ports window is displayed, as shown in Figure 63.

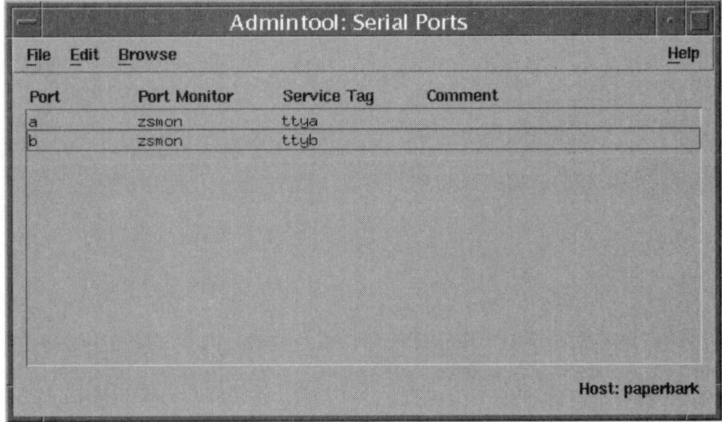

Figure 63 The Admintool: Serial Ports Window

3. Click on one of the ports to highlight it, and choose Modify from the Edit menu. The Admintool: Modify Serial Port window is displayed, as shown in Figure 64.

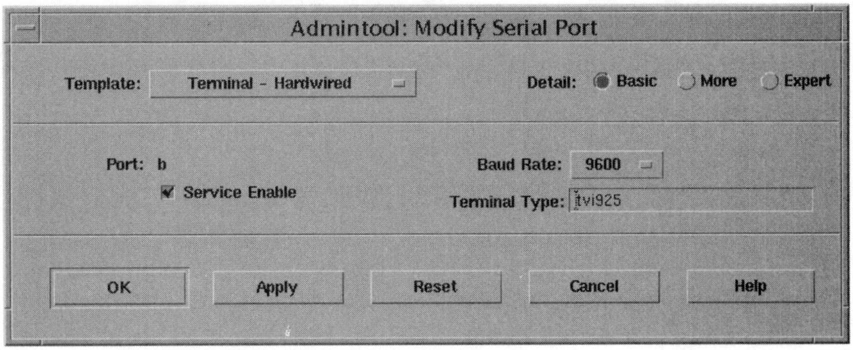

Figure 64 The Admintool: Modify Serial Port Window

This window shows information at three different levels: Basic, More, and Expert. Figure 65 shows the Expert options.

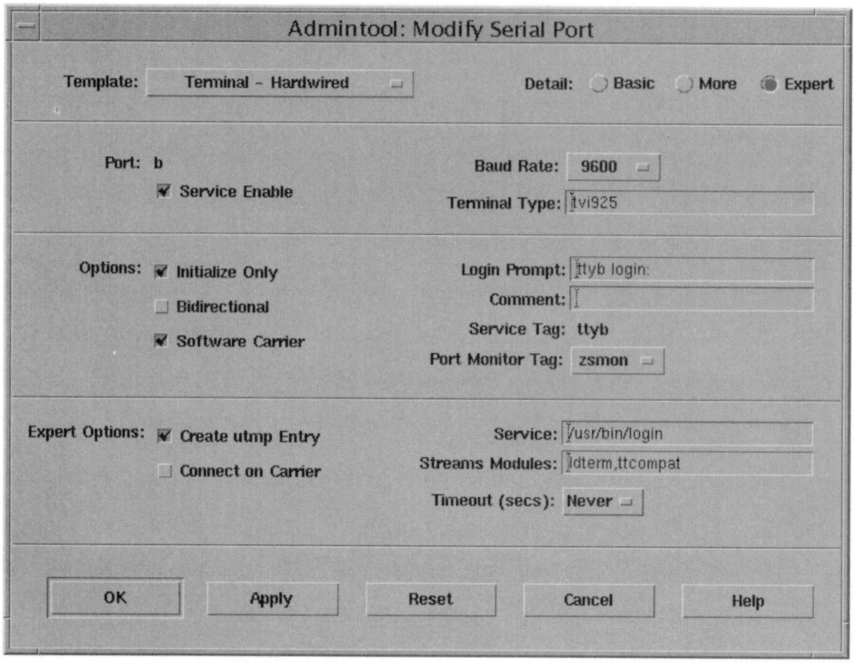

Figure 65 The Admintool: Modify Serial Port Window with Expert Options

Port Monitors and Service Access

A *port monitor* is a program that continuously watches out for requests to log in or requests to access printers or files. When a port monitor detects a request, it sets the parameters that are needed to establish communication between the operating system and the device that is requesting service. Then, the port monitor transfers control to other processes that provide the services needed.

The Solaris Operating Environment provides two types of port monitors: `listen` and `ttymon`. The *listen port monitor* controls access to network services, fielding remote print and file system requests. The *ttymon port monitor* controls access to login services. You need to set up a `ttymon` port monitor (using SAF) to process login requests from modems.

> *NOTE. The* `ttymon` *port monitor replaces the SunOS 4.*x `getty` *port monitor. A single* `ttymon` *can replace multiple* `gettys`.

SAF Control of Port Monitors and Services

You use three SAF commands to administer modems and alphanumeric terminals: `sacadm`, `pmadm`, and `ttyadm`.

The `sacadm` command adds and removes port monitors. This command is your main link with the Service Access Controller (SAC) and its administrative file (`/etc/saf/_sactab`).

The `pmadm` command adds or removes a service and associates a service with a particular port monitor.

The `ttyadm` command formats information for inclusion in various SAF administrative files. A `ttyadm` command often is embedded within a `sacadm` or `pmadm` command to provide some of the data needed by those commands. Table 63 lists the commands associated with specific SAF functions. See the manual pages for more information about each command.

Table 63 SAF Functions and Associated Commands

Function	Command	Description
Overall administration	`sacadm`	Command for adding and removing port monitors.
Service Access Controller	`sac`	SAF's master program.
Port monitors	`ttymon`	Monitor serial port login requests.
	`listen`	Monitor requests for network services.
Port monitor service administrator	`pmadm`	Command for controlling port monitors' services.
Services	logins; remote procedure calls; other	Services to which SAF provides access.

Setting Up Printer Port Monitors

This section provides steps for setting up port monitors for printing. Each Solaris print server and print client must have the port monitor configured to be able to handle network printing requests. If you use the Printer Manager (available with SunOS 5.1), you do not need to follow these steps. The Printer Manager automatically sets up the port monitors as part of the printer configuration process.

1. Become superuser.
2. All on one line, type **sacadm -a -p tcp -t listen -c "/usr/lib/saf/listen tcp" -v `nlsadmin -V` -n 9999** and press Return.

   The network listen service that listens for incoming TCP/IP requests is started. The options are described in Table 64.

Table 64 The sacadm Command Options

Option	Description
-a	Add the -p port.
-t	Identify the type of service.
-c	Tell which command to use to start the port monitor.
-v	Indicate the version of the network listen process.
-n	Specify the number of times the Service Access Controller restarts the process if it dies.

3. Type **sacadm -l** and press Return. Look at the output to verify that the network listen status is enabled, as shown in the following example.

```
# sacadm -l
PMTAG        PMTYPE    FLGS RCNT STATUS     COMMAND
tcp          listen     -    9999 ENABLED    /usr/lib/saf/listen tcp #
#
```

NOTE. It may take several minutes before the network listen service is enabled.

4. Type **lpsystem -A** and press Return.

   The system's universal address is displayed, as shown in the following example.

```
# lpsystem -A
000202038194180e0000000000000000
#
```

The universal address has four parts, as shown in Figure 66. The last part, RFU, means Reserved for Future Use and could be used for other families of addresses (for example, Open Systems Interface) in the future.

PostScript error (invalidfor

Figure 66 Parts of the Universal Address

The first four digits identify the Internet family. The fifth through eighth digits identify the TCP port. For the modified version, replace the fifth through eighth digits with 0ACE. The following example shows the modified version of the universal address shown in the example above.

```
00020ACE8194180e0000000000000000
```

NOTE. You must type the characters **\x** *at the beginning of the universal (or modified universal) address in the next steps exactly as shown. In addition, the address must be enclosed in single quotation marks so the backslash is not stripped off.*

Use the following steps to set up a printer port monitor.

1. To register listen service 0, all on one line, type **pmadm -a -p tcp -s 0 -i root -m `nlsadmin -c /usr/lib/saf/nlps_server -A '\x*modified_address*'` -v `nlsadmin -V`** and press Return.

   The port monitor is configured to listen for requests from listen service 0.
2. To receive print requests from SunOS 5.0 print clients, all on one line, type **pmadm -a -p tcp -s lp -i root -m `nlsadmin -o /var/spool/lp/fifos/listenS5` -v `nlsadmin -V`** and press Return.

   The port monitor is configured to listen for requests from `listenS5`, which registers print requests from Solaris print clients.
3. To receive print requests from SunOS 4.x print clients, all on one line, type **pmadm -a -p tcp -s lpd -i root -m `nlsadmin -o /var/spool/lp/fifos/listenBSD -A '\xaddress'` -v `nlsadmin -V`** and press Return.

   The port monitor is configured to listen for requests from `listenBSD`, which registers print requests from SunOS 4.x print clients.
4. Type **cat /var/saf/tcp/log** and press Return. Examine the messages displayed to make sure that the services are enabled and initialized.

In the following example, all three network listen services are registered.

```
# lpsystem -A
00020203819418Oe0000000000000000
# pmadm -a -p tcp -s lp -i root -m `nlsadmin -o
/var/spool/lp/fifos/listenS5` -v `nlsadmin -V`
# pmadm -a -p tcp -s lpd -i root -m `nlsadmin -o
/var/spool/lp/fifos/listenBSD -A
'\x00020203819418Oe0000000000000000'` -v `nlsadmin -V`
# pmadm -a -p tcp -s Ø -i root -m `nlsadmin -c
/usr/lib/saf/nlps_server -A
'\x00020ACE8194180e0000000000000000'` -v `nlsadmin -V`
# cat /var/saf/tcp/log
10/28/91 10:22:51; 178; @(#)listen:listen.c     1.19.9.1
10/28/91 10:22:51; 178; Listener port monitor tag: tcp
10/28/91 10:22:51; 178; Starting state: ENABLED
10/28/91 10:22:51; 178; Service 0: fd 6 addr
  \x00020ACE8194180e0000000000000000
10/28/91 10:22:51; 178; Service lpd: fd 7 addr
  \x00020203819418Oe0000000000000000
10/28/91 10:22:52; 178; Net opened, 2 addresses bound, 56 fds free
10/28/91 10:22:52; 178; Initialization Complete
#
```

See “Solaris Print Manager” on page 361 for information on how to add printers.

Setting Up a Bidirectional Modem

To set up a bidirectional modem you need information for these variables.

- *port-name*—The port to which the modem is connected (typically, `ttya` or `ttyb`).
- *svctag*—The name of the port monitor service (for Sun systems, `zsmon`).
- *port-device-name*—The name of the device for the port (typically `/dev/cua/a` or `/dev/cua/b`).
- *short-port-device-name*—The name, without the complete path, for the port.
- *modem-label*—The entry in the `/etc/ttydefs` file that is used to set the proper baud rate and line discipline.
- *modem-type*—The type of the modem from the `/etc/uucp/Dialers` file. For example, the type for a Hayes modem is `hayes`.

Use the following steps to connect a modem.

1. Halt the system.
2. Make sure hardware carrier detect is disabled.

On Sun systems, you can use the `eeprom` command or type **`setenv ttyb-ignore-cd=false`** and press Return.

3. Reboot the system.
4. Connect the modem and make sure any modem switches are set to allow bidirectional use.

Use the following steps to configure a bidirectional modem. **New!**

1. Type `admintool&` and press Return.
   Admintool is started.
2. From the Browse menu, choose Serial Ports.
   The Serial Ports menu is displayed, as shown in Figure 67.

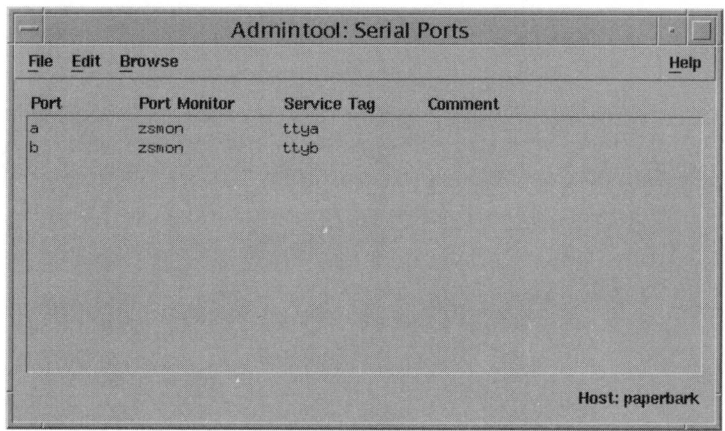

Figure 67 Admintool: Serial Ports Menu

3. Click on the port the modem is connected to.
4. From the Edit menu, choose Modify.
   The Modify Serial Port window is displayed in Basic Detail mode, as shown in Figure 68.

Admintool: Modify Serial Port
Template: Terminal - Hardwired
Detail: Basic More Expert
Port: b
Service Enable
Baud Rate: 9600
Terminal Type: tvi925
OK Apply Reset Cancel Help

Figure 68 Admintool: Modify Serial Port Window

5. Click on Expert to display all of the available settings.
   The Expert Detail window is displayed, as shown in Figure 69.

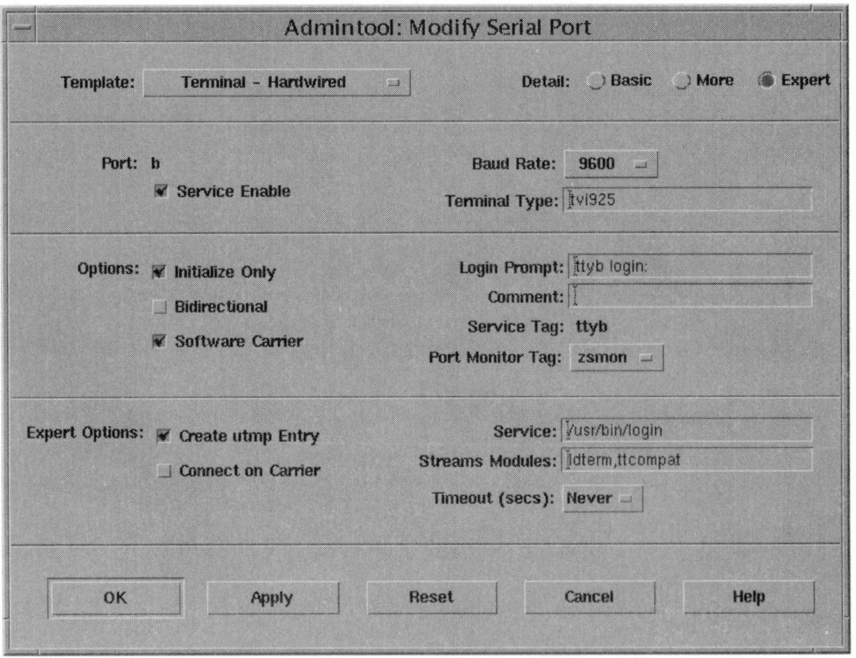

Figure 69 Admintool: Modify Serial Port Window, Expert Detail

6. Click on the Bidirectional check box.
7. Change other values of the template entries if appropriate.
8. Click on the OK button to configure the port.

9. Type **pmadm -l -s *port-number*** and press Return.

   Review the output to verify that the modem service is configured.

Using a Modem

To connect through the modem, type **tip *-baudrate phonenumber*** and press Return. When the software on the connecting system is configured properly, the remote system dials the modem phone number and the modem answers automatically.

The following example uses the information phone number, which is not a dial-in modem number.

```
oak% tip -9600 5551212
dialing ... connected
Login messages>
```

8

Administering Systems

This chapter describes commands that are specific to individual systems. It also shows how to configure additional swap space and how to create a local mail alias.

Displaying System-Specific Information

Use the commands in this section to find system-specific information such as the host ID number, hardware type, processor type, OS release level, system configuration, length of time the system has been up, and system date and time. The following sections also describe how to set the system date and time and change the time zone for a system.

Determining the Host ID Number (sysdef -h)

To find a system's host ID number, type **sysdef -h** and press Return. The host ID for the system is displayed. This command replaces the SunOS 4.x `hostid` command.

```
oak% sysdef -h
*
* Hostid
*
  554095cc
oak%
```

Determining the Hardware Type (uname -m)

To find the hardware type of a system, type **uname -m** and press Return. The hardware type (architecture) for the system is displayed. The SunOS 4.x arch command, which provided similar information, is not available in the Solaris Operating Environment.

```
oak% uname -m
sun4u
oak%
```

Determining the Processor Type (uname -p)

To find the processor type for a system, type **uname -p** and press Return. The processor type for the system is displayed. This command replaces the SunOS 4.x mach command.

```
oak% uname -p
sparc
oak%
```

Determining the OS Release (uname -r)

To find the OS release level for a system, type **uname -r** and press Return. The OS (kernel) release is displayed.

```
oak% uname -r
5.8
oak%
```

Displaying System Configuration Information (prtconf)

To display the configuration information for a system, type **prtconf** and press Return. The system configuration information is displayed.

```
paperbark% prtconf
System Configuration:  Sun Microsystems  sun4u
Memory size: 128 Megabytes
System Peripherals (Software Nodes):

SUNW,Ultra-2
    packages (driver not attached)
        terminal-emulator (driver not attached)
        deblocker (driver not attached)
        obp-tftp (driver not attached)
        disk-label (driver not attached)
        sun-keyboard (driver not attached)
        ufs-file-system (driver not attached)
```

```
    chosen (driver not attached)
    openprom (driver not attached)
        client-services (driver not attached)
    options, instance #0
    aliases (driver not attached)
    memory (driver not attached)
    virtual-memory (driver not attached)
    counter-timer (driver not attached)
    sbus, instance #0
        SUNW,CS4231 (driver not attached)
        auxio (driver not attached)
        flashprom (driver not attached)
        SUNW,fdtwo (driver not attached)
        eeprom (driver not attached)
        zs, instance #0
        zs, instance #1
        sc (driver not attached)
        SUNW,pll (driver not attached)
        SUNW,fas, instance #0
            sd (driver not attached)
            st (driver not attached)
            sd, instance #0s
            sd, instance #1
            sd, instance #2 (driver not attached)
            sd, instance #3 (driver not attached)
            sd, instance #4 (driver not attached)
            sd, instance #5 (driver not attached)
            sd, instance #6 (driver not attached)
            sd, instance #7 (driver not attached)
            sd, instance #8 (driver not attached)
            sd, instance #9 (driver not attached)
            sd, instance #10 (driver not attached)
            sd, instance #11 (driver not attached)
            sd, instance #12 (driver not attached)
            sd, instance #13 (driver not attached)
            sd, instance #14 (driver not attached)
        SUNW,hme, instance #0
        SUNW,bpp (driver not attached)
    SUNW,UltraSPARC (driver not attached)
    SUNW,ffb, instance #0
    pseudo, instance #0
paperbark%
```

An alternative way to display system configuration information and show the state of tunable parameters is to type **sysdef** and press Return. System configuration information is displayed.

```
paperbark% sysdef
*
* Hostid
*
  807d79d4
*
* sun4u Configuration
*
*
* Devices
*
packages (driver not attached)
        terminal-emulator (driver not attached)
        deblocker (driver not attached)
        obp-tftp (driver not attached)
        disk-label (driver not attached)
        sun-keyboard (driver not attached)
        ufs-file-system (driver not attached)
chosen (driver not attached)
openprom (driver not attached)
        client-services (driver not attached)
options, instance #0
aliases (driver not attached)
memory (driver not attached)
```

```
virtual-memory (driver not attached)
counter-timer (driver not attached)
sbus, instance #0
        SUNW,CS4231 (driver not attached)
        auxio (driver not attached)
        flashprom (driver not attached)
        SUNW,fdtwo (driver not attached)
        eeprom (driver not attached)
        zs, instance #0
        zs, instance #1
        sc (driver not attached)
        SUNW,pll (driver not attached)
        SUNW,fas, instance #0
                sd (driver not attached)
                st (driver not attached)
                sd, instance #0
                sd, instance #1
                sd, instance #2 (driver not attached)
                sd, instance #3 (driver not attached)
                sd, instance #4 (driver not attached)
                sd, instance #5 (driver not attached)
                sd, instance #6 (driver not attached)
                sd, instance #7 (driver not attached)
                sd, instance #8 (driver not attached)
                sd, instance #9 (driver not attached)
                sd, instance #10 (driver not attached)
                sd, instance #11 (driver not attached)
                sd, instance #12 (driver not attached)
                sd, instance #13 (driver not attached)
                sd, instance #14 (driver not attached)
        SUNW,hme, instance #0
        SUNW,bpp (driver not attached)
SUNW,UltraSPARC (driver not attached)
SUNW,ffb, instance #0
pseudo, instance #0
        clone, instance #0
        ip, instance #0
        ip6, instance #0
        tcp, instance #0
        tcp6, instance #0
        udp, instance #0
        udp6, instance #0
        icmp, instance #0
        icmp6, instance #0
        arp, instance #0
        sad, instance #0
        conskbd, instance #0
        wc, instance #0
        consms, instance #0
        iwscn, instance #0
        ptsl, instance #0
        rts, instance #0
        tl, instance #0
        keysock, instance #0
        sysmsg, instance #0
        cn, instance #0
        mm, instance #0
        kstat, instance #0
        log, instance #0
        sy, instance #0
        vol, instance #0
        pm, instance #0
        ptm, instance #0
        pts, instance #0
        devinfo, instance #0
        ksyms, instance #0
*
* Loadable Objects
*
* Loadable Object Path = /platform/sun4u/kernel
*
dacf/consconfig_dacf
dacf/sparcv9/consconfig_dacf
drv/dma
drv/ebus
drv/fd
```

```
drv/ledma
drv/pci_pci
drv/pcipsy
drv/power
drv/rootnex
drv/sbus
drv/sbusmem
drv/simba
drv/stc
drv/su
drv/zs
drv/zsh
drv/cgsix
drv/tod
drv/bwtwo
drv/cgthree
drv/ffb
drv/sf
drv/cpc
        hard link:  sys/cpc
drv/sparcv9/dma
drv/sparcv9/ebus
drv/sparcv9/fd
drv/sparcv9/ledma
drv/sparcv9/pci_pci
drv/sparcv9/pcipsy
drv/sparcv9/power
drv/sparcv9/rootnex
drv/sparcv9/sbus
drv/sparcv9/sbusmem
drv/sparcv9/simba
drv/sparcv9/stc
drv/sparcv9/su
drv/sparcv9/zs
drv/sparcv9/zsh
drv/sparcv9/cgsix
drv/sparcv9/tod
drv/sparcv9/ffb
drv/sparcv9/cpc
        hard link:  sys/sparcv9/cpc
genunix
unix
misc/bootdev
misc/consconfig
misc/forthdebug
misc/md5
misc/obpsym
misc/pcmcia
misc/platmod
misc/vis
misc/cpr
misc/sparcv9/bootdev
misc/sparcv9/consconfig
misc/sparcv9/forthdebug
misc/sparcv9/md5
misc/sparcv9/obpsym
misc/sparcv9/pcmcia
misc/sparcv9/platmod
misc/sparcv9/vis
misc/sparcv9/cpr
sparcv9/genunix
sparcv9/unix
strmod/kb
strmod/sparcv9/kb
cpu/SUNW,UltraSPARC-II
cpu/sparcv9/SUNW,UltraSPARC-II
cpu/sparcv9/SUNW,UltraSPARC-IIi
cpu/sparcv9/SUNW,UltraSPARC
cpu/SUNW,UltraSPARC-IIi
cpu/SUNW,UltraSPARC
tod/todmostek
tod/todstarfire
tod/sparcv9/todmostek
tod/sparcv9/todstarfire
*
* Loadable Object Path = /kernel
```

```
*
strmod/bd
drv/sparcv9/arp
        hard link:  strmod/sparcv9/arp
drv/sparcv9/bpp
drv/sparcv9/clone
drv/sparcv9/cn
drv/sparcv9/conskbd
drv/sparcv9/consms
drv/sparcv9/dad
drv/sparcv9/devinfo
drv/sparcv9/esp
drv/sparcv9/icmp
drv/sparcv9/icmp6
drv/sparcv9/ip
drv/sparcv9/ip6
drv/sparcv9/ipsecah
drv/sparcv9/ipsecesp
drv/sparcv9/isp
drv/sparcv9/iwscn
drv/sparcv9/keysock
drv/sparcv9/le
drv/sparcv9/lebuffer
drv/sparcv9/llc1
drv/sparcv9/lofi
drv/sparcv9/log
drv/sparcv9/mm
drv/sparcv9/openeepr
drv/sparcv9/options
drv/sparcv9/poll
drv/sparcv9/pseudo
drv/sparcv9/ptc
drv/sparcv9/ptsl
drv/sparcv9/qe
drv/sparcv9/qec
drv/sparcv9/rts
drv/sparcv9/sad
drv/sparcv9/sd
drv/sparcv9/sgen
drv/sparcv9/st
drv/sparcv9/sy
drv/sparcv9/sysmsg
drv/sparcv9/tcp
drv/sparcv9/tcp6
drv/sparcv9/tl
drv/sparcv9/uata
drv/sparcv9/udp
drv/sparcv9/udp6
drv/sparcv9/wc
drv/sparcv9/fp
drv/sparcv9/ses
drv/sparcv9/pln
drv/sparcv9/soc
drv/sparcv9/ssd
drv/sparcv9/fcp
drv/sparcv9/fas
drv/sparcv9/hme
drv/sparcv9/pcic
drv/sparcv9/pcelx
drv/sparcv9/pcs
drv/sparcv9/pem
drv/sparcv9/stp4020
drv/sparcv9/pcmem
drv/sparcv9/pcram
drv/sparcv9/pcser
drv/sparcv9/pcata
drv/sparcv9/qfe
drv/sparcv9/nca
drv/sparcv9/rtvc
exec/sparcv9/aoutexec
exec/sparcv9/elfexec
exec/sparcv9/intpexec
misc/kgss/gl_kmech_krb5
genunix
misc/kgss/do_kmech_krb5
drv/arp
```

```
        hard link:  strmod/arp
drv/bpp
drv/clone
drv/cn
drv/conskbd
drv/consms
drv/dad
drv/devinfo
drv/esp
drv/icmp
drv/icmp6
drv/ip
drv/ip6
drv/ipsecah
drv/ipsecesp
drv/isp
drv/iwscn
drv/keysock
drv/le
drv/lebuffer
drv/llc1
drv/lofi
drv/log
drv/mm
drv/openeepr
drv/options
drv/poll
drv/pseudo
drv/ptc
drv/ptsl
drv/qe
drv/qec
drv/rts
drv/sad
drv/sd
drv/sgen
drv/st
drv/sy
drv/sysmsg
drv/tcp
drv/tcp6
drv/tl
drv/uata
drv/udp
drv/udp6
drv/wc
drv/xbox
drv/fp
drv/ses
drv/pln
drv/soc
drv/ssd
drv/fcp
drv/fas
drv/hme
drv/socal
drv/pcic
drv/pcs
drv/pem
drv/stp4020
drv/pcelx
drv/pcmem
drv/pcram
drv/pcser
drv/pcata
drv/qfe
drv/nca
drv/rtvc
exec/aoutexec
exec/elfexec
exec/intpexec
fs/cachefs
fs/fifofs
fs/hsfs
fs/lofs
fs/mntfs
```

```
fs/nfs
        hard link:  sys/nfs
fs/procfs
fs/sockfs
fs/specfs
fs/tmpfs
fs/ufs
fs/autofs
fs/udfs
misc/busra
misc/consconfig
misc/dada
misc/des
misc/ipc
misc/klmmod
misc/klmops
misc/krtld
misc/md5
misc/nfs_dlboot
misc/nfssrv
misc/rpcsec
misc/scsi
misc/seg_drv
misc/seg_mapdev
misc/strplumb
misc/swapgeneric
misc/tlimod
misc/ufs_log
misc/fctl
misc/kgssapi
misc/cis
misc/cs
misc/rpcsec_gss
sched/TS
sched/TS_DPTBL
fs/sparcv9/autofs
fs/sparcv9/cachefs
fs/sparcv9/fifofs
fs/sparcv9/hsfs
fs/sparcv9/lofs
fs/sparcv9/mntfs
fs/sparcv9/nfs
        hard link:  sys/sparcv9/nfs
fs/sparcv9/procfs
fs/sparcv9/sockfs
fs/sparcv9/specfs
fs/sparcv9/tmpfs
fs/sparcv9/ufs
fs/sparcv9/udfs
strmod/atun
strmod/authmd5h
strmod/authsha1
strmod/bufmod
misc/sparcv9/busra
misc/sparcv9/consconfig
misc/sparcv9/dada
misc/sparcv9/des
misc/sparcv9/ipc
misc/sparcv9/klmmod
misc/sparcv9/klmops
misc/sparcv9/krtld
misc/sparcv9/md5
misc/sparcv9/nfs_dlboot
misc/sparcv9/nfssrv
misc/sparcv9/rpcsec
misc/sparcv9/scsi
misc/sparcv9/seg_drv
misc/sparcv9/seg_mapdev
misc/sparcv9/strplumb
misc/sparcv9/swapgeneric
misc/sparcv9/tlimod
misc/sparcv9/ufs_log
misc/sparcv9/fctl
misc/sparcv9/kgssapi
misc/sparcv9/cis
misc/sparcv9/cs
```

```
misc/sparcv9/rpcsec_gss
strmod/connld
strmod/dedump
strmod/ldterm
strmod/ms
strmod/pckt
strmod/pfmod
sched/sparcv9/TS
sched/sparcv9/TS_DPTBL
strmod/pipemod
strmod/ptem
strmod/redirmod
strmod/rpcmod
        hard link:  sys/rpcmod
strmod/timod
strmod/tirdwr
strmod/sparcv9/atun
strmod/sparcv9/authmd5h
strmod/sparcv9/authsha1
strmod/sparcv9/bufmod
strmod/sparcv9/connld
strmod/sparcv9/dedump
strmod/sparcv9/ldterm
strmod/sparcv9/ms
strmod/sparcv9/pckt
strmod/sparcv9/pfmod
strmod/sparcv9/pipemod
strmod/sparcv9/ptem
strmod/sparcv9/redirmod
strmod/sparcv9/rpcmod
        hard link:  sys/sparcv9/rpcmod
strmod/sparcv9/timod
strmod/sparcv9/tirdwr
strmod/sparcv9/ttcompat
strmod/sparcv9/tun
misc/kgss/sparcv9/gl_kmech_krb5
strmod/sparcv9/bd
misc/kgss/sparcv9/do_kmech_krb5
strmod/ttcompat
strmod/tun
sys/sparcv9/c2audit
sys/sparcv9/doorfs
sys/sparcv9/inst_sync
sys/sparcv9/kaio
sys/sparcv9/msgsys
sys/sparcv9/pipe
sys/sparcv9/pset
sys/sparcv9/semsys
sys/sparcv9/shmsys
sys/c2audit
sys/doorfs
sys/inst_sync
sys/kaio
sys/msgsys
sys/pipe
sys/pset
sys/semsys
sys/shmsys
strmod/hwc
*
* Loadable Object Path = /usr/kernel
*
drv/sparcv9/audiocs
drv/sparcv9/dbri
drv/sparcv9/dump
drv/sparcv9/kstat
drv/sparcv9/ksyms
drv/sparcv9/lockstat
drv/sparcv9/logindmux
drv/sparcv9/ptm
drv/sparcv9/pts
drv/sparcv9/llc2
drv/sparcv9/pm
drv/sparcv9/vol
drv/sparcv9/winlock
drv/sparcv9/ipd
```

```
drv/sparcv9/ipdcm
drv/sparcv9/ipdptp
drv/sparcv9/tnf
drv/sparcv9/ppp
misc/audiosup
misc/diaudio
misc/mixer
misc/sparcv9/audiosup
misc/sparcv9/diaudio
misc/sparcv9/mixer
drv/dump
drv/kstat
drv/ksyms
drv/lockstat
drv/logindmux
drv/ptm
drv/pts
drv/audio
drv/audiocs
drv/dbri
drv/winlock
drv/llc2
drv/pm
drv/vol
drv/ipd
drv/ipdcm
drv/ipdptp
drv/tnf
drv/ppp
exec/javaexec
fs/fdfs
fs/namefs
fs/pcfs
sched/IA
sched/RT
sched/RT_DPTBL
sys/sysacct
strmod/u8koi8
strmod/u8lat1
strmod/u8lat2
strmod/rlmod
strmod/telmod
strmod/ppp_diag
exec/sparcv9/javaexec
strmod/sparcv9/u8koi8
strmod/sparcv9/u8lat1
strmod/sparcv9/u8lat2
fs/sparcv9/fdfs
fs/sparcv9/namefs
fs/sparcv9/pcfs
strmod/sparcv9/rlmod
strmod/sparcv9/telmod
strmod/sparcv9/ppp_diag
sched/sparcv9/IA
sched/sparcv9/RT
sched/sparcv9/RT_DPTBL
sys/sparcv9/sysacct
*
* System Configuration
*
  swap files
swapfile             dev  swaplo blocks   free
/dev/dsk/c0t0d0s1   32,1      16 1048784 1048784
*
* Tunable Parameters
*
 2506752        maximum memory allowed in buffer cache (bufhwm)
    1914        maximum number of processes (v.v_proc)
      99        maximum global priority in sys class (MAXCLSYSPRI)
    1909        maximum processes per user id (v.v_maxup)
      30        auto update time limit in seconds (NAUTOUP)
      25        page stealing low water mark (GPGSLO)
       5        fsflush run rate (FSFLUSHR)
      25        minimum resident memory for avoiding deadlock (MINARMEM)
      25        minimum swapable memory for avoiding deadlock (MINASMEM)
*
```

```
* Utsname Tunables
*
     5.8  release (REL)
paperbark  node name (NODE)
   SunOS  system name (SYS)
 Generic  version (VER)
*
* Process Resource Limit Tunables (Current:Maximum)
*
          Infinity:Infinity              cpu time
          Infinity:Infinity              file size
          Infinity:Infinity              heap size
0x0000000000800000:Infinity              stack size
          Infinity:Infinity              core file size
0x0000000000000100:0x0000000000000400   file descriptors
          Infinity:Infinity              mapped memory
*
* Streams Tunables
*
      9  maximum number of pushes allowed (NSTRPUSH)
  65536  maximum stream message size (STRMSGSZ)
   1024  max size of ctl part of message (STRCTLSZ)
*
* IPC Messages module is not loaded
*
*
* IPC Semaphores module is not loaded
*
*
* IPC Shared Memory
*
   1048576      max shared memory segment size (SHMMAX)
      1  min shared memory segment size (SHMMIN)
    100  shared memory identifiers (SHMMNI)
      6  max attached shm segments per process (SHMSEG)
*
* Time Sharing Scheduler Tunables
*
60      maximum time sharing user priority (TSMAXUPRI)
SYS     system class name (SYS_NAME)
paperbark%
```

Determining How Long a System Has Been Up (uptime)

To find out how long a system has been up, type **uptime** and press Return. The time, number of users, and load average are displayed for the local system.

```
castle% uptime
  1:16pm  up  4:57,  1 user,  load average: 0.12, 0.06, 0.04
castle%
```

To find out when a system was booted, type **who -b** and press Return. The month, day, and time of the last boot are displayed.

```
oak% who -b
  . system boot Jul 14 08:49
oak%
```

Determining the System Date and Time (date)

To display the system date and time, type **date** and press Return. The system date and time are displayed.

```
castle% date
Sat July  1 13:17:03 WST 2000
castle%
```

Setting the System Date and Time (date)

Use the following steps to reset the system date and time.

1. Become superuser.
2. Type **date *mmddhhmmyy*** and press Return, where *mm* is the month, *dd* is the day, *hh* is the hour, *mm* is the minute, and *yy* is the year. The system date and time are reset using the month, day, hour, minute, and year that you specify.

```
# su
Password:
# date
Sat Jul 1 16:07:01 WST 2000
# date 07011552
Sat Jul 1 15:52:00 WST 2000
#
```

Changing the System Time Zone (/etc/TIMEZONE)

The time zone is set in the `/etc/TIMEZONE` file. The available U.S. time zone variables are shown below. Look in the `/usr/share/lib/zoneinfo` directory for a complete list of time zone variables.

```
Alaska
Aleutian
Arizona
Central
East-Indiana
Eastern
Hawaii
Michigan
Mountain
Pacific
Pacific-New
Samoa
```

Use the following steps to change the system time zone.

1. Become superuser.
2. Edit the `/etc/TIMEZONE` file, change the `TZ=`*`time-zone`* variable, and save the changes. The time zone is reset.
3. Reboot the system.

The following example shows the `/etc/TIMEZONE` file for a system set to Australia West standard time. Note that `/etc/TIMEZONE` is now a symbolic link to `/etc/default/init`.

```
paperbark% more /etc/TIMEZONE
# @(#)init.dfl 1.5 99/05/26
#
# This file is /etc/default/init.  /etc/TIMEZONE is a symlink to this file.
# This file looks like a shell script, but it is not.  To maintain
# compatibility with old versions of /etc/TIMEZONE, some shell constructs
# (i.e., export commands) are allowed in this file, but are ignored.
#
# Lines of this file should be of the form VAR=value, where VAR is one of
# TZ, LANG, or any of the LC_* environment variables.
#
TZ=Australia/West
CMASK=022
LANG=C
paperbark%
```

The following example changes to US/Eastern.

```
oak% su
Password:
# vi /etc/TIMEZONE
TZ=US/Eastern;export TZ
:w!
# reboot
oak% date
Tue Jul 1 14:24:52 EST 2000
oak%
```

NOTE. You may need to make your text editor do a confirmed write of the file. For example, in `vi` *use the command* `:w!` *to write the changes even if the permissions normally would not allow it.*

Configuring Additional Swap Space (mkfile, swap)

To create and add additional swap space without reformatting a disk, you first create a swap file with the `mkfile` command. You can specify the size of the swap file in kilobytes (the default) or in blocks or megabytes by using the `b` and `m` suffixes, respectively. The swap file can either be on a local disk or be NFS-mounted. Then, you add the swap space with the `swap` command.

To list available swap files, type **swap -l** and press Return. A list of available swap files is displayed. The swap command replaces the SunOS 4.x swapon command.

```
drusilla% swap -l
swapfile             dev  swaplo blocks   free
swapfs                -        0  94520  93512
/dev/dsk/c0t3d0s1   32,25      8  65512  45048
drusilla%
```

Use the following steps to create a swap file.

1. Become superuser. You can create a swap file without root permissions, but it is a good idea to have root be the owner of the swap file so that other processes cannot access it.
2. Type **mkfile** ***nnn*****[k|b|m]** ***file-name*** and press Return. The letter following the number you specify indicates kilobytes, blocks, or megabytes. The swap file of the size and file name you specify is created. The following example creates a 1-Mbyte swap file named SWAP.

```
oak% su
Password:
# mkfile 1m /files1/SWAP
#
```

Use the following steps to add the swap file.

1. Become superuser.
2. Type **swap -a** ***path-name*** and press Return. You must use the absolute path name to specify the swap file. The swap file is added and becomes available.
3. Type **swap -l** to verify that the swap file is added.

```
# swap -a /files1/SWAP
# swap -l
swapfile             dev  swaplo blocks   free
swapfs                -        0  94520  93512

/dev/dsk/c0t3d0s1   32,25      8  65512  45048

/files1/SWAP   -  8   2040   2040
#
```

Use the following steps to remove a specified swap file from use.

1. Become superuser.
2. Type **swap -d *path-name*** and press Return. When the swap file is no longer in use, it is removed from the list so that it is no longer available for swapping. The file itself is not deleted.

```
oak% su
Password:
# swap -d /files1/SWAP
# swap -l
swapfile             dev  swaplo
blocks   free
swapfs                -        0
94520  93512

/dev/dsk/c0t3d0s1   32,25      8
65512  45048
# ls -l /files1/SWAP
-rw-------   1 root   root      1048576 Jan 31 13:56 SWAP
#
```

When you create additional swap space, if you want the swap space to remain available when the system is rebooted, you must add the entry to the `/etc/vfstab` file. Use the following steps to add a swap file entry to the `/etc/vfstab` file.

1. Become superuser.
2. Edit the `/etc/vfstab` file and add the following line. Be sure the line follows the entry for the partition where the swap file was created.

```
path-name - - swap - no -
```

The next time the system is rebooted, the swap file is added automatically.

The following example adds the swap file `/files1/SWAP` to the `/etc/vfstab` file after the entry that mounts the file system `/files1`.

```
/files1/SWAP - - swap - no -
```

Creating a Local Mail Alias (/etc/mail/aliases)

In a network environment, you probably have a central way to administer mail aliases. In addition, users frequently want to set up local aliases for use from their systems. Use the following steps to create mail aliases on a local system.

1. Become superuser.
2. Edit the `/etc/mail/aliases` file.
3. At the end of the file, under the Local Aliases category, type ***`aliasname:username1,username2,...`*** and press Return after the last *`username`*.
4. Save the changes.

For example, if you want to create an alias called `friends`, edit the `/etc/mail/aliases` file and add an entry like the following.

```
friends:dexter@elm,ogden@willow,mary@maple
```

9

ADMINISTERING NETWORK SERVICES

This chapter contains information about checking on remote system status, logging in to a remote system, transferring files between systems, and administering the Network Information Service Plus (NIS+) databases. It also introduces the IPv6 Internet protocol, new in the Solaris 8 release, and describes how to display network and configuration information. New!

Checking on Remote System Status

This section describes commands you use to find out the status of remote systems: `rup`, `ping`, and `rpcinfo -d`.

Determining How Long a Remote System Has Been Up (rup)

To find out how long a system has been up and to determine the load average, type **rup *system-name*** and press Return. The host name, uptime, and load average are displayed.

```
oak% rup ash
ash    up 59 days,  3:42, load average: 0.12, 0.12, 0.01
oak%
```

You can also display a list of all remote hosts in the subnet by typing **rup** and pressing Return. If you display a list, you can use the options shown in Table 65 to sort the output.

Table 65 Options to the rup Command

Option	Description
-h	Sort the display alphabetically by host name.
-l	Sort the display alphabetically by load average.
-t	Sort the display by uptime.

In the following example, the output is sorted alphabetically by host name.

```
oak% rup -h
ash     up  1 day,   1:42,   load average: 0.00, 0.31, 0.34

elm     up 14 days,  0 min,  load average: 0.07, 0.01, 0.00

maple   up 32 days,  14:39,  load average: 0.21, 0.05, 0.00

oak     up  8 days,  15:44,  load average: 0.02, 0.00, 0.00
oak%
```

Determining Whether a Remote System Is Up (ping, rup, rpcinfo -p)

Use the following steps to determine whether a remote system is up and to log in to the remote system.

1. Type **ping *system-name*** and press Return.

   The message `*system-name* is alive` means the system is accessible over the network. The message `ping: unknown host *system-name*` means the system name is not known on the network. The message `ping: no answer from *system-name*` means the system is known on the network but is not up at this time.
2. Type **rup *system-name*** and press Return.

   Information about how long the system has been up and the load average is displayed.
3. Type **rpcinfo -p *system-name*** and press Return.

   Information about RPC services is displayed.
4. Type **rlogin *system-name*** and press Return.

   You are logged in to the remote system.

```
cinderella% ping drusilla
drusilla is alive
cinderella% rup drusilla
   drusilla     up  3 days,  15:10    load average: 0.07, 0.08, 0.09
cinderella% rpcinfo -p drusilla
program  vers proto port   service
100000    3   udp     111  portmapper
100000    2   udp     111  portmapper
100000    3   tcp     111  portmapper
100000    2   tcp     111  portmapper
100007    3   tcp    1029  ypbind
100007    3   udp    1025  ypbind
100021    1   tcp    1030  nlockmgr
100021    1   udp    1026  nlockmgr
100024    1   tcp    1028  status
100024    1   udp    1027  status
100021    3   tcp    1030  nlockmgr
100021    3   udp    1026  nlockmgr
100020    2   tcp    4045  llockmgr
100020    2   udp    4045  llockmgr
100021    2   tcp    1030  nlockmgr
100021    2   udp    1026  nlockmgr
100087   10   udp    1031  adm_agent
100011    1   udp    1034  rquotad
100002    1   udp    1037  rusersd
100002    2   udp    1037  rusersd
100012    1   udp    1041  sprayd
100008    1   udp    1043  walld
100001    2   udp    1046  rstatd
100001    3   udp    1046  rstatd
100001    4   udp    1046  rstatd
100068    2   udp    1049  cmsd
100068    3   udp    1049  cmsd
100083    1   tcp    4049
cinderella% rlogin drusilla
Password:
Last login: Mon Mar  2 10:31:55 from cinderella
drusilla%
```

You can also use `ping` with a system's IP address by typing **`ping`** ***`IP-address`*** and pressing Return. The message *`IP-address is alive`* means the system is accessible over the network. The message `ping: no answer from` *`IP-address`* means the system is not available to the network. The message `ping: unknown host` *`IP-address`* means the system name is not known on the network.

```
oak% ping 129.144.52.119
129.144.52.119 is alive
oak% ping 129.137.67.234
ping: unknown host 129.137.67.234
oak% ping 129.145.52.119
ping: no answer from 129.145.52.119
oak%
```

Logging In to a Remote System (rlogin)

Use the following steps to log in to a remote system.

1. Type **`rlogin`** ***`system-name`*** and press Return. You may be prompted for a password.
2. If you have a local account on that system, type your local password. Otherwise, type your NIS or NIS+ password.

   Unless you have a home directory that is accessible on the remote system (because it is local on that system or because it is hard-mounted or automounted), you log in to the root (/) directory.

```
oak% rlogin ash
Password:
No directory!  Logging in with home=/
Last login: Tue Sep 17 13:54:28 from 129.144.52.119
Sun Microsystems, Inc. SunOS 5.8     Generic February 2000
ash%
```

New!

Authentication for Remote Logins (rlogin)

The remote system or the network environment can perform authentication to establish who the user is for `rlogin` operations.

The main difference between these forms of authentication is in the type of interaction they require from the user and the way the authentication is established. If a remote system tries to authenticate a user, the user is prompted for a password unless the user is included in the `/etc/hosts.equiv` or `.rhosts` file on the remote system. If the network authenticates the user, no password is required because the network already knows who the user is.

NOTE. Network authentication usually supersedes system authentication.

Remote System Authentication

When the remote system tries to authenticate a user, it relies on information in its local `/etc/hosts.equiv` or `.rhosts` files. If the user's system or host name is included in the remote system's `/etc/hosts.equiv` file, authentication is automatic and the user can use the `rlogin` command without typing a password. Alternatively, authentication is automatic with the `rlogin` command when the user has a remote home directory with a `.rhosts` file that includes the user's system name and user name.

The /etc/hosts.equiv File The `/etc/hosts.equiv` file contains a list of trusted hosts for a remote system, one entry per line. If a user tries to log in remotely with the `rlogin` command from one of the hosts listed in this file and if the remote system can access the password entry for the user, the remote system enables the user to log in without a password.

A typical `hosts.equiv` file has the following structure.

```
host1
host2 user_a
+@engineering
-@marketing
```

When the `/etc/hosts.equiv` file contains an entry consisting of just a host name, such as the `host1` entry above, the host is trusted and so is any user at that system.

If the user name is also mentioned, as in the second entry above, then the host is trusted only for that specified user.

A group name preceded by a plus sign (+) means that all the systems in that netgroup are considered trusted.

A group name preceded by a minus sign (-) means that none of the systems in that netgroup are considered trusted.

A single line of + in the `/etc/hosts.equiv` file indicates that every known host is trusted.

The `/etc/hosts.equiv` file presents a security risk, especially if it contains a + entry. If you maintain an `/etc/hosts.equiv` file on a system, include only trusted hosts in your network. Do not include any host that belongs to a different network or any systems that are in public areas. For example, do not include a host for which you do not have administrative control.

The .rhosts File The `.rhosts` file is the user equivalent of the `/etc/hosts.equiv` file. It contains a list of host-user combinations instead of hosts in general. If a host-user combination is listed in this file, the specified user is granted permission to log in remotely from the specified host without having to supply a password.

> *NOTE. A* `.rhosts` *file must reside at the top level of a user's home directory.* `.rhosts` *files located in subdirectories are not consulted.*

Users can create `.rhosts` files in their home directories. Using the `.rhosts` file is another way to enable trusted access between an individual's user accounts on different systems without using the `/etc/hosts.equiv` file.

Unfortunately, the `.rhosts` file presents a major security problem. While the `/etc/hosts.equiv` file is under the control of system administrators and can be managed effectively, any user can create a `.rhosts` file granting access to whomever the user chooses without the system administrator's knowledge. The only secure way to manage `.rhosts` files is to completely disallow them.

Use the following procedures to search and remove `.rhosts` files.

1. Become superuser.
2. All on one line, type **find *home-directories* -name .rhosts -print -exec rm{} \;** and press Return.

   The `find` command starts at the designated directory and searches for any file named `.rhosts`. If any `.rhosts` files are found, the path is printed on the screen and the file is removed.

The following example removes all `.rhosts` files in the users' home directories located in the `/export/home` directory.

```
paperbark% su
Password:
# find /export/home -name .rhosts -print -exec rm{} \;
/export/home/ray/.rhosts
/export/home/des/.rhosts
#
```

Network Authentication

Network information is stored in NIS maps or NIS+ tables. Network authentication relies on one of the following two methods.

- A trusting network environment that has been set up with the user's local network information service and the automounters.
- One of the network information services pointed to by the `/etc/nsswitch.conf` file on the remote system that contains information about the user.

What Happens After You Log In Remotely

When you log in to a remote system, the `rlogin` command tries to find your home directory. If the `rlogin` command can't find your home directory, it assigns you to the root (`/`) directory on the remote system and the following message is displayed.

```
Unable to find home directory, logging in with /
```

If the `rlogin` command finds your home directory, it sources both the `.cshrc` and `.login` files for the C shell or the `.profile` file for the Bourne shell. Therefore, your prompt on the remote system is your standard login prompt and the current directory is the same as for a local login. For example, if your usual prompt is your system name followed by the percent (%) sign, such as paperbark%, when you log in to a remote system, the remote system name is displayed as the login prompt.

In the following example, user winsor remotely logs in to the system castle and displays the current working directory.

```
paperbark% rlogin castle
Password:
Last login: Tue Jun 20 14:02:01 from :0
Sun Microsystems Inc.   SunOS 5.7       Generic October 1998
You have mail.
castle% pwd
/export/home/winsor
castle%
```

Logging Out From a Remote System

New!

You use the exit(1) command to log out from a remote system.

The following example shows the user winsor logging out from the system castle.

```
castle% exit
castle% logout
Connection closed.
paperbark%
```

Transferring Files Between Systems (rcp, ftp)

If the automounter is set up for your site, you can transfer files between systems by using commands such as cp and mv. This section describes how to use the rcp and ftp commands to transfer files between systems.

Using the rcp Command

To transfer a file from a remote system to your system with the remote copy command, type **rcp** ***system-name:source-pathname destination*** and press Return. If you have proper security to access the remote system, the file is copied to the destination you specify.

In the following example, the file quest is copied from the /tmp directory on the system ash to the current working directory on the system oak.

```
oak% rcp ash:/tmp/quest .
oak%
```

To transfer a file from a local system to a remote system, type **`rcp`** ***`pathname system-name:destination-pathname`*** and press Return. If you have proper security to access the remote system, the file is copied from the local system to the remote destination you specify.

In the following example, the file `quest` is copied from the current working directory on the system `oak` to the `/tmp` directory on the system `ash`.

```
oak% rcp quest ash:/tmp
oak%
```

If you want, you can rename the file as part of the destination path name. For example, to rename the file `quest` to `questions` and put it in the `/tmp` directory, type **`/tmp/questions`** as the destination path name.

Using the File Transfer Program (ftp)

Use the following steps to transfer files from your local system to a remote system by using the file transfer program.

> *NOTE. You may need to have an account on each system to use the file transfer program. Some systems allow read-only* `ftp` *access to anybody who logs in as* `anonymous` *and types a login name at the password prompt.*

If you have an NIS or an NIS+ account, you can use your login name and network password to access a remote system by using `ftp`.

1. Type **`ftp`** and press Return.

   The `ftp>` prompt is displayed.
2. Type **`open`** ***`remote-system-name`*** and press Return.

   System connection messages are displayed, and you are asked for a user name.
3. Type the user name for your account on the remote system and press Return.

   If a password is required, you are asked to enter it.
4. Type the password (if required) for your account on the remote system and press Return.

   A system login message and the `ftp>` prompt are displayed.
5. Type **`bin`** to set binary format or **`asc`** to set ASCII format and press Return.

The file type is set. ASCII is the default format.

6. Type **put *local-filename destination-filename*** and press Return to transfer a single file.

   File transfer messages and the ftp> prompt are displayed.

7. Type **quit** and press Return.

   A goodbye message and the command prompt are displayed.

The following example establishes an ftp connection from the system oak to the system elm, specifies ASCII format, puts the file quest from oak into the /tmp/quest directory on elm, and quits the session.

```
oak% ftp
ftp> open elm
Connected to elm
220 elm FTP server (UNIX(r) System V Release 4.0) ready.

Name (elm:ignatz): ignatz
331 Password required for ignatz.
Password:
230 User ignatz logged in.
ftp> asc
ftp> put quest /tmp/quest
200 PORT command successful.

150 ASCII data connection for /tmp/quest (129.144.52.119,1333).

226 Transfer complete.
ftp> quit
221 Goodbye.
oak%
```

You can use the send command as an alternative to the put command. You can copy multiple files by using the mput command. There is no msend command. See the ftp(1) manual page for more information.

NOTE. You must have an account on each system to use the file transfer program.

If you have an NIS or an NIS+ account, you can use your login name and network password to access a remote system with ftp. Use the following steps to transfer files from a remote system to your local system by using the file transfer program.

1. Type **ftp** and press Return.

   The ftp> prompt is displayed.

2. Type **open *remote-system-name*** and press Return.

   System connection messages are displayed, and you are asked for a user name.

3. Type the user name for your account on the remote system and press Return.

   If a password is required, you are asked to enter it.

4. Type the password (if required) for your account on the remote system and press Return.

   A system login message and the ftp> prompt are displayed.

5. Type **bin** to set binary format or **asc** to set ASCII format and press Return.

   The file type is set. ASCII is the default format.

6. Type **get** ***remote-filename destination-filename*** and press Return.

   File transfer messages and the ftp> prompt are displayed.

7. Type **quit** and press Return. A goodbye message and the command prompt are displayed.

The following example establishes an ftp connection from the system oak to the system elm, specifies ASCII format, gets the file quest from elm, puts it into the /tmp/quest directory on oak, and quits the session.

```
oak% ftp
ftp> open elm
Connected to elm
220 elm FTP server (UNIX(r)System V Release 4.0) ready.

Name (elm:ignatz): ignatz
331 Password required for ignatz.
Password:
230 User ignatz logged in.

ftp> asc
ftp> get quest /tmp/quest
200 PORT command successful.
150 ASCII data connection for /tmp/quest (129.144.52.119,1333).
226 Transfer complete.

ftp> quit
221 Goodbye.
oak%
```

NOTE. You can copy multiple files by using the mget *command. See the* ftp*(1) manual page for more information.*

Administering NIS+ Databases

NIS+ provides a central store of information for network resources such as hosts, users, and mailboxes. NIS+ replaces NIS (Network Information Service) and provides the following enhancements.

- An organizational framework that is simpler to administer in large companies.
- Improved security.
- Improved distribution time to propagate changes through the network.

In addition, the Solaris Operating Environment provides a nameservice switch file, `/etc/nsswitch.conf`, that lets you use several different network information services at once. The `/etc/nsswitch.conf` file also lets you specify which service provides which type of information. In previous SunOS releases, selection of the nameservice was hard-coded into the services, which made it difficult to switch to a new nameservice. The `/etc/nsswitch.conf` file defines the order in which local files and network databases are searched for information. Describing how to set up NIS+ is beyond the scope of this book.

Using NIS+ Tables

NIS+ tables correspond to NIS maps. The Solaris Operating Environment provides 16 types of tables (shown in Figure 70) that store the network information used by NIS+.

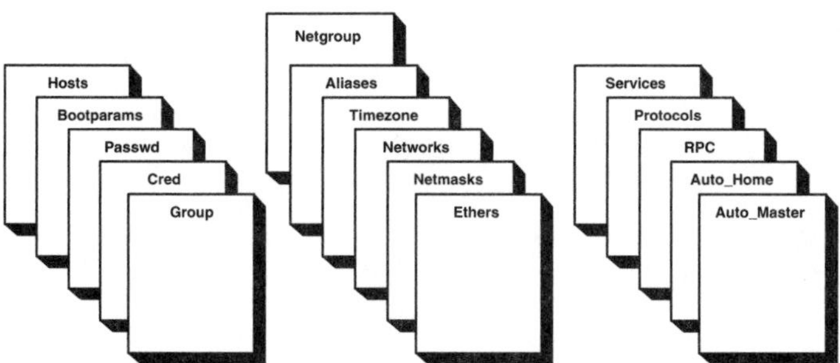

Figure 70 The 16 NIS+ Tables

Each table stores a different type of information about users, workstations, or resources on the network. For instance, the Hosts table stores the host name and network address of every workstation in the domain; the Bootparams table stores the location of the root, swap, and dump directories of the diskless clients in the domain.

Each domain can have its own set of these NIS+ tables, which store all the NIS+ information for that particular domain. Table 66 lists the 16 NIS+ tables and the information they store.

You can access information in NIS+ tables either by entry row or by column, as shown in Figure 71.

Table 66 NIS+ Tables

Table	Information in the Table
Hosts	Network address and host name of every workstation in the domain.
Bootparams	Location of the root, swap, and dump partition of every diskless client in the domain.
Password	Password information about every NIS+ principal in the domain, plus a pointer to the shadow file.
Cred	Credentials for principals who have permission to access the information or objects in the domain.
Group	Password, group ID, and members of every group in the domain.
Netgroup	The netgroups to which workstations and users in the domain may belong.
Aliases	Information about the aliases of workstations in the domain.
Timezone	The time zone of every workstation in the domain.
Networks	The networks in the domain and their canonical names.
Netmasks	The networks in the domain and their associated netmasks.
Ethers	The Ethernet address of every workstation in the domain.
Services	The names of IP services used in the domain and their port numbers.
Protocols	The list of IP protocols used in the domain.
RPC	The RPC program numbers for RPC services available in the domain.
Auto_Home	The location of all users' home directories in the domain.
Auto_Master	Automounter map information.

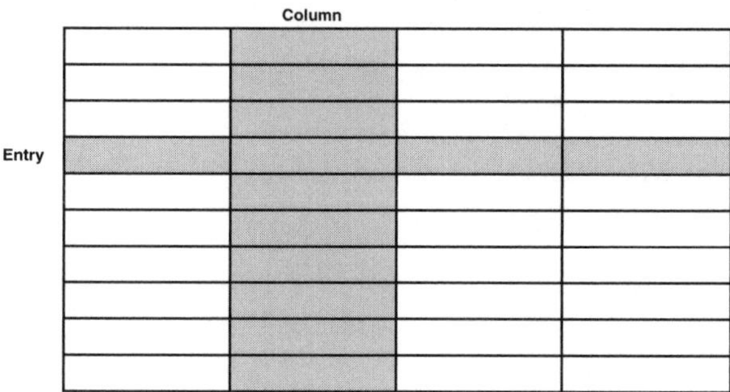

Figure 71 Entry Row and Columns in a Table

For example, if you want to find the network address of a workstation named `drusilla`, you can ask a search program to look through the `hostname` column until it finds `drusilla`, as shown in Figure 72. The program then searches the `drusilla` entry row to find its network address, as shown in Figure 73.

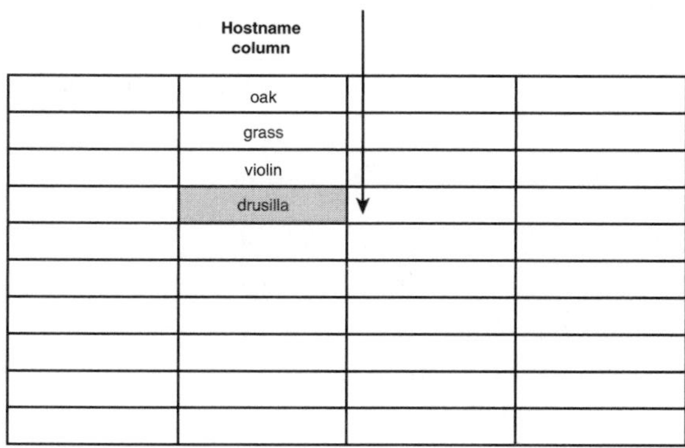

Figure 72 Searching the Hostname Column

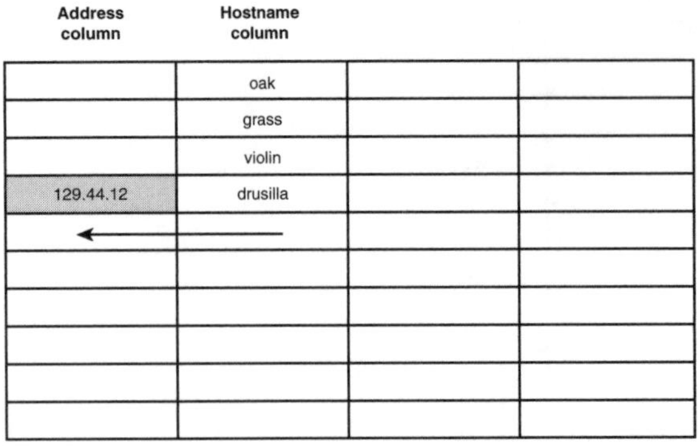

Figure 73 Finding a network Address

You can use NIS+ commands to perform these types of searches for you. Table 67 lists the NIS+ administrative commands.

Table 67 NIS+ Administrative Commands

Command	Description
`nistbladm`	Display, add, modify, and delete information in an NIS+ table.
`nisgrep`	Search for information in an NIS+ table.
`nismatch`	Search for information in an NIS+ table.
`niscat`	Display the entire contents of an NIS+ table.

See the manual pages for information about how to use these commands.

NIS+ Security

NIS+ uses a security authorization model that is similar to the UNIX file system model. It specifies that each item in the namespace as well as each record, each column, and each row has associated with it a set of access rights that are granted to four broad classes of principals.

- The owner of the item.
- A group owner of the item.
- All other principals.
- `nobody`—the class of users not defined in the NIS+ domain or those users accessing NIS+ resources from NIS clients.

The specific access rights are different from the traditional read, write, and execute rights of file systems because of the nature of information services. Refer to your system manual for more information about NIS+ security.

Solstice Host Manager

New!

In previous Solaris releases, you may have used Admintool to manage server and client support. In the Solaris 2.5 through Solaris 7 releases, you can use the Solstice Host Manager tool, which offers ease of use and provides support for the following nameservices.

- NIS+ tables.
- NIS maps.
- Local `/etc` files.

In the Solaris 8 Operating Environment, you can use AdminSuite 3.0 to administer the Aliases, Auto_Home, Passwd, and Groups databases. See Chapter 4, "Administering User Accounts and Groups," for information on how to edit these databases with AdminSuite. No functionality exists yet to enable you to use AdminSuite to edit the Locale, Netgroup, Protocols, RPC, Services, or Timezone databases. Refer to Table 19 on page 77 for a comparison of the Solstice AdminSuite 2.3 and AdminSuite 3.0 products. The following section describes how to use the AdminSuite Computers/Networks tool.

Solaris AdminSuite 3.0 Computers/Networks Tools

In the Solaris 8 release, the Solstice Host Manager is not supported. Instead, you can use the AdminSuite Computers/Networks tools to administer the Hosts, Ethers, Netmasks, and Networks NIS+ tables. Solaris AdminSuite 3.0 is part of the Admin Pack tools, which are available for free download from the Solaris System Administrator Portal at the following URL.

`www.sun.com/bigadmin/content/adminPack`

NOTE. The AdminSuite 3.0 Computers / Networks tool excludes management of different clients such as AutoClient and stand-alone systems, diskless and dataless clients, and JavaStations that was previously provided by the AdminSuite 2.3 Host Manager.

With the Computers/Networks tool you can add a new network, add new computers to an existing network or subnetwork, define a multihomed host, and rename, modify, or delete existing computers and networks.

Adding a New Network

The Computers/Networks tools enable you to add a new network in the current domain. When you define a new network, an entry is made for it in the networks or netmasks table.

1. Refer to "Accessing Solaris AdminSuite 3.0" on page 79 for instructions on how to access the AdminSuite 3.0 window shown in Figure 74.

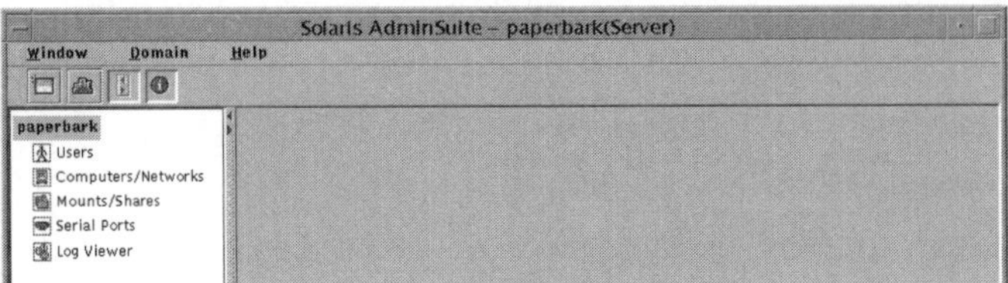

Figure 74 AdminSuite Window

2. Click on the Computers/Networks folder in the navigation pane.

   The contents of the Computers/Networks folder are displayed in the right pane, as shown in Figure 75.

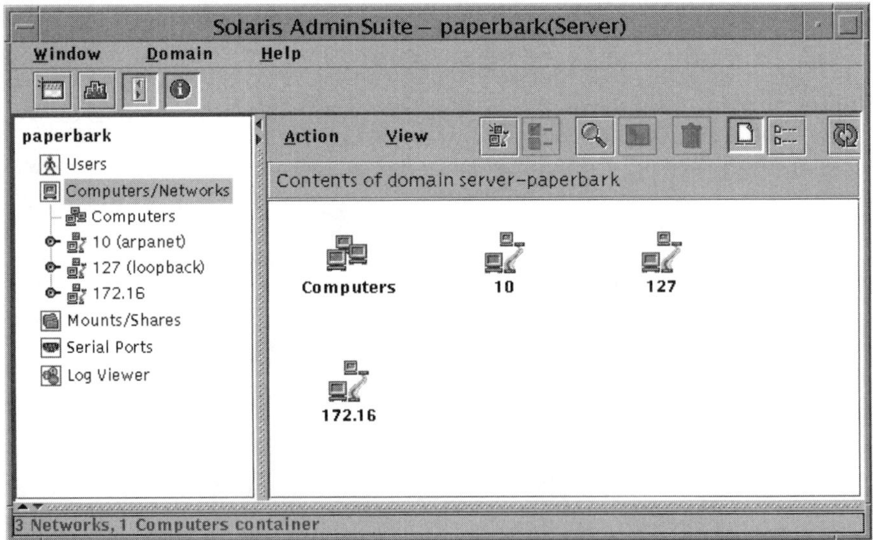

Figure 75 Contents of the Computers/Networks Folder

3. From the Action menu choose Add Network as shown in Figure 76.

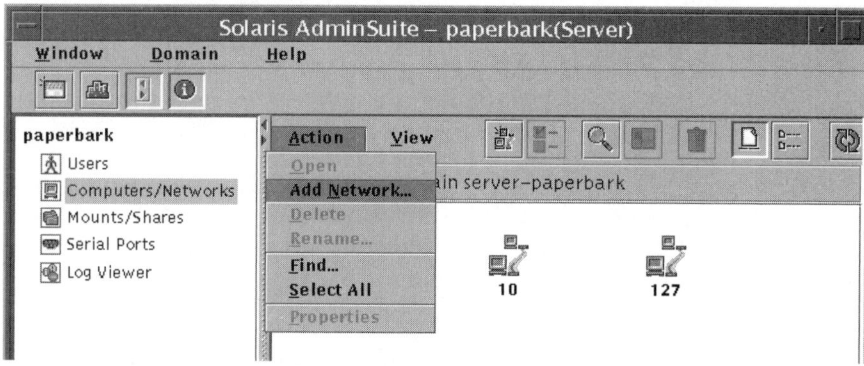

Figure 76 Choose Add Network from the Action Menu

The Add Network window is displayed, as shown in Figure 77.

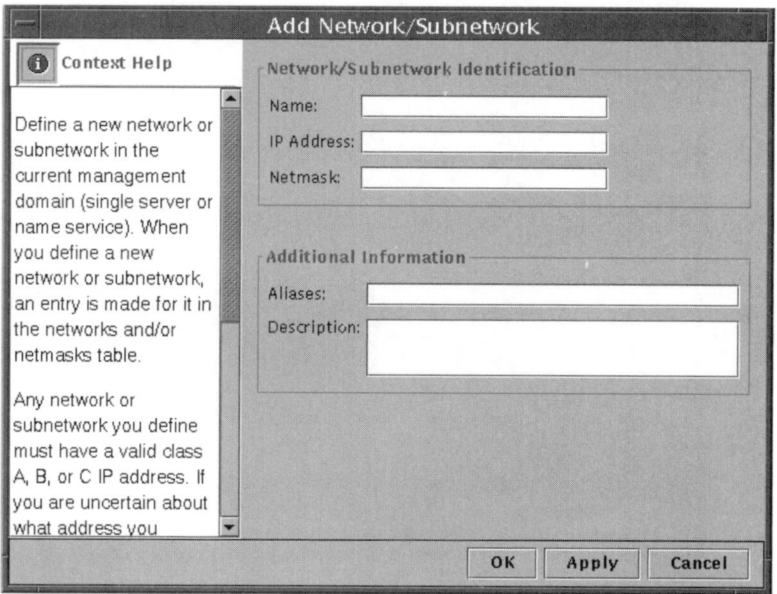

Figure 77 Add Network/Subnetwork Window

4. Use this window to define a new network or subnetwork.

   You must assign a valid A, B, or C class IP address. If you are defining a subnetwork, you must specify a netmask here. If you are creating a subnetwork or a network with no subnetworks, you can leave the Netmask field empty.

5. When you have entered the information for the new network or subnetwork, click on the OK button.

The network or subnetwork is added to the list in the Computers/Network pane and appropriate entries are added to the Networks or Netmasks tables.

Adding a Multihomed Host

The AdminSuite Computers/Networks tool enables you to add a multihomed host alias for servers with multiple network interfaces. If a server has more than one IP address because it is on multiple networks, it is considered a multihomed host. With the Computers/Networks tool, you can specify more than one IP address for a host to make it a multihomed host.

1. Refer to "Accessing Solaris AdminSuite 3.0" on page 79 for instructions on how to access the AdminSuite 3.0 window shown in Figure 78.

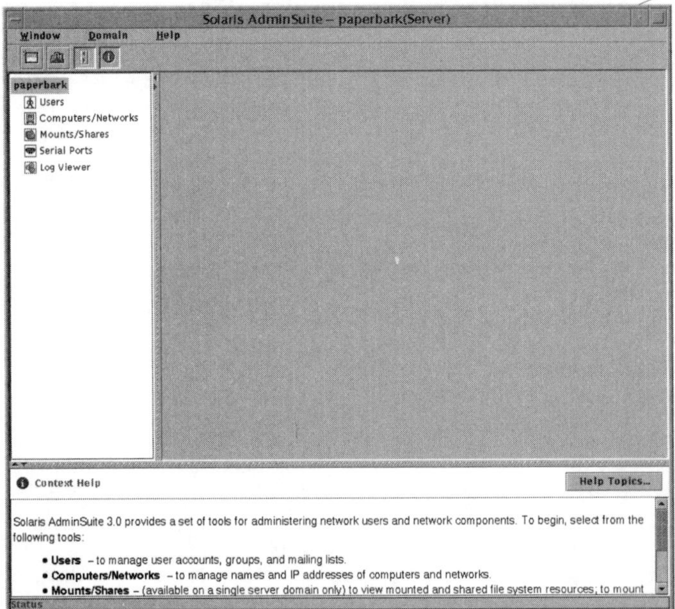

Figure 78 AdminSuite Window

2. Click on the Computers/Networks folder in the navigation pane.

   The contents of the Computers/Networks folder are displayed in the right pane, as shown in Figure 79.

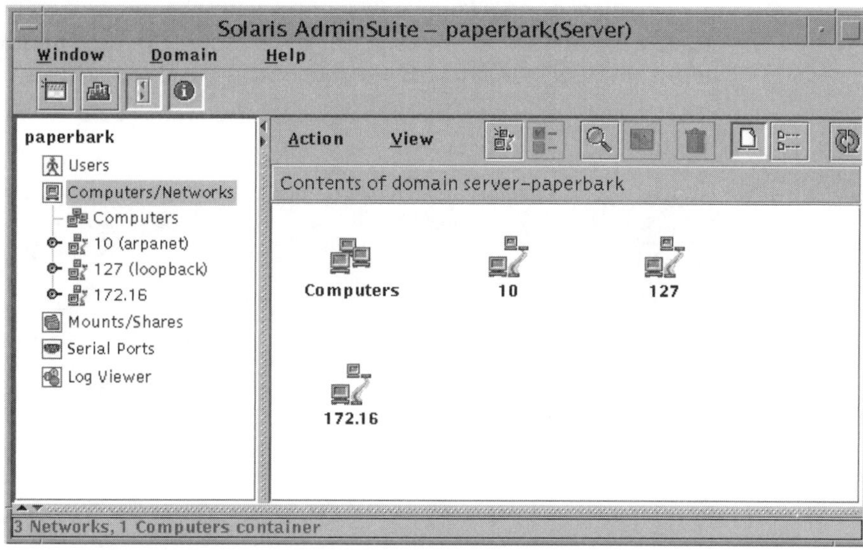

Figure 79 Contents of the Computers/Networks Folder

3. Double-click on the Computers icon.

   The Set Initial View window is displayed the first time you enter the Computers/Networks tool, as shown in Figure 80.

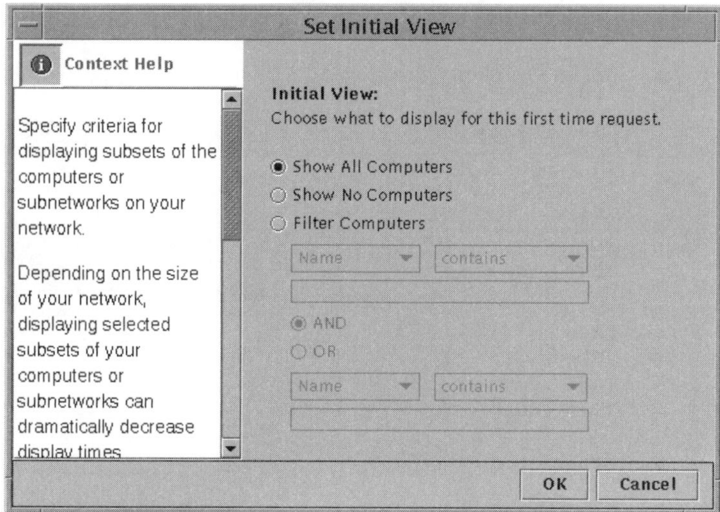

Figure 80 Set Initial View Window

4. Use the Set Initial View window to filter the amount of information displayed in the Computers/Networks tool. Choose the filtering you want and click on the OK button.

   The list of computers is displayed in the right pane, as shown in Figure 81.

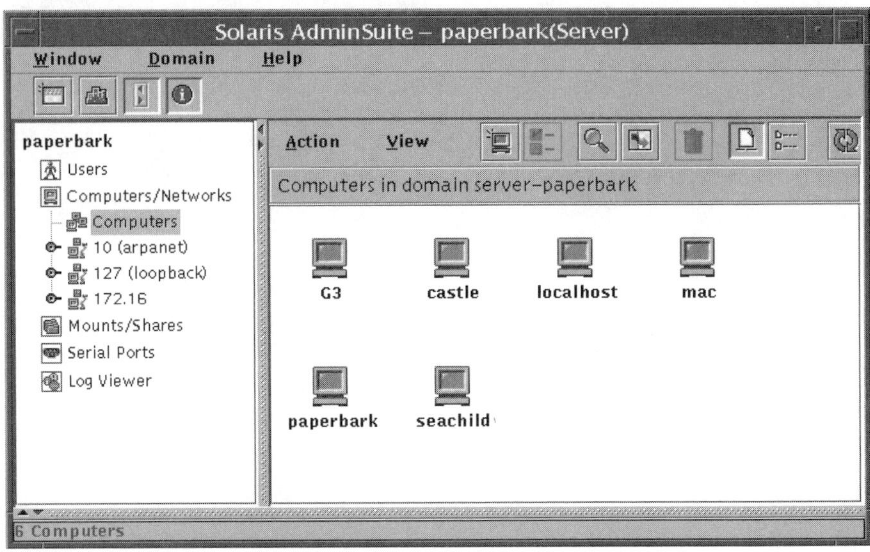

Figure 81 Computers in the Network

5. From the Action menu choose Add Computer, as shown in Figure 82.

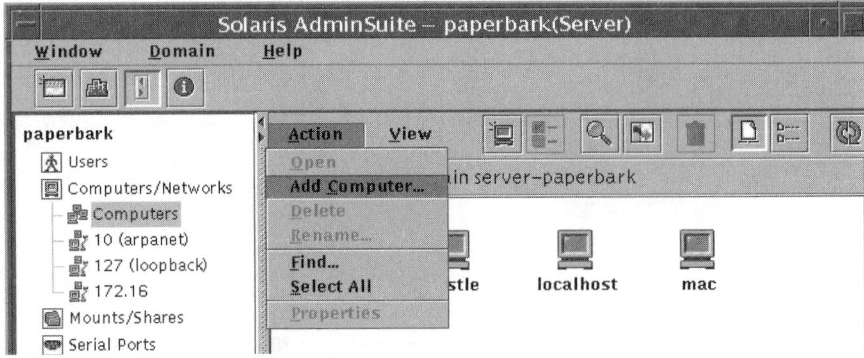

Figure 82 Choose Add Computer from the Action Menu

The Add Computer window is displayed, as shown in Figure 83.

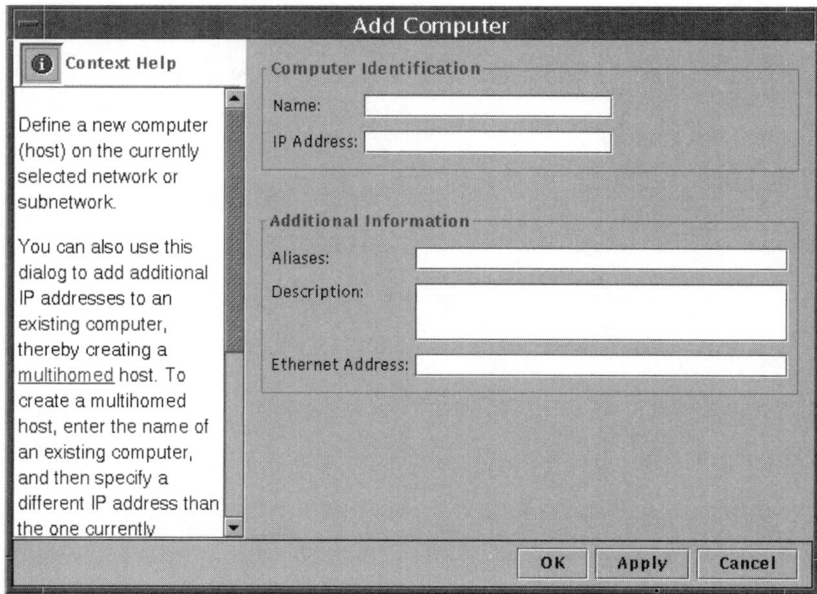

Figure 83 Computers in the Network

6. Use this window to define a new computer on the current network or subnetwork or to add additional IP addresses to an existing computer to create a multihomed host.
7. When you have entered the information for the new computer or multihome computer, click on the OK button.

   The computer is added to the list in the Computers/Network pane and the relevant database files are updated.

Renaming a Computer

You can use the Computers/Networks tool to rename an existing computer.

1. With the list of computers displayed in the right pane, click on the computer you want to rename to highlight it.
2. From the Action menu, choose Rename, as shown in Figure 84.

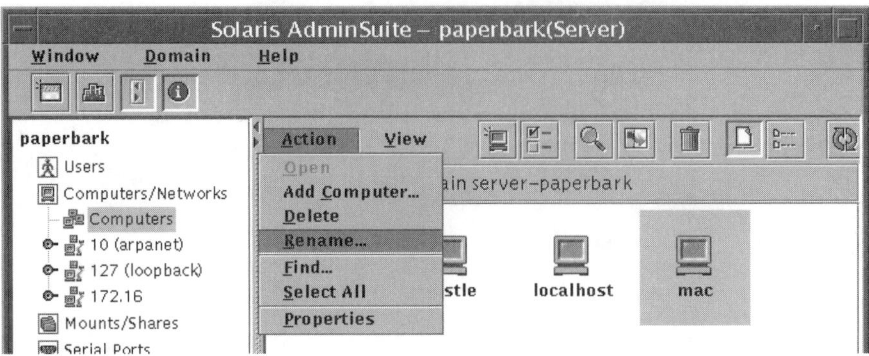

Figure 84 Computer Properties Window

The Rename Computer window is displayed, as shown in Figure 85.

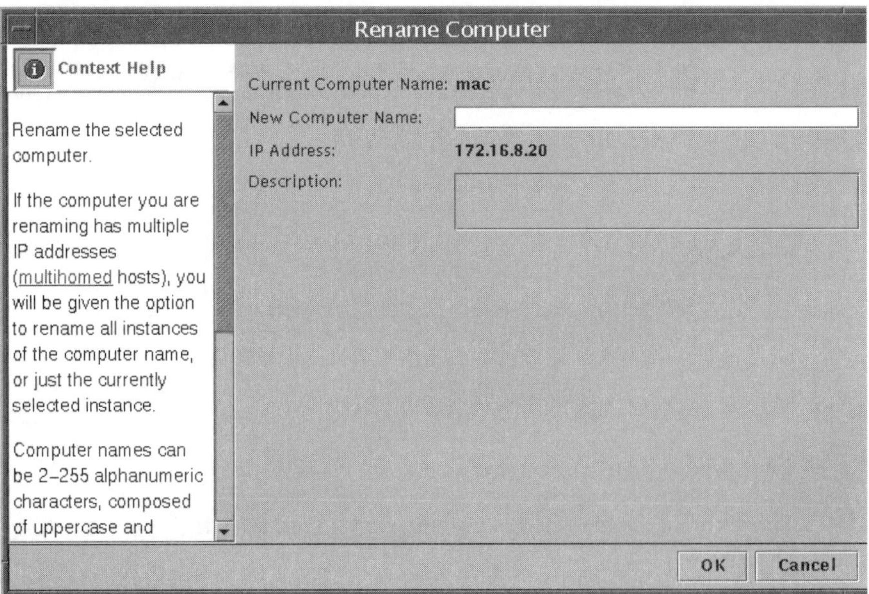

Figure 85 Rename Computer Window

3. Type the name of the new computer.

   Refer to the context help in the left pane for details about requirements for computer names. Make sure the new computer name is unique on the network.
4. Click on the OK button.

   The name of the computer is changed in the Computers/Networks pane, and the Hosts database is updated to reflect the new name.

Modifying Settings for a Computer

You can use the Computers/Networks tool to modify properties for an existing computer.

1. With the list of computers displayed in the right pane, double-click on the computer you want to modify.

   The Computer Properties window is displayed, as shown in Figure 86.

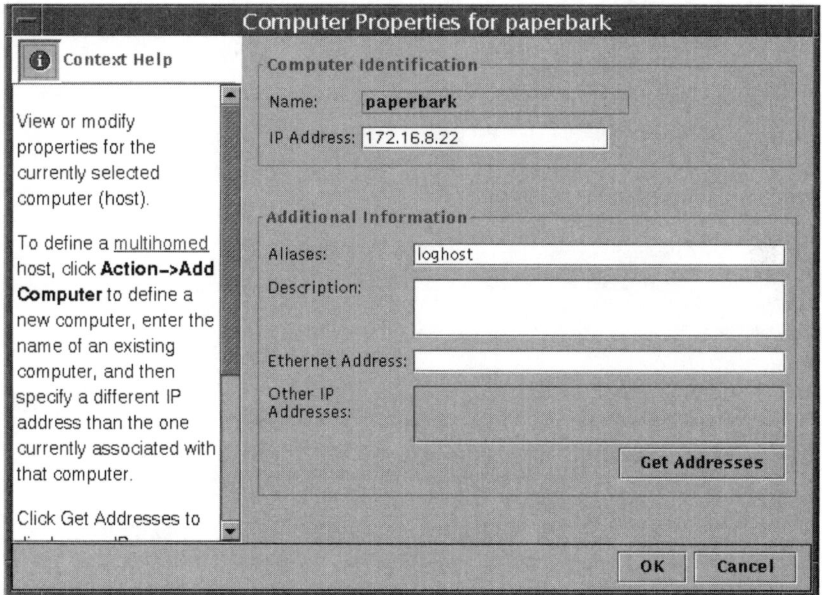

Figure 86 Computer Properties Window

   Alternatively, you can highlight the computer and choose Properties from the Actions menu.

2. Modify the settings as appropriate and click on the OK button.

   The computer settings are changed, and the appropriate databases are updated.

Deleting a Computer

You can use the Computers/Networks tool to delete a computer from a network or subnetwork.

1. With the list of computers displayed in the right pane, click on the computer you want to delete to highlight it.
2. From the Actions menu, choose Delete, as shown in Figure 87.

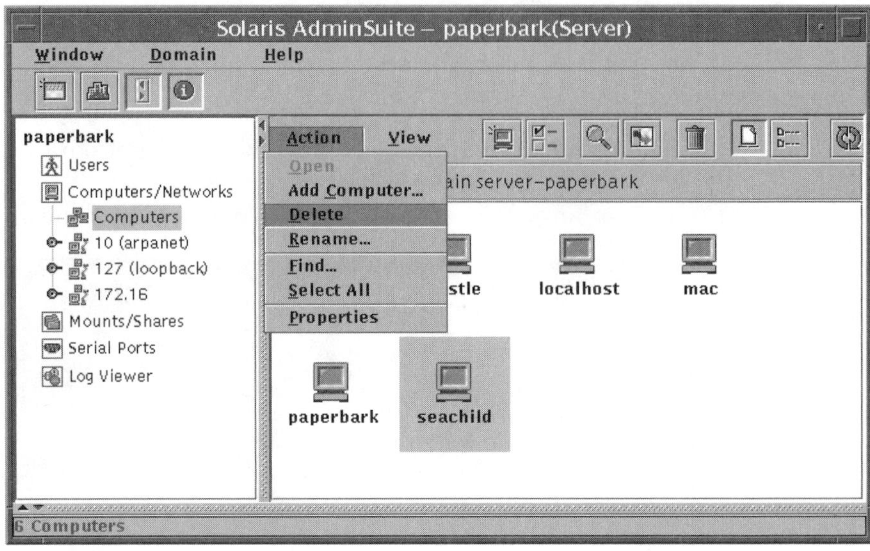

Figure 87 Choose Delete from the Actions Menu

A warning notice is displayed, as shown in Figure 88, asking you to confirm that you want to delete the computer.

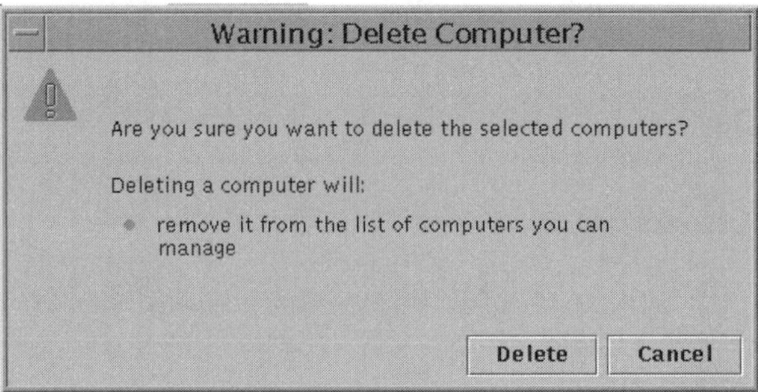

Figure 88 Delete Computer Warning Message

3. Click on the Delete button to delete the computer or the Cancel button to cancel the operation.

   If you click on Delete, the computer is removed from the list of computers that you can manage.

Introducing the IPv6 Internet Protocol

New!

The Solaris 8 release introduces the Internet Protocol, version 6 (IPv6). This new protocol version is evolved from the current IPv4 version, which is also supported in the Solaris 8 Operating Environment. IPv6 adds increased address space and improves Internet functionality by using a simplified header format, support for authentication and privacy, autoconfiguration of address assignments, and new quality-of-service capabilities. Networking commands in the Solaris 8 release have been amended to include support for both the IPv4 and IPv6 network protocols.

You can enable IPv6 on a system when you install the Solaris 8 software. If you answer yes to enable the IPv6 during the installation process, you do not need to enable IPv6 manually. Describing how to enable IPv6 manually is beyond the scope of this book. Refer to Sun's *System Administration Guide, Volume 3*, for more information.

The IPv6 protocol changes are summarized below.

Expanded Routing and Addressing Capabilities

IPv6 increases the IP address size from 32 bits to 128 bits to support more levels of addressing hierarchy, provide more addressable nodes, and use simpler autoconfiguration of addresses.

A scope field improves the scalability of multicast routing to multicast addresses.

IPv6 supports three types of addresses: `unicast`, `anycast`, and `multicast`. The new `anycast` address is defined to identify sets of nodes, where a packet sent to an `anycast` address is delivered to one of the nodes. The use of `anycast` addresses in the IPv6 source route enables nodes to control the path over which their traffic flows.

IPv6 has no broadcast addresses. Multicast addresses are used instead.

Simplified Header Format

Some IPv4 header fields have been dropped or made optional to reduce the common-case processing cost of packet handling. Bandwidth cost of the IPv6 header is kept as low as possible, despite the increased size of the addresses. Even though the IPv6 addresses are four times longer than IPv4 addresses, the IPv6 header is only twice the size of the IPv4 header.

Improved Support for Options

IP header options are encoded to enable more efficient forwarding, less stringent limits on the length of options, and greater flexibility for introducing new options in the future.

Quality-of-Service Capabilities

A new capability enables the labeling of packets belonging to particular traffic flows for which the sender requests special handling, such as nondefault quality of service or real-time service.

Authentication and Privacy Capabilities

IPv6 includes the definition of extensions that provide support for authentication, data integrity, and confidentiality.

New! Showing Network Status (netstat)

You can use the `netstat`(1M) command to display the following network status information.

- A list of active sockets for each protocol.
- The state of the interfaces.
- The routing table.
- The multicast routing table.
- The state of DHCP on one or all interfaces

The Solaris release supports both the IPv4 and IPv6 network interfaces. In the Solaris 8 release, the `netstat` command has been updated to include the IPv6 interfaces.

Displaying Status of Active TCP and UDP Ports

Use the `netstat` command with no arguments to display the status of active TCP and UDP ports. The following example shows the output of the `netstat` command with no arguments, which displays the status of active TCP and UDP ports.

```
paperbark% netstat

TCP: IPv4
   Local Address        Remote Address    Swind Send-Q Rwind Recv-Q  State
-------------------- -------------------- ----- ------ ----- ------ -------
localhost.32786      localhost.32773      32768      0 32768      0 ESTABLISHED
localhost.32773      localhost.32786      32768      0 32768      0 ESTABLISHED
localhost.32789      localhost.32784      32768      0 32768      0 ESTABLISHED
localhost.32784      localhost.32789      32768      0 32768      0 ESTABLISHED
localhost.32792      localhost.32791      32768      0 32768      0 ESTABLISHED
localhost.32791      localhost.32792      32768      0 32768      0 ESTABLISHED
localhost.32795      localhost.32784      32768      0 32768      0 ESTABLISHED
localhost.32784      localhost.32795      32768      0 32768      0 ESTABLISHED
localhost.32798      localhost.32797      32768      0 32768      0 ESTABLISHED
localhost.32797      localhost.32798      32768      0 32768      0 ESTABLISHED
localhost.32813      localhost.32784      32768      0 32768      0 ESTABLISHED
localhost.32784      localhost.32813      32768      0 32768      0 ESTABLISHED
localhost.32816      localhost.32815      32767      0 32768      0 ESTABLISHED
localhost.32815      localhost.32816      32768      0 32768      0 ESTABLISHED
paperbark.32891      G3.ftp               17520      0 24820      0 ESTABLISHED
paperbark.8888       paperbark.32904      32768      0 32768      0 TIME_WAIT
paperbark.32905      paperbark.32779      32768      0 32768      0 TIME_WAIT

Active UNIX domain sockets
Address  Type          Vnode     Conn  Local Addr      Remote Addr
707f1d90 stream-ord 705b89e0 00000000 /tmp/.X11-unix/X0
707f1ea8 stream-ord 00000000 00000000
paperbark%
```

Displaying the Status of Network Interfaces

Use the `-i` option to the `netstat` command to display the status of network interfaces. The following example uses the `netstat -i` command on the system `paperbark` to display the status of network interfaces.

```
paperbark% netstat -i
Name  Mtu  Net/Dest      Address        Ipkts  Ierrs Opkts  Oerrs Collis Queue
lo0   8232 loopback      localhost      11787  0     11787  0     0      0
hme0  1500 paperbark     paperbark      8      0     5      0     0      0

paperbark%
```

Displaying Kernel Routing Tables

Use the `-r` option to the `netstat` command to display kernel routing tables, and use the `-n` option to display network addresses as numbers. The following example uses the `netstat -r -n` command to display the kernel's routing tables with the network addresses as numbers.

```
paperbark% netstat -r -n

Routing Table: IPv4
  Destination           Gateway           Flags  Ref   Use   Interface
-------------------- -------------------- ----- ----- ------ ---------
172.16.8.0           172.16.8.22           U        1      0  hme0
224.0.0.0            172.16.8.22           U        1      0  hme0
127.0.0.1            127.0.0.1             UH      16  11150  lo0
paperbark%
```

Refer to the netstat(1M) manual page for more information.

New! Displaying Network Interface Parameters (ifconfig)

You can use the ifconfig command to display information about specific interfaces, assign an address to a network interface, or configure network interfaces. The /etc/rc2.d scripts run ifconfig at boot time to define the network address of each interface present on a machine. You can also use ifconfig at a later time to redefine an interface address or other operating parameters. Refer to the ifconfig(1M) manual page for complete information. The following sections describe how to use the ifconfig command to display information about specific interfaces.

The ifconfig command has been modified in the Solaris 8 release to create the IPv6 stack and to support new parameters.

Displaying Information About All Interfaces on a System

Use the -a option of the ifconfig command to display information about all interfaces on a system. The following example shows the interfaces on the system paperbark.

```
paperbark% ifconfig -a
lo0: flags=1000849<UP,LOOPBACK,RUNNING,MULTICAST,IPv4> mtu 8232 index 1
        inet 127.0.0.1 netmask ff000000
hme0: flags=1000843<UP,BROADCAST,RUNNING,MULTICAST,IPv4> mtu 1500 index 2
        inet 172.16.8.22 netmask ffffff00 broadcast 172.16.8.255
paperbark%
```

The flags section shows the status of the interface. The mtu field tells you the maximum transfer size in octets. Information on the second line includes the IP address of the host you are using, the netmask currently being used, and the IP broadcast address of the interface.

The following example shows the interfaces on the system castle.

```
castle% ifconfig -a
lo0: flags=849<UP,LOOPBACK,RUNNING,MULTICAST> mtu 8232
        inet 127.0.0.1 netmask ff000000
le0: flags=863<UP,BROADCAST,NOTRAILERS,RUNNING,MULTICAST> mtu 1500
        inet 172.16.8.19 netmask ffff0000 broadcast 172.16.255.255
castle%
```

Displaying Information About Specific Interfaces

Use the following syntax to display information about the configuration of a specific interface.

```
ifconfig interface-name [protocol-family]
```

The following example displays information about the `hme0` interface.

```
paperbark% su
Password
# ifconfig hme0
hme0: flags=1000843<UP,BROADCAST,RUNNING,MULTICAST,IPv4> mtu 1500 index 2
        inet 172.16.8.22 netmask ffffff00 broadcast 172.16.8.255
        ether 8:0:20:7d:79:d4
#
```

The `flags` section shows that the interface is configured `UP`, capable of broadcasting, and not using trailer link-level encapsulation. The `mtu` field tells you that this interface has a maximum transfer size of 1500 octets. Information on the second line includes the IP address of the host, the netmask currently being used, and the IP broadcast address of the interface. The third line gives the machine address (in this case, Ethernet) of the host.

10

ADMINISTERING PRINTING

The printing service consists of the LP print service software, any print filters (programs that process data before printing) you provide, the hardware (the printer, workstation, and network connections), and the Admintool and Solaris Print Manager tools that you can use to administer printing. New!

This chapter briefly describes the LP print service; it lists the files, daemons, and logs used by the LP print service; describes tools available for administering printing; provides steps for setting up print servers and clients; and describes the basic commands used for printing.

What's New in Printing New!

This section describes new printing features in the Solaris 8 Operating Environment.

Solaris Print Manager

The Solaris Print Manager, previously available as part of the Solstice AdminSuite Package, is a Java-based graphical user interface that enables you to manage local and remote printers. You can use the Solaris Print Manager with NIS, NIS+, NIS+ with Federated Naming Service (`xfn`), and `files` nameservices. You must be superuser to use this tool. See "Setting Up

Printing Services" on page 383 for more information about the Solaris Print Manager.

Print Naming Enhancement to the Nameservice Switch File

The Solaris release supports the `printers` database in the `/etc/nsswitch.conf` nameservice switch file. The `printers` database provides centralized printer configuration information to print clients on the network.

See "Print Naming Enhancement" on page 382 for more information.

Enabling or Disabling Global Banner Page Printing

The Solaris 8 Operating Environment adds the `-banner` option with arguments of `always`, `never`, and `optional` to the `lpadmin` command. When banner page printing is set to `optional`, the banner is printed by default, but users can disable banner page printing by using the `lp -o nobanner` command. See "Controlling the Printing of Banner Pages" on page 399 and `lpadmin`(1M) for more information.

Solaris Print Package Redesign

This section describes the redesign of the Solaris print packages starting with the Solaris 2.6 release and the additional features that were added with that release.

Redesign of Print Packages

Starting with the Solaris 2.6 release, print packages have been redesigned to provide greater flexibility and modularity of print software installation and to enable installation of a smaller footprint for the print client.

Solaris 2.6 print software includes the following features.

- Redesign of print packages.
- Print protocol adapter.
- SunSoft print client.
- Network printer support.

The Solaris 2.6 print software has the following limitations.

- No support for print servers defined as S5 (the System V print protocol) in previous Solaris releases.
- No print filtering on print clients.

With the Solaris 2.6 redesign, the default is to install all the print packages. Print servers require installation of all packages, including both client and server. For print clients, you can choose to install only the print client packages. PostScript filter software is provided in its own print package. Table 68 describes the new set of print packages.

Table 68 Solaris Packages

Package	Base Directory	Description
SUNWpcr	root (/)	SunSoft Print—Client.
SUNWpcu	/usr	SunSoft Print—Client.
SUNWpsr	root (/)	SunSoft Print—LP Server.
SUNWpsu	/usr	SunSoft Print—LP Server.
SUNWPSF	/usr	PostScript filters.
SUNWscplp	/usr	SunSoft Print—Source compatibility.
SUNWppm	/usr/sadm/admin/bin	Solaris Print Manager (new in the Solaris 8 release).

New!

The following print packages were removed from the Solaris 2.6 release.

- `SUNWlpr`—LP print service (`root`).
- `SUNWlpu`—LP print service—Client (`usr`).
- `SUNWlps`—LP print service—Server (`usr`).

Print commands from `SUNWscpu` have been moved into the `SUNWscplp` (SunSoft Print— Source Compatibility) package.

Print Protocol Adaptor

The Solaris 2.6 print protocol adapter replaces the Service Access Facility (SAF), the network listener, and `lpNet` on the inbound side of the LP spooler with a more modular and modern design.

The print protocol adapter provides the following features.

- The complete `BSD` print protocol and extended Solaris functionality are implemented.

- Multiple spooling systems can coexist on the same host and have access to the BSD print protocol.
- Third-party application developers can extend the print protocol adapter to support other printing protocols such as Apple and Novell.

The new print protocol adapter is compatible with print clients set up in previous Solaris releases if the BSD protocol was used to configure these clients. If the BSD protocol was not used, you must modify the previous Solaris print client configuration to use the BSD protocol by using Admintool, Solaris Print Manager, or the `lpsystem` command.

SunSoft Print Client

Starting with the Solaris 2.6 release, the SunSoft Print Client software is bundled with the Solaris Operating Environment as packages `SUNWpcr` and `SUNWpcu`. This software was previously released as an unbundled product. It was available on the Solaris Migration CD and as part of the Solstice AdminSuite suite of administration products.

The SunSoft Print Client software uses an NIS map, an NIS+ table, or a single file to provide centralized client administration in the Solaris 2.6 release. The Print Client software includes the following features.

- Replacing the `/etc/lp` directory structure with a configuration database that can be stored in a user file (`$HOME/.printers`), a system file (`/etc/prints.conf`), an NIS map (`printers.conf.byname`), or an NIS+ FNS context.
- Using a more streamlined implementation that provides reduced client overhead and quicker and more accurate responses to print status requests.
- Using the `lpset`(1M) command to create the `printers.conf` file.
- Reducing the size of the package (183 Kbytes total) from previous Solaris releases.
- Providing interoperability with the BSD protocol available with SunOS 4.x, Solaris 2.x, HP-UX, and other systems, as described in RFC-1179.

Enhanced Network Printer Support

Starting with the Solaris 2.6 release, print software provides better support for network printers than in previous Solaris releases. The following new features are included.

- A new interface script, `/usr/lib/lp/model/netstandard`, which is specifically designed to support network printers. This script collects the spooler and print database information needed to perform network printing and passes it to the print output module.
- A new print output module, `netpr`, is called from the netstandard interface script to print the print job. It opens a network connection to the printer, creates the correct protocol instructions, and sends the data to the printer. The `netpr` program currently supports two protocols: BSD print protocol and a TCP pass-through.
- New arguments to the `lpadmin -o` command to specify destination name, protocol, and time-out values for the network printer.
- Solaris Print Manager, now included in the Solaris 8 Operating Environment, can set up and manage network printers.

Print Administration Tools in the Solaris 2.6 Environment

Starting with the Solaris 2.6 release, the Solaris Operating Environment printing software provides an environment for setting up and managing client access to printers on a network. The Solaris printing software contains the following components.

- *SunSoft Print Client software*, previously available only with the Solstice AdminSuite set of administration tools, enables you to make printers available to print clients by using a nameservice.
- *Admintool*, a graphical user interface, assists you in managing printing on a local system.
- *The LP print service commands*, a command-line interface used to set up and manage printers, provide additional functionality not available with the other print management tools.
- *The Solaris Print Manager*, a graphical user interface used to manage printers in a nameservice environment, is available with the Solaris 8 Operating environment.

New!

NOTE. If you do not use the Solaris Print Manager to set up and manage printing, you must use some combination of the other components to completely manage printing in the Solaris Operating Environment.

Table 69 summarizes the features of the printing components, all of which are available in the Solaris 8 Operating Environment.

Table 69 Solaris Printing Component Features

Component	Graphical User Interface	Configure Network Printers	Manage Print Clients and Servers	NIS, NIS+, or NIS+ (xfn) Support
Solaris Print Manager	Yes	Yes	Yes	Yes
Admintool	Yes	No	Yes	No
LP commands	No	Yes	Yes	No

Choosing a Method to Manage Printers

In the Solaris 8 Operating Environment, adding printer information to a nameservice makes access to printers available to all systems on the network and generally makes printer administration easier because all printer information is centralized.

The Solaris print client software and Solaris Print Manager application offer a graphical solution for setting up and managing printers on a network. You can also use the `lpadmin` command to configure printers on individual systems.

Admintool provides an alternative method to install printers in the Solaris environment. Admintool is a graphical user interface for the LP print service commands that simplifies tasks for setting up and managing local printers.

You must run Admintool on the system the printer is connected to, that is, you cannot make changes to a remote system by using Admintool. When you set up a printer, Admintool makes the appropriate changes in the `/etc/printers.conf` file and `/etc/lp` directories on the system, as required. You can use Admintool to set up a system as a print server or print client only if it is running the Solaris operating system.

You can accomplish most printing configuration tasks with Solaris Print Manager. However, if you need to write interface scripts or add your own filters, you can use the LP print service commands directly to accomplish these tasks.

Introducing the LP Print Service

The LP print service is a set of software commands that enables users to print files while they continue to work. The print service consists of the LP print service software and spooler—spool is an acronym for system peripheral operation off-line. The LP print service performs the following functions.

- Administers files and schedules local print requests.
- Schedules network requests.
- Filters files (if necessary) so that they print properly.
- Starts programs that interface with the printers.
- Tracks the status of jobs.
- Tracks forms mounted on the printer.
- Tracks print wheels that are currently mounted.
- Delivers alerts to mount new forms or different print wheels.
- Delivers alerts about printing problems.

Administering Files and Scheduling Print Requests

The LP print service has a scheduler daemon, called `lpsched`. The scheduler daemon updates the LP system files with information about printer setup and configuration, as shown in Figure 89.

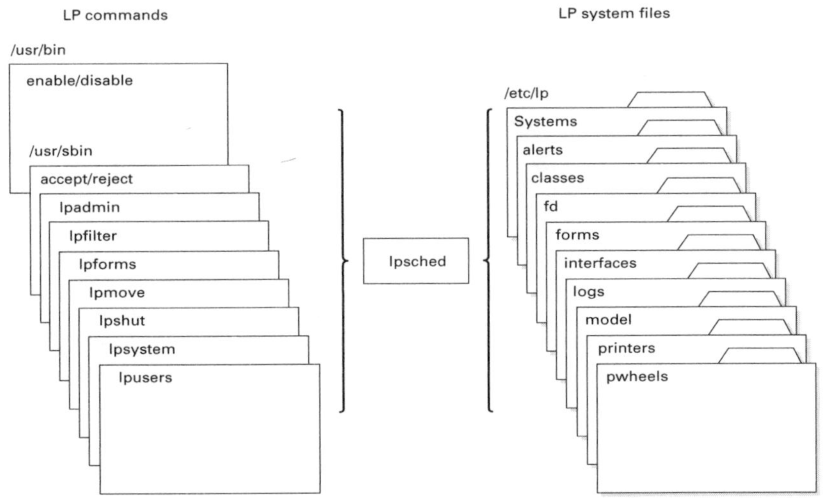

Figure 89 The lpsched Scheduler Upates the LP System Files

Starting with the Solaris 2.6 release, all of the LP commands except for enable and disable have been moved from /usr/bin into /usr/sbin. The enable and disable commands are located in /usr/bin and /usr/lib/lp/local and are symbolically linked to the accept and reject commands.

The lpsched daemon also schedules all local print requests, as shown in Figure 90, regardless of whether the requests are issued by users from an application or from the command line. In addition, the scheduler tracks the status of printers and filters. When a printer finishes printing a request, the scheduler schedules the next request if one is in the queue.

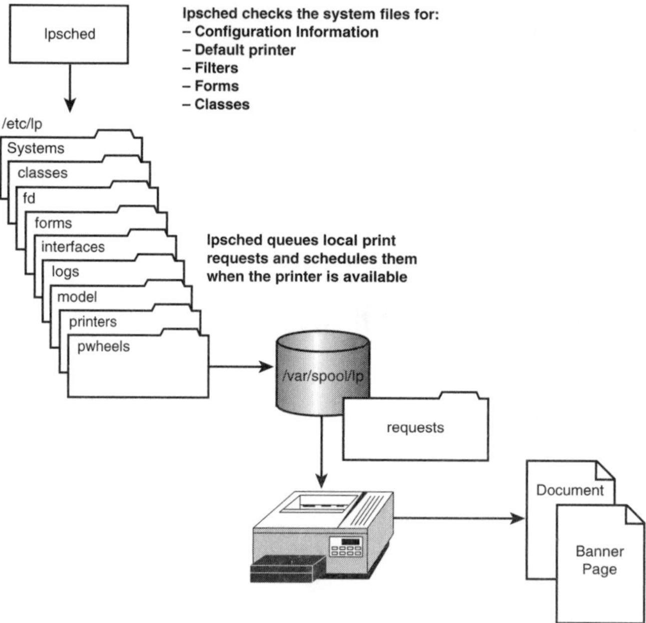

Figure 90 The `lpsched` *Scheduler Schedules Local Print Requests*

Each print client and print server must have only one LP scheduler running. The scheduler is started when a system is booted (or enters run level 2) by the control script /etc/rc2.d/S80lp. Without rebooting the system, you can stop the scheduler with the /usr/sbin/lpshut command and restart the scheduler with the /usr/lib/lp/lpsched command. The scheduler for each system manages its own print requests. It waits for requests issued by the LP commands and then handles the requests in an appropriate manner.

Scheduling Network Print Requests

Each print client and print server must have at least one (and may have several) `lpNet` daemon. The `lpNet` daemon schedules network print requests. The `lpNet` daemon is also started when a system is booted. If you stop and restart the scheduler (using the `lpshut` and `lpsched` commands), the `lpNet` daemon is also stopped and restarted.

Although the Service Access Facility—`sacadm`(1M), `pmadm`(1M)— is not part of the LP print system, the `lpNet` daemon needs a configured port monitor and registered listen services to handle incoming network requests on each print server running Solaris system software. See "Understanding the Service Access Facility" on page 303 for more information about the Service Access Facility.

NOTE. Starting with the Solaris 2.6 release, the `lpnet` *daemon does not schedule network requests. Instead, network scheduling is handled by the* `inetd` *Internet services daemon. The* `inetd` *daemon listens for a request and starts* `in.lpd`*. Then,* `in.lpd` *looks at the request and loads* `bsd_lpsched.so`. `in.lpd` *passes the request through* `bsd_lpsched.so` *to* `lpsched` *for local printing.*

Filtering Print Files

Print filters are programs that convert the content of a file from one format to another so that it can be printed. In network printing, print filters process the file on the print client before it gets transmitted to the server. The LP print service uses filters to perform the following tasks.

- Convert a file from one data format to another so that it can be printed properly on a specific type of printer.
- Handle the special modes of printing that users may request with the `-y` option to the `lp` command—for example, two-sided printing, landscape printing, draft- or letter-quality printing.
- Detect printer faults and notify the LP print service of them so that the print service can deliver alerts.

Not every print filter can perform all of these tasks. However, because each task is printer specific, it can be implemented separately.

A print filter can be as simple or as complex as needed. The Solaris Operating Environment provides print filters in the `/usr/lib/lp/postscript` directory to cover most PostScript printing situations where the destination printer requires the data to be in PostScript format. You have to create and add filters to the system for non-PostScript printers.

Starting the Printer Interface Program

The LP print service uses a standard printer interface program to interact with other parts of the operating system to perform the following tasks.

- Initialize the printer port if necessary. The standard printer interface program uses the `stty` command to initialize the printer port.
- Initialize the printer. The standard printer interface program uses the `terminfo` database and the `TERM` shell variable to find the appropriate control sequences.
- Print a banner page if necessary.
- Print the correct number of copies specified by the print request.

The LP print service uses the standard interface program (found in the `/usr/lib/lp/model` directory) unless you specify a different one. You can create custom interface programs, but you must be careful that the custom program does not terminate the connection to the printer or interfere with proper printer initialization.

Tracking the Status of Print Jobs

The `lpsched` daemons on both the print server and the print client each keep a log of every print request that is processed and note any errors that occurred during the printing process. This log is kept in the `/var/lp/logs/lpsched` file. Every night, the `lp cron` job renames `/var/lp/logs/lpsched` to a new file `lpsched.`*n* and starts a new log file. If errors occur or jobs disappear from the print queue, you can use the log files to determine what `lpsched` has done with a print job.

The following example shows the end of the `/var/lp/logs/lpsched` file.

```
# tail /varl/lp/logs/lpsched
06/01 14:51:50: Print services started.
06/01 16:52:27: Print services stopped.
06/02 15:43:44: build info: 01/08/00:18:06:11
06/02 15:43:44: Print services started.
06/02 17:04:25: Print services stopped.
06/04 10:34:00: build info: 01/08/00:18:06:11
06/04 10:34:00: Print services started.
06/04 16:53:05: Print services stopped.
06/05 09:34:59: build info: 01/08/00:18:06:11
06/05 09:34:59: Print services started.
#
```

Tracking Forms

The LP print service helps you track which forms are mounted on each printer and notifies you when it cannot find the description of how to print on a form. You are responsible for creating form descriptions and mounting and unmounting the paper form in each printer, either as part of setting up a printer or in response to alerts from the LP print service.

Users can specify the form on which they want a job to print. You (root) can mount a specific form and then tell the LP print service that the form is available and on which printer it is mounted. Alternatively, users can submit print requests specifying a particular form and requesting that the form be mounted. When the LP print service receives the request, it sends an alert message to the system administrator (root) requesting that the form be mounted.

Tracking Print Wheels

The procedure for tracking print wheels is similar to the procedure for tracking forms. Some printers (usually letter-quality printers) have removable print heads, such as daisy wheels or print balls, that provide a particular font or character set. A user can request a named character set. If that character set is not available, the LP print service notifies the system administrator (root) of the request. The job is stored in the print queue until the print wheel is changed.

Receiving Printing Problem Alerts

The LP print service performs sophisticated error checking. If a printing problem occurs, alerts are sent to the originator of a print request or to the system administrator, depending on the nature of the problem and what is required to fix it. Users are notified when a print request cannot be completed. Users can request notification by e-mail when a job is successfully completed. Administrators are alerted to problems with printers and to requests for filters, forms, or character sets.

For problems that require an administrator's attention, the LP print service default is to write an alert message to the system administrator's console window (that is, to the terminal on which root is logged in).

As the system administrator, you can change the policy to receive alert messages via e-mail or a program of your choice. Or, you can choose to receive no alerts when printing problems occur.

Understanding the Structure of the LP Print Service

The following sections explain the structure and directory hierarchy for the LP print service. The many files of the LP print service are distributed among several directories, as shown in Table 70.

Table 70 Directories for the LP Print Service

Directory	Description
/usr/bin	The lp, lpstat, enable, and disable commands.
/etc/lp	A hierarchy of LP configuration files.
/usr/share/lib	The terminfo database directory.
/usr/sbin	The accept, reject, lpadmin, lpfilter, lpforms, lpmove, lpshut, lpsystems, and lpusers LP commands.
/usr/lib/lp	The LP daemons, directories for binary files and PostScript filters, and the model directory (which contains the standard printer interface program).
/var/lp/logs	The logs for LP activities.
lpsched.*n*	Messages from lpsched.
/var/spool/lp	The spooling directory where files are queued for printing.
requests.*n**	Information about completed print requests.

* Moved from /var/lplogs starting with the Solaris 2.6 release. Note that the lpNet log was removed completely from the /var/lp/logs directory because the lpNet daemon is replaced by inetd, starting with the Solaris 2.6 release.

User Commands

The /usr/bin directory contains the lp and lpstat commands, with which users submit and monitor print requests. The directory also contains the enable and disable commands used to enable and disable printers.

Users can customize their print requests by using options for the lp command, specifying forms, character sets, filters, titles, banners, and so forth. Table 71 summarizes the frequently used options for the lp command. These options can be used individually or combined in any order on the command line. When combining options, use a space between options and repeat the dash (-). For example, the following command specifies a destination printer, requests e-mail notification, and prints six copies of a file.

```
% lp -d printer-name -m -n6 filename
%
```

Table 71 Summary of Frequently Used lp Command Options

Option	Name	Description
-d	Destination	Specify a destination printer by name.
-m	Mail	Send e-mail to the user who submitted the print request when the file has been printed successfully.
-n	Number	Specify the number of copies to be printed.
-t	Title	Specify a title for a print request (printed only on the banner page).
-o nobanner	Option	Suppress printing of the banner page for an individual request.
-h	Header	Put a header on each page of the print request.
-c	Copy	Copy the file before printing.
-w	Write	Write a message to root's terminal when the file has printed successfully.

See the `lp`(1) manual page for a complete list of options.

LP Configuration Files

The scheduler stores configuration information in LP configuration files located in the `/etc/lp` directory. These configuration files serve the function of the `/etc/printcap` file in SunOS 4.1. You can check the contents of these files, but you should not edit them directly. The LP administrative commands provide input for the configuration files in the `/etc/lp` directory. The `lpsched` daemon administers and updates the configuration files. You should use the administrative commands any time you need to update any configuration file. Table 72 describes the contents of the /etc/lp directory.

Table 72 Contents of the /etc/lp Directory

Name	Type	Description
alerts	Directory	Contains form, jobdone, printer, and sendMsg scripts for sending print system alerts to users.
classes	Directory	Contains files that identify classes provided by the lpadmin -c command.
fd	Directory	Contains descriptions of existing filters.
forms	Directory	Is the location in which to put files for each form. Initially, this directory is empty.
interfaces	Directory	Contains printer interface program files.
logs	Link to /var/lp/logs	Contains log files of printing activities.
model	Link to /usr/lib/lp/model	Contains the standard printer interface program.
printers	Directory	Contains directories for each (remote or local) printer setup. Each directory contains configuration information and alert files for an individual printer.
pwheels	Directory	Contains print wheel or cartridge files.

The printers directory has a subdirectory for each printer (local or remote) known to the system. The following example shows the subdirectories for the printers pinecone and sparc1.

```
% ls -l /etc/lp/printers
drwxrwxr-x 2 lp lp 512 Jan 23 23:53 pinecone
drwxrwxr-x 2 lp lp 512 Jan 11 17:50 sparc1
%
```

Within each of the printer-specific directories, the following files can describe the printer.

- `alert.sh`—Shell to execute in response to alerts.
- `alert.vars`—Alert variables.
- `configuration`—Configuration file.
- `users.deny`—List of users who are denied printer access.
- `comment`—Printer description.

The following example shows a typical configuration file for the printer `pinecone`, `/etc/lp/printers/pinecone/configuration`.

```
Banner: on: Always
Content types: PS
Device: /dev/term/b
Interface: /usr/lib/lp/model/standard
Printer type: PS
Modules: default
```

Printer Definitions

The LP print service uses the `terminfo` database to initialize a local printer; to establish a selected page size, character pitch, line pitch, and character set; and to communicate the sequence of codes to a printer. The `terminfo` database directory is located in `/usr/share/lib`.

Each printer is identified in the `terminfo` database with a short name. If necessary, you can add entries to the `terminfo` database, but it is a tedious and time-consuming process. Describing how to add entries to the `terminfo` database is beyond the scope of this book.

Daemons and LP Internal Files

The `/usr/lib/lp` directory contains daemons and files used by the LP print service, as described in Table 73.

Table 73 Contents of the /usr/lib/lp Directory

Name	Type	Description
`bin`	Directory	Contains files for generating printing alerts, slow filters, and queue management programs.
`local`	Directory	Contains LP executables for the local system.
`locale`	Directory	Contains locale information.
`lpsched`	Daemon	Manage scheduling of LP print requests.

Table 73 Contents of the /usr/lib/lp Directory (Continued)

Name	Type	Description
`model`	Directory	Contains the standard printer interface program.
`postscript`	Directory	Contains all PostScript filter programs provided by the Solaris LP print service. These filters come with descriptor files in the `/etc/lp/fd` directory that tell the LP print service the characteristics of the filters and where to locate them.

LP Administrative Commands

The commands used to set up and administer the LP print service are in the `/usr/sbin` directory; they are listed in Table 74.

Table 74 The LP Commands in the /usr/sbin Directory

Command	Purpose
`accept` `reject`	Accept print requests into the printer's queue or reject print requests.
`lpadmin`	Define printer names, printer types, file content types, print classes, printer devices, and printer comments; remove printers or print classes; specify fault recovery, interface programs (either custom or standard), printing options, banner/no banner; mount forms; mount print wheels or cartridges; define allow and deny user lists.
`lpfilter`	Add, change, delete, and list filters.
`lpforms`	Add, change, delete, and list forms.
`lpmove`	Move queued print requests from one printer to another.
`lpshut`	Halt the LP print service (the `lpsched` command, which starts the LP print service, is in the `/usr/lib/lp` directory).
`lpsystem`	Register print servers and print clients with the LP print service.
`lpusers`	Set queue priorities for users.

Log Files

The LP print service maintains two sets of log files: a list of current requests that are in the print queue (`/var/spool/lp`) and an ongoing history of print requests (`/var/lp/logs/requests`).

Print Queue Logs

The scheduler for each system keeps a log of print requests in the directories `/var/spool/lp/requests/`*`system`* and `/var/spool/lp/tmp/`*`system`*. Each print request has two files (one in each directory) that contain information about the request. The information in the `/var/spool/lp/requests/`*`system`* directory can be accessed only by root or `lp`. The information in the `/var/spool/lp/tmp/`*`system`* directory can be accessed only by root, `lp`, or the user who submitted the request.

The following example shows the contents of the `/var/spool/lp/tmp/pine` directory. See Table 75 on page 378 for an explanation of the LP requests log codes.

```
pine% ls /var/spool/lp/tmp/pine
20-0 21-0
pine% cat 21-0
C 1
D slw2
F /etc/default/login
P 20
t simple
U winsor
s 0x1000
```

These files remain in their directories only as long as the print request is in the queue. Once the request is finished, the information in the files is combined and appended to the `/var/lp/logs/requests` file, which is described in the next section.

Use the information in the `/var/spool/lp` logs if you need to track the status of a print request that is currently in the queue.

History Logs

The LP print service records a history of printing services in three log files: `lpNet`, `lpsched`, and `requests`. These log files are located in the `/var/lp/logs` directory. You can use the information in these logs to diagnose and troubleshoot printing problems. The following example shows the contents of the `/var/lp/logs` directory.

```
# cd /var/lp/logs
# ls
lpsched.1    requests    requests.2
lpsched      lpsched.2   requests.1
#
```

The files with the .1 and .2 suffixes are copies of logs for previous days. Each day, the lp cron job cleans out the lpsched and requests log files; it keeps copies for two days.

The most important log file for troubleshooting is the lpsched log, which contains information about local printing requests.

The requests log contains information about print requests that have completed and are no longer in the print queue. Once a request is finished printing, the information in the /var/spool/lp log files is combined and appended to the /var/lp/logs/requests file.

The requests log has a simple structure, and you can extract data by using common UNIX shell commands. Requests are listed in the order they are printed and are separated by lines showing their request IDs. Each line below the separator line is marked with a single letter that identifies the kind of information contained in that line. Each letter is separated from the data by a single space.

The following example shows the contents of a requests log.

```
# pwd
/var/lp/logs
# tail requests.2
= slw2-20, uid 200, gid 200, size 5123, Thu Nov 18 01:24:01 EST 2000
z slw2
C 1
D slw2
F /etc/motd
P 20
t simple
U irving
s 0x0100
#
```

Table 75 shows the codes in the LP requests log.

Table 75 Codes in the LP Requests Log

Character	Content of Line
=	The separator line. It contains the following items, separated by commas: the request ID, the user ID and group IDs of the user, the total number of bytes in the original (unfiltered) files, and the time when the request was queued. The user ID, group IDs, and file size are preceded by the words uid, gid, and size.
C	The number of copies printed.
D	The printer or class destination, or the word any.
F	The name of the file printed. The line is repeated for each file printed; files were printed in the order shown.

Table 75 Codes in the LP Requests Log (Continued)

Character	Content of Line
`f`	The name of the form used.
`H`	One of three types of special handling: `resume`, `hold`, and `immediate`. The only useful value found in this line is `immediate`.
`N`	The type of alert used when the print request was successfully completed. The type is the letter `M` if the user was notified by e-mail or `W` if the user was notified by a message to the terminal.
`O`	The `-o` options.
`P`	The priority of the print request.
`p`	The list of pages printed.
`r`	This single-letter line is included if the user asks for raw processing of the files (the `-r` option of the `lp` command).
`S`	The character set or print wheel (or cartridge) used.
`s`	The outcome of the request, shown as a combination of individual bits expressed in hexadecimal form. Although several bits are used internally by the print service, the most important bits are listed below.
	`0x0004` Slow filtering finished successfully.
	`0x0010` Printing finished successfully.
	`0x0040` The request was cancelled.
	`0x0100` The request failed filtering or printing.
`T`	The title placed on the banner page.
`t`	The type of content found in the file(s).
`U`	The name of the user who submitted the print request.
`x`	The slow filter used for the print request.
`Y`	The list of special modes to give to the print filters used to print the request.
`z`	The printer used for the request. This printer differs from the destination (the `D` line) if the request was queued for any printer or a class of printers, or if the request was moved to another destination.

Spooling Directories

Files queued for printing are stored in the /var/spool/lp directory until they are printed. Table 76 shows the contents of the /var/spool/lp directory.

Table 76 Contents of the /var/spool/lp Directory

File	Type	Description
SCHEDLOCK	File	Lock file for the scheduler. Check for this file if the scheduler dies and won't restart.
admins	Directory	Linked to /etc/lp.
bin	Directory	Linked to /usr/lib/lp/bin.
fifos	Directory	Contains pipes that convey networked print requests to and from the lpNet daemon.
logs	Link	Linked to ../lp/logs where completed print requests are logged.
model	Link	Linked to /usr/lib/lp/model.
requests	Directory	Contains a directory for each configured printer where print requests are logged until printed. Users cannot access this log.
system	Directory	Contains a print status file for the system.
temp	Link	Linked to /var/spool/lp/tmp/*printer-name*, which contains the spooled requests.
tmp	Directory	Contains a directory for each configured printer where print requests are logged until printed. Changes to existing print requests are also recorded in this log.

Using the SunSoft Print Client

This section describes how the SunSoft print client works. Starting with the Solaris 2.6 release, the SunSoft print client is provided as part of the Solaris Operating Environment. It was available previously only as an unbundled product.

A system becomes a SunSoft print client when you install the SunSoft print client software and enable access to remote printers on the system. The

SunSoft print client commands have the same names and produce the same output as the print commands of the previous Solaris releases.

The SunSoft print client commands use a greater number of options to locate printer configuration information than in the previous Solaris Operating Environment, and the client communicates directly with the print server.

The print command locates a printer and printer configuration information in the following sequence.

1. It checks whether the user specified a destination printer name or printer class in one of the three valid styles.
2. If the user did not specify a printer name or class in a valid style, the command checks the user's `PRINTER` or `LPDEST` environment variable for a default printer name.
3. If neither environment variable for the default printer is defined, the command checks the `.printers` file in the user's home directory for the `_default` printer alias.
4. If the command does not find a `_default` printer alias in the `.printers` file, it then checks the SunSoft print client's `/etc/printers.conf` file for configuration information.
5. If the printer is not found in the `/etc/printers.conf` file, the command checks the name service (NIS or NIS+) if any.

The client does not have a local print queue. The SunSoft print client sends its requests to the queue on the specified print server. The client writes the print request to a temporary spooling area only if the print server is not available or if an error occurs. This streamlined path to the server decreases the print client's use of resources, reduces the chance for printing problems, and improves performance.

Printer Configuration Resources

This section describes the resources that the SunSoft print client commands use to locate printer names and printer configuration information.

The SunSoft print client commands can use a nameservice, which is a shared network resource, for storing printer configuration information for all printers on the network. The name service (either NIS, NIS+, and in the Solaris 8 release, NIS+ with FNS) simplifies the maintenance of printer configuration information. When you add a printer in the nameservice, all SunSoft print clients on the network can access it. New!

The SunSoft print client software locates printers by checking the following resources.

- Atomic, POSIX, or context-based printer name or class.
- User's PRINTER or LPDEST environment variable for the default printer.
- User's .printers file for a printer alias.
- SunSoft print client's /etc/printers.conf file.

- Nameservice (NIS, NIS+, or NIS+ with FNS).

Print Naming Enhancement

The Solaris 8 Operating Environment supports the printers database in the /etc/nsswitch.conf nameservice switch file. The printers database provides centralized printer configuration information to print clients on the network.

With the printers database and corresponding sources of information in the nameservice switch file, print clients can automatically access printer configuration information without having it added to their own systems. Table 77 shows the default printers entry for each of the nameservice environments.

Table 77 Default printers Entries in the /etc/nsswitch.conf File

Nameservice	Default printers Entry
files	printers: user files
nis	printers: user files nis
nis+	printers; user nisplus files xfn

For example, if the nameservice is NIS, print client configuration information is looked up in the following order.

- user—The $home/.printers file for the user.
- files—The /etc/printers.conf file.
- nis—The printers.conf.byname table.

If the nameservice is NIS+, print client configuration information is looked up in the following order.

- user—The $home/.printers file for the user.
- nisplus—The printers.org_dir table.
- files—The /etc/printers.conf file.
- xfn—The FNS printer contexts.

Submitting Print Requests

Users submit a print request from a SunSoft print client by using either the `lp` or `lpr` command. The user can specify a destination printer name or class in any of three styles.

- *Atomic style*, which is the print command and option followed by the printer name or class and the file name.
  lp -d *printer-name filename*
- *POSIX style*, which is the print command and option followed by *server:printer* and the file name.
  lpr -P *server-name:printer-name filename*
- *Context-based style*, as defined in the *Federated Naming Service Guide* in the *Solaris Software Developer AnswerBook*.
  lpr -d *dept-name/service-name/printer-name filename*

Summary of the SunSoft Print Client Process

The following list summarizes how the SunSoft print client process works.

1. A user submits a print request from a SunSoft print client by using a SunSoft print client command.
2. The print client command checks a hierarchy of print configuration resources to determine where to send the print request.
3. The print client command sends the print request directly to the appropriate print server. A print server can be any server that accepts BSD printing protocol, including SVR4 (LP) print servers and BSD print servers such as the SunOS 4.x BSD print server.
4. The print server sends the print request to the appropriate printer.
5. The print request is printed.

Setting Up Printing Services

You need to decide which systems have local printers directly cabled to them and which systems connect to printers over the network. The system that has the printer connected to it and makes the printer available to other systems is called a *print server*. The system that has its printing needs met by a print server is called a *print client*.

Setting up printing services comprises three basic tasks.

- Setting up local printers.
- Setting up print servers.
- Setting up print clients.

You can have the following client/server combinations, as illustrated in Figure 91.

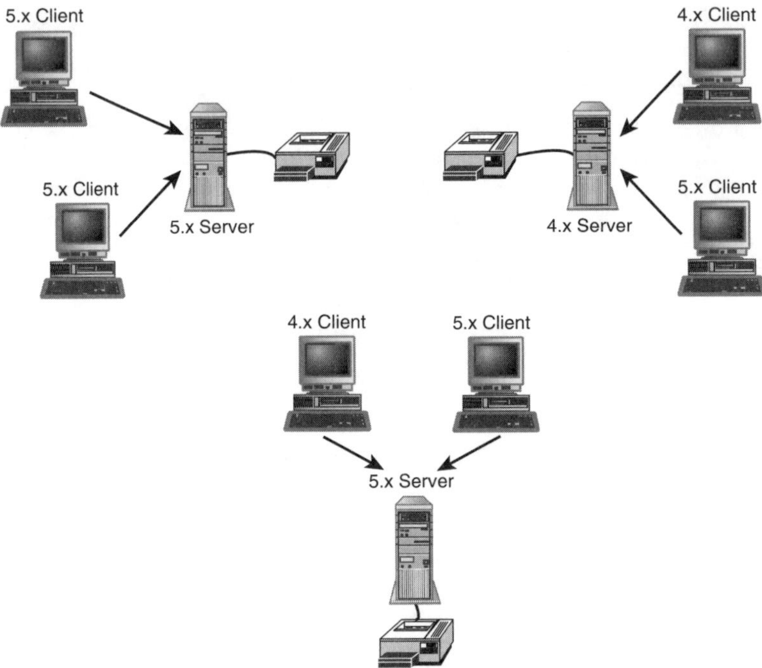

Figure 91 Print Client/Server Configurations

- SunOS 5.0 print clients with a SunOS 5.0 print server.
- SunOS 5.0 and SunOS 4.1 print clients with a SunOS 5.0 print server.
- SunOS 5.0 and SunOS 4.1 print clients with a SunOS 4.1 print server.

This section describes how to set up a Solaris print client.

New! Introducing Solaris Print Manager

In the Solaris 8 release, the Solaris Print Manager is the preferred method for managing printers because this Java-based graphical user interface centralizes printing information when used in conjunction with a nameservice. Using a nameservice to store printer configuration information centralizes printer information and makes printer information available to all systems on the network.

You can use Print Manager in the following nameservice environments.

- `files`.
- NIS.
- NIS+.
- NIS+ with Federated Naming Service (`xfn`).

In the Solaris 8 release, you can use the Solaris Print Manager to manage printer configuration information in the NIS+ nameservice without the underlying `xfn` application layer. Eliminating the underlying `xfn` application layer provides better performance when accessing printer configuration information. See “Converting Printer Configuration in NIS+ (xfn) to NIS+ Format” on page 392 for more information

You must be superuser or belong to a role that enables you to manage printing functions to use the Solaris Print Manager. See Chapter 5, “Administering Roles,” for more information about roles.

Solaris Print Manager recognizes existing printer information on the printer servers, print clients, and in the nameservice databases. You do not need to convert print clients to use the new Solaris Print Manager as long as the print clients are running either the Solaris 2.6 release or compatible versions.

Using Solaris Print Manager to perform printer-related tasks automatically updates the appropriate printer databases. Solaris Print Manager also includes a command-line console that displays the `lp` command line for the add, modify, and delete printer operations. Errors and warnings are also displayed when Printer Manager operations are performed.

You can run Solaris Print Manager on a remote system with the display sent to the local system. See “Managing Printing Services” in *System Administration Guide, Volume II,* for instructions on setting the `DISPLAY` environment variable.

See `printmgr`(1M) for more information.

Starting Solaris Print Manager

The command to start Solaris Print Manager is `/usr/sadm/admin/bin/printmgr&`. If you use Solaris Print Manager frequently, you may want to add `/usr/sadm/admin/bin` to your path.

Use the following steps to access the Print Manager.

1. Become superuser.
2. Type **/usr/sadm/admin/bin/printmgr&** and press Return to start the Print Manager.

   The window that is displayed asks you to choose the naming service, as shown in Figure 92.

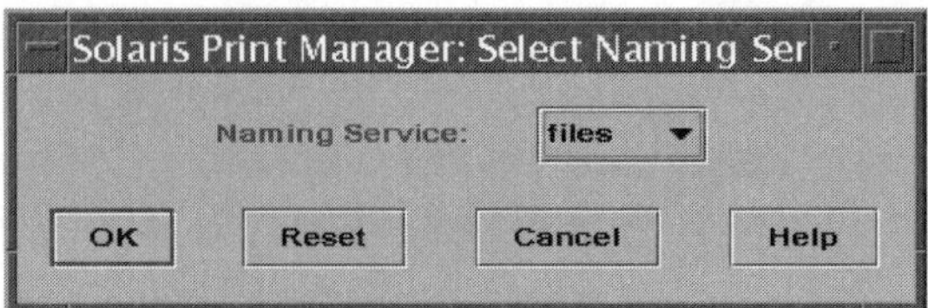

Figure 92 Print Manager Select Naming Service Window

3. Choose the appropriate nameservice from the Naming Service menu and click on the OK button.

   The Print Manager window is displayed, as shown in Figure 93.

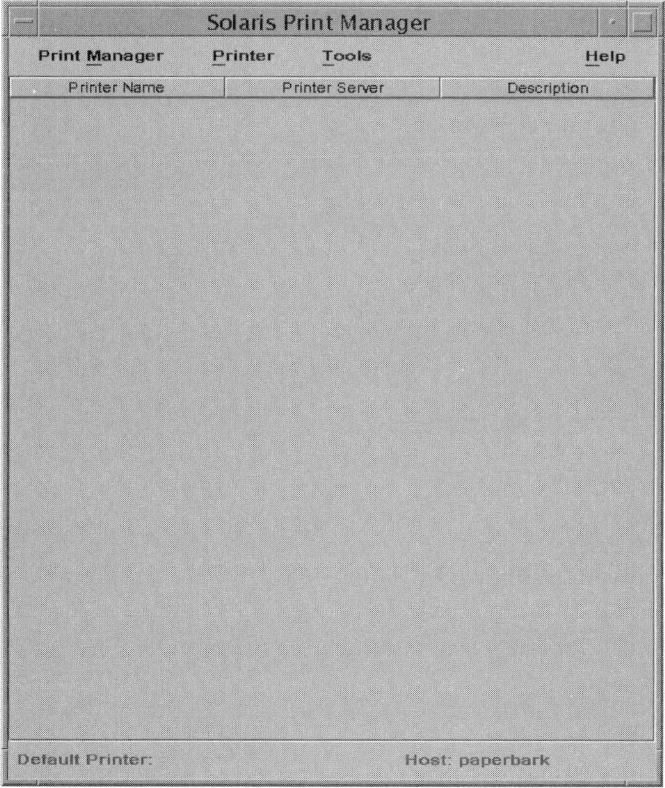

Figure 93 Solaris Print Manager Window

Adding Access to a Printer with the Print Manager

New!

To add access to a printer, you need the following information.

- Printer name.
- Print server name.
- Description of the printer.
- Whether this printer is the default printer.

Use the following steps to add access to a printer.

1. Start the Print Manager (if necessary).
   See "Starting Solaris Print Manager" on page 385 for more information.

2. From the Printer menu, choose Add Access to Printer, as shown in Figure 94.

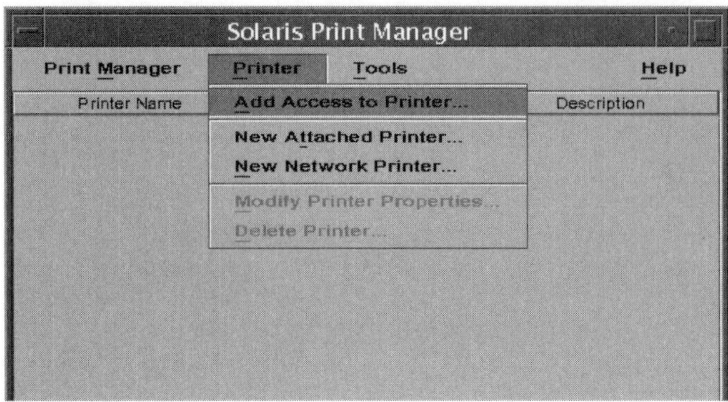

Figure 94 Printer Menu

The Solaris Print Manager Add Access to Printer window is displayed, as shown in Figure 95.

Figure 95 Solaris Print Manager Add Access to Printer Window

3. Type the printer name, name of the printer server, and description in the text fields. If you want this printer to be the default printer, click on the Default Printer check box.
4. Click on the OK button.

   The printer is configured, the printer information is added to the list in the Solaris Print Manager window, and the relevant files are updated. The name of the default printer is displayed at the bottom of the window, as shown in Figure 96.

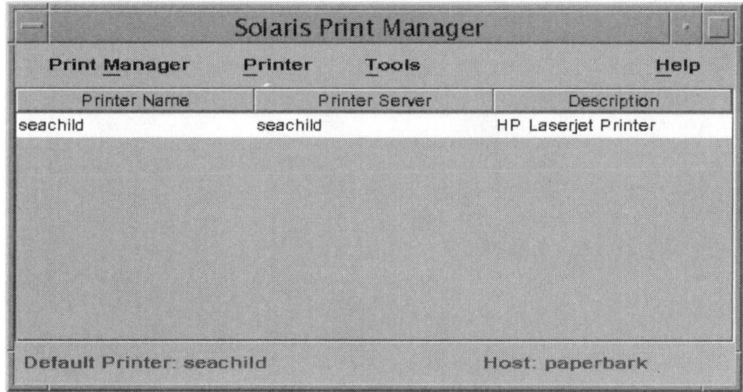

Figure 96 Solaris Print Manager Window

Adding a New Attached Printer with Print Manager

New!

To add a new printer attached to a print server, you need the following information.

- Printer name.
- Description.
- Printer port.
- Printer type.
- File contents.
- Fault notification policy.
- Whether this printer is the default.
- Whether to always print banners.
- User access list.

Once you have physically attached the printer to the computer, use the following steps to make the printer available to the local computer.

1. Start the Print Manager (if necessary).

   See "Starting Solaris Print Manager" on page 385 for more information.
2. From the Print menu, choose New Attached Printer, as shown in Figure 97.

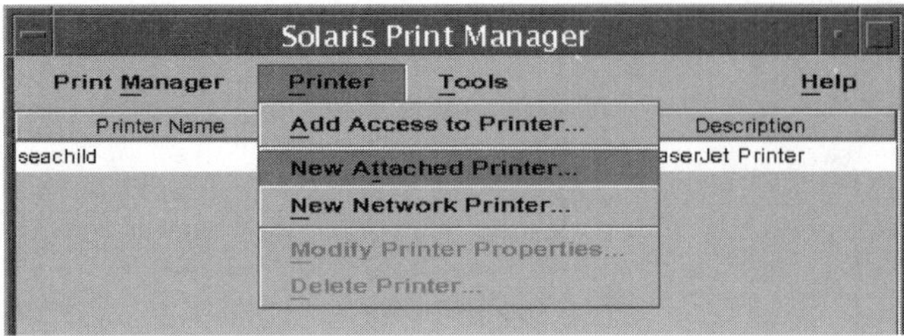

Figure 97 Choose New Network Printer from the Print Menu

The New Attached Printer window is displayed, as shown in Figure 98.

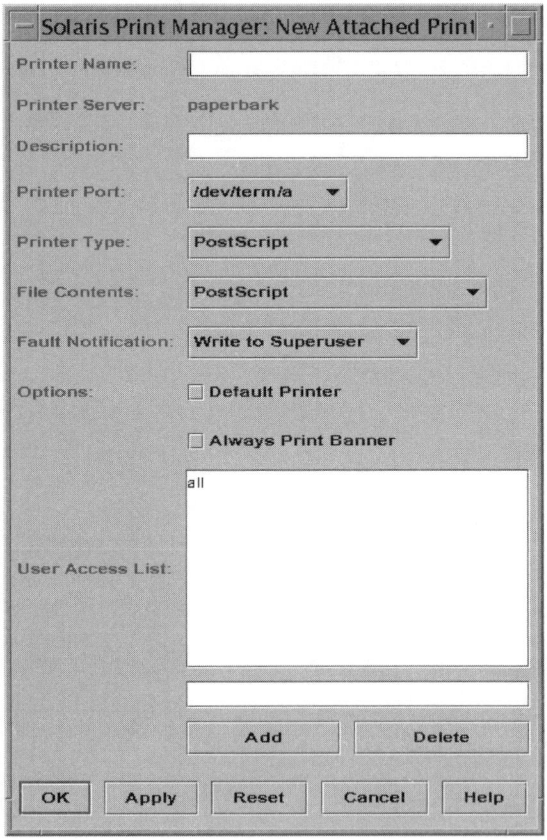

Figure 98 Add New Network Printer Window

Click on the Help button if you need help with details about values that are required for the text fields.

3. Fill in the form and click on the OK button.

   The printer is added to the Print Manager and the appropriate databases and files are updated.

Adding a New Network Printer with Print Manager

New!

To add a new network printer, you need the following information.

- Printer name.
- Description.
- Printer type.
- File contents.
- Fault notification policy.
- Destination.
- Protocol.
- Whether this printer is the default.
- Whether to always print banners.
- User access list.

Use the following steps to add a new network printer.

1. Start the Print Manager (if necessary).

   See "Starting Solaris Print Manager" on page 385 for more information.
2. From the Print menu, choose New Network Printer, as shown in Figure 99.

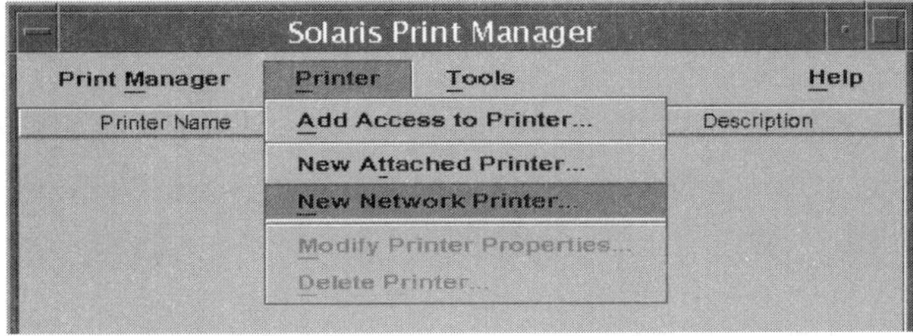

Figure 99 Choose New Network Printer from the Print Menu

The New Network Printer window is displayed, as shown in Figure 100.

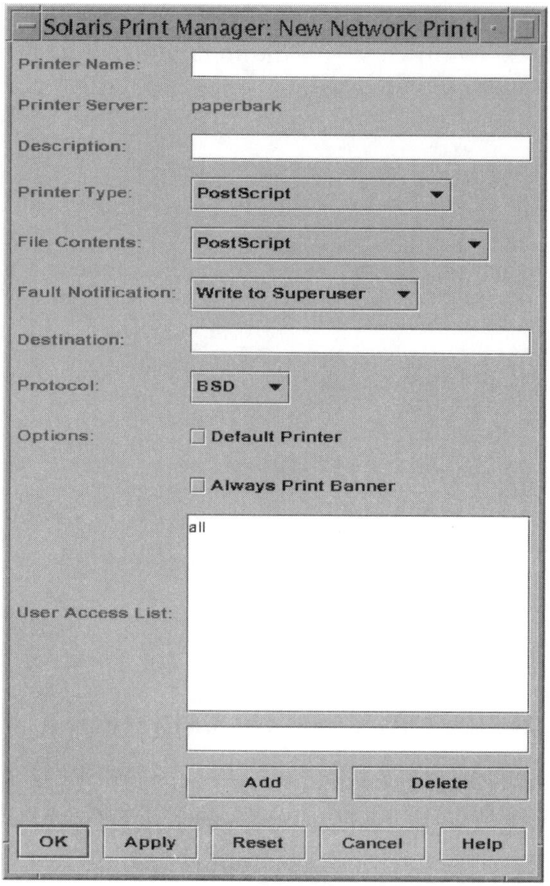

Figure 100 New Network Printer Window

Click on the Help button if you need help with details about values that are required for the text fields.

3. Fill in the form and click on the OK button.

   The printer is added to the Print Manager and the appropriate databases and files are updated.

New! Converting Printer Configuration in NIS+ (xfn) to NIS+ Format

This section describes how to convert printer configuration information in NIS+ (`xfn`) format to NIS+ format. You can run the following conversion script only on a system running the Solaris 8 Operating Environment.

1. Log in as superuser on the NIS+ master.
2. Copy the following conversion script and name it something like /tmp/convert.

```
#!/bin/sh
        #
        # Copyright (C) 1999 by Sun Microsystems, Inc.
        # All Rights Reserved
        #
        PRINTER=""
        for LINE in `lpget -n xfn list | tr "\t " "Control A Control B?"` ; do
         LINE=`echo ${LINE} | tr "Control A ControlB" "\t " | sed -e 's/^
  \t//g'`
         case "${LINE}" in
          *:)
           PRINTER=`echo ${LINE} | sed -e 's/://g'`
           ;;
          *=*)
           lpset -n nisplus -a "${LINE}" ${PRINTER}
           ;;
         esac
        done
```

3. Type **chmod 755 /tmp/convert** and press Return.

   The script is executable.
4. Type **/tmp/convert** and press Return.

Setting Up Access to a Printer with Admintool

You can use Admintool to set up access to a printer or to configure a local printer. To use the Admintool: Printers windows, you must be a member of the UNIX sysadmin group (GID 14).

NOTE. If you access Admintool through the Solaris Management Console, you must log in as root or as a member of a role that grants you superuser permissions to run Admintool. Only then can you use Admintool to edit local password databases. See "Using AdminSuite 3.0 to Grant Access Rights to Users" on page 190 for more information. The Solaris Management Console does not recognize membership in GID 14.

To set up a print client, you need the following information.

- Printer name.
- Print server name.
- Description.
- Whether this is the default printer for the print client system.

Use the following steps to access a network printer.

1. Type **`admintool&`** and press Return to start Admintool (if necessary).
2. From the Browse menu, choose Printers.

   The Admintool: Printers window is displayed, as shown in Figure 101.

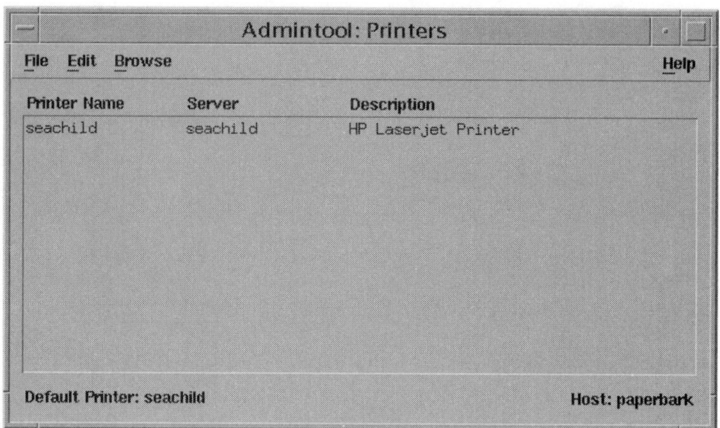

Figure 101 The Admintool: Printers Window

3. From the Edit menu, choose Add and Access to Printer.

   The Admintool: Add Access To Printer window is displayed, as shown in Figure 102.

Admintool: Add Access To Printer
Print Client: paperbark
Printer Name:
Print Server:
Description:
Option: Default Printer
OK Apply Reset Cancel Help

Figure 102 The Admintool: Add Access to Printer Window

4. Enter the printer name, print server name, and description.
5. If you want this printer to be the default printer, click on the Default Printer check box.

6. Click on the OK button. The printer is configured and the printer information is added to the list in the Admintool: Printers window.

Setting Up A Local Printer with Admintool

You can use Admintool to set up a local printer. To use the Admintool: Printers windows, you must be a member of the UNIX `sysadmin` group (GID 14).

NOTE. If you access Admintool through the Solaris Management Console, you must log in as root or as a member of a role that grants you superuser permissions to run Admintool. Only then can you use Admintool to edit local password databases. See "Using AdminSuite 3.0 to Grant Access Rights to Users" on page 190 for more information.The Solaris Management Console does not recognize membership in GID 14.

To set up a local printer, you need the following information.

- Printer name.
- Print server name.
- Description.
- Printer port.
- Printer type.
- File contents.
- Type of fault notification.
- Whether this is the default printer for the print client system.
- Whether you always print a banner page.
- Whether to specify a custom user access list.

Use the following steps to add a local printer.

1. Type **`admintool&`** and press Return to start Admintool (if necessary).
2. From the Browse menu, choose Printers.
3. From the Edit menu, choose Add and Local Printer.

   The Admintool: Add Local Printer window is displayed, as shown in Figure 103.

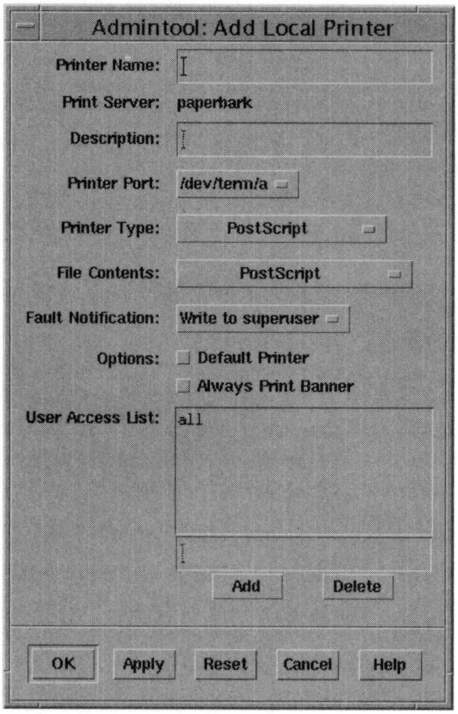

Figure 103 The Admintool: Add Local Printer Window

4. Enter the printer name and description.
5. Choose the printer port, printer type, file contents, and fault notification.
6. If you want to specify this printer as the default printer, click on the Default Printer check box.
7. If you want to always print the banner, click on the Always Print Banner check box.
8. If necessary, modify the user access list.
9. When you have completed all of the setup, click on the OK button.

   The printer is configured and the printer information is added to the list in the Admintool: Printers window.

Setting Up a Print Server (Solaris Operating Environment)

This section describes how to add a network printer by using LP commands.

You need the following information to set up a Solaris print server.

- Printer name.
- Server name.
- Network printer access name, sometimes qualified by a port name.
- IP address for the printer.
- Protocol. The print subsystem uses the `BSD` print protocol and raw TCP to communicate with the printer. In general, the TCP protocol is more generic. The printer vendor documentation provides the information about which protocol to use.
- Timeout value. The `timeout` option specifies the amount of time in seconds to wait between successive attempts to connect to the printer. The default is 10 seconds. Some printers have a long warm-up time, so a longer timeout is advised.
- Printer type. The default is PostScript.
- File content type. The default is PostScript
- Fault notification policy for this print server. The default is write to superuser.

Use the following steps to set up a print server.

1. Set switches and ensure appropriate cabling.

   Consult the printer vendor installation documentation for information about hardware switches and cabling requirements.
2. Connect the printer to the network and turn on the power to the printer.
3. Get an IP address and select a name for the printer node.

   These procedures are equivalent to those for adding any new node to the network.
4. Become superuser.
5. Type **`lpadmin -p`** ***`printer-name`*** **`-v /dev/null`** and press Return.

   This step defines the printer name and the port device the printer uses. The device to use is `/dev/null`.
6. All on one line, type **`lpadmin -p`** ***`printer-name`*** **`-i /usr/lib/lp/model/netstandard`** and press Return.

   This step defines the interface script the printer uses.

7. All on one line, type **lpadmin -p *printer-name* -o dest=*access-name:port* -o protocol=*protocol* -o timeout=*value*** and press Return.

   This step sets the printer destination, protocol, and timeout values.
8. All on one line, type **lpadmin -p *printer-name*-I *content-type* -T *printer-type*** and press Return.

   This step specifies the file content type and the printer type.
9. Type **cd /etc/lp/fd** and press Return.

   Focus is in the filter directory.
10. Type **for filter in *.fd;do** and press Return.
11. At the > prompt, type **name='basename $filter .fd'** and press Return.
12. At the > prompt, type **lpfilter -f $name -F $filter** and press Return.
13. At the > prompt, type **done** and press Return.

    You have installed filters.
14. Type **accept *printer-name*** and press Return.

    The printer is able to accept requests.
15. Type **enable *printer-name*** and press Return.

    The printer is enabled to print the requests.
16. Type **lpstat -p *printer-name*** and press Return.

    This step verifies that the printer is configured correctly.
17. Set up any print clients that should have access to this printer.

The following example sets up a print server by supplying the following information.

- Printer name: `seachild`
- Network printer access name: `nimquat:9100`
- Protocol: `tcp`
- Timeout: `5`
- Interface: `/usr/lib/lp/model/netstandard`
- Printer type: `PS`
- Content types: `postscript`
- Device: `/dev/null`

```
# lpadmin -p seachild -v /dev/null
# lpadmin -p seachild -i /usr/lib/lp/model/netstandard
# lpadmin -p seachild -o dest:nimquat:9100 -o protocol=tcp -o timeout=5
# lpadmin -p seachild -I postscript -T PS
# cd /etc/lp/fd
```

```
# for filter in *.fd;do
   > name='basename $filter .fd'
   > lpfilter -f $name -F $filter
   > done
# accept castle
destination ' 'castle' ' now accepting requests
# enable castle
printer ' 'castle' ' now enabled
# lpadmin -p castle -D "PostScript printer"
# lpstat -p castle
  printer castle is idle. enabled since Thu Sep 15 08:45 1997.
available
#
```

Controlling the Printing of Banner Pages

New!

A banner page identifies the person who submitted the print request, the print request ID, and the date and time the request was printed. Banner pages also have a modifiable title to help users identify their printouts.

By default, the print service forces banner pages to be printed. However, in the Solaris 8 Operating Environment, by using the new `-o banner=` option to the `lpadmin` command, you can specify whether a banner is `always` printed, `never` printed, or is `optional`. Alternatively, you can use Admintool to set up a print server and control the printing of banner pages. as listed in Table 78.

Table 78 Behavior of Banner Page Printing

Command	Behavior of Banner Page Printing	Overridden

`lpadmin -p` *printer* `-o banner`
or
`lpadmin -p` *printer* `-o banner=always`
	Required and printed.	If you are root or `lp`, the `nobanner` argument is honored. The `nobanner` argument is ignored for all other users.

`lpadmin -p` *printer* `-o nobanner` `lpadmin -p` *printer* `-o banner=optional`	On by default but can be disabled for each print request with the`lp -o nobanner` command.	N/A.
`lpadmin -p` *printer* `-o banner=never`	Disabled.	No.

Making Banner Pages Optional

When you specify `optional`, the banner is printed by default but users can disable banner printing with the `lp -o banner` command.

Use the following steps to make banner pages optional.

1. Become superuser or `lp` on the print server.
2. Type **`lpadmin -p`** ***`printer`*** **`-o banner=optional`** and press Return.

   The banner page setting is entered in the `/etc/lp/printers/`*`printer`*`/configuration` file on the print server.
3. Type **`lpstat -o`** ***`printer`*** **`-l`** and press Return.

   Review the output to verify that the `Banner not required` line is displayed.

The following example makes banner pages optional for the printer `seachild`.

```
seachild% su
# lpadmin -p seachild -o banner=optional
# lpstat -p seachild -l
printer seachild is idle. enabled since Thu Jan  3 18:20:22 PST 2000.
 available.
        Content types: PS
        Printer types: PS
        Description:
        Users allowed:
                (all)
        Forms allowed:
                (none)
        Banner not required
        Character sets:
                (none)
        Default pitch:
        Default page size:
#
```

New!

Turning Off Banner Pages

Use the following steps to turn off the printing of banner pages.

1. Become superuser or `lp` on the print server.
2. Type **`lpadmin -p`** ***`printer`*** **`-o banner=never`** and press Return.

   The banner page setting is entered in the `/etc/lp/printers/`*`printer`*`/configuration` file on the print server.
3. Type **`lpstat -o`** ***`printer`*** **`-l`** and press Return.

   Review the output to verify that the `Banner not required` line is displayed.

The following example turns off banner pages for the printer seachild.

```
seachild% su
# lpadmin -p seachild -o banner=never
# lpstat -p seachild -l
printer seachild is idle. enabled since Thu Jan  3 18:20:22 PST 2000.
  available.
        Content types: PS
        Printer types: PS
        Description:
        Users allowed:
                (all)
        Forms allowed:
                (none)
        Banner not printed
        Character sets:
                (none)
        Default pitch:
        Default page size:
#
```

Setting Up a PostScript Print Client with LP Commands

This section describes how to set up a Solaris print client to print on a SunOS 4.x print server that has a PostScript printer installed. You must complete the following tasks so the print client can use the printer connected to the print server.

- Identify the printer and server system to which the printer is connected.
- Define the characteristics of the printer.
- Set up the print filters.

You must have a network that enables access between systems to set up print clients. If your network is running NIS or NIS+, follow the appropriate procedures for enabling access between systems. If your network is not running NIS or NIS+, you must include the Internet address and system name for each print client in the /etc/hosts file on the print server. You must also include the Internet address and system name of the print server in the /etc/hosts file of each print client system.

Before you start, you need superuser privileges on the print client system. You also need the name of the printer and the name of the print server system. You do not need to specify a printer type or file content type for a printer client. If no printer type is specified, the default is unknown. If no file content type is specified, the default is any, which allows both PostScript and ASCII files to be printed on a PostScript printer.

Use the following steps to set up a PostScript print client.

1. Become superuser on the print client system.
2. Type **lpsystem -t bsd** ***server-system-name*** and press Return. The print server system is identified as a BSD (SunOS 4.x) system.
3. Type **lpadmin -p** ***printer-name*** **-s** ***server-system-name*** and press Return. The printer and the server system name are registered with the client LP print service.
4. Type **cd /etc/lp/fd** and press Return.
5. Type **lpfilter -f download -F download.fd** and press Return.
6. Type **lpfilter -f dpost -F dpost.fd** and press Return.
7. Type **lpfilter -f postio -F postio.fd** and press Return.
8. Type **lpfilter -f postior -F postior.fd** and press Return.
9. Type **lpfilter -f postprint -F postprint.fd** and press Return.
10. Type **lpfilter -f postreverse -F postreverse.fd** and press Return.

    The PostScript filters are installed.
11. Type **accept** ***printer-name*** and press Return.

    The printer is now ready to begin accepting (queuing) print requests.
12. Type **enable** ***printer-name*** and press Return.

    The printer is now ready to process print requests in the print queue.
13. (This step is optional but recommended.) Type **lpadmin -d** ***printer-name*** and press Return.

    The printer you specify is established as the default printer for the system. You should define a default printer even if there is only one printer configured for a system.
14. Type **lpstat -t** and press Return. Check the messages displayed to verify that the printer is accepted and enabled.
15. Type **lp** ***filename*** and press Return. If you have not specified a default printer, type **lp -d** ***printer-name filename*** and press Return.

    The file you choose is sent to the printer.

If you want to set up Solaris print clients and print servers in addition to setting up the LP print system, you must also configure the port monitors by using the Service Access Facility. See "Understanding the Service Access Facility" on page 303 for information on how to set up the port monitors. If you use the Solaris Print Manager, the port monitors are configured for you automatically. To set up a Solaris print client, in place of step 2 in the procedure described above, type **lpsystem** ***server-system-name*** and press Return. The print server system is identified as a Solaris system.

Using Printing Commands

The following sections describe how to use `lp` to submit requests from a command line. When a request is made, the LP print service places it in the queue for the printer, displays the request ID number, and then redisplays the shell prompt. The `lp` command has many options that can modify the printing process, as summarized in Table 71 on page 373. For a complete list of options, see the `lp`(1) manual page.

Printing to the Default Printer

When the LP print service is set up with a default printer, users can submit print requests without typing the name of the printer. Type **lp** ***filename*** and press Return. The file specified is placed in the print queue of the default printer, and the request ID is displayed.

The following example prints the `/etc/passwd` file.

```
pine% lp /etc/passwd
request id is pinecone-8 (1 file)
pine%
```

Printing to a Printer by Name

Regardless of whether a default printer has been designated for your system, you can submit print requests to any printer that is configured for your system. To submit a print request to an individual printer, type **lp -d** ***printer-name filename*** and press Return. The file specified is placed in the print queue of the destination printer, and the request ID is displayed.

The following example prints the `/etc/passwd` file on the printer `acorn`.

```
pine% lp -d acorn /etc/passwd
request id is acorn-9 (1 file)
pine%
```

If you submit a request to a printer that is not configured on your system, an information message is displayed, as shown in the following example.

```
pine% lp -d thorn /etc/passwd
UX:lp: ERROR: Destination "thorn" is unknown to the
              LP print service.
pine%
```

Requesting Notification When a File Has Been Printed

When you submit a large file to be printed, you may want the LP print service to notify you when printing is complete. You can request that the LP print service notify you either via an e-mail message or via a message to your console window.

To request e-mail notification, use the `-m` option when you submit the print request. Type **`lp -m`** ***`filename`*** and press Return.

To request that a message be written to your console window, use the `-w` option when you submit the print request. Type **`lp -w`** ***`filename`*** and press Return.

Printing Multiple Copies

You can print more than one copy of a file. When you request more than one copy, the file is printed the number of times you specify by the `-n` option to the `lp` command. The print request is considered as one print job, and only one banner page is printed if banner printing is enabled. To request multiple copies, type **`lp -n`*`number filename`*** and press Return.

The following example prints four copies of the `/etc/passwd` file.

```
pine% lp -n4 /etc/passwd
request id is pinecone-9 (1 file)
pine%
```

Determining Printer Status

Use the `lpstat` command to find out about the status of the LP print service. You can check on the status of your own jobs in the print queue, determine which printers are available for you to use, or determine request IDs of your jobs if you want to cancel them.

The Status of Your Print Requests

To find out the status of your own spooled print requests, type **lpstat** and press Return. A list of the files that you have submitted for printing is displayed.

In the following example, on the system `pine`, one file is queued for printing to the printer `pinecone`.

```
pine% lpstat
pinecone-10              fred             1261    Mar 12 17:34 on pine
pine%
```

The `lpstat` command displays one line for each print job, showing the request ID and followed by the name of the user who spooled the request, the output size in bytes, and the date and time of the request.

Availability of Printers

To find out which printers are configured on your system, type **lpstat -s** and press Return. The status of the scheduler is displayed, followed by the default destination and a list of the systems and printers that are available to you.

In the following example, on the system `elm`, the scheduler is running, the default printer is `pinecone`, and two network printers are available.

```
elm% lpstat -s
scheduler is running
system default destination: pinecone
system for pinecone: pine
system for acorn: oak
elm%
```

Display of All Status Information

The `-t` option for `lpstat` gives you a short listing of the status of the LP print service. To display a short listing of all status information, type **lpstat -t** and press Return. All available status information is displayed.

In the following example, no jobs are in the print queue. When files are spooled for printing, the status of those print requests is also displayed.

```
elm% lpstat -t
scheduler is running
system default destination: tom
system for slw2: bertha
system for slw1: bertha
device for tom: /dev/term/b
slw2 accepting requests since Thu May 11 11:01:54 EDT 2000
slw1 accepting requests since Sat May 27 16:26:38 EDT 2000
tom accepting requests since Sat Jun  3 14:25:41 EDT 2000
printer slw2 is idle. enabled since Thu May 11 11:01:55 EDT 2000. available.
```

```
printer slw1 is idle. enabled since Thu May 27 16:26:38 EDT 2000. available.
printer tom is idle. enabled since Sat Jun  3 14:25:41 EDT 2000. available.
character set usascii
character set english
character set finnish
character set japanese
character set norwegian
character set swedish
character set germanic
character set french
character set canadian_french
character set italian
character set spanish
character set line
character set security
character set ebcdic
character set apl
character set mosaic
elm%
```

The -l option for lpstat, when used with one of the other options, gives you a long listing of the status of the LP print service. To display a long listing of all status information, type **lpstat -tl** and press Return. All available status information is displayed.

In the following example for the same system, additional information is displayed. When files are spooled for printing, the status of those print requests is also displayed.

```
{:44} lpstat -tl
scheduler is running
system default destination: tom
system for slw2: bertha
system for slw1: bertha
device for tom: /dev/term/b
slw2 accepting requests since Thu May 11 11:01:54 EDT 2000
slw1 accepting requests since Sat May 27 16:26:38 EDT 2000
tom accepting requests since Sat Jun  3 14:25:41 EDT 2000
printer slw2 is idle. enabled since Thu May 11 11:01:55 EDT 2000. available.
        Content types: any
        Printer types: unknown
        Description:
        Users allowed:
                (all)
        Forms allowed:
                (none)
        Banner not required
        Character sets:
                (none)
        Default pitch:
        Default page size:

printer slw1 is idle. enabled since Sat May 27 16:26:38 EDT 2000. available.
        Content types: simple
        Printer types: unknown
        Description: Located in ia lab
        Users allowed:
                (all)
        Forms allowed:
                (none)
        Banner not required
        Character sets:
                (none)
        Default pitch:
        Default page size:

printer tom is idle. enabled since Sat Jun  3 14:25:41 EDT 2000. available.
        Form mounted:
```

```
        Content types: PS
        Printer types: la100
        Description: hi
        Connection: direct
        Interface: /usr/lib/lp/model/standard
        After fault: continue
        Users allowed:
                 (all)
        Forms allowed:
                (none)
        Banner required
        Character sets:
                usascii
                english
                finnish
               japanese
              norwegian
                swedish
               germanic
 french
        canadian_french
                italian
                spanish
                   line
               security
                 ebcdic
                    apl
                 mosaic
        Default pitch: 10 CPI 6 LPI
        Default page size: 132 wide 66 long
(More information not shown in this example)
```

Display of Status for Printers

You can request printer status information for individual printers by using the `-p` option to `lpstat`. This option shows whether the printer is active or idle, when it was enabled or disabled, and whether it is available to accept print requests.

To request status for all printers on a system, type **`lpstat -p`** and press Return. In the following example, two printers are idle, enabled, and available, as shown in the following example. If one of those printers had jobs in the print queue, those jobs would also be displayed.

```
elm% lpstat -p
printer pinecone is idle. enabled since Sat Jan  1 18:20:22 PST 2000.
 available.
printer acorn is idle. enabled since Thu Mar  2 15:53:44 PST 2000. available.
elm%
```

To request status for an individual printer by name, type **`lpstat -p`** ***`printer-name`*** and press Return.

Display of Printer Characteristics

To see all of the characteristics for a printer, use the `-p` option together with the `-l` (long) option to `lpstat`. This command can be especially useful for finding the printer type and content type.

To show characteristics for all printers on a system, type **lpstat -p -l** and press Return. A table shows all the configuration information that is used by the LP print service for each printer.

In the following example, all the fields are blank except for the content type and the printer type of the printer pinecone.

```
elm% lpstat -p pinecone -l
printer pinecone is idle. enabled since Sat Jan  1 18:20:22 PST 2000.
  available.
         Content types: PS
         Printer types: PS
         Description:
         Users allowed:
                  (all)
         Forms allowed:
                 (none)
         Banner not required
         Character sets:
                  (none)
         Default pitch:
         Default page size:
elm%
```

Summary Table of lpstat Options

You can request different types of printing status information by using the lpstat command. Table 79 summarizes the frequently used options for the lpstat command. Use these options individually or combine them in any order on the command line. When you combine options, use a space between options and repeat the dash (-). For example, to show a long list of status for an individual printer, type **lpstat -p *printer-name* -l** and press Return. See the lpstat(1) manual page for a complete list of options.

Table 79 Summary of Frequently Used Options to the lpstat Command

Option	Description
-a	Accept. Show whether print destinations are accepting requests.
-c	Class. Show classes and their members.
-d	Destination. Show default destination.
-f	Forms. Show forms.
-o	Output. Show status of output.
-p [*list*] [-D] [-l]	
	Printer/description/long list. Show status of printers.
-r	Request. Request scheduler status.
-R	Show position of job in the queue.

Table 79 Summary of Frequently Used Options to the lpstat Command (Continued)

Option	Description
`-S`	Sets. Show character sets.
`-s`	Status. Show status summary.
`-u [`*`username`*`]`	
	User. Show requests by user.
`-v`	Show devices.

Cancelling a Print Request

Use the `cancel` command to cancel a print request while it is in the queue or while it is printing. To cancel a request, you need to know its request ID. The request ID always includes the name of the printer, a dash, and the number of the print request. When you submit the print request, the request ID is displayed. If you do not remember your request ID, type **`lpstat`** and press Return. Only the user who submitted the request, or someone logged in as root or `lp`, can cancel a print request.

Cancelling of Print Request by ID Number

To cancel a print request, type **`cancel`** ***`request-ID`*** and press Return. A message is displayed telling you that the request is cancelled. The next job in the queue begins printing.

In the following example, two print requests are cancelled.

```
elm% cancel pinecone-3 pinecone-4
request "pinecone-3" cancelled
request "pinecone-4" cancelled
elm%
```

Cancelling by Printer Name a File That Is Currently Printing

You can also cancel just the job that currently is printing (if you were the submitter) by typing the printer name in place of the request ID. Type **`cancel`** ***`printer-name`*** and press Return. A message is displayed telling you that the request is cancelled. The next job in the queue begins printing.

In the following example, the currently printing job has been cancelled.

```
elm% cancel pinecone
request "pinecone-3" cancelled
elm%
```

As system administrator, you can log in as root or `lp` and cancel the currently printing job by using the printer name as the argument for the `cancel` command.

11

Recognizing File Access Problems

This chapter describes how to recognize problems with search paths, permissions, and ownership.

Users frequently experience problems—and call on a system administrator for help—because they cannot access a program, a file, or a directory that they could formerly access. Whenever you encounter such a problem, investigate one of the following areas.

- The user's search path may have been changed.
- The directories in the search path may not be in the proper order.
- The file or directory may not have the proper permissions or ownership.

This chapter briefly describes how to recognize problems in each of these areas and suggests possible solutions.

Recognizing Problems with Search Paths

If a user types a command that is not in the search path, the message `Command not found` is displayed. The command might not be found because the command is not available on the system or the command directory is not in the search path.

If the wrong version of the command is found, a directory with a command of the same name is in the search path. In this case, the proper directory may be found later in the search path or may not be present at all.

To diagnose and troubleshoot problems with search paths, use the following procedure.

1. Display the current search path.
2. Edit the file where the user's path is set (`.cshrc` or `.login` for the C shell, `.profile` for the Bourne and Korn shells). Add the directory or rearrange the order of the path.

NOTE. For the C shell, always check both the `.cshrc` *and* `.login` *files to make sure the path information is set all in one place. Duplicate entries can make the search path harder to troubleshoot and makes search times less efficient for the user.*

3. Source the file to activate the changes. See "Sourcing Bourne and Korn Shell Dot Files" and "Sourcing C Shell Dot Files" on page 413 for more information.
4. Verify that the command is found in the right place.
5. Execute the command.

The tasks you use to follow this procedure are described in the following sections.

Displaying the Current Search Path

To display the current search path, type **echo $PATH** and press Return. The current search path is displayed.

```
cinderella% echo $PATH
/sbin:/usr/sbin:/usr/bin:/etc
cinderella%
```

Setting the Path for Bourne and Korn Shells

The path for the Bourne and Korn shells is specified in the user's `$HOME/.profile` file in this way.

```
PATH=/usr/bin:/$HOME/bin:.;export PATH
```

The dot (`.`) at the end of the path specifies that the current working directory is always searched last.

Sourcing Bourne and Korn Shell Dot Files

When you have changed information in the `.profile` file, you must source the file to make the new information available to the shell. To source the `.profile` file, type **`. .profile`** and press Return.

```
$ . .profile
$
```

Setting the Path for the C Shell

The path for the C shell is specified in the user's `$HOME/.cshrc` or `.login` file (with the `set path` environment variable) in this way.

```
set path =  (/usr/bin $home/bin .)
```

The dot (`.`) at the end of the path specifies that the current working directory is always searched last.

Sourcing C Shell Dot Files

When you have changed information in the `.cshrc` or `.login` file, you must source the file to make the new information available to the shell. To source the `.cshrc` file, type **`source .cshrc`** and press Return. To source the `.login` file, type **`source .login`** and press Return.

```
castle% source .cshrc
castle% source .login
castle%
```

Verifying the Search Path

When you have changed a user's path, use the `which` command to verify that the shell is finding the proper command. The `which` command looks in the `.cshrc` file for information. The `which` command may give misleading results if you execute it from the Bourne or Korn shell and the user has a `.cshrc` file that contains aliases for the `which` command. To ensure accurate results, use the `which` command in a C shell. Alternatively, from the Korn shell you can use the `whence` command instead of the `which` command.

To verify the search path, type **`which`** ***`command-name`*** and press Return. If the command is found in the path, the path and the name of the command are displayed.

The following example shows that the OpenWindows executable is not in any of the directories in the search path.

```
oak% which openwin
no openwin in . /home/ignatz /sbin /usr/sbin /usr/bin /etc/home/ignatz/bin
  /bin /home/bin /usr/etc
oak%
```

The following example shows that the executable for OpenWindows is found among the directories in the search path.

```
oak% which openwin
/usr/openwin/bin/openwin
oak%
```

If you cannot find a command, look at the manual page to find its path name. For example, if you cannot find the `lpsched` command (the LP printer daemon), the `lpsched`(1M) manual page tells you the path is `/usr/lib/lp/lpsched`.

Executing a Command

To execute a command, type ***command-name*** and press Return. The command is executed if it is in the search path. You can always execute a command that is not in the search path by typing the full path name for the command.

Recognizing Problems with Permissions and Ownership

When users cannot access files or directories that they used to be able to access, the most likely problem is that permissions or ownership on the files or directories has changed.

Frequently, file and directory ownerships change because someone edited the files as root. When you create home directories for new users, be especially careful to make the user the owner of the dot (`.`) files in the home directory. When users do not own the dot (`.`) files, they cannot create files in their own home directory.

Another way access problems can arise is when the group ownership changes or when a group of which a user is a member is deleted from the `/etc/groups` database.

Changing File Ownership

NOTE. You must own a file or directory (or have root permission) to be able to change its ownership. If the {_POSIX_CHOWN_RESTRICTED} *configuration option is enabled (the default), you must be superuser to change ownership of a file, even if you own it. See "Changing File Ownership or Permissions (chown, chmod, chgrp)" on page 67 for more information.*

Use the following steps to change file ownership.

1. Type **ls -l *filename*** and press Return. The owner of the file is displayed in the third column.
2. Become superuser.
3. Type **chown *new-owner filename*** and press Return. Ownership is assigned to the new owner you specify, in this case, ignatz.

```
oak% ls -l quest
-rw-r--r--   1 fred    staff    6023 Aug  5 12:06 quest
oak% su
Password:
# chown ignatz quest
# ls -l quest
-rw-r--r--   1 ignatz   staff    6023 Aug  5 12:06 quest
#
```

Changing File Permissions

You use the chmod command to change file permissions. You can change permissions in two ways. If you use letters, use the following syntax.

```
chmod [who]operator[permission(s)] file-name
```

For *who*, you can specify u, g, or o (for user, group, or other). You can specify a to change all operators. If you do not specify who the permissions are for, permissions are changed for all three groups. The operator is either + to add permission or – to take away permission. The permissions are r, w, or x, for read, write, or execute. See the chmod(1) manual page for more information.

For example, to grant read, write, and execute permissions to everyone, type **chmod +wrx *filename*** and press Return.

```
oak% chmod +wrx kookaburra
oak% ls -l kookaburra
-rwxrwxrwx  1     janice    staff    54  Jul 7  11:33  kookaburra
oak%
```

To grant read and execute permissions to everyone, type **chmod +rx *filename*** and press Return.

```
oak% chmod +rx kookaburra
oak% ls -l kookaburra
-r-xr-xr-x  1    janice    staff    54  Jul 7  11:34  kookaburra
oak%
```

Another way to change the permissions to read and execute only would be to deny write permission to everyone. Type **chmod -w *filename*** and press Return.

```
oak% chmod -w kookaburra
oak% ls -l kookaburra
-r-xr-xr-x  1    janice    staff    54  Jul 7  11:35  kookaburra
oak%
```

To change ownership for a specific group, type the letter for the group followed by the operator and the permission. In the following example, read, write, and execute permissions have been granted for the owner to the file kookaburra.

```
oak% chmod u+wrx kookaburra
oak% ls -l kookaburra
-rwxr-xr-x  1    janice    staff    54  Jul 7  11:36  kookaburra
oak%
```

To deny execute permissions to group and other, type **chmod go-x *filename*** and press Return.

```
oak% chmod go-x kookaburra
oak% ls -l kookaburra
-rwxr--r--  1    janice    staff    54  Jul 7  11:37  kookaburra
oak%
```

With the chmod command, you can also use a numeric argument that describes the user class and permission to change as a sequence of bits. Table 80 shows the octal values for setting file permissions. You use these numbers in sets of three to set permissions for owner, group, and other. For example, the value 644 sets read/write permissions for owner, and read-only permissions for group and other.

Table 80 Octal Values for File Permissions

Value	Description
0	No permissions.
1	Execute-only.

Table 80 Octal Values for File Permissions (Continued)

Value	Description
2	Write-only.
3	Write, execute.
4	Read-only.
5	Read, execute.
6	Read, write.
7	Read, write, execute.

Use the following steps to change permissions on a file.

1. Type **`ls -l`** ***`filename`*** and press Return.

   The long listing shows the current permissions for the file.
2. Type **`chmod`** ***`nnn filename`*** and press Return.

   Permissions are changed according to the numbers you specify.

NOTE. You can change permissions on groups of files or on all files in a directory using metacharacters such as `*` *and* `?` *in place of file names or in combination with them.*

The following example changes the permissions of a file from `666` (read/write, read/write, read/write) to `644` (read/write, read-only, read-only).

```
oak% ls -l quest
-rw-rw-rw-   1 ignatz   staff    6023 Aug  5 12:06 quest
oak% chmod 644 quest
oak% ls -l quest
-rw-r--r--   1 ignatz   staff    6023 Aug  5 12:06 quest
oak%
```

Changing File Group Ownership

If a file has an incorrect group owner, users of the group won't be able to make changes to the file. To change file group ownership, you must either be a member of the group, own the file, or change it as root.

To change the group ID for a file, type **`chgrp`** ***`gid filename`*** and press Return. The group ID for the file you specify is changed. With the Solaris Operating Environment, the `ls -l` command shows the owner and the group for the file. You can display only the group owner by using the `ls -lg` command.

```
$ ls -lg junk
-rw-r--r-- 1 other 0 Oct 31 14:49 junk
$ chgrp 10 junk
$ ls -lg junk
-rw-r--r-- 1 staff 0 Oct 31 14:49 junk
$
```

The group ID is found in the `Group` database or the local `/etc/group` file.

Glossary

Admintool

A CDE and OpenWindows tool from which you can edit `/etc` files on a local system.

AnswerBook2

A collection of Sun online documents that you can view with a Web browser. You can search, bookmark, and print the information.

archive

A copy of files, on secondary media, that have been removed from the system because they are no longer active.

autoconfiguration **New!**

The automatic loading of kernel modules as they are needed.

Auto_home database

The database that you use to add home directories to the automounter. In SunOS 4.x releases, this database is a file named `auto.home`.

automounter

Software that automatically mounts a directory when a user changes to that directory and unmounts the directory when it is no longer in use.

backup schedule

The schedule you establish for a site to determine when you regularly run the `ufsdump` command at different levels to back up user files and essential file systems. See full backup, incremental backup.

bang

An exclamation point (`!`) that acts as a single-character UNIX command or as a separator between the routes of a route-based e-mail address.

New! *BIOS*

Basic Input/Output System (BIOS) is the firmware interface on a PC.

boot block

An 8-Kbyte disk block that contains information used during booting: Block numbers point to the location of the boot program on that disk. The boot block directly follows the disk label.

booting

The process of powering up a system, testing to determine which attached hardware devices are running, and bringing the operating system kernel into memory and operation at the run level specified by the `boot` command.

New! *Bourne-Again shell*

A Bourne-shell-compatible language interpreter that executes commands read from the standard input or from a file. `bash` incorporates useful features from the Korn and C shells.

Bourne shell

The default shell for the Solaris Operating Environment. The Bourne shell is a small shell for general-purpose use. It also provides a full-scale scripting language that you can use to develop shell scripts to capture frequently performed commands and procedures.

C shell

A shell completely different from the Bourne and Korn shells with its own C language syntax. The most important advantages of the C shell are command history, command editing, and aliases.

cache

A small, fast memory area that holds the most active part of a larger and slower memory.

CDE

Common Desktop Environment is a windowing system based on the Motif graphical user interface.

core file

An image of the state of a software program when it failed; used for troubleshooting. A core file can be created by any program, including the operating system kernel.

crash

A situation when a system panics and dies. See also hang.

crash dump

A core file image of the operating system kernel that is saved in the swap partition when a system crashes. If crash dumps are enabled, the core image is written from the swap partition to a file.

cylinder group

One or more consecutive disk cylinders that include inode slots for files.

cylinder group map

A bitmap in a UFS file system that stores information about block use and availability within each cylinder. The cylinder group replaces the traditional free list.

daemon

A type of program that, once activated, carries out a specific task without any need for user input. Daemons are typically used to handle jobs, such as printing, mail, and communication, that have been queued.

disc New!

An optical disc, a CD-ROM, or a DVD-ROM.

disk

A hard-disk storage device.

diskette

A nonvolatile storage medium used to store and access data magnetically. Solaris Operating Environment supports 3.5-inch, double-sided, high-density (DS, HD) diskettes.

diskless client

A system with no local disk drive that instead relies on an NFS server for the operating system, swap space, file storage, and other basic services.

disk quotas

A mechanism for controlling how much of a file system's resources any individual user can consume. Disk quotas are optional and must be configured and administered to be used.

domain

A hierarchical directory structure for e-mail addressing and network address naming. Within the United States, top-level domains include `com` for commercial organizations; `edu` for educational organizations; `gov` for governmentsl; `mil` for the military; `net` for networking organizations; and `org` for other organizations. Outside the United States, top-level domains designate the country. Subdomains designate the organization and the individual system.

domain addressing

Using an address to specify the destination of an e-mail message.

DS, HD

Double-sided, high-density signifies the type of 3.5-inch diskettes supported by the Solaris Operating Environment.

dump

The process of copying directories onto media (usually tape) for off-line storage by using the `ufsdump` command. The `ufsdump` command is an enhanced version of the SunOS 4.x `dump` command.

New! *dynamic reconfiguration*

The capability, available on certain SPARC servers, to remove and replace hot-pluggable system I/O boards in a running system, eliminating the time lost in rebooting.

New! *DVD*

Digital Versatile Disc or Digital Video Disc uses the UDFS format for storing information.

e-mail

Electronic mail. A set of programs that transmit mail messages from one system to another.

environment variable

A system- or user-defined variable that provides information about the operating environment to the shell or a program.

failover New!

The process of selecting a server from a list of servers supporting a replicated file system. Normally, the next server in the sorted list is used unless it fails to respond.

file system

A hierarchical arrangement of directories and files organized on a portion of a magnetic or optical disk.

floppy diskette

See diskette.

free list

See cylinder group map.

full backup

A complete, level 0 backup of a file system done with the `ufsdump` command. See incremental backup.

fully qualified domain name

The complete domain name that contains all the elements needed to specify one particular system in the world. See also domain.

gateway

A system that handles e-mail traffic between different communications networks.

GID

The group identification number used by the system to control access to files and directories owned by other users.

Group database

The database that you use to create new group accounts or to modify existing group accounts.

group ID

See GID.

hang

A condition in which a system does not respond to input from the keyboard, a mouse, or the network.

home directory

The part of the file system that is allocated to an individual user for private files.

Hosts database

The database you use to control network security.

New! *hot-plugging*

The ability to physically add, remove, or replace system components while a system is running. See dynamic reconfiguration.

incremental backup

A partial backup of a file system that is performed by the `ufsdump` command. The backup includes only those files in the specified file system that have changed since a previous backup at a lower level. See full backup.

initialization files

The dot files (files prefixed with `.`) in a user's home directory that set the path, environment variables, windowing environment, and other characteristics to enable users to use the system.

init state

One of the seven initialization states, or run levels, a system can be running in. A system can run in only one init state at a time.

inode

An entry in a predesignated area of a disk that describes where a file is located on that disk, the size of the file, when it was last used, and other identification information.

input variables

The environment variables that CDE's `dtsearchpath` reads.

IP address

A unique Internet protocol number that identifies each system in a network.

New! *IPv4*

Internet Protocol, version 4. The default protocol for the Solaris 7 and earlier releases.

IPv6 New!

Internet Protocol, version 6 adds increased address space and improves Internet functionality to the IPv4 protocol by using a simplified header format, support for authentication and privacy, autoconfiguration of address assignments, and new quality-of-service capabilities.

kernel

The master program set of Solaris software that manages all the physical resources of the computer, including file system management, virtual memory, reading and writing files to disks and tapes, scheduling of processes, printing, and communicating over a network.

Korn shell New!

A shell that uses the same syntax as the Bourne shell but provides more built-in functions that can be defined directly from the shell and a sophisticated form of command editing.

login name

The name assigned to an individual user that controls user ID access to a system.

manual pages

Online technical references for each Solaris command.

metacharacter

A symbol used in file names and extensions to represent another character or string of characters. An asterisk (*) matches any number of characters. A question mark (?) matches a single character.

monitor

The program in the PROM that provides a limited set of commands that can be used before the kernel is available. See PROM.

mount point

A directory in the file system hierarchy where another file system is attached to the hierarchy.

netmask New!

A setting that determines how many and which bits in the host address space represent the subnet number and how many and which represent the host number. See also subnet mask.

NFS

The default Solaris distributed file system that provides file sharing among systems. NFS servers can also provide kernels and swap files to diskless clients.

NIS

The SunOS 4.x network information service.

NIS+

The Solaris network information service.

OpenWindows

A windowing system based on the OPEN LOOK graphical user interface.

parse

To resolve a string of characters or a series of words into component parts to determine their collective meaning. Virtually every program that accepts command input must do some sort of parsing before the commands can be acted on. For example, the `sendmail` program divides an e-mail address into its component parts to decide where to send the message.

partition

A discrete portion of a disk, configured with the `format` program. Also referred to as slice.

Passwd database

The database that you use to add, modify, or delete user accounts.

path

The list of directories that are searched to find an executable command.

path name

A list of directory names, separated with slashes (`/`), that specify the location of a particular file.

port

A physical connection between a peripheral device (such as a terminal, printer, or modem) and the device controller.

port monitor

A program that continuously watches for requests to log in or requests to access printers or files. The `ttymon` and `listen` port monitors are part of the Service Access Facility.

power cycling

Turning off the power to a system and then turning it on again.

preen

To run `fsck` with the `-o p` option, which automatically fixes any basic file system inconsistencies normally found when a system halts abruptly but does not repair more serious errors.

process

A program in operation.

PROM

Programmable read-only memory is a chip containing permanent, nonvolatile memory and a limited set of commands used to test the system and start the boot process.

remap New!

To make use of a new server with NFS client failover. Through normal use, the clients store the path name for each active file on the remote file system. During the remap, these path names are evaluated to locate the files on the new server.

root

The highest level of a hierarchical system. As a login ID, the user name of the system administrator or superuser who has responsibility for an entire system. Root has permissions for all user files and processes on the system. See also superuser.

run level

See init state.

runaway process

A process that progressively uses more and more CPU time.

server

A system that provides network services such as disk storage and file transfer; a program that provides such a service.

Service Access Facility (SAF)

The part of the system software that is used to register and monitor port activity for modems, terminals, and printers. SAF replaces `/etc/getty` as a way to control logins.

New! *shell*

The command interpreter for a user, specified in the `Passwd` database. The Solaris Operating Environment supports the Bourne (default), C, and Korn shells. The Solaris 8 Operating Environment also provides the freeware Bourne Again, TC, and Z shells.

slice

An alternative name for a partition. See also partition.

spooling directory

A directory where files are stored until they are processed.

spooling space

The amount of space that is allocated on a print server for storing requests in the printer queue.

stand-alone system

A system that has a local disk and can boot without relying on a server.

state flag

A flag in the superblock that the `fsck` file-system check program updates to record the condition of a file system. If a file-system state flag is clean, the `fsck` program is not run on that file system.

New! *subnet mask*

A setting that determines the bits in the host IP address bytes that are applied to subnet addresses and those applied to host addresses. See also netmask.

superuser

A user who is granted special privileges by supplying the correct password with the `su` command or when logging in as root. For example, only the superuser can edit major administrative files in the `/etc` directory. See also root.

swap file

A disk partition or file used to temporarily hold the contents of a memory area until it can be loaded back into memory.

symbolic link

A file that contains a pointer to the name of another file.

system New!

A computer with a keyboard and terminal. A system can have either local or remote disks and can have additional peripheral devices such as CD-ROM players, DVD-ROM players, tape drives, diskette drives, and printers.

TC shell New!

An enhanced and completely compatible variation of the Berkeley UNIX C shell, `csh(1)` that can be used as an interactive login shell and a shell script command processor. It includes a command-line editor, programmable word completion, spelling correction, a history mechanism, job control, and a C-like syntax.

UFS

UNIX file system. The default disk-based file system for the Solaris Operating Environment.

UID

The user identification number assigned to each login name. UID numbers are used by the system to identify, by number, the owners of files and directories.

Univeral Disc Format file system New!

The UDFS file system is the industry-standard format for storing information on the optical media technology called DVD (Digital Versatile Disc or Digital Video Disc).

user account

An account set up for an individual user in the `Passwd` database that specifies the user's login name, UID, GID, login directory, and login shell.

user ID

See UID.

user mask

The setting that controls default file permissions that are assigned when a file or directory is created. The `umask` command controls the user mask settings.

virtual memory

A memory management technique that is used by the operating system for programs that require more space in memory than can be allotted to them. The kernel moves only pages of the program currently needed into memory; unneeded pages remain on the disk.

New! *Z shell*

A UNIX command interpreter that you can use as an interactive login shell and as a shell script command processor. The Z shell most closely resembles the Korn shell with enhancements. The Z shell provides command-line editing, built-in spelling correction, programmable command completions, shell functions (with autoloading), a history mechanism, and a host of other features.

zombie

A process that has terminated but remains in the process table because its parent process has not sent the proper exit code. Zombie processes do not consume any system resources and are removed from the process table when a system is rebooted.

INDEX

B

C

V

W

X

Y

Z

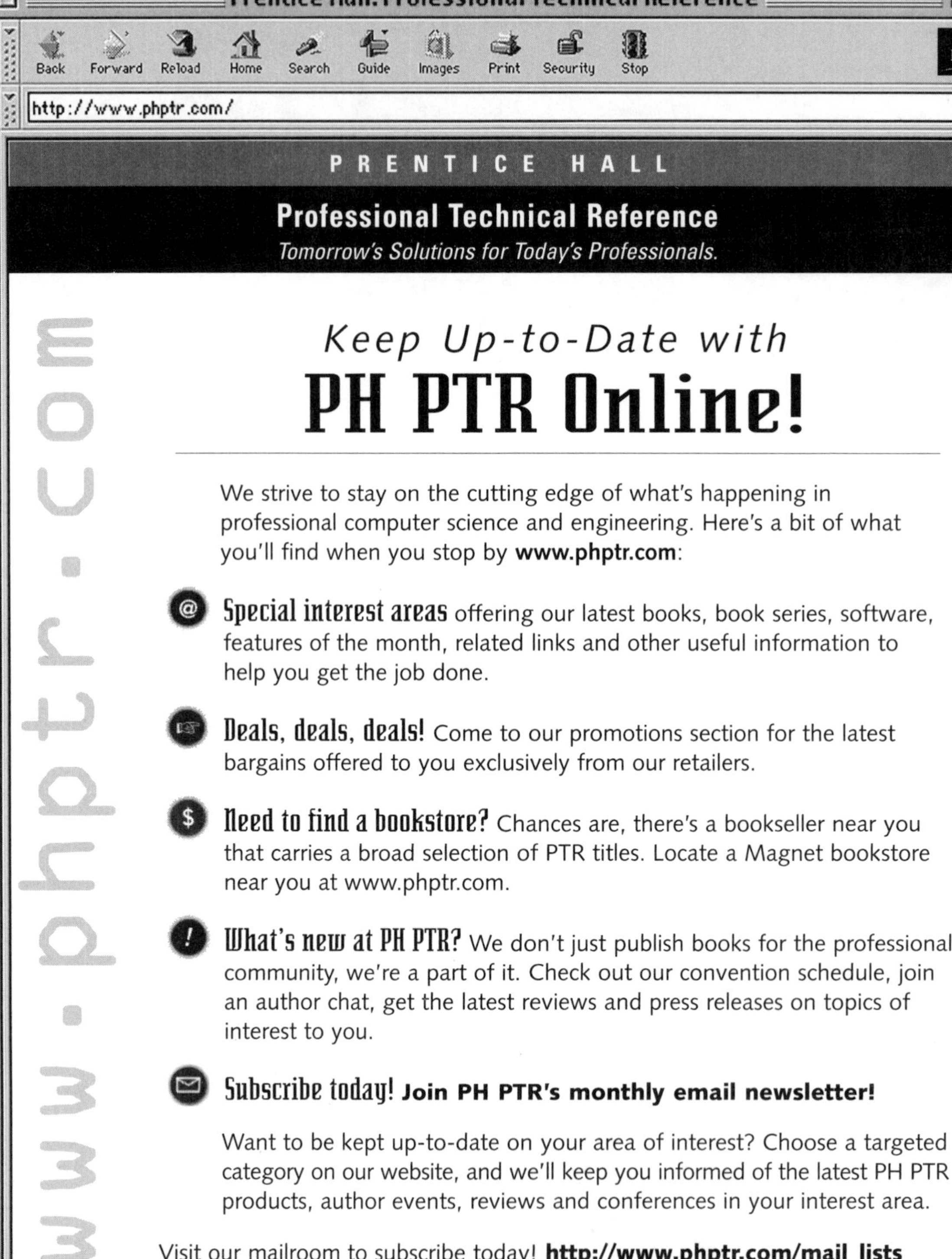